The New Standard Book of

DOG CARE *and* TRAINING

The New Standard Book of
DOG CARE
and
TRAINING

Abridged Edition

1001 QUESTIONS ANSWERED

by

JEANNETTE W. CROSS
and
BLANCHE SAUNDERS

HAWTHORN BOOKS, INC.
Publishers / NEW YORK

Acknowledgments

Lloyd Sandford prepared most of the drawings in this book, except those on trimming of dogs' coats. The poodle-trimming
illustrations were made by Jeannette W. Cross; the trimming
diagrams for the twelve other breeds and a few others are repro-
duced here through the courtesy of the Durham-Enders Razor
Corporation of Mystic, Conn., and Mr. D. H. Henderson. Fred-
erick Lewis provided the photographs of dog bathing (by
Dean), the English setter bitch and puppies, the cocker spaniel
puppy, and the pointer in action (by Harold M. Lambert), and
the obedience class (by Ewing Krainin); also the photographs
of the Siberian husky, beagle puppy, boxer puppies, smooth
dachshund puppies, Irish terrier puppies, Chihuahua, Irish
water spaniel, mastiff, Komondor, Bouvier des Flandres, otterhound, harrier, affenpinscher, English foxhound, Eskimo, Mexican hairless, American foxhound, Staffordshire terrier, Sussex
spaniel, American water spaniel, flat-coated retriever, view of
judging rings at Westminster Kennel Club, Labrador retriever
in action, and the boy with Irish Setter—all by Percy Jones-
M. E. Browning.

About This Book

LOVING YOUR DOG is not enough. Affection and good intentions, important as they are, will not assure your dog of health and happiness, or you of a devoted, pleasant, and well-trained canine friend. For that, you need solid, practical know-how every step of the way.

The New Standard Book of Dog Care and Training has been planned to make the care of your dog, from puppyhood to old age, more enjoyable and free of needless headache and heartache. Not only should it spare you worry—it has been designed to spare you wasted effort as well, and to save you money. Here are some of the reasons why it will do these things for you:

The information in it is practical, authoritative, and up-to-date. The authors, Jeannette W. Cross and Blanche Saunders, enjoy a national reputation as breeders, raisers, and trainers of dogs. Many of the dogs they have raised are champions. In this book they have combined their rich fund of knowledge, based on years of day-to-day contact with dogs of all breeds, to show you how to give your dog the best of care. Their book tells you, in full detail, what you should know about dogs and their selection, training, feeding, general care and management, medical care, and grooming. It explains breeding thoroughly, and gives you an understanding of the mechanics and meaning of dog shows and field trials. It is valuable not only as a how-to guide, but also as a book for general reading and as a work of reference.

This book is easy to use. It is presented in the form of questions asked by dog owners, with clear, to-the-heart-of-the-matter answers by the authors. You can read the book through from start to finish or quickly locate, by means of the ready-reference index, the subject on which you require information. The questions are printed in boldface type, and there are many headings, making it easier for you to find what you want. A dictionary of dog terms and phrases, at the end of the book, defines words that may be unfamiliar to you. In addition, there are scores of helpful explanatory illustrations.

This is a book for every dog owner. The questions concern real dogs and the problems they cause their owners. Often these questions are amusing, and sparkle with human—and dog—interest. The authors enliven their answers with stories about real dogs, too. They write as they talk, in the simple, down-to-earth language that one dog owner uses to another. Throughout, you will feel that they are talking directly to you as they show you better, easier ways to give your dog the excellent care he needs and deserves.

THE PUBLISHERS

Contents

7

has "blue ribbon" parents—dogs for children—good watchdogs—the best American herd dog—breeds that bark less—dogs for different climates—toy dogs—what you should know about terriers—how to find something special—dogs by mail order—registration and what it means.

The foods your dog must have—foods your dog should never have—starch in your dog's diet—diets and different breeds—about commercial dog foods—dog biscuits—why dogs must have meat—bones for your dog—fish and eggs—milk, the perfect food—fat in your dog's diet—a dish for the dogs—the big meal of the day—kibble and how to prepare it—preparing food mixtures—underweight and overweight—diets right and wrong—variety in your dog's diet—when your cupboard is bare—when your dog is very hungry—rest periods before mealtime—why some dogs eat manure—why sweets are not recommended—facts about vitamins—how to treat the finicky feeder.

Why your dog should have a balanced diet—ingredients and preparation of milk formula for puppies—feeding charts for all breeds, arranged according to breed size—Menus for morning, noon, late afternoon, and evening meals, for dogs three months old—for dogs at four and five months—at six, seven, and eight months—nine months to one year—from twelve months on—substitutions and additions to the feeding charts.

Keeping your dog clean—how to bathe your dog—the "dry bath"—how to dry your dog—the doghouse and bedding—fencing for the dog yard—what to do where fences are forbidden—formula for a spray that will help keep the doghouse free of fleas—when your dog sleeps indoors—exercise means health to your dog—how to exercise your dog—wardrobes for dogs—the best collar for your dog—when to use a muzzle—free advice from commercial sources—your dog's drinking habits—how to control fleas—hot-weather care—preventing foot trouble—problems of country life—care of your dog's nails—care of your dog's teeth—combing and brushing—formula for skin-dressing mixture to beautify your dog's coat—ridding the dog of lice —the difference between clipping and stripping the coat—hair over a sheepdog's face—when to use electric clippers—if your dog has one ear up and one ear hanging—traveling with your dog—things to take along for the dog—if you travel by train—shipping-crate sizes for all breeds—special care for old dogs.

Part Two: HOW TO TRAIN YOUR DOG

Part Three:

DOG BREEDING, SHOWS, AND FIELD TRIALS

ing problems—nursing fits—when and how to wean puppies—care of the newborn puppies—docking puppy tails—tail-docking chart—cropping puppies' ears—raising orphans—canine birth control—false ideas about breeding—inbreeding and line-breeding—registering the litter—breeding as a business.

Part One

●

YOUR DOG

His Selection, Feeding, and General Care

CHAPTER 1

First Facts About Dogs

Over ten thousand years ago a man and a wolflike dog hunted in a great forest together. They did not know each other very well, and now and then cold distrust glittered in their eyes. But the dog kept scenting prey where the starving man thought there was none, and chased it till it could run no further, while the man, breathless, lagged behind. On the other hand, the man was craftier, and he knew how to use weapons to subdue large beasts against which the dog was powerless. Each grew in esteem in the other's eyes. After a while the man's rough blows felt more like pats, and the wolflike dog found himself less and less inclined to snap at his companion. Sometimes, on cold nights particularly, the dog even nuzzled up close when the man was sleeping, and one body took warmth from the other.

In some way such as this, there grew up the sturdiest friendship that history has ever seen between man and beast. Time has only served to draw the bond tighter. The dog has become not only man's fellow-hunter, but the protector of his flocks, the guardian of his home, his closest companion, and his greatest admirer. Small wonder that the dog is the most popular animal in the world today.

Every dog is different from the next, although all have certain things in common. There are over three hundred distinct breeds today, many of them produced by man to excel at special tasks and to conform to special standards of strength and beauty. No other domesticated animal shows such diversity of body and temperament.

15

This great variety of breeds is often bewildering to the person who simply wants to buy a dog as a pet or companion. Probably the most frequent question which is put to breeders, dog trainers, veterinarians, judges, writers about dogs, and, in fact, almost anyone who is considered at all informed on canine matters, is: "What is the best breed?" This is what the late Franklin D. Roosevelt used to call an "iffy" question, for the answer depends on many factors—the two most important being the personal taste of the individual and the purpose for which the dog is desired.

Broad statements about the character or disposition of an individual breed are likely to be inaccurate. When we describe a breed as exceptionally intelligent or unusually loyal, we simply mean that the majority of the dogs of that breed show these traits. Even in one litter you will find vastly differing temperaments. A puppy that is bold to the point of rashness may have a brother who is afraid of his own shadow and an exceptionally bright dog can have a littermate with the lowest of I.Q.s. A remark such as, "All Wire-haired Terriers are wild-acting hoodlums with no sense at all," reveals that the speaker does not know much about dogs, Wire-haired Terriers in particular. It is as inaccurate as the popular myth that mongrels are smarter than purebred dogs.

Dogs are by nature affectionate and teachable creatures. Given a healthy environment, understanding treatment, and proper training, 99 per cent of them will develop into delightful pets, no matter what their breed. Just as most juvenile delinquency is caused by misguided or irresponsible parents, so is most canine wrongdoing traceable to careless owners. It is not a dog's breed, but the way he is brought up that will determine whether he is to be a hoodlum or a heart-warming source of pride and pleasure to his owner.

Breeds Raised in America

How many breeds are raised in America?

At the present time, the American Kennel Club recognizes 115 breeds. These breeds are divided into six groups: Sporting Dogs,

Hounds, Working Dogs, Terriers, Toy Dogs, and Nonsporting Dogs. In Part Four of this book we shall give you a good idea of the appearance, characteristics, history, and uses of all these breeds and more.

The names of the various groups (with the exception of the confusingly named Nonsporting Group) indicate fairly well the purposes for which the breeds comprising each group have been developed. The Sporting Group is made up of bird dogs and retrievers, keen-nosed finders and fetchers of feathered game; the Hound Group, of breeds which are fleet pursuers and patient trackers of fur-bearing animals. The Working Group contains the breeds that excel at guard and patrol duty, the herding of livestock, leading the blind, and other responsible jobs; the Terrier Group, all the many types of varmint-destroying terriers that are characterized by their gameness, pep, and good nature. The Toy Group comprises those miniature breeds which have been bred for their attractive appearance and affectionate dispositions. The Nonsporting Group is a diverse collection of breeds, too large in size to be classified as Toys, which are now mostly pets, though several of them have sporting or working backgrounds, as for example the Poodle which was originally a retriever, and the Schipperke which was, in spite of his small size, once used as a watchdog.

These groups, which have been set up by the American Kennel Club for bench-show purposes, denote the backgrounds of the various breeds and the uses for which, by inheritance, they are likely to prove most adaptable. Within each group, however, are breeds which differ from one another greatly in size, coat, conformation and temperament. The Working Group, for instance contains both the statuesque and dignified Great Dane, and that cocky little busybody the Welsh Corgi. The only group displaying any uniformity even of size is the Toy Group, all the members of which are diminutive.

Besides the American Kennel Club breeds, there are several American breeds, well established as individual types, which are recognized and registered by other organizations. The United Kennel Club, of Kalamazoo, Michigan, registers a number of this group—the Toy Fox Terrier, the Spitz (or American Eskimo), the English Shepherd, the Plott Hound, the Redbone Hound, the Bluetick Hound, the English Coonhound and the Treeing Walker Hound. The North American Sheepdog Society maintains the stud book of the Border Collie, and there are at least seven organizations located in the southern and western states which register Foxhounds and Coonhounds of various types not accepted for listing by the American Kennel Club.

Popular Favorites

What breeds are the most popular in America?

The top ten breeds according to recent American Kennel Club registrations are: Poodles, Beagles, Dachshunds, Chihuahuas, German Shepherds, Pekingese, Collies, Cocker Spaniels, Boston Terriers and Pomeranians, in that order. This is not a complete picture, however, for there are three favorite American breeds that are mainly registered with other organizations, though they are recognized by the A.K.C. and its stud book is open to them. They are American Foxhounds, Pointers and English Setters. If the Pointers and Setters, annually entered in the Field Dog Stud Book, and the American Foxhounds, listed in the five stud books open to them, were taken into consideration, the over-all result would in all probability show these breeds among the first ten.

What do people mean when they talk about a breed being fashionable? Isn't that the same thing as being popular?

No, not quite. Poodles, for instance, particularly the Miniature and Toy are extremely fashionable. These dogs are great favorites with Parisians and with the people who set fashions in this country. Consequently, they were considered exceedingly chic even before the breed ranked among the ten most popular here. On the other hand, the Beagle is a popular breed but not particularly fashionable and does not sell for the fancy prices commanded by Poodles.

How do you account for the great popularity of the Cocker Spaniel for so many years?

The popularity of the Cocker Spaniel seems to be living proof of the old saw about "Love begets love." Other breeds may be more useful, keener mentally, more impressive looking, but no breed is more sweetly devoted and adoring than the Cocker. When it's love that's in demand—and when isn't it?—the Cocker Spaniel is the dog to fill the bill.

What are the main differences between the English Cocker Spaniel and the American type?

According to Joseph C. Quirk, a respected authority on sporting dogs, the most noticeable contrasts between the two are these: the English Cocker should be a larger, leggier dog than the American type, with a longer, narrower head, lengthier muzzle, and a less profusely feathered coat.

Recently I read a magazine article about dogs which stated that the Collie is among the ten most popular breeds. Do you think the Lassie movies and television shows are the reason for this?

Movie-hero dogs undoubtedly have a strong effect in promoting the popularity of various breeds. The tremendous demand for German Shepherds during the 1920s was due partly to the breed's distinguished service record in World War I, but was even more strongly affected by the movies starring the German Shepherds, Rin-Tin-Tin and Strongheart. The Lassie movies have probably enhanced the Collie's position a good deal, although this breed's popularity is nothing new. Collies have been near the top in popularity, both in this country and England, for more than fifty years. Queen Victoria admired Collies, and her liking for them gave them great prestige as long ago as the 1860s. Albert Payson Terhune's novels and short stories about Collies still further glorified the breed. Such a long period of public favor as the Collie has known does not come about by chance. Helpful publicity often gives a breed a temporary boost, but the Collie's good looks, intelligence, and dependable disposition are the real reasons for the breed's enduring popularity.

Is the popularity of a breed built up by specimens of that breed winning high awards at dog shows?

It never hurts the prestige of a breed when one of its representatives wins top honors in an important show, but too small a percentage of the general public pays much attention to dog-show results for this one factor to raise a breed to any great height of popular approval. The puppies that are sold as pets and companions are the most potent good-will ambassadors for a breed. When these youngsters are consistently of attractive appearance, good disposition, and sound health they do more to bring attention to their breed's merits than any number of show wins.

Don't men prefer different breeds of dogs than women do?

Apparently they do. *Esquire* magazine once conducted a poll to determine men's favorite breeds and the results showed wide variation from the American Kennel Club's popularity rankings. This is how it came out:

Ten Most Popular Breeds with Men According to Esquire	Rank of Men's Preferences in A.K.C. Registrations	Most Popular Breeds According to A.K.C. Registrations
1. Boxer	11th	1. Poodle
2. Great Dane	28th	2. Beagle
3. German Shepherd	5th	3. Dachshund
4. Cocker Spaniel	8th	4. Chihuahua
5. Collie	7th	5. German Shepherd
6. Standard Poodle	1st	6. Pekingese
7. Wire-haired Fox Terrier	13th	7. Collie
8. Dachshund	3rd	8. Cocker Spaniel
9. Irish Setter	27th	9. Boston Terrier
10. English Springer Spaniel	20th	10. Pomeranian

No one has conducted a poll which would indicate the breeds which women like best, but the results would probably place more of the toy breeds among the first ten, and show less of a preference for big dogs.

The streets of the city where I live always seem to be full of people walking their dogs, but I seldom see a Beagle. If Beagles are so popular, where are they all?

In small towns, farm districts, rural areas—in fact, any place where there are rabbits to be hunted—you will find Beagles. People don't seem to think of Beagles as being suitable for city living, though dog owners who have tried it have found that the cheerful little hound is as pleasant a pal for big-town life as one could desire.

Male or Female?

If we buy a female dog, is it true that we will be continually annoyed by the male dogs she will attract?

The *only* time a female dog is attractive to male dogs is when she is in season. Most bitches come in season at six-month intervals and the period usually lasts from two to three weeks. During this time she is most enticing to males and must be closely confined in order that an undesirable mating does not take place. At other times male dogs will pay no more attention to a bitch than they would to another male.

Is it true that a female dog is a better pet than a male?

People who really know dogs often prefer a female as a house pet. They feel a female is usually more affectionate, less likely to rove, and a more dependable watchdog. Breeders who have a whole kennel full of dogs from which to choose their house dogs almost always have a female or two in the house as their special pets.

Facts About Females

We are buying a female Dalmatian puppy. Our home is in a small village where all the dogs in town run loose and as we are not interested in raising puppies, are thinking of having our Dalmatian spayed. A friend has told us that if she is spayed she will become very unattractive—fat, lazy, and mentally dull. Is this true?

No, it isn't. A spayed bitch is a wonderful pet and if her diet is properly controlled she will keep her figure. As for the spaying operation affecting her mentality, that's nonsense. Few people, aside from kennel owners, are able to give an unspayed bitch the careful confinement necessary at the times she is in season in order to prevent her from presenting her owner with a litter of unwanted mongrels. It is hard to understand how the theory that a spayed bitch is ruined as a pet or watchdog became so prevalent. Any dog or bitch will become fat and sluggish if it is overfed, and a bitch that has been spayed will also resemble a pig if her loving owner gives her too much to eat. A spayed bitch, given proper care, is just as pleasant as a companion and alert as a guardian as any other dog and can be given as much freedom as a male. In other words, she combines the virtues of both sexes and is less inclined to the vices of either.

I live in a city where all dogs must, because of a city law, be kept on leash at all times. Would you advise me to have my female Cairn Terrier puppy spayed?

No. If you lived in an area where your Cairn were turned loose to roam it would be safer, but as long as she is leading the sheltered life of a city pet there is no reason for spaying her.

Why is it that so many people refuse to own a female dog as a pet and that even the word bitch is a term of contempt?

The feeling against female dogs dates back to the time of the Crusades. One of the beliefs of the Moslem religion is that the dog is an unclean animal. Another of its tenets is that women are lowly creatures, worthy of no consideration whatsoever, and are just one jump ahead of the dogs as far as social position is concerned. Consequently, the unfortunate combination of being both canine and female made the bitch an animal held in great disdain by the natives of Asia Minor. This lamentable intolerance was brought back to Europe by the returning Crusaders and only within the past fifty or sixty years has begun to die a well-deserved death.

Aside from this ancient prejudice, the general public still holds several misconceptions about female dogs. One is that they are a constant source of sexual allurement to male dogs and the ownership of a bitch means one's house is in a continual state of siege by canine suitors. The truth is that a bitch is interesting to male dogs at *no time* except when she is in season. She has no unpleasant odor about her at this time and, furthermore, will fight off the advances of a male dog, except during a period of four or five days in the middle of that period. The rest of the time she is the sweetest pet in the world. The majority of those who have owned bitches as pets like them so much that they will always choose a female in preference to a male dog as a companion.

Why is a bitch considered a more dependable watchdog than a male dog?

It is believed that a female dog is less easily distracted from her job than a male. There have been numerous cases in which male watchdogs have been lured from their posts by bitches in heat used by housebreakers and thieves who are aware of this male weakness. Rudyard Kipling's lines, "The female of the species is more deadly than the male," apply as much to canines as to other animals.

The Purebred Dog

What is the difference between a purebred dog and a thoroughbred dog?

There is no such thing as a thoroughbred dog. A thoroughbred is a type of horse. A purebred dog is a dog whose ancestry is known to consist of many generations of the same breed, with no admixture of blood from any other breeds.

Is a purebred dog the same thing as a registered dog?

No. In order to be eligible for registration with the American Kennel Club, a dog *must* be purebred, but not all purebred dogs are registered.

What is meant by a breed's being "recognized" by the American Kennel Club?

It means that the American Kennel Club maintains stud records and a registration system for a particular breed. Any dog show which is rated as an "all-breed" show must offer classes for all recognized breeds.

Why are some breeds not accorded American Kennel Club recognition?

Usually because there are not enough dogs of these breeds in the United States to warrant records being kept on them or classes offered for them at shows.

If a dog is a purebred, is he eligible for registration in a recognized stud book?

Yes, if his sire and dam were registered.

Why are some imported purebred dogs accepted for registration with the American Kennel Club while others are not?

Whether or not an imported dog is eligible for registration with the American Kennel Club depends upon the availability of authentic records from the dog's country of origin. Records, stud books, and breeding files were lost or destroyed in many European countries during World War II. Consequently, dogs from those countries cannot be registered, though they are obviously purebreds.

Will you please explain the difference between a pedigreed dog and one that is registered?

A pedigree is the record of a dog's ancestors. Even a mongrel could have a pedigree if someone took the trouble to puzzle out his family tree and put down the names of his forebears. A registered dog is one whose pedigree shows that his ancestors were of pure breeding and were registered in a recognized stud book.

I understand what is meant when I hear of or read about a dog being of some particular breed, but sometimes a dog is described as being of some special variety. What is the difference between a breed and a variety?

A variety is a division within a breed. For instance, Fox Terriers are considered one breed, but may be either one of two varieties, the Smooth Fox Terrier or the Wire-haired Fox Terrier. Another breed which is divided into varieties is the Cocker Spaniel. In this case there are three classifications which are made according to color—solid black, any solid color other than black, and particolor. Some of the other breeds which have variety divisions according to height, color or coat type are Bull Terriers, Collies, Dachshunds, Poodles, and Beagles.

What is a "made" breed?

A "made" breed is a breed that has been created by man in order to fulfill a specific purpose. With a definite picture in mind of the new breed to be brought into being, breeders have scientifically crossbred dogs of different breeds, until a type was established which would breed true. The Bull Mastiff and the Doberman Pinscher are examples of "made" breeds.

The sad-faced docile-looking dogs that appear in the drawings of James Thurber have always amused me and made me wish to own such an animal. Are there any real dogs that look like Mr. Thurber's pictures?

Yes, there are. Bloodhounds, Basset Hounds and Newfoundlands look very much like Thurber dogs. All these breeds are very gentle, have affectionate dispositions, and make wonderful pets.

There's a billboard that I pass on my way to work every day and last week there was a beer ad on it, showing a dog that looked to me like a miniature Airedale. Is there such a breed?

What you saw was a Welsh Terrier. This breed does resemble a scaled-down Airedale, as both breeds have the same black-and-tan coloring, wiry coat, and squared-off outlines.

Photographs of the British royal family often show them accompanied by small dogs? What kind of dogs are they?

They are Pembroke Welsh Corgis. The royal family owns several Corgis, a fact which has enhanced the breed's popularity a great deal in recent years.

Facts About Mongrels

Is a dog that is the result of the mating of two purebred dogs of different breeds just as much of a mongrel as one whose parents were both mongrels?

Yes, as far as being eligible for registration is concerned. However, when both parents of a puppy are known to be purebreds, though of different breeds, the offspring is frequently referred to as a "crossbred" rather than a mongrel.

Many people claim that mongrels are smarter and healthier than purebred dogs. Is this true?

No. It's nonsense. If mongrels were smarter than purebreds, institutions that train guide dogs for the blind would not insist on using only purebreds for this work. And sportsmen would not pay big prices for purebred bird dogs and retrievers if mongrels were just as capable. As for the health angle, any practicing veterinarian will affirm the fact that mongrels are just as vulnerable to the ravages of distemper germs, skin ailments, and worms as are their purebred relatives.

My grocery man has a litter of three-month-old puppies which he says are part Collie and part some kind of Terrier. They are very cute and he wants to give me one, but how can I tell what it will look like when it grows up?

You can't. That's the trouble with mongrels. All puppies are tremendously appealing, but when you take on a puppy of mixed breeding, your chances of having it develop into a dog you'll be proud of are questionable. A mongrel may resemble either or neither of its parents, or may even inherit the more unattractive features of both.

Is it true that if the roof of a dog's mouth is black he is a pure-bred?

No, it doesn't mean anything at all. Many a mongrel, descended from a long line of mongrels, has a mouth with a black roof.

Is there anything at all to be said in favor of mongrels, or mutts, as most people call them?

Certainly there is. Mongrels are often very attractive dogs, highly intelligent, loyal and loving. They can usually be acquired for little or no money. They are generally fairly hardy physical specimens, for were they not, they would never survive their casual origins. There is one great disadvantage—mutts are not replaceable when lost through old age, sickness, or accident, because no two mongrels are alike. The owner of a purebred who loses his dog can get another dog of the same breed, which, of course, will not be *exactly* like the one he has lost, but will at least be very much the same in appearance and, possibly, in character too.

What kind of a dog is "Daisy" that belongs to Dagwood and Blondie Bumstead in the funny papers?

In spite of her heart of gold, Daisy's ancestry appears to be about as mixed as the contents of one of Dagwood's sandwiches. She is pure kiyoodle.

Viciousness In Dogs

Is viciousness common among our modern dogs?

No. American breeders have made a sincere effort to breed dogs of reliable temperament, and viciousness is quite rare. European breeders, the Germans in particular, have emphasized "sharpness" in the large breeds which are used for police duty. These same breeds, in the hands of Americans who have put stress on good dispositions, have become trustworthy companions.

When the K-9 Corps was training dogs for service with the armed forces during World War II, the dogs had to be *taught* to attack, and a great many of them could not be induced to bite anyone no matter how much training they received.

Occasionally specimens of the "police duty" breeds mentioned above have an excess of nervous driving energy which may lead to trouble if the dogs are improperly trained, not trained at all, or permitted too much unsupervised freedom. Any of these conditions may produce a dog that would be unsafe in the hands of most owners. In fairness to the dogs, though, it should be mentioned that bad dispositions are more often the result of environment than heredity.

The Oldest, The Biggest, The Smallest

What is the most ancient breed?

That is a disputed point. In the opinion of most authorities it is either the Afghan Hound or the Saluki. Pictures and carvings of dogs which bear a strong resemblance to these two breeds have been found in ancient Egyptian tombs which date back to 4000 B.C. The Saluki probably has the edge in this argument, for recent excavations in Eridu, Mesopotamia, which has been termed by archeologists the oldest city in the world, uncovered a tomb containing the remains of a young boy and his favorite hound which had been buried with him. The dog was unmistakably a Saluki and its skeleton gave evidence that this breed has remained unchanged for thousands of years.

Which breed is the biggest?

The tallest breed is the Irish Wolfhound. Many specimens of this breed stand thirty-four to thirty-six inches at the shoulder. Mastiffs and St. Bernards often weigh more than the Irish dogs for they are much more heavily built.

What is the smallest breed of dog?

The Chihuahua. Specimens of this breed weighing between two and four pounds are considered correct in size. Breeders strive consistently to produce puppies who will be in this weight range on maturity, making them the pocket pieces of dogdom.

Which Breeds Live Longer

Are some breeds inclined to live longer than others?

In most cases, dogs of the small breeds seem to be longer-lived than representatives of the large breeds. This is a reversal of the laws of nature that affect other animals, for most species that take a long time to reach maturity are long-lived (the elephant is a good example of this), while those that achieve maturity quickly are short-lived. In spite of the fact that dogs of the large breeds are two or three years of age before they are completely developed, they show signs of age much sooner than specimens of the small breeds, which reach their full growth when one year or eighteen months old.

Is it true that one year in the life of a dog is equal to seven years of a human's life?

It was formerly believed that the ratio of a human being's age to that of a dog's is seven to one, but the prevailing theory is this: At one year of age a dog corresponds in development to a human being sixteen years of age; at two years, to a human of twenty-four; at three, to a human of thirty; and when a dog is four, he is comparable to a human being thirty-five years old. After he is four years old, each following year in a dog's life is equivalent to a period of five years in a human being's life.

Your Dog and Your Morale

*Those who love dogs maintain that owning a dog is mentally
and emotionally beneficial to the owner. Is this really so?*

Sociologists say that dogs have often an important influence
on the mental health of humans, for these reasons: A dog is an
outlet for affection which need not be concealed or disguised
in any way. A dog's demonstration of friendliness or love is
gratifying because there is never any question about the honesty
of his emotions—duplicity is foreign to the canine character.

Children who own dogs and are entrusted with their complete care, develop a sense of responsibility which would be difficult to instill by any other method. A dog can build up the
deflated ego of the individual whose days are spent obeying the
orders of others, for in the dog he finds a creature that *he* can
command and control. For the lonely, the defeated, the misfit,
the painfully shy, the isolated, the dog provides the solace of
loyal, uncritical, responsive companionship.

A striking demonstration of the role which dogs can play in
the building up of human morale took place during World War II
at the Army Air Forces' Convalescent Hospital at Pawling, New
York. Many of the patients were men whose war experiences had
left their nerves so shaken that they were completely unfitted for
return to civilian life. Cases of this type were characterized by
a withdrawn sort of melancholia and an indifferent attitude
toward making a recovery. Psychiatric investigation uncovered
one subject that struck a spark of interest—dogs.

Through the untiring efforts of the late Mrs. Marvin Preston,
a breeder of Chows, purebred dogs of the breeds the men wanted
were obtained and presented to those patients who indicated
they would enjoy having a pet. A kennel was set up on the
hospital grounds and put in the charge of an experienced manager, Richard Farnham, who supervised the dogs' diets and kept
an eye on their health. At times there were as many as forty
dogs "in residence" at the hospital. The dogs were with their
convalescent owners during all their waking hours, returning to
the kennels only to sleep.

The results of the program were almost miraculous. The wagging tails and friendly eyes of their pets seemed to act as a tonic to the men, who found in the affectionate companionship of the dogs a happy distraction from their illnesses. Mental attitudes changed from gloom to optimism and hospital authorities credited the dogs with having speeded up recovery rates to the point where men were being released as cured months ahead of the dates that had been predicted. The story has a happy ending too, for each man's dog was his for "keeps" and when he finally left the hospital for home his dog went with him.

Your Character and Your Dog

My father always claimed that he could tell a great deal about a man's character by the breed of dog he owned or liked. Is this a sound theory?

Your father must have believed completely in John Ruskin's dictum, "Tell me what you like, and I'll tell you what you are," but it doesn't really hold true in regard to dogs. A dog's behavior is a more accurate indication of his owner's character than is his breed. Certainly, no man or boy who prided himself on being very much of a he-man would be expected to go in for raising Pomeranians, nor would the very feminine and fastidious type of woman care much for having a Chesapeake Bay Retriever for a pet, but a survey of the owners of any one breed would show only slight conformity of disposition, background or general type. Breed clubs, which are organizations of fanciers interested in the same kind of dog, show great diversity in their memberships. In fact, about the only thing that most of the members have in common is that they happen to like the same breed.

People Who Should Not Own Dogs

Do you believe there are people who should not own a dog?

There certainly are. Careless people who think their only responsibility toward a dog is to feed it have no right to own dogs. Usually the dogs belonging to people of this sort are the flea-ridden creatures that roam the streets, raid garbage cans, kill cats and chickens, tear up lawns and gardens, and keep the neighbors awake with nocturnal yowling. Some people like dogs and insist on owning one, refusing to accept the fact that they really haven't time enough for a dog. An example of this is the person whose job keeps him away from home all day, while his dog leads a life of lonely, boring confinement. The type of housekeeper known as "nasty nice" is never a happy dog owner. Any dog, no matter how well trained, will occasionally bring in dirt on his feet, scuff up rugs, shed hair, or cause other disorder, which will annoy the overfussy housewife.

Then there are unspeakable individuals who adopt a dog from a city pound or humane society shelter, keep it while they spend the summer in the country, and then abandon the poor animal when they return to the city in the fall.

Dogs belonging to the ultrafashionable and wealthy are not as lucky as one might think. Owners of this sort frequently regard a dog as a plaything with which to entertain themselves. Much of the time the dog is in the charge of servants who may resent the extra work of feeding, exercising, and grooming, and take their resentment out on the animal. To sum it up, those who are unwilling or unable to give a dog time, attention, care, and affection should not own one.

Why is it that some people apparently like to own a big, mean-acting dog?

A person with an inferiority complex might conceivably derive feelings of importance and power from owning and controlling a large, savage dog which frightens other people. It is not unknown for a neurotic owner actually to encourage ferocity in a dog, for the more menacing the dog's behavior, the more like Superman the owner feels.

A Dog's Mind and Aptitudes

What is the most intelligent breed? This claim is made for so many breeds that it's hard to know what to believe.

There is no pat answer to this one. Certain breeds have certain aptitudes, but statements about one particular breed being more

PLAYMATES

The child who owns a dog not only has a wonderful playmate, but learns, through taking care of the dog, to accept responsibilities. The dog shown here is an Irish Setter, one of the most beautiful of all breeds.

THE AMERICAN KENNEL CLUB
CHAMPIONSHIP CERTIFICATE

This certifies that

Dachshund — Hardway Welcome Stranger — owned by Mrs. John W. Cross, Jr. — having been awarded 15 points in Winners Classes, under The American Kennel Club rules, is a

CHAMPION OF RECORD

No. H-110609

Dated May 19, 1951

P. B. Everett
Secretary

A CHAMPION AND HIS CERTIFICATE

An American Kennel Club Certificate of championship is a prized possession. The holder of this one is Hardway Welcome Stranger, champion Dachshund.

intelligent than all others are ridiculous. Who can say which is the cleverest—the Setter that finds and points birds, the German Shepherd that leads a sightless human being, the Bloodhound that can follow an intricate trail, or the Border Collie that rounds up and controls a herd of sheep? Each of these dogs is outstanding in his own field of performance but would be lost if called on to do the job that another breed learns easily.

There was an argument at my house last night about which is the more intelligent animal—dog or monkey. I said the dog is, and my guests claimed that monkeys are smarter than dogs. Who is right?

Your guests are. Scientists rate the monkey to be above the dog in mental ability. The dog is a more easily trained animal though, for he alone, of all animals, will respond to praise or reprimand from his master. Of course, many other animals can be trained, but they obey because of fear of punishment, as in the case of the horse, or in the hope of reward in the form of food, an instance of this being the trained seal that is fed pieces of fish as he goes through his routine. Only the dog will obey simply for love of a human being.

Is there any explanation for the fact that the dog is more popu-lar as a pet than any other animal?

There is a psychological reason, and it is this: The dog and the human being are very similar in emotional make-up. When a dog's owner tells you that the dog can sense his moods, don't snicker. It's perfectly true. Because of these emotional bonds, there is a responsiveness between dogs and humans that does not exist between other living creatures.

Why is it that some breeds are inclined to be high-strung and excitable while others are easygoing?

The emotional behavior of a breed, as a whole, is determined by hereditary organic factors. The breeds which are typified by high-tension temperaments have larger thyroid and adrenal glands

than those whose general behavior is characterized by steadiness
and placidity.

The idea of a dog's being a "one-man dog" has always sounded
  good to me. Are some breeds more likely to have this type
  of disposition than others, and, if so, what are they?

As mentioned before, it's dangerous to make flat statements
about the disposition of any one breed. There are several breeds,
however, that have a tendency toward the reserved "one-man dog"
type of temperament. They are: the Chow Chow, the Doberman
Pinscher, the German Shepherd, the Scottish Terrier, the Chesapeake Bay Retriever, the Gordon Setter, the Standard Schnauzer
the Giant Schnauzer, the Borzoi, and the Pekingese.

People often credit dogs with having a sense of humor. Are
  there breeds which are noted for this characteristic?

There are a few. Welsh and Irish Terriers have the sort of
roguishness that indicates a sense of humor. Dachshunds are often
born clowns, so are Poodles. Most Sealyham Terriers are willing
to make fools of themselves for their owner's entertainment, and
many Old English Sheepdogs are inclined to be comedians. Individuals of many other breeds have a droll turn of mind, but the
characteristic seems most prevalent in the breeds mentioned above.

What is meant when a breed is described as having a "senti-
  mental" disposition? And which breeds have this sort of
  temperament?

When a dog is described as being sentimental, it means he
is sweetly loving by nature and his attitude toward his master
is one of worshipful affection. Spaniels and Setters are noted
for this type of disposition.

Do some breeds of dogs dislike certain other breeds? My Boxer
  a friendly and playful dog, goes for every Collie he sees.

Certain dogs appear to have a strong animosity toward some
breeds and definite preference for others, but their attitude is

probably due to past associations and experiences with individual
dogs rather than deep-dyed, inbred hatred.

*Have short-faced breeds, that is, breeds with pushed-in noses
such as Boxers, Boston Terriers, Bulldogs, as good scenting
powers as long-nosed breeds?*

Usually not. The breeds with the keenest scenting powers
almost all have long, deep muzzles with large, widely-opened
nostrils.

*Are German Shepherds the only breed used as guide dogs for
the blind?*

Probably more German Shepherds are used for this work
than any other breed, as they are more likely to have the combination of intelligence, initiative, and steadiness which is needed
for such a serious job. The Doberman Pinscher has proven
himself a reliable guide dog too and in some few cases Boxers
and Labrador Retrievers have been successfully used.

*Aren't Poodles supposed to be very intelligent? Why, then,
aren't they used for leading blind people?*

Poodles are smart all right, but they are clowns and show-offs,
too, and their playfulness makes them unreliable for such responsible work as leading the blind. A Poodle wouldn't be bothered
leading a blind person around an obstacle which he himself
could clear. He'd jump just for the fun of it and let his master
make out as best he could. Then, too, the Poodle prefers to
be led rather than do the leading.

What breeds are best for obedience training?

Fine obedience work is done by many breeds. The brilliant
exhibition of obedience-trained dogs at a recent Westminster
Kennel Club Show had nineteen different breeds participating,
and it would be hard to single out the representative of any one

breed as having put on the best performance. Generally speaking, the working breeds, because they are more serious-minded, are the most reliable obedience performers.

Dogs and Their National Origins

Do you think that there is anything in the theory that the country of a breed's origin has some bearing on the type of temperament which is typical of that breed?

To some extent, yes. Certainly the Irish Setter has the gay devil-may-care temperament which is considered Irish, and the Kerry Blue Terrier and Irish Terrier both personify Irish pluck and gameness. The Scottish Terrier has a reserved and dour disposition, which bears out his Highland origin, and the Dandie Dinmont's independence and dignity are typically Caledonian too. The Bulldog's tenacity quite properly symbolizes the English ability to "carry on." It is easy to understand why the Poodle is frequently (and wrongly) called the "French Poodle," for this breed has the quick intelligence, gaiety, and humor which are the special attributes of the French people. German Shepherds and Dobermans usually exhibit the amenability to discipline which is a German trait, while the Dachshund has the persistence which is thought of as Teutonic. Chows have the aloof dignity of the Chinese aristocrat. The list of such instances could be almost endless, but these few examples should be sufficient to prove that there is something in the theory of a breed's country of origin being reflected in its disposition.

What breeds are of American origin?

The Boston Terrier is a made-in-America product, as are the Chesapeake Bay Retriever and the American Water Spaniel. The Black-and-Tan Coonhound and the American Foxhound were brought to their present form in this country too. The American-type Cocker Spaniel, though developed from imported foundation stock, is also the result of the work of American breeders.

What country has produced or developed the greatest number of breeds?

England, with twenty-seven breeds.

What are the rarest breeds in this country?

There are several breeds so rare that sometimes a year or two goes by without a single specimen being registered with the A.K.C. This does not mean that a breed is extinct, but simply that it is in the hands of a very few owners who do not breed their dogs extensively. Here are some of the most infrequently-seen breeds: Mexican Hairless, Affenpinscher, Field Spaniel, Komondor, Harrier, Eskimo, Clumber Spaniel, Sussex Spaniel, Wire-haired Pointing Griffon, Bernese Mountain Dog, Flat-coated Retriever, Curly-coated Retriever, and Otterhound.

Words Used to Describe a Dog

Why is it that the official standards of many dog breeds use so much "horse language," such as "hocks," "withers," "stifles," in speaking of the various points of the dog's anatomy?

The first people who took the trouble to make note of the physical structure considered correct for the different dog breeds were sportsmen and horsemen familiar with the conformation of horses. It was only natural for them, therefore, to apply the names used for the parts of the horse to the corresponding points of the dog. Even now, breeders of English Foxhounds speak of a male Foxhound used for breeding purposes as a "stallion hound."

Facts About Hunting Dogs

What is the most popular bird-dog breed for practical hunting use in this country?

According to William F. Brown, editor of *The American Field* and a top authority on bird dogs, this honor is divided about evenly between the Pointer and the English Setter.

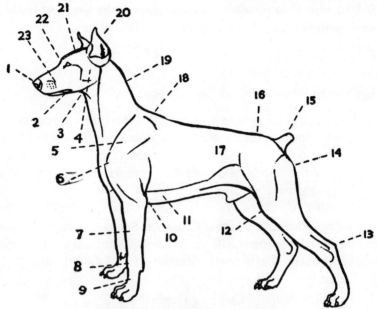

POINTS OF THE DOG'S BODY

(1) Nose. (2) Lips or flews. (3) Dewlap. (4) Cheek. (5)
Shoulder. (6) Point of shoulder. (7) Forearm. (8) Knee.
(9) Pastern. (10) Elbow. (11) Chest. (12) Stifle. (13) Hock.
(14) Point of rump. (15) Tail. (16) Rump or croup. (17)
Loin. (18) Withers. (19) Arch or crest. (20) Ear. (21) Skull.
(22) Stop. (23) Muzzle.

*Why is it that so many more Pointers than Setters compete in
bird-dog field trials?*

Field-trial enthusiasts have come to prefer the Pointer because
as a breed the Pointer develops faster than the Setter and is
consequently ready for training and field-trial competition at an
earlier age.

*Has the English Setter any advantages over the Pointer as a gun
dog?*

The Setter's heavier coat makes it possible for him to stand
much colder weather than can the Pointer, and also protects
him from being scratched and cut by briars and heavy underbrush.

Is it true that Pointers are such great natural hunters that they are liable to go off and hunt on their own if given much freedom?

There is no getting around the fact that Pointers are very enthusiastic hunters, and many of them become incurable roamers when allowed to run loose. This is liable to occur with a dog of any of the large hunting breeds that has no opportunity to exercise his ability in the field.

Are there any breeds besides the English Setter and the Pointer that will find and point birds?

The English Setter and the Pointer are the two best-known pointing breeds, but there are several other sporting breeds which will point birds. They are: Irish Setter, Gordon Setter, Wirehaired Pointing Griffon, German Shorthaired Pointer, Brittany Spaniel, and Weimaraner.

What is a sight-hound?

All hound breeds are classified either as sight-hounds or scent-hounds depending on their manner of hunting. Those which run down game by using their noses to follow the trail are called scent-hounds. Beagles, Bloodhounds, and Fox Hounds are three of the breeds which hunt this way. Hounds which use their eyes to follow their prey are called sight-hounds, and seem to have much keener vision than other breeds. The Greyhound, the Afghan Hound, and the Borzoi are examples of hounds which hunt by sight.

What breed is considered best for duck-hunting use?

Chesapeake Bay Retrievers are specialists on ducks. They have great natural aptitude as swimmers and will plunge without hesitation into rough and icy water, displaying tremendous endurance and courage. As a willing, tireless retriever of waterfowl the Chesapeake is supreme.

What breed is considered the best gun dog for use on pheasants?

The English Springer Spaniel is a specialist on pheasant and most sportsmen prefer that breed above all others for hunting this crafty game bird.

Do pointing breeds and spaniels hunt in the same way?

No. Pointing breeds are expected to cover a wide range in seeking feathered game, to find and point birds, and then remain steady on point while the hunter shoots. Spaniels should hunt within range of the handler's gun, find and flush birds, mark the spot where shot birds fall, and then retrieve them.

What is a Llewellin Setter?

This is not a separate breed, as many people seem to think, but is an English Setter whose pedigree traces back to the original foundation stock of the breed owned by Mr. R. L. Purcell Llewellin of Pembrokeshire, South Wales. Mr. Llewellin is credited with the establishment of the modern field-trial type English Setter, and the Setters descended from the dogs he developed are referred to as being of the Llewellin strain. Many of today's field-trial winning English Setters are of Llewellin lineage.

Why isn't the Irish Setter used for hunting purposes as extensively as the English Setter?

The Irish Setter has been the victim of his own good looks. The breed's handsomeness, gaiety and personality make him an ideal show dog and pet. For many years breeders have entirely ignored the Irishman's hunting ability and concentrated entirely on producing specimens of great physical beauty. Consequently, except for a few isolated cases, the Irish Setter's aptitude as a bird dog is no longer utilized to any degree.

Is a "nonslip" retriever a special breed of hunting dog?

No. There are several breeds which are used as nonslip retrievers. The term "nonslip" refers to the work a dog has been trained to do in the hunting field or duck blind. The job of the nonslip retriever is to stay right with the handler, walking quietly at heel in the field, or sitting in the duck blind, and to find and retrieve fallen game on order. Labrador, Chesapeake and Golden Retrievers, and some of the Spaniel breeds, are used in this way by hunters.

Which breed has the best record in retriever trials?

The Labrador has won more first places in these contests than all the other breeds combined.

I've been told that if hunting dogs—retrievers, bird dogs, spaniels, hounds—are pets they are liable to lose their desire to hunt. Is this so?

Not at all. Henry P. Davis, a top authority on sporting dogs and one of America's most respected judges of bird-dog field trials, has stated that "the hunting instinct is an inborn trait of the hunting dog and its development in the highest degree can only be attained when there is complete understanding— and affection—between the hunter and his dog," and "the way to get the most out of your dog is to win his affection and gain his confidence and respect. The shortest cut to this is to make a 'pet' of him." Further proof of the fact that a dog can be a pet and a good hunting dog at the same time is shown by the fact that many of the greatest field-trial winners have been house dogs who got plenty of affection and attention from their owners or handlers.

Great Danes

The other day in an elevator I overheard someone talking about a Harlequin Great Dane. What on earth is that?

In general, Great Danes may show one of five color variations: brindle (dark streaks on a golden brown background), blue (bluish steel gray), fawn, black, or harlequin. The standard of the Great Dane describes the Harlequin as follows: "Base color: pure white with black torn patches irregularly and well-distributed over the entire body; pure white neck preferred. The black patches should never be large enough to give the appearance of a blanket nor so small as to give a stippled or dappled effect." This striking coloring, in combination with the Dane's imposing size and proud carriage, makes a good Harlequin an eye-filling sight.

A Word About Bulldogs

The terms Boston Bulldog, English Bulldog, and French Bulldog confuse me. Are these all names for the same breed, varieties of the same breed, three separate breeds, or what?

They are three separate breeds. Maybe this will help you to keep them straight. The Boston is the smallest of the three breeds, and his correct name is Boston *Terrier*, not Bulldog. He is distinguished by his dark brindle or black coat, with a white band around the muzzle, white blaze running up his face between the eyes, white chest and collar markings, and white feet. His ears are usually cropped to stand in thin, erect points.

The French Bulldog is a larger-boned, more solidly-built dog than the Boston. He has more variation of color. Brindle; fawn; white; and brindle with white are all acceptable Frenchie colors. His flaring ears are his most unusual feature. Known as "bat ears," they are broad at the base, long, roundtipped and are carried erect.

The largest of the three breeds is the Bulldog, symbol of the British Empire and for this reason erroneously called the English Bulldog. His projecting lower jaw, sour expression, broad chest and low-slung, massive body make him easily identified. His ears are carried folded back rather than erect.

Is it just by process of natural evolution that the English Bulldog has such a massive head and a pushed-in face, or were these physical characteristics developed by breeders for some special reason?

The English Bulldog was originally used for the barbarously cruel sport of bullbaiting. It was important that the dog be able to hang on to the bull once he had gotten a firm hold. Heavy powerful jaws and a nose set back deeply between the eyes (enabling the dog to breathe easily while keeping his grip) were desirable features. Bulldogs have been carefully bred to maintain this head construction, even though the sport for which the breed was once used has been outlawed for over a hundred years.

We owned two Bulldogs and loved them dearly, but both of them snored something awful. Was it just a coincidence that both of our Bulldogs did this, or is it a peculiarity of the breed?

It was not a coincidence. Any dog with a short, flat, pushed-in nose is liable to snuffle and snore, and the bigger the dog, the bigger the noise. Pekingese, Pugs, Boxers, Bulldogs, Boston Terriers, French Bulldogs, Japanese Spaniels, Brussels Griffons, and English Toy Spaniels all have the short, flat noses that tend to make them snorers.

The German Shepherd Dog

Is the German Police Dog the same breed as a German Shepherd Dog?

Yes. "German Police Dog" is a commonly used, but incorrect, name for the German Shepherd. The use of the term "police dog" to describe the German Shepherd came into general usage because the breed has been used extensively for police and patrol duty. It would be just as accurate to call Airedales, Boxers, and Doberman Pinschers "police dogs," for these breeds have also seen ample service as assistants to law-enforcement officers.

Dogs of War

What breeds were used by the K-9 Corps during World War II?

When the Corps was first organized many different breeds were put in training, the only limitation being as to size and age. To be acceptable, dogs had to measure not less than twenty-four inches or more than twenty-eight inches at the shoulder, and be from fourteen months to three and a half years of age. Experience showed that only a few breeds were really well-fitted for army duty and the list of eligible breeds was accordingly restricted. The eligible breeds for sentry work, scouting duty, and messenger service were the German Shepherd, Doberman Pinscher, farm-type Collie, Giant Schnauzer, Airedale, and Rottweiler. The breeds which were considered qualified for use as sled and pack dogs were the Alaskan Malamute, the Eskimo, and the Siberian Husky.

Dalmatian: The Firehouse Dog

How did the Dalmatian come to be known as the "firehouse dog"?

The tradition started back in the days when fire-fighting apparatus was horse-drawn. For generations, horses and Dalmatians have been the best of friends. In the days when transportation was by coach-and-four, the Dalmatian would run ahead of the coach clearing the way for the horses, or sometimes he would run along under the rear or front axle, driving off stray dogs that bothered the horses. When horses were waiting outside an inn while the occupants of a coach or carriage paused for refreshment, the Dalmatian stayed outside guarding them. No fine stable was considered really complete unless it owned a Dalmatian or two to accompany the horses whenever they went out. Naturally, fire companies which took great pride in their swift, well-trained horses and fine equipment felt that a handsomely spotted Dalmatian lent the crowning touch of elegance to their outfit. Today, even though fire-fighting equipment has been motorized for many years, the Dalmatian is still the traditional pet of the firehouse.

Sled Dogs

Are all sled dogs Huskies?

Almost all sled dogs do seem to be referred to as Huskies, but actually the Siberian Husky is only one of four breeds which are used as draft animals in snowy regions. The other three are the Alaskan Malamute, the Eskimo, and the Samoyed.

A great many people seem to think that the arctic sled-dog breeds are part wolf. Is there any truth in this?

While there probably have been innumerable cases of sled dogs mating with wolves, purebred specimens of the Arctic breeds carry no wolf blood.

How The Dog Became Domesticated

Do scientists know for sure just when and how the dog ceased to be a wild animal and became the domesticated companion of mankind?

Most anthropologists believe that the domestication of the dog took place during the last part of the period known as the Old Stone Age, about ten thousand years ago, and that the process was a very gradual one. George R. Stewart, a professor at the University of California at Berkeley, wrote a book called *Man: An Autobiography,* in which the story of mankind through the ages is told in the first person. That Mr. Stewart has a warm appreciation of the fellowship between human beings and dogs is indicated by the book's dedication, *To Canis, my oldest friend.* His account of how the dog came to be man's first animal friend seems as credible and apperceptive as any that one is likely to discover. He wrote:

"I, Man, from very early times had known the wolf. While I was still a forager, his packs may sometimes have hung on the flanks of my bands, cutting off a straggler, or snapping up a baby, as still happens in India. After I became a hunter, my bands and the wolf-packs must have lived in something like armed neutrality; each was too clever and dangerous for the other to hunt, and it was easier for each to prey upon more stupid and safer animals.

"I do not know just where the next step occurred. I think it was well to the south in some warm country, for in the northern forests he was a big-boned and long-fanged fighter—'that gray beast, the wolf of the weald.' When I suddenly came upon him in the oak-glade, he stood bristling, or even sprang at my throat. But in hot jungle and desert-scrub, he was smaller. When he saw me, he scuttled with tail between legs, as a beast should before a spearman.

YOUR DOG'S WILD RELATIVES
Your dog has a great many wild relatives. Five of the best-known are: (1) the red fox, (2) the coyote, (3) the timber wolf, (4) a wild dog of Australia called the dingo, and (5) the Cape or South African hunting dog.

"Then I invented the bow. After that, I had more meat than ever, and perhaps killed off so much game that the wolf went hungry. In the evenings I began to see his eyes shining, as he crept up close to the fire, and I heard him crunching hungrily at the half-picked bones which I in my wastefulness had thrown away. I was not afraid of him; he was not even worth an arrow. Perhaps out of my riches, I even threw the poor wolf a bone, with a lordly gesture. (For I was flattered to have a hanger-on, and I have always loved doling out charity, after I myself was full of good meat.)

"Then, being hungry, he began to turn up before it was dark, to see what pickings could be had. I let him gnaw on the sheep's head and guts. He kept his distance, and learned to judge for himself how far I could throw a stone, and whether I was going to throw one. We got along rather well because we thought much the same about various matters, and had really much in common. We both hunted in packs; we spiced our courage with cowardice; we both hated all the slinking and self-sufficient cats; we ate much the same food; and both of us had intelligence. Often as I looked at him sitting with alertly cocked head, I must have said in thick accents, 'Why, he looks almost human!'

"Then, too, I sometimes found a lost puppy in the forest—a roly-poly and trusting bit of fur which wiggled on its fat stomach and looked up with big eyes. I lowered the raised ax and brought him to the camp. He played with the children for a while. When he grew his fangs, a wilder light began to glow in his eyes. Then perhaps he snapped at a child or eyed a baby too minutely, and the long-delayed ax crashed down. More often he merely slipped off to join the gray circling ones at the edge of the firelight. But such a wolf was never quite the same. He crept closer to the fire than the others, and remembered the children who had patted him.

"Yes, as centuries slipped by, we got to know each other better. I was the leader always, chiefly because I could think more quickly and clearly. I was the cleverer hunter. Following my band, he often ate the leavings of my kill; I rarely was forced to eat his. I dominated him—by being taller and looking down, by the miracle of fire, by my fearful power to detach a stone or arrow from myself and strike from far off. (He never quite understood about this, and even yet any normal dog scuttles off when I even pretend to pick up a stone.)

"Yet he had gifts that I admired too. He ran faster. When a deer escaped into a thicket where I lost the trail, he went to it directly by his own private miracle. Also, I blundered in the dark, but he got along as well by night as by day. I admired his great power of jaw too, by which he even cracked bones. This matter of the bones was still another point at which we fitted well together, for he could eat what I most often threw away.

"One thing else brought us together and gave me the leadership. Ever since I had learned to talk, I had tried speaking to animals and things. 'Have pity!' I cried to the lightning. 'Fly well, little one!' I whispered as I loosed the arrow. But only when I began to talk to my new hanger-on did I get much response. He had the clever mind to understand, and the ear for tone. When I rapped the captured puppy over the snout, I said 'No!' without thinking. After a while, I noticed that merely to say the word was enough. This was wonderful! At first he only snarled and howled in reply; at last he learned to bark, but that was the closest his stiff throat could ever come to talking.

"Soon also, those gray shapes in the twilight began to pay me back many times over for the poor leavings I threw them. Their sudden outcry in the night let me know that tigers were prowling close, and I had time to throw dry sticks on the fire. When he was following and I ran foul of a she-bear, his quick snap at her heels turned her and let me get an arrow into her flank. Most of all, the pack joined in my hunt; being natural hunters, they learned when to crouch silent, when to follow by scent, and when to leap forward in full cry on the trace of the wounded stag.

"It is a strange part of my story, hardly to be imagined, if it had not really happened. There is much more to it perhaps than I have told. I have always loved puppies, the mothers and children especially. And the faster growing-up of the puppies was important. A little child might be the master and protector of a young puppy, but in two years the full-grown dog (now I may call him by that name) felt himself the protector of the child. Thus by mutual give-and-take we grew together, although it was, I think, more by slow coming closer of the band and the pack than by the taming of pets.

"As for the changes that the dog brought to my life—there was something of "practical" advantage, although this was by no means the equal of what the bow had brought. He helped with hunting, and thus insured a fuller food-supply. In the starving time, he also might become food-supply himself. As a scavenger, he kept the camp-sites a little more sanitary and less smelly, but I was not at all conscious of such details. As a watcher also he brought me a new security. Of more importance, I think, he served as an example. If I could gain power over one animal, I might over another, and so the way was pointed to much in the future.

"But most of all, the dog brought actual pleasure to my individuals. He at last gave proof of what I must often already have asserted: that I was lord over the animals. In his eyes (and how it has flattered me ever since!) I imagined myself to be a god.

"So, as the centuries passed, the hanger-on came to be watchman, and fellow-hunter, and friend—and crept in closer to the fire. (And still lies by the fire, importantly cocking an ear at a strange sound, then deciding it is only the boy next door coming home, falling asleep to dream ancient dreams of chasing tigers, and awaking to eye suspiciously that newcomer, the house-cat.) " *

Dogs and the Supernatural

Do dogs really exhibit supernormal perception?

Dogs have been known to go almost insane with joy before the homecoming of a beloved master, though the owner may have been away for weeks and no one in the household expected his return.

Man: An Autobiography, by George R. Stewart. New York: Random House. Reprinted by permission of Random House, Inc. Copyright 1946, by George R. Stewart.

Intelligent, educated, truthful people have reported instances of dogs howling at the approach of death. We know personally of two such happenings. In the first case, a strange dog appeared at the front door of a house where the owner lay dying and drove the family frantic with its dismal wailing. The dog was driven away repeatedly but persisted in returning. Shortly before the master of the house died the dog disappeared and was never seen in the neighborhood again.

The second situation involved a home where the owner was stricken with a fatal heart attack in the middle of the night. The dog, which was his particular pet, was not in her master's room at the time of the attack but she bolted from the house, crashing straight through a closed screen door and stayed outside of the house, howling. These accounts are from people who were present at the time.

The authors also know firsthand of another instance where a dog apparently sensed imminent death. A well-known New England handler took a Gordon setter to the home of the owner of a bitch that was to be mated. The male dog was an ardent and experienced stud, and the bitch was in full heat and willing, but the male refused even to look at her. All efforts to interest the indifferent stud were useless. Thinking that the dog might be having an "off day" the handler left, promising to return. The next day another attempt was made, but this time the stud went over to the bitch, sniffed, and then lifted his leg and wet on her, an unheard-of piece of behavior. The handler, disgusted by now, put the male in the station wagon and drove home, thinking gloomy thoughts about the lost stud fee. That evening the phone rang. It was the owner of the bitch who said that half an hour before the dog had been lying on the living-room floor, apparently asleep, when suddenly she raised her head, gave a deep sigh and died. The male dog had never refused to breed a bitch before this incident, nor did he afterwards.

The powers of perception seem to vary greatly with individual dogs. Some dogs seem to be unable to find their way home from two blocks distance. Others have become separated from their owners when hundreds of miles from home and have found their way back. Even more remarkable are the verified cases of dogs whose owners have moved great distances, leaving dogs behind with friends or relatives, and the dogs have found their owners' new living places. There is the well-known case of a dog finding his way from Idaho to a town near Oakland, California, to catch up with his owners who had moved there. Only abilities beyond those of which we have any knowledge would enable an animal to travel across several states to a place completely new to him, in order to be reunited with those he loves.

CHAPTER 2

How to Choose Your Dog

What kind of dog do you like? A shaggy, comfortable-looking fellow with a placid disposition? A frisky, short-haired chap? An aloof aristocrat with elegant lines? Before you buy a dog, you will be wise to decide exactly what kind will suit you best. Having decided, you must find a kennel that offers the breed of your choice.

For the person who simply wants a nice Cocker Spaniel puppy, this is relatively easy. At present, this breed is in such great demand that there are Cocker breeders in practically every village and hamlet in the country. Scan the classified section of almost any newspaper and you will probably find an ad for "Cocker Spaniels for Sale." If you have your heart set on a Keeshond, though, or a Skye Terrier, or some other of the lesser known breeds, things will not be quite so simple. Unless you live in an area where there are many kennels, it is likely that a little reconnaissance work will be necessary in order to find just what you want.

A visit to a dog show is a fine way to find a well-bred puppy. The average show, with four or five hundred dogs entered, will generally have representatives of forty to sixty different breeds. A tour of the benches will reveal that many of the exhibiting kennels have puppies for sale. Few breeders keep all the puppies they raise, and almost all of them have young stock available from time to time. If none of the exhibitors or handlers has young stock for sale, they usually know of someone who does. Don't be timid about asking for advice—most dog people are friendly and will be glad to help you with information and suggestions.

For the person who lives in an area where there are no dog shows, and who wants a puppy of one of the more unusual breeds, the American Kennel Club is an excellent source of information. The club maintains an up-to-date and complete file of hundreds of kennels. A letter of inquiry addressed to that organization at 51 Madison Avenue, New York, New York 10010, will receive a prompt reply, giving the addresses of kennels specializing in whatever breed may be desired.

Another means of getting in touch with reputable breeders is through a breed club. These are organizations of fanciers and breeders which have been formed in order to promote the interests of some particular breed, and most of them maintain a register of their members who have puppies or young stock for sale. The American Kennel Club will supply the name and address of the secretary of the club devoted to the breed you are interested in.

Above all, make haste slowly when you are buying a dog. If several breeders in your area are offering the kind of puppy you want, go to *all* the places, look over the pups carefully—then think about it a little. Should you be planning to buy a puppy as a birthday gift, don't wait until the day before the birthday to start on a frantic search. You may not be able to find what you want at all or you may get a lemon. Bear in mind that the puppy you select is going to be a close companion for many years. The time you devote to locating a healthy, good-looking youngster of the breed you want will certainly be well-spent.

Deciding On a Breed

What are the most important considerations in choosing a breed?

Probably the *most* important is where you live. This will be the deciding factor as to what size dog will best fit your mode of living. Unless some member of your family is willing to make a career of dog-walking, keeping a large dog in the city is liable to prove a headache. Big dogs need plenty of exercise. Giving them enough workouts to keep them healthy and in good trim is a full-time job in areas where they must, for their own protection—and in some communities by police order—be walked on a leash. Even the suburbs are not the best place to keep a very large dog. Your fellow commuters will not take kindly to having a Great Dane or Newfoundland galumphing across their lawns and gardens. Dogs are often the source of ill-feeling between neighbors in closely built-up suburbs, and the owners of large dogs who live in such areas often find themselves obliged to keep their dogs as closely confined as though they were living in the city.

Dog lovers who live in ranch, farm, or estate areas, or real open country are usually safe in choosing almost any breed that they happen to like, their choice being governed primarily by their pocketbooks. The puppies of some breeds cost more than others, and the feeding of the bigger breeds runs into more money, naturally than that of the medium-sized or small breeds.

The age and physical condition of the prospective owner is another matter which requires some thought. The companionship of a dog can mean a great deal to an elderly person or to one who is not in good health, as long as the dog is not very large or active, but coping with an oversized, bumptious canine is only for those who are sound of wind and limb.

It is well to remember too that the coats of some breeds require a certain amount of care. Many of the terrier breeds look raggle-taggle if they are not trimmed at regular intervals. Poodles need frequent combing and brushing, and a clipping job at least every two months. Without this attention they look frowsy and their coats become matted. The Collie's coat, if left uncombed, develops feltlike wads and a ragged shabbiness. This is also true of the Chow Chow, the Pomeranian, the Afghan Hound, the Pekingese, and all the other breeds having long, profuse coats. Nothing speaks more of neglect than a white dog whose coat is tattle-tale gray. If you live in an area where there is a smoke or soot problem, a white dog is not for you. In order to keep the dog in a respectable-looking condition, it would be necessary to bathe him almost daily, a procedure detrimental to the dog's health, not to mention the strain on the owner.

Ask yourself a few questions before trying to make a decision. How large a dog can your living quarters accommodate? How big a dog are you willing and able to exercise and feed? Do you mind if his coat is going to need a little attention? Will a "live-wire" disposition amuse you or annoy you? Would you find a calm, quietly behaved dog good company? Your answers may add up to the fact that the breed for you should be small and short-haired. There are easily fourteen or fifteen breeds that answer this description, and surely one of them will appeal to your eye and heart as well as your sense of practicability. On the other hand it might turn out that you can perfectly well own something as big as a colt, as white as snow, and as shaggy as a buffalo, in which case the sky is the limit and you can consider anything you like—from a Great Pyrenees to a Toy Manchester Terrier.

My wife and I want to get a dog but are having trouble deciding what breed we want. How can we make up our minds?

The best way to come to a decision would be to attend an all-breed dog show or, better yet, several. This would give you an opportunity to look over representative specimens of most of the better-known breeds and decide which appeals to you the most. In one recent year there were 355 all-breed dog shows held in this country, so the chances are good that there will be one in your locality which you can attend.

Advice From Experts and Fanciers

I would like to get some firsthand information about the disposition and the care involved·with the various kinds of dogs. There is a long-established and apparently well-run boarding-kennel not far from our house, and I was thinking that the fellow who runs it might be a good person to consult. Do you agree?

Operators of boarding-kennels, professional trainers, and handlers usually have a wide knowledge of the temperament and general care of the different breeds. The advice of a person in one of these professions is, as a rule, more impartial than that of a one-breed fancier and is founded on practical experience with a great many breeds.

Why are authorities on dogs usually so cagey about recommending any one particular breed to a prospective pet owner?

Because it's very much like trying to decide for someone else which is the prettiest ornament on the Christmas tree, or what flavor of ice cream tastes the best. An adviser can point out certain obvious facts, such as that it would be a waste of time to try to train a Bulldog to herd sheep, or that a St. Bernard would be too much dog in a one-room apartment, but he would have to be familiar with the questioner's living quarters, family activities, and finances to be able to make definite suggestions.

About three or four weeks ago I went to a dog show with the intention of looking over the various breeds on exhibit and possibly buying a puppy. I got into conversation with a lady who was showing some Cocker Spaniels and asked her opinion of some of the breeds I had found attractive. She advised me not even to consider anything but a Cocker, and went on to point out that every other breed was either nervous, shy, liable to be vicious, delicate in health or untrainable. By the time I was through listening to all this I was so confused that I went home not knowing what kind of dog I wanted, if any. Should I believe all the things I was told, or ignore them?

Dog fanciers are usually so completely sold on their own breed that they are not very reliable sources of information. If you had talked to a German Shepherd fancier or a breeder of Miniature Schnauzers, the result probably would have been about the same, except the German Shepherd or Miniature Schnauzer would have been depicted as *the* perfect breed and all the other breeds would have been described as half-witted, overexcitable, yappy or sickly.

No one breed and no one individual dog is perfect, but there is a breed to suit almost anyone's taste—unless the person is an out-and-out dog hater. Forget the admonitions of the Cocker Spaniel fancier and buy whatever dog most appeals to you. The way you feed, train and care for your dog is what will make him a dog you will be proud of and love.

Factors That Influence Your Choice

What do you think influences people most strongly in their selection of a breed?

There are so many factors that may cause a person to select one breed rather than another that it would be difficult to single out any one of them as the most potent. The breed of the dog (or dogs) one owned or knew as a child is often the breed for which one has a lifelong affectionate feeling. If a friend, a neighbor, or a relative owns a dog that is especially good-looking or intelligent, one is likely to decide that a dog "just like that nice Springer Spaniel of Cousin Joe's" is the one to buy. Sometimes there is an unreasonable and indescribable sort of affinity existing between a human being and a certain breed. An individual of this type couldn't any more explain why he is drawn to this particular breed than he could analyze his zest for pineapple cheese cake, but an attraction of this sort is usually both genuine and enduring.

Best Breeds for Learning Tricks

I'm sold on the idea of owning a purebred dog, but would like one that could be taught a few tricks. What breeds would be good for this?

The Smooth Fox Terrier and the Poodle (either Miniature or Standard) are both good trick dogs. These two breeds are quick to learn, and once they know a few tricks, seem to enjoy showing off their accomplishments.

Breeds and Carsickness

Are some breeds of dogs more susceptible to carsickness than others? I do a great deal of traveling and want a dog that I can take around with me.

It is not so much the breed as the temperament of the dog. Just as some human beings always cross the Atlantic flat on their backs with seasickness, certain dogs react unfavorably to the motion of a car. Nervous dogs are the ones most liable to have this trouble. Dogs that have been taken for repeated short rides while still very young (preferably held on someone's lap, as contact with a human being seems to instill confidence), rarely suffer any bad effects from motoring.

When you choose a dog for a companion on your travels you would be well-advised to select one of the small breeds. Few hotels will welcome you if you arrive accompanied by a sixty- or seventy-pound canine side-kick.

Buying a Purebred Dog

When a person buys a purebred dog, how can he tell whether he is getting a representative specimen of the breed?

Every recognized pure breed has a standard which describes the various physical characteristics considered desirable, and the faults which are rated as serious or disqualifying for that breed. A prospective puppy buyer, who is interested in a Scottie, for example, would do well to read over the Scottish Terrier standard and familiarize himself with the salient points of the breed. Standards, of course, describe the correct appearance of fully developed, mature dogs. Puppies, naturally, cannot (and should not) look like grown-up dogs. However, if he had read the breed standard, the Scottie purchaser would know that a puppy with large, round, yellow eyes or extensive white markings was a faulty specimen and not worth more than a very modest price. The American Kennel Club's official publication, *The Complete Dog Book,* contains the authentic standard of every recognized A.K.C. breed. Most public libraries have a copy of this book.

Consider His Temperament and Health

Is there any way to judge a puppy's temperament in order to be sure that he will have a good disposition when he grows up?

Not with very young pups, but by the time a puppy is four or five months old an observant person can usually spot a bad disposition. A good temperament manifests itself in curiosity, friendliness, and playful aggressiveness. Don't condemn a pup who isn't particularly sociable with you, a stranger, but if he shies away from his owner, beware! The pup that huddles in the corner of the pen and doesn't join in the romping of his litter mates is often a shy one. If you want to be dead sure of a good disposition buy a puppy six or seven or eight months of age. Then you can be certain of what his temperament will be.

If I buy a puppy, how can I choose a healthy one?

A healthy puppy is plump and well-fed-looking, with no ribs or hipbones protruding. When a puppy is thin and potbellied, it usually means he has worms. The coat should be shiny, if the breed is smooth-coated; thick in texture, if the breed is long-coated. The skin should not be dry and scaly, or show any sore patches or areas resmbling a rash. A mucous discharge from the eyes or nose is usually a sign of serious trouble, probably distemper. The eyes should be clear. A bluish cast or white spots indicate either injury or disease of the eye. Healthy puppies are full of energy, so beware of one that is listless or inactive. Diarrhea is an indication of many disorders, so look out for that. If you can manage it, watch the puppies when they are fed. A puppy with a good appetite is usually robust. When in doubt, ask the seller to take the puppy's temperature and let you see the thermometer. It should register around 101.5, although anything from 101 to 102 degrees is considered normal. If the person selling the puppies refuses to take the temperature or claims he or she has no thermometer, be on your guard. Anyone who is raising puppies without checking temperatures is either ignorant or careless.

My brother bought a Dalmatian puppy which has turned out to be stone deaf. I'm going to get a puppy soon myself but I certainly don't want a deaf one. Are there some breeds which are inclined to deafness? And is there any way to test a puppy's hearing?

Deafness seems to be linked with pigmentation and is often evidenced in dogs of those breeds which are white or mostly white and blue merle in color. White Bull Terriers, Dalmatians, blue merle Collies and Shelties, white Great Danes, and white Boxers are all predisposed to defective hearing.

A puppy's hearing can be tested by separating him from his litter-mates and watching his reaction to a whistle, a snap of the fingers, or a high-pitched squeaking noise from a place he cannot see. If he cocks his head and looks toward the source of the sound, his hearing is probably all right. If he appears not to notice the noise, his hearing may be defective, as puppies are rarely blasé about sounds which are strange to them.

What information should a puppy-buyer obtain about his new puppy?

First, find out what steps have been taken to immunize the puppy against distemper. Then ask if the shots were of the temporary or permanent type, and also if any further injections are needed and, if so, when they will be due. Inquire as to whether or not the pup has been wormed and if any more worming treatments are necessary. Get the seller to write out the puppy's diet for you.

A Large or Small Puppy?

All the dog books I've ever read say that it's a mistake to pick either the largest or smallest puppy in a litter. Why is this?

That advice is meant mostly for people who are looking for a show prospect and does not apply to those who are solely interested in selecting a healthy, attractive pet. The largest puppy in a litter is frequently the most robust and the least liable to be timid. The smallest puppy often has merits too, from a pet owner's viewpoint. Many times the runt of a litter has an especially engaging personality, as though to make up for his lack of size. Then, too, a runt sometimes turns out to be not a runt at all when he gets a home of his own and no longer has to battle his brothers and sisters for every bite of food.

Choosing from a Litter

We are getting a male Cocker pup from a friend who has a litter of seven. I've been to see them twice and still can't pick one. There are four males and three females, all solid black and all nice and plump and healthy. I can't tell them apart. How should I go about choosing one?

Do it the way the judge at a dog show judges a class—by elimination. As long as you're buying a male, ask the owner to take the females out of the pen. Then watch the remaining four pups. If you see one whose expression you don't like, or one that seems less bright than the others, remove him. In this way you can whittle your choice down to one or two. If you can't decide between two, take the one that seems the most friendly. Once you have selected your pup, take a pair of scissors and trim the whiskers from one or both sides of his muzzle, then you won't get him mixed up with the other puppies when they are put back in the pen.

Will His Color Change?

Do some dogs change the color of their coats as they get older? We have a black Poodle pup but were told by his breeder that his coat will be silver-gray when he is full-grown.

Certain breeds change color upon maturity. Blue-gray and silver-gray Poodles are born black. The color starts to change when the puppies are six to eight weeks old. The coats of gray Bedlington Terriers and Kerry Blue Terriers go through the same change from black to a lighter shade. Dalmatians are born pure white and get their spots later. Weimaraner puppies often

have stripes at birth which disappear upon maturity. Colors such
as dark brown, deep red, cream, and apricot usually get lighter
as the dog gets older.

One Dog or Two?

*We have a Setter, Reddy, who has been with the family for
years. If we get a new puppy, will Reddy's feelings be hurt?*

Not if you handle the matter correctly. An older dog sometimes resents the intrusion of a youngster, so you must expect
a certain period of readjustment. Your attitude can help make
this phase as painless as possible. Don't allow your older dog to
feel he is being pushed into the background. Give him precedence
in all matters. For example, when you come home and both
dogs run to greet you, pet Reddy first; if both dogs are to be
taken for a walk, put on the old-timer's collar and leash first;
when the dogs are fed, put down the older dog's pan first and
then keep watch to be sure the pup doesn't steal any of his
food. Never make an affectionate fuss over the new dog without
giving the other dog some attention too. In a short time Reddy
will probably come to enjoy the company of the youngster and
the two will be good friends.

*A relative has given us a Smooth Fox Terrier puppy and now
we are thinking about buying another one to keep our first
pup company. Don't you think it's true that a dog is lonely
without another dog for a playmate?*

Dogs seem to crave the attention and companionship of human
beings more than they do the company of other dogs, and we
doubt that your dog will mind being an "only dog." If your
Terrier has to be left alone very much he might enjoy having
a friend of his own age. When planning on acquiring two pups,
it is best not to try to house-train them both at once. You are
liable to find yourself never being sure of just which one has
misbehaved and rather than chastise the innocent one, end up
by disciplining neither of them. Get one of them fairly well

started on his house manners before you bring the other into your house.

About Kennels

How can I size up a kennel in order to judge whether or not it is a good place to buy a puppy?

A good kennel is Dutch clean. The runs and pens are not littered with droppings that have obviously been there for some time. There should be no odor about the place. Don't be fooled by a strong odor of disinfectants, as they are often used to cover up less attractive smells. The whole place—buildings and grounds —should have a neat, well-kept look, not necessarily elaborate or expensive-looking, but the general aspect should be tidy and workmanlike. What tells the real story is the appearance of the puppies and older dogs. Do they look well-fed? Nicely groomed? Clear-eyed? Active? If the answer to these questions is "yes," then the kennel is probably a well-run establishment and a good place to buy a pup.

Wouldn't a puppy from a kennel where the main interest is in show dogs be very expensive?

No. The breeder who raises dogs for show purposes retains only a small percentage of the puppies he breeds, because no matter how many litters a year he may raise very few of his puppies are likely to be promising enough to be considered show prospects. The rest he sells for pets at current pet-stock prices. Puppies from a show kennel are generally healthy, good-looking youngsters, because in a kennel of this type all the puppies are treated as potential champions and the care, feeding and general treatment are the best that can be provided.

Not long ago I visited a kennel and was shown several nice-looking puppies. I wanted to go through the whole kennel and see all the dogs but the owner said he would rather I

*didn't. It made me wonder if he had something to hide. What
do you think?*

Most kennel owners use an office or some sort of reception room
as a place for showing their puppies to prospective buyers for
two reasons. First, the presence of strangers in their living
quarters often gets dogs in a dreadful uproar (and, for all you
know, the kennel may be having neighbor trouble). Second, if
visitors have been calling at other kennels they may be the
innocent carriers of distemper or other disease.

*In going through a dog magazine I noted that many of the
kennels had a line in their ads saying, "Dogs shown by
appointment only." Isn't this a rather high-hat attitude?*

It isn't meant that way. Kennels are often subjected to the
casual calls of people who seem to think that the owner will be
delighted to see them at mealtime, bedtime, or in the midst of
departing for a dog show. A phone call in advance makes a visit
to a kennel pleasanter for all concerned.

*One Sunday a few weeks ago we went around to several kennels
looking at puppies. In a few places we were asked not to
handle the puppies. We didn't ask why and have been wondering ever since what the reason was for this request.*

Germs are often carried from one kennel to another on the
hands, shoes, and clothing of visitors. The kennel owners who
asked you not to handle their puppies were trying to protect
their youngsters from possible exposure to disease.

*Is it better to buy a puppy from a large kennel which raises a
great many dogs or from a small breeder who only has one
or two litters a year?*

The large kennel usually has a greater selection on hand at
all times than a small breeder. Puppies raised by the breeder
who brings them up in his own house, and who never has more
than a few at a time, usually have had more handling and may,

LOOKING AT NEW SIGHTS

Adjusting to a new environment will be less difficult for this trio of Smooth Dachshunds, who have the comfort of each other's company, than for the Beagle puppy (*left*), separated from his littermates. Some petting and cuddling will reassure the lone pup and put his mind at rest.

BOXER PUPPIES

(*Right*) Healthy puppies, like these Boxers, have a well-fed look. Their coats are clean and shiny, their eyes clear and alert. They are active and have a healthy curiosity about their surroundings.

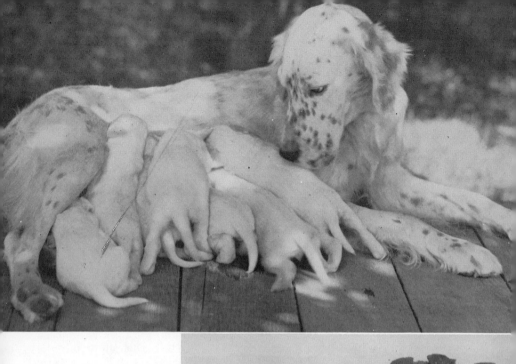

AN ENGLISH SETTER WITH HER PUPPIES

(*Above*) English Setter puppies are pure white when very young. Not until they are older will their coats show the flecks of color which are typical of their breed.

DISPOSITIONS DIFFER

These Irish Terriers (*above*) will make ideal pets for anyone who likes dogs that are frisky and full of pep, while the Cocker Spaniel (*left*) is recommended to those who want a merry but gentle and devoted companion.

therefore, be more adaptable to family life than kennel-raised puppies. Because a breeder operates on a small scale, don't make the mistake of thinking that his puppies are not well-bred. Some of the finest dogs this country has seen, from both bench-show and field-trial standpoints, have been bred by fanciers whose breeding stock consists of but a few dogs and whose puppies are kitchen-raised.

Buying Your Puppy at a Pet Shop

Why do most authorities on dogs warn against buying a puppy from a pet shop?

Because the majority of pet-shop puppies have had such a poor start in life that they have little chance of achieving full growth and good health. Reputable breeders don't dispose of their puppies to be resold through pet shops, so most of the young stock in such places are the results of careless wholesale breeding operations and can only be labeled culls. There is no way of telling how many different hands a puppy may have passed through before he lands in a dealer's show window, and every change in food and environment is a setback to a young animal.

To the person who runs a pet shop, puppies are merchandise. They are usually fed as cheaply as possible. Worm treatments and distemper shots are neglected because they entail expense and bother. There probably are people in the pet-shop business whose business ethics are admirable, but the fact is that a very high percentage of the puppies sold in such establishments are poor specimens to begin with, wormy, undernourished and, if not actually sick, completely lacking in resistance to disease.

What would you do if you saw a puppy in a pet-shop window, fell hopelessly in love with it and felt you just had to buy it?

We would make a cash deposit on the pup to insure its not being sold to someone else and then run, not walk, to the nearest veterinarian and make a date with him to go back to the pet shop with us and examine the pup. If he okayed the pup, we'd buy it. If he said the pup was in poor condition but not actually sick, we might still buy it, if we were willing to incur the inevitable vet's bills and take the risk of losing the pup because of its lack of resistance to disease. If the veterinarian found the pup diseased, we would ask that our deposit be returned and try to forget the poor little thing.

Dogs Sold on Approval

Is it a common practice for dogs to be sold on approval?

Some of the larger kennels will sell a dog on a week or ten days approval, provided the buyer assumes full responsibility should anything happen to the dog during that period. A dissatisfied customer reflects on the reputation of a kennel and the owner may feel that permitting a puppy or dog to be taken on trial is good business policy. Pet-shop owners and small private breeders frequently are not of this opinion and when a sale is made the deal is considered closed.

Buying a Dog on the Installment Plan

Are dogs ever sold on the installment plan? I would like to buy a Setter puppy and pay half the cost this month and half next month.

The usual understanding is that a dog is paid for in full at the time his new owner takes him home. Occasionally an agreement is made whereby a dog may be paid for in two or more installments, but such an arrangement is strictly between the buyer and the seller and is not a general practice.

Meeting the Puppy's Parents

When going to a kennel to see puppies that are for sale, isn't it a good idea to get a look at the pup's parents?

It certainly is. If you can see one or both of a puppy's parents you can get an idea of what he may be expected to look like when mature. Remember, though, that if the puppies are very young, six or eight weeks old for instance, the dam will not be looking her best. Most bitches are rather shabby and rundown in appearance after raising a litter, particularly if it was a large one.

Most Breeders Are Honest, But—

What do breeders do with the puppies they raise that have disqualifying faults from a show standpoint?

They sell them. The honest breeder, because he recognizes that a specimen with serious faults is useless for his showing or breeding program, sells such dogs as pets, at relatively low prices. Dealers, more interested in making a profit than they are in fairly representing their wares, sometimes try to foist off puppies so imperfect as to be culls, claiming they are very unusual and desirable. A Boxer, for example, whose white markings exceed more than one-third of his body area is known as a "check" and is disqualified from show competition. Reputable breeders either destroy such puppies or else neuter them and give them away to anyone who can offer a good home. Dishonest breeders have been known to advertise "Boxers for sale. Including the rare white ones." The best protection a puppy buyer can have against an unscrupulous dog dealer of this sort is to read the breed standard and find out for himself the faults that are considered so serious that they render a dog of little value.

Yesterday we went to a place where they are raising Beagle puppies. We found a little male that suited us perfectly. The woman who owned the puppies said she wanted to keep him for a few days before we took him home because he was due for a worming, so we paid a deposit and said we would be back the next week. Now I'm wondering if maybe we weren't foolish. How do we know the woman is honest?

A dishonest person would have sold you the puppy worms and all. Anytime a breeder wants to keep a puppy for a short time in order to make sure that it gets a distemper shot or a treatment for worms, you may be certain that he or she is a trustworthy person. Unscrupulous dealers are always in a great hurry to sell their puppies and get them out of their kennels or shops as fast as possible.

What happens when a person buys a pup and the puppy gets sick very shortly after arriving at his new owner's home? Does the buyer get his money back?

If you buy a puppy from a reputable breeder and the puppy shows signs of illness within a very few days or a week after you get him, the breeder will probably make some sort of an adjustment, either replacing the pup or returning your money. If, on the other hand, the pup picks up rat poison or is accidentally injured, the responsibility is yours and you are not entitled to a refund.

When to Buy a Puppy

We are planning on getting a Basset Hound pup for a pet, but are in no hurry about it. What is the best time of year to bring a new puppy into the house?

From the viewpoint of convenience to the owner the best time to get a puppy is during the late spring or summer. Because pleasant weather may be expected at this time of year, the dangers of exposing a puppy to cold, wet weather while house-training him are avoided, and the puppy's health will be benefited by the additional hours of sunshine, fresh air and exercise.

Our children have been promised a Spaniel puppy and we are trying to make up our minds whether we should give it to them at Christmastime or wait until later. What do you advise?

Although the Christmas puppy is an established institution, the truth of the matter is that Christmas is just about the worst time a family could select to bring a new pup into the house. In most parts of the country the weather during December is severe, and the difficulties and risks of house-training are doubled. The average household is in a state of excitement and confusion at Christmas, in no condition to take on the responsibility of a young, untrained pet. The coming and going of guests, the commotion and general to-do are liable to intimidate the pup to such an extent that it may take him a much longer than usual time to become accustomed to his new home. Our advice is to put off getting a puppy until after the holidays or, even better, until spring.

The Best Age

What age puppy would you advise me to buy for a pet?

One from four to six months of age is about right, but don't reject a puppy of eight or nine months as being too old. By the time he has reached four months a puppy can be started on house-training, he can be permanently inoculated against distemper and his first cycle of wormings should be completed.

Why do so many breeders and dealers offer six- and eight-week-old puppies for sale?

If a dealer can dispose of a puppy before he has had to feed it for several weeks the profit is much greater. The selling of just-weaned puppies is fine from the viewpoint of the seller but for the buyer it is a disadvantage. A six-week-old puppy is too young for house-training; he should have antidistemper serum every two weeks; he usually needs worming; he requires four feedings a day; discipline at this age is liable to cow him permanently. In other words, he's an adorable nuisance, but more nuisance than adorable.

Haven't a great many people bought very young puppies—five or six weeks old—and raised them successfully?

Yes, they have, but probably twice as many have bought just-weaned puppies only to have them die, because the owners either did not know how to or could not give them the necessary care and attention. A young puppy is like a young baby, practically a twenty-four-hour-a-day job.

If I buy a puppy when he's very young, say eight or nine weeks old, won't he love me more than if I get him when he's six months old?

Not at all. An older puppy will love you just as quickly and just as much as will one eight weeks old. As for your side of it, you will get more pleasure and fun out of an older puppy than a very young one.

We saw an adorable Cocker puppy at a kennel in our town and want to buy him, but he is only six weeks old and we would rather not take a pup that is so young. We are afraid that if we don't buy him someone else will get him. What to do?

Buy the pup now and arrange to leave him with the breeder for another six weeks or two months. The charges for his board won't amount to much while he is so little, and you will be spared the trouble of caring for such a young puppy. Be sure to mention that you want the pup to have distemper shots and that you will pay for them.

Do you think it a mistake to buy an adult dog or accept one as a gift?

It depends entirely on the dog. If you have a friend or relative who wants to find a home for a dog, and you are reasonably sure the dog has a good disposition, there would be no reason against taking it. If you give the dog a good home and treat him affectionately, he will probably come to like you as well as he did his former owner. Dogs of three or four years of age that have been kennel dogs sometimes (but not always) do not adjust themselves so easily to the life of a house dog. However, with enough patience and attention one can usually make even a kennel dog into a nice pet. Certainly no one would recommend that a person acquire a grown dog with a mean disposition or incorrigible bad habits. A week's trial will usually show whether a dog will fit into your household, so if you are considering acquiring a grown dog let it be "on approval" for a week or ten days before you make a final decision.

We don't feel we can afford to pay the price of a good purebred puppy. Our little boy is so anxious to have a dog that we are going to adopt a homeless one from our local Humane Society shelter. Should we choose a grown dog or a puppy?

The majority of the canine waifs at the Humane Society shelters are mongrels, and in case you have no choice except to take a dog of mixed breeding, you had better try to select one that is full-grown but still fairly young. By doing this you will be able to judge the size of the dog you are getting, how he is going to look, and what sort of disposition he has. Mongrel pups can be awfully cute, but there is always the possibility that they will develop into yellow-eyed monstrosities of uncertain temper, so it is a risky venture to take on a sweet little bundle of fluff whose mother was almost a Poodle and whose father was a traveling man. Quite often animal shelters have nice looking purebreds for adoption. If you aren't in too big a hurry you may be able, by waiting, to acquire a dog which you will be proud to own. You will be expected to make a small contribution to the support of the shelter and to offer proof that you will give the dog you adopt a good home.

What You Can Expect to Pay

How much should I have to pay for a purebred puppy?

The average price range on purebred pet stock of most breeds is from fifty to a hundred and fifty dollars. If you took your time about it, you might be able, by bargain hunting, to pick up a nice healthy puppy for as little as thirty-five dollars. Watch the classified ads in your local newspapers. Occasionally an entire kennel is broken up because of the age or ill-health of the operator, and when this occurs, puppies are offered at clearance sale prices. Generally speaking, you can't expect to get a well-bred pup for much less than fifty to seventy-five dollars. Show stock, that is, puppies and youngsters showing unusual promise as show specimens, sell for relatively stiff prices. Breeders ask (and get, incidentally) from two to fifteen hundred or even two thousand dollars for top-flight show prospects.

Why are female puppies usually sold for lower prices than males?

Because the dog-owning public has an unfounded prejudice against keeping bitches as pets, female pups of pet stock quality are usually sold at slightly lower prices than males. In the case of high-grade show and breeding stock, females command prices as high or higher than those asked for male dogs. The wise breeder knows that his fine brood bitches are the very lifeblood and foundation of his breeding program, and for this reason he will often refuse to sell them at all or will demand very high prices for them.

Why should a puppy of a very small breed, such as a Miniature Pinscher, cost just as much as a Boxer or a German Shepherd puppy?

The law of supply and demand sets the prices for puppies. The small breeds usually have small litters, three or four puppies being the usual number. Because many of the small breeds are very popular, the kennels that raise them often have more customers than they have puppies, and for this reason are in a position to set comparatively high prices. Large breeds are inclined to have large litters and, if one considers the amount of food, distemper serum, worm medicine, and hard work required to care for a litter of nine or ten German Shepherd pups, it is easy to understand why breeders sell them for reasonable prices rather than be obliged to continue spending time and money on pups which they do not plan to keep for show or breeding purposes.

*How much should I have to pay for a six-month-old Dober--
man that is a promising show prospect, housebroken, gentle
with children, and intelligent enough to be obedience-
trained successfully?*

A puppy such as you describe would probably not be for sale
at any price. If it were, the price would be in the hundreds and
you would be fortunate indeed to have found a breeder who
was willing to part with such a paragon. Young dogs that show
promise of becoming champions are seldom sold for less than
two hundred dollars and usually bring much more. The fact
that a youngster of championship quality was house-trained, of
reliable temperament, and showed evidence of aptitude for obedience work, would still further enhance his value. If you wrote
a letter to a breeder, describing a dog like this and mentioning
a hundred dollars as your top price, we doubt that you would
get an interested reply.

*Is it true that puppies that have been sold as pets for rather
modest prices often turn out to be valuable show dogs?*

It happens so rarely that when such a case does occur it is
written up in all the dog magazines as a nine-day wonder. If a
person wants a dog that is a fine enough specimen to do some
winning at dog shows, he would be better off to get the advice
of an experienced fancier and pay the price of a good show dog,
than to buy a fifty-dollar puppy hoping that by some miracle
it will develop into a show specimen.

*We have been shopping around for a male Collie pup. One
place we visited had two litters for sale, both about the
same age. One litter was sired by a well-known champion
and the pups were priced at seventy-five dollars. The pups
in the other litter, which was sired by a young dog that has
not won a championship, were sixty dollars. Would it be
worth it to pay the extra fifteen dollars to buy one of the
puppies whose father is a champion?*

Not if you are interested solely in an attractive, well-bred pet.
Of course there is a certain amount of pride to be derived from

the ownership of a dog whose sire is a famous winner, and many people are willing to pay a little extra for that pleasure. If you were buying a female puppy with the idea of possibly going into breeding sometime in the future, we would advise you to purchase a pup from the litter sired by the champion.

How to Recognize a Bargain

In the past week I have gone to see three litters of Boxer puppies. The first litter belonged to a couple who lived in a three-room apartment. There were seven pups and I could have bought any of them for fifty dollars. The next litter was at a large kennel and the pups were priced at one hundred dollars apiece, except for one which the owner considered a show prospect and planned to keep. The third litter was owned by a woman living out in the country. She said that she had paid three hundred dollars for the mother of the pups and had paid a seventy-five dollar stud fee when she bred the bitch and felt that the pups were worth two hundred and fifty dollars each. All of these dogs were about the same age (four months), all were purebred, eligible for registration with the American Kennel Club, and seemed healthy and well-fed. What I can't understand is why there is such a wide variation in prices. Can you explain it?

Quite often people who decide to make a brood matron of their house pets put prices on the puppies which are ridiculously low or much too high. The people who offered you the puppies at fifty dollars have probably found out (as have many would-be breeders before them) that an apartment is no place to raise dogs.

A litter of Boxer puppies can raise havoc in small living quarters, the food costs are staggering, and the work of cleaning and feeding is endless. Those apartment-raised puppies are really distress merchandise and are a bargain, because the owners are probably about ready to give them away rather than keep them any longer. They will lose money by selling puppies of a large breed at such low prices, but that is their concern, not yours.

The hundred-dollar puppies you saw at the kennel are priced about right for healthy, well-bred pups. The owner will be making a reasonable profit but not a spectacular one when you consider the cost of stud fees, ear cropping, food, labor and so on.

The woman who thinks her puppies are worth two hundred and fifty dollars apiece is obviously a beginner at breeding who has the idea that the raising of dogs is the royal road to riches. Because the dam of her puppies cost three hundred dollars does not make the puppies worth the price she has set. Only an established kennel with a fine record for producing high-class show stock gets prices in the hundreds for young puppies. If she refuses to sell her puppies for less than the amount you mention, she will probably find herself keeping them until they are nine or ten months old and then selling them for whatever price she can get—at a loss.

Why Agreement to Exhibit May Be Part of the Sale

There is a fellow in our town who raises prize-winning English Setters. My wife and I have seen a beautiful puppy at his place and want to buy it. Although we are willing to pay the price he asks, the breeder says it is the best puppy he has ever bred and won't sell it to us unless we promise to show it. We aren't interested in dog shows and feel the man is being very unfair to refuse us the dog. Don't you agree?

Nothing is more painful to a breeder than to sell a dog of unusually good show quality to people who will not exhibit it. It takes time, money and effort to produce a champion, or a dog that could be a champion, if shown. When a breeder has such a dog he wants to be sure that it goes to someone who will give it an opportunity to become a winner, for a kennel's reputation is made by the dogs of its breeding which attract favorable notice in show competition. Even though a kennel should breed dogs of outstanding quality, it will remain unknown and unhonored if those dogs are in the hands of people who never show

them. The English Setter breeder probably feels that the puppy
you want is too good to be merely an ornament for your back-
yard and for that reason won't sell him to you.

When the Puppy Has "Blue Ribbon" Parents

*A local kennel advertises puppies whose parents are blue-
ribbon winners. Does this make the pups especially valuable?*

No. Almost any purebred dog can win a blue ribbon if he
is taken to enough dog shows, for sooner or later he'll be the
only entry in his class at some show or other and will be given
a blue ribbon. A blue ribbon won at Westminster, or Morris
and Essex, or one of the other big shows can mean that a dog
was a winner in fairly tough competition and may have had to
beat more dogs in order to win it than he might have to defeat
in order to win a purple-and-gold best-of-breed ribbon at a small
show. Puppies whose parents are champions are considered worth
more than those from nonchampion breeding stock, and the offspring of sires and dams which are proved producers of champion quality offspring are very valuable indeed.

Dogs for Children

*Both my wife and I like Terriers and want to get a dog for
our two sons. The boys are as active and bumptious as Terriers themselves, so we want a fairly good-sized dog that can
take plenty of rough-and-tumble playing. Would an Airedale
be a good choice?*

An Airedale would be a grand pal for your boys, so would a
Kerry Blue Terrier.

*My nine-year-old daughter has had an illness which restricts
her activities. We have promised her a dog but it must be
small and rather sedate in behavior. What would be best?*

There are several of the toy breeds that fit those qualifications. The Pekingese, the Pug, the Papillon, the English Toy

Spaniel, and the Toy Poodle. Have your little girl look at the pictures and read the descriptions of these breeds. She will be sure to find one that will please her.

Are there any breeds which are not suitable companions for youngsters?

A dog of almost any breed will be gentle with children if he has grown up with them. There are individuals of every breed (particularly older dogs who are unaccustomed to children) that will resent teasing, roughness or mauling, and will bite rather than put up with it.

We own a summer place on a river and think it would be fun to have a dog that would play in the water with the children, retrieve, and be a generally good water dog. I know that some breeds have a natural liking for water and are good swimmers, but which are they?

Chesapeake Bay Retrievers take to water like ducks. So do most Labrador Retrievers, Otter Hounds, standard-size Poodles, Irish Water Spaniels, and American Water Spaniels. The Newfoundland is a wonderful swimmer too and would be a trustworthy pal and guardian for your children.

Now that our little girl is two years old, my husband wants to get a dog for her, as he says all children should grow up with a dog. He is talking about a Boxer pup. Do you think this is a good idea?

It sounds very much as though your husband wants a Boxer for himself and not for your little girl. In twelve months your Boxer puppy will be a big, bumptious, active young dog, weighing around seventy pounds, and your child will still be very much of a toddler—not very well-matched playmates. A child of two is too young to take much real interest in any dog, but if your husband insists, try and talk him into getting a smaller dog. Most Boxers are good-natured, but because of their habit of using their paws when frolicking are liable to knock over a

small child or inflict deep scratches just in play. For an older
child, nine or ten years of age, a Boxer would be ideal.

Good Watchdogs

*I am planning on giving my sister a dog for her birthday. She
is a widow, living alone in an isolated country house, and
wants a large dog that will be a really good watchdog. What
breed do you suggest?*

A German Shepherd or a Doberman Pinscher would be a
good choice, as both of these breeds have highly developed protective instincts and are natural guard dogs. A Collie, Boxer,
Newfoundland, Great Pyrenees, St. Bernard, or Great Dane would
be worth considering too, for while these breeds are perhaps
not as aggressive as the first two mentioned, they are large
enough to frighten unwelcome intruders or trespassers by their
appearance alone.

*The night watchman at the plant where I am manager has
asked if we will provide him with a dog to accompany him
on his rounds. He is a partially disabled war veteran, and
because of his physical handicap would have trouble keeping
up with a fast-moving dog, such as a German Shepherd or
a Doberman Pinscher. He has been reading up on dogs and
has decided that a Bull Mastiff would be about perfect for
his purposes. We are willing to get a dog for him but want
to be sure we're getting the right breed. What do you think
of his choice?*

His choice is a very good one. The Bull Mastiff was created
as a guard dog to help keep game preserves free of the depreda-
tions of poachers and was originally known as the "Gamekeeper's
Night-Dog." They have a natural guarding instinct and are
sensible and teachable. A Bull Mastiff can be very agile when
the occasion demands, but is, generally speaking, a slower-moving
dog than the other two breeds you mentioned and would be easier
for your night watchman to keep up with and handle. The

breed's ferocious looks are also an asset for a dog used for guarding purposes.

The Best American Herd Dog

My farm helper and I have been thinking for some time of getting a dog that could be trained to help us handle sheep and cattle. What is considered the best dog for such purposes?

One of the best breeds for use as a herd dog is the Working Border Collie. The dogs are usually black with white markings, weigh from thirty to fifty pounds, and resemble the larger Collie in general outline, except for having heads which are proportionately shorter and more blunt-nosed and less profuse coats. For practical farm and herding use this breed is tops, for they have such a strong herding instinct that they will not only work sheep and cattle but chickens and ducks as well.

The breed is not recognized by the American Kennel Club, but its breeding records are maintained by the North American Sheep Dog Society of Wooster, Ohio. Only dogs whose parents have been awarded a "Certificate of Proven Working Ability" are eligible for registration with this organization. Consequently, the breed's capability as useful, working sheep dogs has been kept uniformly high. Another fine herding breed is the English Shepherd. This breed is not A.K.C. recognized either, but is registered by the United Kennel Club.

Breeds That Bark Less

A magazine I recently read made reference to a barkless dog. Is there such a breed?

The Basenji, a member of the hound group, is the barkless dog you read about. This breed, while not mute, never really barks, though they do make a noise which is described as a sort of chortle or yodel, and are capable of growling too.

We have cranky neighbors who would probably complain if we had a dog which barked very much. What breeds should we consider and which should we avoid?

If you don't want a Basenji, you might do well to choose one of the breeds of easygoing phlegmatic temperament. The larger sporting and hound breeds are seldom noisy. Newfoundlands, Great Pyrenees, and St. Bernards are quiet breeds too. Breeds to watch out for, under your circumstances, are the Welsh Corgi, the Collie, the Miniature Poodle, most of the Terriers, and nearly all the Toy breeds.

Dogs for Different Climates

My brother's business makes it necessary for him to live in Central America. He wants me to send him a dog, and mentioned that he thought he'd like a Bulldog. I have been told that Bulldogs can't stand heat, so maybe that wouldn't be a wise choice. Are there other breeds that should be avoided for the same reason?

Short-faced breeds, Bulldogs and French Bulldogs especially, are very liable to succumb to the effects of a hot climate. Breeds with long, heavy coats are troublesome in areas where there is no cold weather, because fleas, ticks, and other parasites are a year-round problem in such places and it is all but impossible to keep a long-coated dog free of these pests. Any of the breeds with a short coat and a normally proportioned long-nosed head would be a good choice. Here are a few suggestions: Whippet, Dachshund, Smooth-haired Fox Terrier, Doberman Pinscher, Basenji, Pointer, Italian Greyhound, Bull Terrier, German Short-haired Pointer, or Dalmatian.

What breeds stand cold weather the best?

The Siberian Husky, the Alaskan Malamute, the Eskimo, the Samoyed, the Chow, the Norwegian Elkhound, the Newfoundland, the Old English Sheepdog, and the St. Bernard are all breeds that seem to thrive on and enjoy cold weather.

Toy Dogs

It seems ridiculous to me for Toy dogs to be considered a pro-tection against burglars. How could anything as small as a dog of a Toy breed scare a housebreaker?

Burglars fear noise and, because the Toy breeds are usually very alert and quick to give the alarm when they sense something is wrong, they are effective watchdogs.

Toy dogs have always appealed to me, but I would rather not have a dog whose coat requires much care. Can you give me some ideas about what breeds might suit me best?

There are several smooth-coated toy breeds whose coats require little attention beyond an occasional brushing. They are the Chihuahua, the Miniature Pinscher, the Pug, the Toy Manchester Terrier, and the Italian Greyhound.

I want some sort of a very small dog, but have heard that many of the Toy breeds are liable to bark too much. Can you suggest a Toy breed that isn't yappy?

An Italian Greyhound would be a good pet for you. They are graceful, active little dogs, not given to excessive barking, and have affectionate bright dispositions.

People who own a Pekingese often claim that these little dogs have a great deal of character and are really very courageous. Is this true?

The Pekingese has a most distinctive personality, as his disposition seems to have been designed for a much larger dog. The Peke is typified by boldness and independence and seldom retreats from either man or beast.

What You Should Know

I like dogs that have plenty of pep and vim, but not too large. What breeds would be my dish?

Probably one of the terrier breeds. As long as you want something in the small to medium-sized range, we suggest the following: Welsh Terrier, Wire-haired or Smooth Fox Terrier, Irish Terrier, Miniature Schnauzer or Miniature Poodle. These are all breeds that are noted for frisky dispositions.

When I was a child I had a Black and Tan Terrier. I haven't heard much about this breed in recent years, although I have occasionally seen a dog that looks like my childhood pet. Has the name of the breed been changed?

The dog that used to be known as the Black and Tan Terrier had its name changed to Manchester Terrier in 1923, but it is the same sporty, sleek little dog you knew as a child.

Would you please suggest three or four of the smaller terrier breeds which make nice pets but do not require a great deal of plucking and grooming in order to look smart and attractive?

The Cairn Terrier, the Dandie Dinmont, the Norwich Terrier, and the West Highland White Terrier all make intelligent, lively pets and have coats that need only an occasional "tidying up" in addition to the usual combing and brushing. The Manchester Terrier is a stylish-looking small-sized terrier too, and his coat requires the minimum of attention as it is short-haired and smooth.

Are terriers really good rat-killers?

Almost all of the terrier breeds are enthusiastic and efficient ratters.

Are terriers more liable to have skin trouble than other breeds?

Several of the wiry-coated terrier breeds are predisposed to hot-weather skin ailments. New treatments and remedies now make canine skin disorders easily prevented or cured, so the problem is not as serious as it used to be.

How to Find Something Special

Hunting is my greatest interest and I'm looking for a Pointer pup from real hunting stock. How can I locate one?

For the kind of puppy you want, write to the Field Dog Stud Book, 222 W. Adams Street, Chicago 6, Illinois. This Stud Book maintains a registry of Pointers and Setters bred for the field, and the kennels they recommend raise puppies of true hunting type.

We are interested in buying a Welsh Terrier that can do some winning at bench shows. How should we go about finding a dog with definite show possibilities?

By attending as many dog shows as possible you should be able to find out which kennels are breeding and showing dogs of the winning type. If you can, make the acquaintance of one or more experienced breeders or fanciers and ask their advice before making a purchase. Then, when you do decide to buy, be prepared to pay a price in keeping with the quality of the dog. Don't approach a breeder saying, "We just want a pet," in hopes that he will sell you a champion by mistake, because he won't. Explain that you are interested in a show dog, and indicate that you are willing to pay a fair price for a good one, and you will probably get one.

Do reputable breeders ever sell puppies with a guarantee that they will grow up to be champions?

No, because many a promising youngster grows up to be a mediocre adult. The only guarantee a conscientious breeder can give the purchaser of a young pup is that the puppy is pure-bred and is healthy at the time of sale. Some puppies are more promising than others and for this reason are priced higher, but few breeders would be willing to stake their reputations on the possibility of a two- or three-month-old pup developing into a show winner.

*We could have plenty of use for a good herd dog on our farm
but don't know how to go about finding one. How can we
locate such a dog?*

Write to the North American Sheepdog Society at Wooster,
Ohio, and ask for a list of breeders who are raising working
sheep dogs. You may not be able to obtain a fully trained adult
dog but you will be given information about finding a puppy
from parents of proven working ability.

*Suppose a person wanted to buy a puppy of one of the rare
breeds, a Clumber Spaniel or a Scottish Deerhound, for
instance. How would he go about finding such a dog?*

By writing to the American Kennel Club, 221 Park Avenue South,
New York 3, N. Y. The Kennel Club maintains an enormous
file of breeders all over the country and will give you the names
and addresses of those who have puppies of the kind you want.

Dog by Mail Order

*I am in the market for a Lakeland Terrier. There are no
Lakeland breeders in my section of the country, but the
Kennel Club has given me the name of a kennel which is
located too far away for me to be able to visit it. Would I
be well-advised to order a puppy by mail?*

Certainly, if the breeder has been recommended to you by the
A.K.C. Thousands of puppies are sold by mail order every year,
and in the vast majority of cases the transaction is perfectly
satisfactory. Some kennels will even ship puppies on approval,
provided the prospective purchaser promises to give the pup
a few days' rest before shipping him back in case he is not
satisfactory.

*Some time ago we bought an Afghan Hound from a breeder
in a distant state. The pup was shipped by air, arrived in
fine condition, and we are delighted with him. Now the
breeder has written asking me to send back the crate in*

which the pup was shipped. I thought the crate went with the pup and that we were entitled to keep it, or am I wrong?

Unless there was a definite understanding that you were to keep the crate, you should ship it back to the breeder immediately. A well-made shipping crate costs from twenty to fifty dollars, depending on the size, or, if homemade, represents many hours of painstaking carpentry. If you really want the crate you could ask the breeder if he would be willing to sell it to you.

I am having a Coonhound shipped to me from another state, but neither the breeder from whom I am buying the pup nor I, know whether or not the puppy has to be inoculated against rabies before he can be sent here. How can I find out?

Most states require a veterinarian's certificate of health to accompany a dog being shipped from another state. Your local Railway Express agency will be able to tell you if your state requires proof of rabies inoculation as well.

I have heard that dogs being shipped into England have to go through a period of six months quarantine before they are admitted to the country. Are there similar restrictions on bringing a dog from another country into America?

There is no quarantine requirement here. There are certain other regulations to be met, though. They are as follows:

"No quarantine restrictions except that dogs intended for use in the handling of sheep or other livestock may be required to undergo a short period of detention in quarantine on arrival in the United States. Veterinary certificates of health are required. A dog being sold to an American and valued at one hundred dollars or more must be accompanied by a Consular Invoice obtained from the American Embassy.

"A dog imported by a citizen of the United States especially for breeding purposes is admitted free of duty provided that no such animal shall be admitted free unless purebred of a recognized breed and duly registered in a book of record, and pedigree of such animal shall be produced and submitted to the Department of Agriculture, duly authenticated by the proper custodian of such book record, together with an affidavit of the owner, agent, or importer that the animal imported is the identical animal described in said certificate of record and pedigree. The Secretary of Agriculture may prescribe such regulations as may be required for determining the purity of breeding and the identity of such animal. And provided further, that the collectors of customs shall require a certificate from the Department of Agriculture stating that such animal is purebred of a recognized breed and duly registered in a book of record recognized by the Secretary of Agriculture for that breed.

"Import licenses are not required and there are no exchange restrictions."

These rules cover the importation of dogs from all foreign countries.

My cousin in England raises Welsh Terriers and is planning on sending me one as a gift. How can we arrange for the dog's shipment?

The easiest way is to arrange such a transaction through a firm which specializes in handling livestock consignments. Here are the addresses of two English companies which have good reputations:

> Spratt's Livestock Shipping Service
> Spratt's Patent Limited
> 41-47 Bow Road
> London, E.3, England

> Cook's Livestock Transport Service
> Berkeley Street
> London, W.1, England

Registration and What It Means

Who attends to the registration of a purebred puppy, the buyer or the seller?

Either the buyer or the seller may register a puppy from a registered litter. An established kennel usually registers all the puppies it breeds, because then the pups will bear the kennel's name, which is a means of identification for the dogs that the kennel has bred. If the breeder of a puppy isn't interested in naming the pup himself, then he gives the purchaser a signed application form which must be sent to the American Kennel Club with the proper fee.

If I buy a purebred puppy, am I entitled to certain papers?

Yes. The seller should either give you the pup's registration certificate, properly signed for transfer to your name, or a signed application blank which you then send to the American Kennel Club. It sometimes happens that a puppy is sold after his registration application has been sent to the A.K.C. and before the breeder has received the certificate in return. In a case of this sort the breeder signs the registration certificate as soon as he gets it from the kennel club and sends it to the new owner. Most kennels also give a puppy a three- or four-generation pedigree, though technically they are not required to do this.

After I have sent my dog's registration application to the kennel club, how soon will I receive his certificate?

Usually in about three or four weeks, perhaps a bit longer if it happens to be one of the occasional periods during which the A.K.C. is snowed under with applications.

Last year we bought a Labrador puppy. We have his registration certificate but no pedigree. The man who sold us the dog has moved away and we have been unable to locate him. Is there any way we can get a pedigree for our dog?

Yes. You can obtain a certified three-generation pedigree by sending your dog's full registered name, his registration number and a check or money order for two dollars to the American Kennel Club. If you want a four-generation pedigree, that costs five dollars.

*We have just bought a Collie pup. We paid eighty dollars and
are more than satisfied with him, but the breeder says that
if we want our dog's papers it will cost us ten dollars. We
don't think this is fair. Do you?*

It is not only unfair, it's dishonest. Any breeder who offers
puppies for sale at two different prices, attempting to get a
higher price if the pups are sold "with papers," is simply trying
to take advantage of the average dog lover's inexperience in
such matters. The American Kennel Club maintains that a
purebred dog's registration certificate is his birth certificate and
whoever is his legal owner is entitled to this testimonial of the
dog's pure-bloodedness. In your case the thing to do is to
demand that the breeder give you either the registration certificate or a properly signed registration application. Should he
refuse, warn him that you are going to report the matter to the
A.K.C. and then do so.

*Are there any circumstances under which the seller of a pure-
bred puppy may rightfully withhold the registration certificate?*

Yes. Once in a while a breeder may have a puppy with a disqualifying fault, such as a Boston Terrier with a Dudley nose or
a mis-marked Cocker Spaniel. Because these faults are known
to be difficult to eradicate in breeding, such puppies are usually
given away (or sold at very low prices) with a written agreement
signed by both buyer and seller that the dog is never to be
registered. This is done as a precaution against the dog's being
used for breeding purposes and perpetrating physical characteristics which are considered undesirable.

*Does the buyer or the seller pay the fee for transferring a regis-
tered dog from one name to another?*

There is no definite rule on this. The larger kennels usually
pay the fee as a matter of courtesy, but they are not required
to do so.

We have a purebred Boston Terrier but have never bothered to send his registration papers to the A.K.C. Is there any point in doing so as long as we don't intend to show him?

When you bought your Boston you probably paid a fairly good price for him. The reason he was worth that much was because he is a purebred dog. By not obtaining his registration certificate you are rejecting something for which you paid. Another reason for registering your dog is that sometime in the future you may have an opportunity to breed him to a purebred bitch for either a stud fee or one of the resulting puppies. If your dog is not registered, the puppies he sires are not eligible for registration either, and are, therefore, of little value.

Is a dog that is registered in the Field Dog Stud Book eligible for registration with the American Kennel Club?

In most cases, yes. So, usually, is a litter of puppies whose sire is A.K.C. registered and whose dam is F.D.S.B. registered, or vice versa. If you own a dog that is registered with the Field and wish to register it with the A.K.C., submit the F.D.S.B. certificate and the dog's pedigree to the Kennel Club together with the proper fee—two dollars if the dog is less than eighteen months of age, four dollars if the dog is eighteen months of age or older.

CHAPTER *3*

Feeding Your Dog

There are probably almost as many theories about dog feeding as there are on how to beat the races. In fact, we have in one day talked to as many as a dozen dog owners and found that no two were feeding their dogs in exactly the same way. Moreover, in spite of their divergent ideas, almost any of them could show you dogs in the pink of condition being fed by *their* special method.

There are breeders who raise puppies on plain meat, milk, and vitamin supplements; there are others who use nothing but prepared commercial feeds; and still others who feed a mixture of broken biscuit and meat. Some kennel operators give their grown dogs two meals a day; others insist that an adult dog is better off with one daily feeding; one Boxer fancier believes in a diet of meat, milk, and vegetables; another says, "No vegetables —give them biscuit." Then there are the breeders who claim that milk is superfluous in dog nutrition; and those who insist that they could not raise youngsters without it and proceed to complicate matters still further by stating that canned milk is so much better than bottled milk that puppies raised on milk out of bottles are starting life with a handicap. Confusing, isn't it?

After all the opinions on the subject have been aired, arguments argued, and examples pointed out, a few facts about dog feeding remain indisputable. One is that the canine digestive system is, for the most part, a fairly tolerant and versatile apparatus, and it is entirely likely that dogs can be kept in good condition on any one of several different diets. Another is that different dogs display great individuality as to the amounts and types of food required for healthy growth while puppies, and for hardiness and vitality when full-grown. Your neighbor's Scottie may thrive on a daily breakfast of milk and corn flakes, while your own Highland Laddie might refuse such a meal entirely, or else eat it with gusto and then heave it on the parlor rug twenty minutes later. In the case of litter-mates getting exactly the same rations, Peter may be sloppy fat while his brother Buster is positively scrawny. The answer is that Buster needs twice as much food to keep in good shape because of his active, high-strung temperament.

There is a long list of foods which are considered good canine nourishment and are easily digested by most dogs. Then there is a list of undesirable items which are liable to cause stomach upsets or even more serious complaints. Both of these lists will be given on pages that follow, together with sample menus and general suggestions; but how hearty or lean a diet *your* dog may require, in order that his contours are neither those of a blimp nor a four-legged hatrack, will be a matter of the individual's needs. So the question of how much will have to be decided by keeping an eye on Towser's figure and then using your own good judgment.

The Foods a Dog *Must* Have and Those He Should *Never* Have

What foods are necessary in a dog's diet for proper growth and good health?

Meat (protein), cereals (carbohydrates), fats, vitamins and minerals.

Would you please give me a list of foods which should not be fed to dogs?

At the very top of the list should be small, easily splintered bones. By this we mean chicken bones, turkey bones (in fact the bones from any poultry at all), rabbit bones, chop bones, small steak bones, and fishbones.

Pork is difficult for dogs to digest.

Freshly baked bread, cake, candy; highly seasoned meats such as salami, bologna, etc.; salted nuts, pastry, and candied fruits are bad news for your dog's stomach too, no matter how much he may like these tidbits.

Vegetables that are liable to cause trouble are Brussels sprouts, cabbage, broccoli, cauliflower, turnips, peas, lima beans, corn, beets, and parsnips.

Starch in the Dog's Diet

I've heard that dogs aren't able to digest starch. Is this true?

Dogs can perfectly well digest cooked starches but in a different way than humans do. The saliva of man contains an enzyme which starts the digestion of starchy foods while they are still in the mouth. The dog's saliva does not contain this enzyme, so starches consumed by a dog are digested when they reach the small intestine.

Should a dog be fed any starchy foods at all?

Certainly, as they serve as a source of energy and, if properly cooked, are easily digested. Kibble and dog biscuits are both basically starchy foods and can constitute one-third to one-half of an adult dog's diet with safety as long as the balance of the diet provides sufficient meat, fat, vitamins, and minerals.

What would happen to a dog fed entirely on potatoes?

He wouldn't get the vitamins and minerals he needed and would probably die of malnutrition. A dog whose diet was one-third potatoes, if the other part was meat, would be well nourished.

Diets and Different Breeds

To me it doesn't make sense that a St. Bernard and a Pekingese should get the same diet. Shouldn't different breeds of dogs be fed different kinds of food?

According to Dr. Clive M. McCay, of Cornell University, a top authority on dog nutrition, there is almost no difference in the maintenance needs of the different breeds. In other words, a St. Bernard and a Pekingese will thrive on the same kinds of food, the only difference being in the amounts needed. The larger breeds, during their period of growth, require proportionately greater amounts of vitamin D (found in cod-liver oil, viosterol, Haliver oil) and minerals (calcium, phosphorus, iron, etc.).

Tomato juice is considered so good for human babies that I've been wondering if I shouldn't give it to my Cocker Spaniel puppy.

The reason tomato juice and orange juice are beneficial to human nutrition is that they are rich sources of vitamin C. Dogs, however, seem able to generate their own vitamin C under most conditions. Except for this, the vitamin requirements of human beings and dogs are almost exactly the same. In fact, the use of dogs in nutritional studies had led to the discovery and isolation of many of the more important vitamins. As for your puppy—small amounts of tomato juice, if he likes it, can do him no harm.

My two-year-old Great Dane seems to need less food now than he did when he was ten months of age. How come?

Once they are mature even the largest dogs don't eat as much as one might think. It is while they are growing that the puppies of the large breeds require a generous diet. When you consider that during his first year a Great Dane can grow to seventy-five times his weight at birth, it's easy to see why the big fellows need good food and plenty of it. Big breeds compress into two years the growth that it takes a human being eighteen to twenty years to achieve.

About Commercial Dog Food

The advertising of the various dog food manufacturers has me confused. They all make different claims about their products and I don't know what to believe. The makers of a dry dog food state in their radio commercials that when a dog owner buys canned dog food what he's getting is mostly water. Is this so?

Statements about how much water canned dog food contains are rather misleading. Meat contains 70 per cent water, and still meat is the most important item in a dog's diet. The price of canned food is rather high in proportion to the amount of actual nourishment contained, but most dogs eat it with relish and will stay in good condition on it if their diet is supplemented with other foods.

When I go to the grocery store I never know which brand of canned dog foods to buy. Can you help me?

The main thing to remember when buying canned dog food is to steer clear of the bargain-priced brands which are of obscure origin and doubtful value. The canned foods which are made by the better-known meat packing firms that produce dog food as a by-product and the big companies which specialize in dog foods are both palatable and nourishing.

Sammy, our Peke, gets canned dog food a couple of days a week. Should I heat it before giving it to him?

Not if the canned food has been on the pantry shelf in a warm kitchen. Leftover food which has been kept in the refrigerator should be slightly warmed in a little soup, gravy, or fat.

Do you advise canned dog food as a steady diet for growing puppies?

No, and not for grown dogs either. Once or twice a week is all right for youngsters. The rest of the time they should be getting meat mixed with dry dog foods or cereals. Grown dogs may be given one of the good brands of canned food two or three times a week.

The market where I shop carries two brands of canned dog food. One kind is mostly horse meat. The other has a statement on the label "Contains no horse flesh." Does the fact that the second brand contains no horse meat make it more desirable? The horse meat kind is a little less expensive.

When the maker of dog food boasts that his product contains no horse flesh he is simply admitting that he is passing up an economical and wholesome source of animal protein. Because horse meat is not used to any extent as food for humans in this country, a good grade of clean horse meat can be purchased for less money than what the very poorest beef scrap would cost. The brand containing horse meat is undoubtedly the better buy, and is just as desirable from the standpoint of being clean and nourishing as the higher-priced brand.

What are the pros and cons of feeding dry meal-type dog food?

The advantages are these: it's cheap; it isn't much trouble, as the only necessary preparation is the addition of liquids; the better brands are fairly well balanced foods. The disadvantages are these: many brands are lacking in "taste appeal" and dogs will not readily eat them; most of them smell unpleasant; when liquids are added to this type of food its consistency is rather mushy and sticky, and dogs dislike eating it as it adheres to the roofs of their mouths; it does not contain enough fat. However, feeding a good grade of meal-type dog food with fat, broth and, if possible, meat added is certainly preferable to a diet of starchy scraps and leftovers consisting mostly of vegetables.

Our Collie-Shepherd thrives on meal-type dog food and I'm in favor of it because of the economic angle. What things should be added to this type of food?

First of all, fat. If you use two cupfuls of dry meal-type food, moisten it with water or broth and then mix in one half cupful of melted or finely ground fat. This will do your dog more good than three cupfuls of dry food with liquid added and no fat. Be sure to give your dog any leftover meat you have too.

*The manufacturer of a well-known dry dog food states that
the food contains 20 per cent meat meal. Just what is meat
meal and is it as good a food for dogs as fresh meat?*

Meat meal is made from scrap meat which has been processed
at high temperatures to extract the fat content and then dried.
The resulting product is used as a source of protein for many
dry dog foods. Meat meal is not as nutritious as fresh meat,
because the value of the protein has been lowered and most of
the vitamin B₁ destroyed by the heat used in rendering and
drying it.

*If the label on a package of dog food says that the food con-
tains a minimum of 18 per cent protein does that mean
that 18 per cent of it consists of meat?*

No, it doesn't even mean that the protein content is necessarily
of animal origin. Cheese, soy-bean meal, fish meal, wheat germ,
meat meal, dried brewer's yeast, and dry skim milk are all used
as protein in dog foods. Only if a label states that a food contains a certain percentage of meat can you be sure that that is
the source of protein content.

*Were the war dogs which served with the armed forces in
World War II fed commercial dog food?*

War dogs were fed a carefully balanced, mixed food. Less than
one-fifth of this mixture was commercial dog food. The War
Department's manual on war dogs gives the following formula
for the daily diet of a sixty-pound dog in training:

> ½ lb. cooked horse meat
>
> ¾ lb. raw horse meat (ground with the bone)
>
> ½ lb. yellow cornmeal cooked for two hours in horse-meat
> broth
>
> ½ lb. commercial dog food
>
> Salt added in amounts to make 1 per cent based on dry
> weight

This may seem like a great deal of food for a sixty pound dog, and it would be if the dog were a sedentary house pet. Because war dogs led extremely strenuous and active lives while in training and on duty, they needed large amounts of food to supply energy and maintain a healthy weight.

Dog Biscuits

Out of curiosity I have eaten dog biscuits once or twice and found them to be absolutely flat and tasteless. Why is it that dogs like them so much?

A dog's sense of taste (which is linked to his scenting powers) is much keener than a human being's; consequently, dog biscuits seem slightly sweet to him. Dog biscuits are composed mostly of second-grade wheat flour. The baking of the biscuits changes the starch in the flour to dextrose, and that's what the dog tastes, and likes, when he eats dog biscuits.

Are dog biscuits a complete and balanced food in themselves?

No, they are a good basic food to which meat and fat should be added, and vegetables too, if you wish. They are convenient, and most dogs like them, but they do not constitute a complete diet by any means.

Why Dogs Must Have Meat

Is there some physical reason for the fact that a dog should get a generous proportion of meat in his diet?

Yes. The dog is a carnivore—a flesh-eating animal. One of the physical characteristics of carnivorous animals is an intestinal tract which is rather small in diameter and short in comparison with that of other zoological species. Because he has this type of digestive apparatus, the dog needs food that is concentrated rather than bulky, and meat fulfills this requirement perfectly.

More About Meat

Should I give my dog, a full-grown Samoyed, chopped meat or meat in chunks?

Most authorities agree that for grown dogs meat in chunks is preferable, because it does not pack down in the stomach and form a solid mass, as chopped meat can. There is one disadvantage in using chunk meat—choosy feeders find it easy to pick out the pieces of meat and leave the cereal or biscuit portions of their food. If your dog starts doing this, change him to chopped meat, which can be so thoroughly mixed with cereal or kibble that he can't pick over his food and sort out the meat from the rest of his dinner.

Which kind of meat is most nutritious for dogs?

The meat that is highest in nutritional value is liver. However, liver has a tendency to produce diarrhea, and if a dog isn't accustomed to it, even a rather small amount is liable to cause an upset of the bowels.

I've heard it claimed that feeding raw meat can cause worms or fits and even make dogs vicious. Is there any truth in this?

Not a bit. Raw meat is better food for your dog than anything else you can give him. It will not cause worms, fits, or meanness.

Because dogs are by nature meat-eating animals, wouldn't an all-meat diet be ideal for them?

No, it wouldn't be as beneficial as one made up of 50 to 60 per cent meat combined with cereals (carbohydrates), fats, vitamins, and minerals. Muscle meat alone (hamburger, beefsteak, horse meat) is not a complete or balanced diet for dogs, any more than a diet of all cereal or all meat would fill the needs of a human being.

Our German Shepherd has always been fed on chopped beef, beef hearts and beef kidneys. We have recently moved to a

*neighborhood where we can obtain good, clean horse meat
very reasonably. Would it do any harm to change her diet
from beef to horse meat?*

None at all, but don't do it too abruptly. For instance, if you've
been feeding two pounds of beef a day, start out by feeding one-
half pound of horse meat mixed with a pound and a half of
the beef, and then gradually increase the proportion of horse
meat a few ounces a day until the change is complete. Don't forget
that horse meat is usually lacking in fat, so be sure to add suet
or meat drippings to it.

*There's a fellow in our neighborhood who goes hunting quite
often and frequently offers us a rabbit or two as a treat for
our spaniels. I don't want to hurt our neighbor's feelings
by refusing his favors but I'm not sure if rabbit meat is
good for dogs, and I don't want a couple of sick Cockers
on my hands. What's the verdict on rabbit meat—is it O.K.?*

Rabbit meat is relished by dogs and is good for them as long
as it is *thoroughly* cooked and cut away from the bone. Never,
never, give your dogs uncooked rabbit meat, as they are almost
sure to become infested with tapeworm as a result.

Is there a disease that dogs are liable to get from eating pork?

Yes, it is trichinosis and it can be contracted from eating raw
pork. Even cooked pork is not recommended for dogs. The fat
in it often causes nausea, and if the dog does keep it down, he
digests it slowly.

*My wife recently bought a five-month-old English Cocker Span-
iel. He's a fine healthy puppy but it puzzles us that he won't
eat raw meat. Isn't this very unusual?*

Puppies that are raised on cooked meat frequently refuse raw
meat because it smells and tastes strange to them. Dogs are so
much creatures of habit that they are often unwilling to accept
foods to which they are unaccustomed. As long as your puppy
is growing and thriving on cooked meat by all means continue
with it.

A local meat-packing firm has been selling stomachs (tripe), lungs, and udders as food for dogs. Are these things really good for dogs?

Yes, if properly prepared. Lungs and udders should always be well-cooked, as they are focal points for tuberculosis. Remember that lungs are spongy, so judge them by weight rather than bulk, or you are liable to underfeed your dog. Stomach meat (or tripe) should be cut up or ground rather fine because of its toughness. All of these organs contain plenty of good nourishment and are relatively inexpensive.

Experts on dog nutrition seem to agree that feeding a dog nothing but meat does not provide a properly balanced diet. Yet the only food that dogs in their wild state could have had was the meat of the game they killed. How, then, did they survive before they were domesticated?

When wild dogs killed an animal the first parts of it they ate were the internal organs, including the stomach and its contents of grain and cereal grasses. Secondly, the body fat, the muscle meat, and finally even the pelt and bones were eaten. The plant products in the animal's stomach provided carbohydrates; the muscle meat, proteins; the body fat, fat; the liver, vitamins; and the bones, minerals. In other words, by eating the entire animal the dog did a good job of providing himself with a balanced diet. When dogs that live in the country catch a rabbit or squirrel, or a woodchuck, they will eat the entire animal the same way that their primitive ancestors did.

Bones for Your Dog

Every so often the butcher sends over a nice big soup bone as a treat for Gus, our Boxer. Should I cook the bones before giving them to Gus?

No. Cooking would only destroy what little nourishment the bones might contain, and Gus will enjoy the bones more if they are raw.

Why are chicken and chop bones forbidden items for dogs? I always hate to throw them out when I think of how our Bucky would enjoy gnawing them.

The chances are that Bucky would enjoy the bones all right, but not for long. Small bones such as chicken and chop bones, easily break into sharp splinters that are liable either to choke a dog or puncture his intestines.

Coyotes, foxes, wolves, and dogs running wild frequently kill chickens, pheasants, quail, and rabbits and eat them, bones and all, with no ill effects. Why then, are poultry bones, chop bones, steak bones, etc. dangerous for dogs?

Because the birds and rabbits that wild canine animals kill and eat are eaten *raw*. Uncooked bones are more flexible and less likely to splinter than those which have been subjected to heat. It is the brittleness of the bones which are left from our dinner tables which makes them unsafe. But take no chances—don't give your dog any of these bones either raw or cooked.

I know chicken bones should never be given to dogs, but what about the meat? Would it make my Pomeranian sick if I gave him a little leftover chicken or turkey occasionally?

Not at all, as long as you carefully pick the meat from the bones. Often a sick or convalescent dog that will refuse all other food can be tempted to eat a little chicken, turkey, or well-cooked rabbit meat.

On the days when our dog is given a bone to gnaw is it neces-sary to give him meat too?

It is, unless the bones are very meaty. Dogs don't derive any real nourishment from bones. It's only the bits of meat that cling to a bone that are of any benefit.

Do bones help to keep a dog's teeth in good condition?

If a dog is given a raw beef bone once a week it should help to keep tartar from forming on his teeth.

Fish and Eggs

Is fish an approved food for dogs?

Fish is a good protein food and also contains iodine which is a necessary and valuable mineral. Fresh fish has its dangers for it's almost impossible to get all of the bones out of some varieties. Canned fish, such as salmon and tuna is better, as the cooking reduces the bones to pulp. If your dog likes these foods and they agree with him, they make a nice variation in his diet.

Eggs are supposed to be very good food for dogs, but which is better, raw eggs or cooked eggs?

If eggs are fed raw, only the yolk should be used. Raw egg white is not only indigestible and liable to cause diarrhea, but acts as a robber to the dog's system by absorbing and carrying away essential vitamins. If eggs are fed whole, they should be cooked—boiled, scrambled, or poached—as cooked egg white is easily digested, and heat destroys none of the nourishment contained in the yolk.

Milk — The Perfect Food

Do you recommend goat's milk for dogs?

There is nothing better, especially for puppies. Goat's milk contains smaller fat globules than cow's milk and is more easily digested.

Isn't fresh cow's milk with the cream mixed in just as nourishing for young puppies as their mother's milk?

No. Bitch's milk is much richer than cow's milk. It contains several times as much fat and casein. This is the reason for using a rich milk formula when feeding growing puppies.

We are the proud owners of a litter of fine English Setter puppies and are anxious to raise them right. When it comes to weaning time should the bottled milk we give them be diluted?

No. You would only be filling them up with water. When you start the puppies on bottled milk give them whole milk — unskimmed and undiluted.

Doesn't giving milk to puppies make them have worms?

Absolutely not. Puppies thrive on milk. Puppies can be born with worms or may become infested shortly after birth, but milk has nothing to do with it.

Which is preferable for puppies, fresh milk or canned milk?

Most breeders prefer canned evaporated milk. It is easily stored and can be fed in either a rich or a diluted mixture, depending on how much water is added to it. Then too, fresh milk may vary from time to time, but canned milk is uniform in flavor and content. This doesn't mean that healthy puppies can't be raised on fresh milk, because untold thousands have been.

Recently I gave our German Shepherd a few laps of butter-milk and he seemed to enjoy it. Is this kind of milk liable to cause an upset stomach?

No. Buttermilk and even sour milk are perfectly all right to give your dog. If he likes these products and you have an oversupply, by all means let him have them.

Fat in the Dog's Diet

Ice cream containing high-grade cream, egg yolks, etc., is sup-posedly full of nourishment and is often given to invalids and children. Why then, is it supposed never to be given to dogs?

A spoonful or two of ice cream won't hurt any dog. A large portion would probably cause stomach cramps or nausea, not because of the ingredients contained in the ice cream but because of its temperature. Icy cold foods or liquids should never be given to dogs, as most of them "fall to" with such zest that the food arrives in the stomach practically all in a lump still thoroughly chilled.

The only kind of meat drippings which we always have on hand is bacon fat. Would it be advisable to use this to supply the necessary fat in our Collie's food?

Yes, it would. Though pork and bacon are not recommended items for dog feeding, bacon fat seems to agree with almost all dogs, and the use of it is a fine means of supplying fat to the diet.

When I don't happen to have any meat drippings or other fat, is there any substitute I could use to mix with the horse meat I feed my dog?

Yes. Mazola or Wesson oil are both good substitutes. Add one and a half tablespoonfuls to each pound of meat.

Is butter good for dogs? I give my Scottie a lick or two once in a while when there is some left on a plate, and he's just crazy about it.

Any time you have a little leftover butter which you don't want to use for cooking, by all means give it to your dog. It's loaded with vitamin A and is wonderful for his coat.

What's the maximum amount of fat that may be fed to a dog with safety?

His diet may be as high as 25 per cent fat by dry weight.

One pair of Cocker Spaniels are a puzzle to me. They are brothers and very similar in temperament, but until we figured out how to feed them, Charlie was plump and sleek and Marty, who got exactly the same diet, was much too thin. Now we give Marty almost twice as much as Charlie gets and he is in good condition, too. Without any differences in disposition to account for the great divergence in their requirements, it's hard to understand. Can you give me an explanation?

The actual efficiency of the digestive apparatus can vary enor- mously between two individuals of exactly the same background and temperament. An illustration of this is the number of thin people who are big eaters and the fat people who really eat very little. In the case of your Cockers, Charlie probably has an exceed- ingly efficient digestive system and is able to transform every bit of food he gets into good solid flesh, while Marty's system, being less efficient, requires more food in order to get enough nourish- ment to stay in good condition.

A Dish for the Dogs

We have a Dachshund and a Cocker Spaniel. As a Christmas present a friend of ours sent the dogs a couple of special feeding dishes. The dishes are quite deep and are so con- structed that a dog can put his head down in them without getting his ears in the food. It works fine for Danny, the Cocker, and keeps his ears from getting messy, but Alfred, the Dachshund, seems really to dislike his dish, picks at his food, and sometimes doesn't eat all of it. What can the trouble be?

Alfred, having a Dachshund's long pointed nose, probably wouldn't like his food from any dish that was very deep because his nostrils would come in contact with the food before his teeth and tongue could reach it. A pie pan, or other shallow vessel, is a much better dish for any dog with a long pointed nose. A deep dish is all right for the Cocker because his muzzle is fairly blunt and he can get at the food without digging his nose into it.

Is there some way I can keep my Afghan Hound from getting his ears in his food when he eats?

Slide a round garter or a man's sleeveband over his head and it will hold his ears against his neck and keep them out of his food when he puts his head down to eat. Be sure the garter or band isn't so tight as to cause discomfort. You can cut the top off a silk or nylon stocking and use it in the same way.

The Big Meal of the Day

Why do most people give their dogs the big meal of the day in the late afternoon or early evening?

The custom probably traces back to when dogs worked hard during the day herding sheep or cattle, or hunting. A dog with a full stomach is inclined to sluggishness, so it became standard practice to feed the dog after his day's work was done, giving him only a snack in the morning.

How can a dog get along on just one meal a day? Twenty-four hours between meals seems like a long time to me.

If you will consider the feeding habits of dogs in their wild state it will be easier to understand why a domestic adult dog can enjoy good health on one daily feeding. When wild dogs (and this goes for wolves and coyotes, too) killed game, they literally gorged themselves with meat and then sought a safe retreat where they would rest and sleep for two or even three days, making no attempt during this period to seek food. The reason the wild dog's feeding habits were as we have described them was that his stomach was designed to accommodate large amounts of hastily gulped food, and the digestive processes were rather slow. The dogs we keep as pets may be extremely civilized creatures, but their digestive tracts and processes are the same as those of their wild ancestors. One generous meal a day of the right food will suffice for almost any normal adult dog.

A few weeks ago one of my daughter's business associates gave us a lovely two-year-old Irish Setter. At the time Timmy was presented to us we were told that he only needed to be fed once a day, so that's what we have been doing—giving him a big meal every afternoon at four. But now he hangs around the kitchen in the morning when I'm getting breakfast and almost drives me crazy pestering me for something to eat. Even though he is full-grown, couldn't he have some sort of a little breakfast snack?

Certainly he can. It's rather hard on a house dog, who is fed only once a day, to have to smell the enticing aromas of food being cooked for the family, when he isn't going to have even a taste. You can give Timmy as much as half of his daily food allotment in the morning and then the other half can be his four o'clock meal.

It would give us a great sense of protection to know that our Collie was on the job as a watchdog at night. Would he be more alert if we gave him his big meal of the day in the morning instead of in the late afternoon?

Yes, he would, because a dog is likely to sleep more soundly after a large meal. Give him his main meal of the day in the morning and a snack in the evening.

Kibble and How to Prepare It

Is it necessary to always soak kibble before feeding it?

Yes. Feeding dry or insufficiently soaked kibble generally causes painful bloating or indigestion.

Should the liquid in which kibble is soaked be hot or cold?

Kibble seems to absorb moisture and soften faster in hot water, but the temperature of the fluid isn't too important. If the dog meat is cold from having been in the icebox, soaking the kibble in boiling water or broth and then mixing it with the meat will take the chill off the meat, and it can be fed without cooking or heating. When the meat is still hot from having been cooked, use cold water for soaking the kibble and it will help cool the meat to a temperature that won't burn Fido's mouth.

How can I tell when kibble has soaked long enough?

Pick out one or two of the larger pieces and crumble them. If the interior is still dry, soak the kibble for another fifteen minutes before feeding.

How much broth or water should be used to soak one cup of kibble?

This you will have to find out for yourself, for some brands seem to "take up" more moisture than others. Try using a cup and a half of fluid to one cup of kibble and letting the mixture soak for half an hour. If the kibble is thoroughly moistened and all the fluid is absorbed at the end of this time, then the amount of liquid is correct. If all the liquid is absorbed and the pieces of kibble are still not wet all the way through, use more fluid. If the kibble is completely soaked and there is still some liquid which is unabsorbed, you're using too much. You'll find it a help if you will always use the same brand of kibble. Then you will become familiar with the correct proportions and won't have to experiment.

Preparing Food Mixtures

My brother and I own a beautiful Greyhound. We are continually arguing about how to fix his food. My brother always wants to give him a meat-and-meal mixture that's very moist and "soupy," and I think the food should be prepared so as to be more like hash in consistency. Which is right?

The food mixture should be crumbly in texture. The correct consistency is just moist enough for easy eating, but never sloppy. In fact "hashlike" is a good description.

Every few days I cook up a sort of stew for our St. Bernard and generally add broken dog biscuit to sop up the juices. Would it be all right to use rice to thicken the stew?

Rice is a good alternate for the biscuit; so is barley. Both rice and barley should be thoroughly cooked. Continue to simmer the stew for at least half an hour after the addition of either of these cereals, and be sure that meat constitutes at least 40 to 50 per cent of the whole mixture.

We feed our three Pointers a combination of meat and a commercially prepared dry dog food. Why can't we mix and bake the dry dog food ourselves?

A nourishing dry dog food contains as many as fourteen or fifteen ingredients which must be carefully measured and blended and then baked or boiled at the proper temperature. It's really quite an undertaking, and wouldn't be worth the time and trouble, unless one were maintaining a very large kennel. Even then it's doubtful that any real economy would be achieved.

During the summer months my two Beagles spend most of their time in a fenced yard at the side of the house. I try to keep fresh, cool water in their pan at all times, but during the warm weather the sun makes the water almost hot, and dust and dirt and bugs get into it, too. Isn't there some way to prevent this?

Ask your grocer for a wooden box such as is used for shipping canned goods. Stand the box on one end, with the solid wood bottom to the south, and set the water pan inside it. This will shade the water and help keep the dust and bugs out of it.

Underweight and Overweight

I'm beginning to think that perhaps I haven't been giving our Old English Sheepdog as generous a diet as he needs, but his coat is so shaggy that it's really hard for me to decide whether or not he's too thin. How can I tell?

Heavy-coated dogs often appear to be in better flesh than they actually are. The next time you bathe your dog and his coat is sopping wet and clinging to him, take a careful look and run vour hands over his ribs and hipbones. If these bones are easily seen and felt you can be sure he's underweight and needs his food allowance increased.

I've been told that cottage cheese is a good food for dogs. Is this true?

Cottage cheese has the same amount of high quality protein as lean meat and is high in all nutrients except calories. In other words, it's fine food for dogs. Because cottage cheese is so low in calories, it is especially recommended for dogs whose waistlines need a little paring down.

Ever since he was two years old our Bulldog has been fat as a pig. How can we get his weight down and keep it down?

The only cure is more exercise and less food. Cut out any meal-type food, biscuit, or cereal for a while. Feed meat (with some fat), cottage cheese, skim milk, eggs, and vegetables. Give him a vitamin capsule every day (the type that contains a mixture of several vitamins). Try this for at least two months. If the dog is lazy and sluggish, force him to exercise by taking him for walks at least twice a day. Don't walk him too far or too fast at first. Increase the speed and distance gradually.

Several breeders I have talked with say that they believe in putting their dogs on half rations one day a week. Is this a good idea?

Feeding very lightly one day a week is a good way to keep a picky eater's appetite keyed up. This practice is not recommended for growing puppies or bitches that are in whelp, but is perfectly all right for adult dogs, especially those that are inclined to go off their feed for no apparent reason.

Diets Right and Wrong

Our hired man feeds my two bird dogs, and lately I discovered that all he's been giving them is dog biscuits soaked in milk or soup. It seems to me that this isn't a very hearty diet for hard-working hunting dogs but Jim, the hired man, says it's plenty good enough for any dog. Is he right?

Jim is apparently still operating on the theory that any old thing is all right to feed the dog. The diet your dogs have been getting is really pretty poor, especially for dogs that are expected to go all day in the field. They should be fed at least 50 per cent meat with one of the good meal or kibble-type feeds mixed with it. If you will improve their diet you'll find that your dogs will give you much more pleasure when hunting. Their pep, stamina, and alertness will be greatly increased.

Isn't it a sound idea to change a dog's diet during the hot summer months?

The ingredients of his menu should be about the same, except for possibly a little less fat. It is sometimes a good plan to reduce the quantity of food during hot weather, as most dogs are fairly inactive when the thermometer soars, and are liable to put on too much weight if kept on a full diet.

Our Boxer discharges such foul-smelling gases that we can hardly stand to have him in the same room with us. Is some-thing in his diet causing this? Is there any way we can correct it?

When a dog is on a diet containing a high proportion of meat and eggs, putrefaction takes place in the intestines, causing obnoxious gases to be given off. If you will cut down the amount of meat and eggs you feed your dog, and give him more kibble or cereal in his diet, you will probably notice a marked improvement.

We are coonhound enthusiasts and always have at least one or two—and sometimes more—full-grown dogs on our place. We feed a meat-and-kibble mixture, and, needless to say, the dogs consume plenty of both. Our dealer has offered us a discount if we buy the kibble in hundred-pound lots. We

*would like to take advantage of this proposition, but we
are worried about possibly attracting rats or mice if we
have large quantities of food around. What would be the
safest way to store the food?*

Buy one or two galvanized metal ash cans with tight-fitting
covers. The tall-size ones will easily hold a hundred pounds of
kibble and keep it dry and safe from vermin. Containers of this
type are preferable to built-in bins, as they are movable and more
easily cleaned, too.

Variety in the Dog's Diet

*Which is better—giving my dog exactly the same food, day
after day, or varying the diet?*

Variety is preferable. When dogs are accustomed to exactly the
same food day in and day out, even slight changes are liable to
upset them. If a dog is accustomed to a variety of food, any changes
in diet which might be necessitated by temporary shortages or
traveling aren't liable to cause stomach or bowel trouble.

*Bessie, our Shetland Sheepdog, seems to enjoy a little variety
in her diet. Would you please suggest a weekly menu which
would be good for her and that she would relish? She's
spoiled anyway, and we might just as well go on indulging
her whims.*

You might try something like this: Give her beef or horse
meat, chopped or in chunks, twice a week, mixing it with shredded
wheat, kibble, or whatever dry dog food she may like. Then
substitute beef kidney for the beef or horse meat once a week,
and heart of beef or pork kidney twice a week. The remaining
two days she could be given canned dog food.

When Your Cupboard Is Bare

*The meat we give our dogs is delivered to us three times a
week by a local dog-food firm. Sometimes during bad winter
weather the delivery man isn't able to get to our house, and*

I have to give the dogs whatever I'm able to concoct from what we have on hand. Have you any suggestions for meeting these emergencies?

The easiest thing to do is to keep a supply of canned dog food on hand. If you should be out of canned food, try this: break up toasted bread in milk and let it soak for a few minutes; then stir two or three eggs into the toast and milk and cook the mixture as you would scramble eggs. This makes a nourishing emergency meal which most dogs enjoy. Canned soup, such as chicken noodle or beef soup, poured over toast or shredded wheat will always do in a pinch too. When using canned soups, don't add any salt until you've tasted the soup yourself, as many of these products are already adequately seasoned.

The Dog That Is Very Hungry

I have a Schnauzer whose table manners are a scandal. Every time she's fed she acts as though she hasn't seen food in a month, and gobbles and gulps her food so that it's a wonder she doesn't choke to death. What's the matter with her?

Nothing is wrong with your dog. She just has a healthy appetite. A great many dogs gulp their food, and it does them no harm because their stomachs are equipped to take care of food which hasn't been chewed. The habit is probably a holdover from ancient times when dogs running in packs would pull down game, and it was every dog for himself. Under those circumstances if a dog didn't grab whatever he could as fast as possible, the other dogs would get all the meat and poor Slowpoke would be out of luck.

My Pointer bitch stays in good condition all year round on what I feed her until the hunting season comes. After two or three weeks of daily workouts in the field she looks like a skeleton she's so thin. What causes this?

The amount of food you give your Pointer is probably adequate for those periods during which she is comparatively inactive, but not sufficient for her requirements when she is exercising strenuously. An active bird dog exerts a great deal of energy, and if you want her to stay in good condition during periods of field work you'll have to increase her diet in accordance with the amount of work she is doing. Bird dogs should be in hard, lean condition when they are hunting, but not so thin as to seem emaciated.

Rest Before Mealtime

When I bring my coonhounds home from hunting, my sister, with whom I live, usually has their food ready and wants to feed them as soon as we get home. The dogs are generally rather hot and excited after a chase, and, in my opinion, it would be better if we let them cool off and calm down before giving them their dinners. What do you think?

Your opinion is correct. Dogs should never be fed immediately following strenuous exercise. Give them at least an hour in which to get over their excitement and stimulation, and then feed them.

Why Dogs Eat Manure

We live near a park where there is a bridle path, and now our dog has the disgusting habit of picking up and eating horse manure at every opportunity. What makes him do this and how can we stop him?

Probably the reason your dog eats manure is to obtain the partially digested grain it contains. While the habit is understandably upsetting to you, as his owner, it actually isn't likely to do the dog any great harm. The first thing to do is to be sure that he is getting enough cereal in his diet so that his craving for carbohydrates will be appeased. Try thoroughly cooked oatmeal as a starter. Then, if you discover him in the act of indulging in his unpleasant habit, treat him as though you had caught him stealing. Scold him sharply and sternly, hold him by the collar and shake him or give him a good whack on the rump.

Sweets Are Not Recommended

I know of plenty of dogs who regularly get cake, candy, canapes, etc., and it doesn't seem to hurt them. Why are such little treats on the forbidden list?

Snacks and tidbits such as you mention are not so harmful in themselves. The trouble is that they contain little or no nourishment which a dog can utilize, and they spoil his appetite for less exciting foods which are necessary for good health and condition.

It's generally agreed that dogs are among the most intelligent of animals. Wouldn't it then be logical to presume that a dog's likes and dislikes in food are sufficient indication of what his diet should be?

A dog's judgment about food isn't any more reliable than a small boy's—and most youngsters, if allowed to choose their own meals, would subsist on chocolate sundaes, hot dogs, and cracker-jack. This doesn't mean that you should starve your dog into eating food that is normally distasteful to him. It's up to you to make selections from the many foods that *are* recommended for dogs and see to it that he gets a properly balanced and palatable ration.

Cinda, my Pug, just loves candy and, although I know I shouldn't do it, I give her a chocolate or a bonbon once in a while. A friend recently told me that giving a dog candy will cause it to have worms. True or false?

False. Sweets won't give a dog worms. Candy may ruin Cinda's appetite and cause her to snoot the meat and other good food which she should have. As long as she eats her regular meals with gusto, and if it gives you pleasure to indulge her on rare occasions, don't let your friend's warning scare you.

Facts About Vitamins

Wheat-germ oil is frequently advertised as being helpful in giving a dog a glossy coat. Is it really of benefit?

Wheat-germ oil is a good source of vitamin E, often called the "skin vitamin." A proper dosage mixed in your dog's food should improve his coat. Don't expect immediate results, though. It may be three or four weeks before you see the hair getting glossy.

Which vitamins are of the greatest importance in the feeding of dogs?

Vitamin A, vitamin B_1 (known as thiamin), vitamin D, and niacin.

I've read that lack of sufficient vitamin A in the diet of a human being is often the cause of night blindness. What effect has the lack of this vitamin on dogs?

Insufficient vitamin A can impair a dog's vision too. Eyes which are runny or contain "matter" often indicate this lack. This vitamin is also of importance for proper growth of young dogs and the functions of reproduction in older dogs. The proper functioning of the kidneys also seems dependent on Vitamin A. It is present in cod-liver oil. Other sources are egg yolks, kidneys, cornmeal, carrots.

Why do all dog experts stress the importance of giving puppies cod-liver oil?

Because fish-liver oils are a rich source of vitamin D. Without this vitamin young animals are unable to assimilate the minerals which are needed in the formation of strong bones and good teeth. A deficiency of vitamin D results in the condition known as rickets, which is characterized by leg bones which are bowed, malformed jaws, and rib bones which have irregularities known as "beads."

*A few days ago I ran out of the haliver oil I've been giving
our Kerry pup. I remembered a bottle of cod-liver oil which
has been in the medicine cabinet for some time and thought
I would use that until I could get more of the haliver oil,
but it smelled so peculiar I decided against it. Does cod-liver
oil "spoil"?*

If cod-liver oil is not kept in a cool place it turns rancid and
loses its vitamin content. You were right not to give the rancid
oil to your puppy, as it would have been of no value and might
have made him sick. The best way to keep fish-liver oils fresh is
to store them in the refrigerator.

*We know our Dalmatian puppy should be getting cod-liver oil,
but when I add it to her food, she won't eat the food. How
can I get it into her?*

There are two things you can do: you can give her the cod-
liver oil separately, administering it as you would liquid medicine, or you can buy haliver oil or viosterol and add that to her
food instead. The second method is preferable, as giving the oil
in daily doses is a nuisance and liable to be a messy business too.
Another alternative is giving the cod-liver oil in capsules, although
the cost of the capsules is rather high.

Can percomorph oil be used in place of cod-liver oil?

Yes. One drop of percomorph oil contains as much vitamins (A
and D) as a teaspoonful of cod-liver oil.

*I've just realized that I've been giving our litter of German
Shepherds about four times as much cod-liver oil as they
should be getting. Do you think I've done them any permanent injury?*

It takes many, many times as much vitamin D to injure an
animal as it does to protect it from rickets. Most likely your
puppies haven't been harmed at all, and the only damage done is

to your bank roll, as good cod-liver oil isn't cheap. Just cut the pups down to the recommended dosage for their age and all will be well.

My sister-in-law has an eleven-year-old Cocker Spaniel. Besides giving him the very best of food she gives him a complete vitamin capsule every day. Isn't that silly?

Not at all. A good complete vitamin pill or capsule every day will often give just enough of a boost to the health of an aged dog so that it makes the difference between his being well and happy, or ailing and enfeebled. Complete vitamin capsules (the kind made for human consumption) are also fine for building up a dog that is recuperating from an illness, or helping along a puppy who has had a setback, or restoring a bitch to good condition after having had puppies.

Do dogs get a disease which is caused by dietary deficiencies similar to pellagra in humans?

They do. The disease is known as "black tongue," and it is caused by an insufficiency of niacin (nicotinic acid). A good mixed diet is the best defense against this ailment. Whole-wheat bread is a rich source of niacin, and that is why this type of bread is recommended when toast is used as part of a dog's meals..

Does loss of appetite sometimes indicate a vitamin deficiency?

Inadequate supplies of vitamin B1 often result in poor appetite and irregular bowel functions. Meat (especially kidneys), whole-wheat bread, and oatmeal provide this vitamin.

Does wrong feeding cause skin trouble (itchiness, hair falling out, etc.) in dogs?

Not usually. A poorly nourished dog or a very fat dog has less resistance to skin trouble, but diet is almost never the primary cause of skin ailments in dogs. A dry, dead-looking coat often results from a diet too low in fats and oils. Many dog owners used to believe that a starchy diet would cause summer eczema (often called "hot spots"), but this idea has been proved false.

How to Treat the Finicky Feeder

I have a Boxer who is a slow, finicky eater. She starts to eat her food and, after a few bites, walks away, wanders around the kitchen, or even goes into another room, then comes back and nibbles a little more and goes away again. This foolishness sometimes goes on for a couple of hours, and even then she doesn't eat all her food. How can I cure her of her silly eating habits?

Dogs which are spoiled and overfed are likely to fool around with their food the way your Boxer does. When you next feed her, put the food down and leave it for half an hour, no longer. At the end of that time, even though she may have taken but very little of it, remove the food and don't let her have anything at all to eat until it is time for her next meal. It won't take long for her to realize that it's a now-or-never proposition when dinner is served. It may help, too, to make her meals smaller until she is readily cleaning up all that you give her.

I have tried feeding my Boston Terrier three different brands of meal-type dry dog food mixed with his meat. He dislikes it so much that even if there is only a couple of spoonfuls of the meal added to the meat he refuses it. He doesn't like cereals much either. Shall I try to starve him into eating the meat-and-meal mixture?

It's never a wise idea to starve a dog into eating any special food. He may eventually eat it, but you're taking the chance of having him get run-down and thin in the process. It is not necessary that the dry food you mix with meat be of the meal type. A good one to try would be the dry food which has been processed so that it resembles noodles in form. This food is nutritious and has a flavor which is tempting to dogs. The chances are that your dog will like it.

CHAPTER 4

Menus for Your Dog

If you want a healthy, happy pet, take a few pains planning his meals. It isn't necessary, of course, to treat your dog as if he were a gourmet, but you should see that he gets his vitamins, proteins, minerals, and other diet essentials. And as a household member in good standing, he deserves a little variety in his fare.

Most of the foods that are good for your dog, as you will see, require a minimum of preparation. More than likely, you will introduce a few innovations of your own into the feeding charts that we are going to give you. Do this with care, for these menus have been devised to give your dog the foods he needs, in the proper balance.

In order to simplify the following feeding charts, the breeds have been grouped into five classes according to their average mature weights. You will find your dog's breed listed in one of these classes. Should your dog not be a purebred, select the group into which he best fits as to size, and then follow the schedule for that group. The amounts indicated are intended as suggestions, not inflexible formulas. Increase or lessen the portion to whatever seems to suit your dog best.

CLASS I: VERY SMALL BREEDS

Affenpinscher, Brussels Griffon, Chihuahua, English Toy Spaniel, Italian Greyhound, Japanese Spaniel, Maltese, Mexican Hairless, Miniature Dachshund (mature weight under nine pounds), Miniature Pinscher, Papillon, Pekingese, Pomeranian, Toy Manchester Terrier, Toy Poodle, Yorkshire Terrier.

CLASS II: SMALL BREEDS

Basenji, Beagle, Bedlington Terrier, Border Terrier, Boston Terrier, Cairn Terrier, Cardigan Welsh Corgi, Cocker Spaniel, Dachshund, Dandie Dinmont Terrier, English Cocker Spaniel, French Bulldog, Irish Terrier, Lakeland Terrier, Lhasa Apso, Manchester Terrier, Miniature Poodle, Miniature Schnauzer, Norwich Terrier, Pembroke Welsh Corgi, Pug, Schipperke, Scottish Terrier, Sealyham Terrier, Shetland Sheepdog, Skye Terrier, Smooth Fox Terrier, Welsh Terrier, West Highland White Terrier, Wire-haired Fox Terrier, Whippet.

CLASS III: MEDIUM-SIZED BREEDS

Airedale Terrier, American Water Spaniel, Basset Hound, Brittany Spaniel, Bulldog, Bullterrier, Chow Chow, Clumber Spaniel, Dalmatian, English Springer Spaniel, Field Spaniel, Harrier, Keeshond, Kerry Blue Terrier, Norwegian Elkhound, Puli, Samoyed, Siberian Husky, Standard Schnauzer, Staffordshire Terrier, Sussex Spaniel, Welsh Springer Spaniel, Wire-haired Pointing Griffon.

CLASS IV: LARGE BREEDS

Afghan Hound, Alaskan Malamute, Belgian Sheepdog, Bernese Mountain Dog, Black and Tan Coonhound, Boxer, Briard, Chesapeake Bay Retriever, Collie, Curly Coated Retriever, Doberman Pinscher, English Setter, Eskimo, Flat Coated Retriever, Foxhound, German Shepherd Dog, German Short-haired Pointer, Giant Schnauzer, Golden Retriever, Gordon Setter, Greyhound, Irish Setter, Irish Water Spaniel, Kuvasz, Labrador Retriever, Old English Sheepdog, Otterhound, Pointer, Saluki, Standard Poodle, Weimaraner.

CLASS V: VERY LARGE BREEDS

Bloodhound, Borzoi, Bouvier des Flandres, Bull Mastiff, Great Dane, Great Pyrenees, Irish Wolf Hound, Komondor, Mastiff, Newfoundland, Rottweiler, Saint Bernard, Scottish Deerhound.

Milk Formula

This is based on the formula which Dr. Edwin R. Blamey, one of the best-known and most respected veterinarians in the New York City area, has recommended for a number of years. This mixture has been used successfully in the rearing of puppies of all breeds.

The easiest way to handle the preparation of the formula is to make up a pint or quart at a time and keep it in the refrigerator, warming whatever amount is needed for each meal.

To Make One Pint: Two teaspoons of sugar of milk
Two cups of whole milk
Two egg yolks
Two teaspoons of lime water
Stir well

Note: The sugar of milk, lime water, and the dicalcium phosphate (the last will appear in suggested menus further along) are all available at any drugstore.

At Three Months

MORNING

Class I. Four or five tablespoons of milk formula mixed with Pablum to make a gruel.

Class II. One-half cup of milk formula with Pablum to make a gruel, or the same amount of beef broth with either one-half of a shredded wheat biscuit or one piece of toast well crumbled.

Class III. Three-quarters to one cup of milk formula with Pablum to make a gruel, or the same amount of beef broth with one shredded wheat biscuit or one and a half pieces of toast.

Class IV. One to one and a half cups of milk formula with one of the following added: enough Pablum to make a gruel, one and a half shredded wheat biscuits, or two pieces of toast. Beef broth may be used in place of milk formula with shredded wheat or toast.

Class V. Two cups of milk formula with one of the following added: enough Pablum to make a gruel, two shredded wheat biscuits or three pieces of toast.

Beef broth may be used in place of the milk formula with shredded wheat or toast.

Note: The milk formula is preferable to the beef broth at this age. If the puppy should not be quite so eager for his breakfast when he reaches five or six months of age, switch to the beef broth.

NOON

Class I. One to one and a half tablespoonfuls of chopped raw beef or horse meat.

Mix in one-half teaspoonful of dicalcium phosphate.

Class II. Two heaping tablespoonfuls of chopped raw beef or horse meat.

Mix in one teaspoonful of cod-liver oil and one teaspoonful of dicalcium phosphate.

Class III. Three to four heaping tablespoonfuls of chopped raw beef or horse meat.

Mix in one teaspoonful of cod-liver oil and one teaspoonful of dicalcium phosphate.

Class IV. Four to five heaping tablespoonfuls of chopped raw beef or horse meat with one-half of a shredded wheat biscuit moistened with milk or broth.

Mix in one and a half teaspoonfuls of cod-liver oil and one and a half teaspoonfuls of dicalcium phosphate.

Class V. One-half pound of chopped raw beef or horse meat with either one to one and a half shredded wheat biscuits moistened with milk or broth, or two pieces of toast crumbled and moistened with milk or broth.

Mix in one tablespoonful of cod-liver oil and one tablespoonful of dicalcium phosphate.

Note: If your puppy doesn't seem to want as much as the amounts given here, don't worry about it. Decrease the amounts, and then gradually build them up again.

LATE AFTERNOON (around four or five o'clock)

For all classes give the same meal as given at noon, including the cod-liver oil and dicalcium phosphate.

EVENING (around bedtime)
For all classes, same as breakfast.

Four and Five Months

MORNING

Class I. Six or seven tablespoonfuls of milk formula with Pablum
added to make a gruel, or the same amount of beef broth with
one-third of a shredded wheat biscuit or one-half piece of well
crumbled toast.

Class II. Three-quarters to one cup of milk formula with Pablum
added to make a thick gruel, or the same amount of beef broth
with either two-thirds of a shredded wheat biscuit or one piece
of well crumbled toast.

Class III. One and a half cups of milk formula with Pablum added
to make a thick gruel, or the same amount of beef broth with
either one to one and a half shredded wheat biscuits or two
pieces of crumbled toast.

Class IV. One and a half cups to two cups of milk formula with
one of the following added: enough Pablum to make a thick
gruel, one and a half or two shredded wheat biscuits, or two or
three pieces of toast. Beef broth may be used in place of the
milk formula and mixed with shredded wheat biscuits or toast.

Class V. Two cups of milk formula with one of the following
added: enough Pablum to make a thick gruel, two and a half
or three shredded wheat biscuits, or four pieces of toast. Soup
or beef broth may be substituted for the milk formula and
mixed with shredded wheat biscuits or toast.

NOON

Class I. Two to three heaping tablespoonfuls of chopped beef or
horse meat with one-third of a shredded wheat biscuit moistened
with soup, broth, or meat juices. Mix in one teaspoonful of
cod-liver oil and one-half teaspoonful of dicalcium phosphate.

Class II. Three to four heaping tablespoonfuls of chopped beef or
horse meat with either two-thirds of a shredded wheat biscuit,
or one piece of toast moistened with soup, broth, or meat juices.

Mix in one and a half teaspoonfuls of cod-liver oil and one teaspoonful of dicalcium phosphate.

Class III. Six or seven heaping tablespoonfuls of chopped beef or horse meat with either one shredded wheat biscuit, or one and a half pieces of toast, moistened with soup, broth, or meat juices.

Mix in two teaspoonfuls of cod-liver oil and one and a half teaspoonfuls of dicalcium phosphate.

Class IV. One-half pound of chopped beef or horse meat with either one and a half shredded wheat biscuits or two pieces of toast moistened with soup, broth, or meat juices.

Mix in two and a half teaspoonfuls of cod-liver oil and two teaspoonfuls of dicalcium phosphate.

Class V. Three quarters of a pound to a pound of chopped beef or horse meat with either two shredded wheat biscuits, or three pieces of toast, moistened with soup, broth, or meat juices.

Mix in one tablespoonful of cod-liver oil and two teaspoonfuls of dicalcium phosphate.

Note: Class V dogs should have their meat ration gradually increased so that by the end of their fifth month they are getting around one and a half pounds of meat with each meal.

LATE AFTERNOON

For all classes, same as noon meal.

EVENING

For all classes, same as morning meal.

Note for All Classes: When your puppy is around five or six months old he may start turning up his nose at his evening milk meal. If this occurs, increase the amount of the late afternoon meal and instead of the regular evening meal give him a few puppy biscuits to munch when you put him to bed.

Six, Seven and Eight Months

MORNING

Class I. One-half cup of milk with one of the following added: Pablum to make a thick gruel, one-third of a shredded wheat biscuit, or one-half piece of toast.

Three times a week mix a raw egg yolk into the milk.

Class II. One cup of milk with either one shredded wheat biscuit or one piece of toast crumbled in it.

Four times a week mix a raw egg yolk into the milk.

Class III. One and a half cups of milk mixed with a raw egg yolk and either two shredded wheat biscuits, or two and a half pieces of toast. Soup or beef broth may be used instead of milk.

Class IV. Two cups of milk mixed with a raw egg yolk and either two shredded wheat biscuits or three pieces of toast.

Soup or beef broth may be used in place of the milk.

Class V. Three to four cups of milk mixed with two egg yolks and either three shredded wheat biscuits or four pieces of toast.

NOON

Class I. Two heaping tablespoonfuls of chopped beef or horse meat.

Mix in one teaspoonful of cod-liver oil and one-half teaspoonful of dicalcium phosphate.

Class II. Four heaping tablespoonfuls of chopped beef or horse meat.

Mix in two teaspoonfuls of cod-liver oil and one teaspoonful of dicalcium phosphate.

Class III. One-half pound of chopped beef or horse meat.

Mix in one tablespoonful of cod-liver oil and two teaspoonfuls of dicalcium phosphate.

Class IV. One-half pound of chopped beef or horse meat.

Mix in one tablespoonful of cod-liver oil and two teaspoonfuls of dicalcium phosphate.

Class V. One and a half pounds of chopped beef or horse meat with either two shredded wheat biscuits, or three pieces of toast, moistened with soup, broth, or meat juices.

Mix in two tablespoonfuls of cod-liver oil and one tablespoonful of dicalcium phosphate.

EVENING

Class I. Three heaping tablespoonfuls of chopped beef or horse meat with one piece of toast moistened with soup, broth, or meat juice.

Mix in one teaspoonful cod-liver oil and one-half teaspoonful dicalcium phosphate.

Class II. Seven or eight heaping tablespoonfuls of chopped beef or horse meat with either one shredded wheat biscuit, or one and a half pieces of toast, moistened with soup, broth, or meat juices.

Mix in two teaspoonfuls of cod-liver oil and one teaspoonful of dicalcium phosphate.

Class III. One-half pound of chopped beef or horse meat with either two shredded wheat biscuits, or three pieces of toast, moistened with soup, broth, or meat juices.

Mix in one tablespoonful of cod-liver oil and two teaspoonfuls of dicalcium phosphate.

Class IV. Three-quarters of a pound to one pound of chopped beef or horse meat with either three shredded wheat biscuits, or four pieces of toast, moistened with soup, broth, or meat juices.

Mix in one tablespoonful of cod-liver oil and two teaspoonfuls of dicalcium phosphate.

Class V. One and a half to two pounds of chopped beef or horse meat with either four shredded wheat biscuits, or five pieces of toast, moistened with soup, broth, or meat juices.

Mix in two tablespoonfuls of cod-liver oil and two tablespoonfuls of dicalcium phosphate.

Note: Class V dogs should have their evening meat ration gradually increased until at the age of nine months they are getting three pounds of chopped beef or horse meat with this meal.

Nine Months to One Year

MORNING

All classes continue to receive the same breakfast as given for the six, seven, and eight months period.

EVENING

Class I. Four to six heaping tablespoonfuls of chopped beef or horse meat with a piece of toast moistened with soup, broth, or meat juices.

Mix in one teaspoonful of cod-liver oil and one-half teaspoonful of dicalcium phosphate.

Class II. One-half pound of chopped beef or horse meat with
either one shredded wheat biscuit, or two pieces of toast,
moistened with soup, broth, or meat juices.

Mix with one tablespoonful of cod-liver oil and two teaspoonfuls of dicalcium phosphate.

Class III. One pound of chopped beef or horse meat with either
two shredded wheat biscuits, or three pieces of toast, moistened
with soup, broth, or meat juices.

Mix in one and a half tablespoonfuls of cod-liver oil and
one tablespoonful of dicalcium phosphate.

Class IV. One and a half to two pounds of chopped beef or horse
meat with either three or four shredded wheat biscuits, or four
or five pieces of toast, moistened with soup, broth, or meat
juices.

Mix in two tablespoonfuls of cod-liver oil and one and a half
tablespoonfuls of dicalcium phosphate.

Class V. Three to four pounds of chopped beef or horse meat with
four or five shredded wheat biscuits, or six or seven pieces of
toast.

Mix in three tablespoonfuls of cod-liver oil and two tablespoonfuls of dicalcium phosphate.

From Twelve Months On

MORNING

Classes I, II, and III. Breakfast may be discontinued for dogs of
these classes at this time, particularly if they appear to be at all
overweight. Dogs which are thin should continue to be given a
morning meal until such time as their weight has come up to
normal.

Class IV. Because of their slower growth rate, dogs of this class
should continue to be fed a morning meal until at least eighteen
months of age. The same breakfast as is suggested for the six,
seven, and eight month period is good, or a meat meal about
one-half the size of the evening meal.

Class V. Dogs of this class should continue to be fed a morning meal until they are eighteen months to two years of age. The same breakfast as is suggested for the six, seven, and eight months period is all right, or a meat meal about one-half the size of the evening meal.

EVENING

For all classes, same evening meal as fed during the nine to twelve month period. Portions should be adjusted according to the dog's condition. Dicalcium phosphate may be discontinued at this time for dogs of Classes I, II and III. Dogs of Classes IV and V should continue to receive cod-liver oil and dicalcium phosphate until eighteen months of age, particularly if this period of their lives occurs during winter months.

Substitutions and Additions

So that the feeding charts may be easily adapted to the convenience of the individual dog owner, the following list of foods is given which may be safely substituted for, or added to, those on the charts.

Instead of Pablum you may use Gerber's or Clapp's dry baby cereal.

In place of toast—which should be whole wheat toast—or shredded wheat, any of the dry breakfast cereals such as corn flakes, Pep, and Wheaties, may be used. The only exception is that those containing a high percentage of bran are not recommended. Other good substitutes for toast or shredded wheat are dry bread, well-cooked oatmeal, cornmeal mush, or Wheatena. Another is ground-up dog biscuit (kibble) which has been soaked for twenty minutes in hot broth or hot water. Use a small size, finely ground kibble for the smaller breeds.

Horse meat may be used in place of beef, but because it lacks fat, very finely ground or melted beef or lamb fat, or fatty meat drippings should be added to it. One to one and a half tablespoons of fat to the pound is about right. Heart of beef, beef kidneys, pigs' hearts, and pigs' kidneys are all easily digested and nourishing meats for dogs. Lamb, lamb hearts and kidneys, and veal hearts and kidneys are fine too, when not too expensive to be practical.

Raw meat is suggested because it is considered by experts to be more easily digested, and it is known that cooking destroys some of the vitamin content of meat. The disadvantage of raw meat is that it does not keep as well as cooked meat. If it is more convenient to buy two or three days' supply of meat at once and cook it, do so, but be sure to give the dog all the juices and broth from the meat.

Meat should be lightly salted. Iodized salt should be used.

Feed your dog vegetables, if you wish, but it has yet to be proved that vegetables are a necessity in dog nutrition, or do much more for a dog than fill him up. What traces of vitamins or minerals they may provide can be more easily supplied in other foods and food supplements. The vegetables which seem to agree best with most dogs are mashed cooked carrots, string beans or celery, and finely chopped lettuce. Small amounts of cooked spinach and mashed boiled onions are acceptable occasionally. Do not regard vegetables as a substitute for the meat or cereal portion of your dog's diet. Think of them as extras or supplements only.

CHAPTER *5*

General Care and Grooming

A snug place to sleep, enough exercise to keep his waistline trim, and regularly scheduled groomings, started at an early age, are important factors in keeping your dog looking and feeling his best.

Your dog's sleeping arrangements may be a fancy dog bed with a tufted mattress, or a doghouse in the back yard, but wherever he sleeps it is essential that his bed be out of drafts and free of any trace of dampness. The floors of most houses and apartments are drafty, and, because of this, dog beds should be raised from the floor or placed in a protected location. A corner of the kitchen or bathroom often proves practical, especially for puppies that are not yet completely housebroken, as these rooms usually have floors that are not damaged by soiling and are easily cleaned. As a matter of fact, it won't hurt your dog's feelings if his bed is in the garage or the basement, provided that the place is clean, dry, and not too cold.

The problem of exercise is one of more concern to city dog owners than to those living in country areas. The increase in popularity of the smaller breeds in recent years is undoubtedly due to the drift of population to the urban centers, where giving a large dog sufficient exercise is more of a problem than most people care to tackle. Continual lack of adequate exercise results in flabbiness, decrease in stamina, and a lowered resistance to disease.

The mention of the word "grooming" often causes pet owners to elevate their eyebrows and exclaim, "Oh, but we don't want

Muffin to be a show dog or to look like a sissy!" Well, Muffin need not be a show dog, or a sissy either, unless his owners have made him one; but that doesn't mean he has to look like a tramp just to prove his manhood. Owning a well-bred dog of good conformation, and failing to keep him neatly groomed is as silly as buying expensive clothes and wearing them in a wrinkled and spotted condition.

Most dogs enjoy being groomed; they like the attention and are amusingly pleased with themselves when turned out to look their best. Naturally, because of the great variety in the coats of the different breeds, some dogs require more care than others, but even the breeds with short, sleek hair need regular groomings. Every dog should have periodic check-ups on his nails, ears, and teeth. His skin should be inspected for parasites, for the sake of his health and comfort. The necessary procedures for keeping a dog smart-looking are not very complicated or time-consuming. It is more of a pleasure to have a dog around who looks as if he is a cherished member of your family rather than a neglected ragamuffin.

Keeping Your Dog Clean

My wife gives our dog a bath almost every week. Isn't this too often?

It certainly is. A dog should be bathed only when necessary— that is, when he is really dirty or has parasites. If the dog gets a thorough combing and brushing two or three times a week, he should not have to be bathed oftener than once in about four weeks. In the case of smooth-coated dogs, baths can be even fewer and farther between than this.

We have a beautiful brown-and-white Collie and would like to keep him looking nice, but he struggles so when we try to bathe him that we dread the whole business. What do you advise?

You should be able to get your dog to submit to bathing with, at least, resignation, if not enthusiasm. Most of his bad behavior is probably caused by fear. He may be afraid of slipping in the tub, or perhaps in the past someone bathed him in water that was too hot, or he may have got soap in his eyes or water in his ears. When next you bathe him, place a door mat or a heavy rubber mat in the bottom of the tub so that he won't slide around. Stuff absorbent cotton in his ears and put a few drops of castor oil or mineral oil in each eye to protect them from soap. Most dogs hate water in their faces, so use a damp cloth to clean that part of him. Use water that is just a little warmer than lukewarm, and if you use a spray hose, don't let the water run with too much force. If possible, get someone to help you by holding the dog while you bathe him. After he has had a couple of baths and found that nothing terrible has happened to him, no restraint should be necessary.

Is it all right to bathe a dog during cold weather?

Yes, but extra care must be taken to see that he is dried thoroughly and kept warm afterwards. Give him a good run outdoors before the bath so that he can be kept indoors for at least two or three hours afterwards.

What can I do when I bathe my English Setter (mostly white) to make him look a nice silvery white?

Any white dog will look better after a bath if bluing is added to the final rinse water. Be careful not to use too much though, or you will have a purple pup on your hands.

What is meant by giving a dog a "dry bath"?

A dry bath or dry shampoo is the process of cleaning a dog without using liquids. There are several good commercial products available for this purpose. Corn meal, cedar sawdust, or fuller's earth also may be used. The cleaning agent is sprinkled and rubbed into the coat and then brushed out again. Cleaning in this manner does a pretty good job on almost all dogs, except those with dense or woolly coats. Dogs of this type can be made really clean only by soap-and-water baths.

*I'm always afraid of using water that is too hot when bathing
our dog. Is it all right to use cool or cold water?*

Water that is just a little hotter than lukewarm is best. Dousing
your dog in cold water is liable to give him the sniffles, and then,
too, you can't work up a good lather in cold water.

*My Dachshund seems to have a very sensitive skin. After he
is bathed he scratches furiously for two or three days and
his coat seems to have dandruff in it. What would be the
best kind of soap to use for him?*

If you use pure castile soap you will avoid the itchy dandruff
condition following a bath. Avoid the soaps which are offered
specially for dogs, as most of them are too strong and harsh in
action for a dog with skin that is easily irritated. Be sure to rinse
him thoroughly in order to remove every trace of soap.

*How deep should I have the water in the tub when bathing
my dog?*

Up to his elbows, no deeper. Plunging a dog in water so deep
that only his head is above the surface may frighten him and make
him hard to handle.

*Which is best to put in my Cocker's eyes when he has a bath—
castor oil, plain petroleum jelly, or mineral oil?*

They are equally good. Use whichever is handiest.

*We have a time keeping our Chow free of fleas. How can we
be sure of killing all the fleas when we bathe him?*

Add Pearson's Creolin to the bath water; then when you start
to wash him, dampen his head and neck first and work up a thick
lather of soapsuds completely encircling his neck, to prevent the
fleas escaping to his head while you are soaping his body. Be sure
to work the soap right down to the roots of his coat.

Does too frequent bathing have a bad effect on a dog's coat?

A few breeds—the water dogs such as Retrievers and Poodles —have so much oil in their coats that even excessive bathing doesn't seem to bother them, but with other breeds too many baths will remove the natural oil from the coat and cause dry, itchy skin.

Drying Your Dog

Whenever I bathe my dog, I dry him carefully and keep him warm afterwards, but he always shows all the symptoms of a cold. In fact his eyes run and he starts sneezing while he's still in the tub. Can you explain this?

If your dog did get a cold as a result of a bath he wouldn't show any signs of it for several hours or even days later. The irritation is probably caused by soap. Put castor oil or white petroleum jelly in his eyes for protection, and use extra care when washing around his nose and head.

Is any further drying necessary other than permitting a dog to shake the water out of his coat?

In hot weather, shaking is all that is necessary. In cold weather, let him shake as much water as possible out of his coat, then follow this up by rubbing him with rough, turkish towels or using a home hair drier. Or, if you have a tank-type vacuum cleaner use that—most of them are designed for use as blowers and make good driers.

Every time we bathe our English Cocker his coat looks awful for days afterwards, because it's so fluffy and stands away from his body. Is there some way to flatten it a little?

Try this—it is what professional handlers do to beautify Spaniels' coats after bathing: While the dog's coat is still quite damp, comb it well. Then, when the coat is nicely straightened out, place a bath towel on his back. The towel should be long enough to reach from the dog's neck to the base of his tail, and wide enough to cross over his chest at the front and under his abdomen at the rear. Use strong safety pins to fasten the towel firmly, lapping it across his chest and under the loin at the other end. Leave the towel in place until the coat is entirely dry, or better yet, let it stay on overnight.

If your dog's coat is full of dead, straggly bunches of hair, even this treatment won't do very much good. Only a proper trimming and thinning of the coat will make it look really sleek.

The Doghouse and Bedding

Will you please give me some suggestions about building a doghouse?

The first consideration is to situate the doghouse on well-drained ground and in a place where it will be shaded in summer. Sunshine during the winter is beneficial and, for this reason, a house that is not too heavy to be moved is desirable. The bottom of the house should never rest on the ground. It may have legs that raise it six to eight inches from the earth, or two or three bricks under each corner will give it sufficient height to eliminate dampness. Insulation of some sort is a good idea, as it will make the house warmer in winter and cooler in summer, and is easy to install at the time it is being assembled. A doghouse with an open doorway which allows the cold winds of winter to blow in directly on the inmate is a poor kind of shelter.

There are three ways to make the house draftproof. A piece of old carpeting can be nailed across the top of the door, forming a sort of curtain to shut out the wind. This is a rather makeshift arrangement but at least furnishes some protection. A vestibule may be built outside the house which will serve as a windbreak. An old packing case with a hole cut in it for a doorway, and its open side placed against the door of the doghouse, will do. The hole in the packing case or box should be cut so that the dog has to make a right angle turn to enter the house from the vestibule. This won't look very stylish but it will do a good job of keeping the doghouse warm. The third plan is to partition the interior of the dog house into two separate compartments with the outer and inner doorways arranged so as not to be in line with one another.

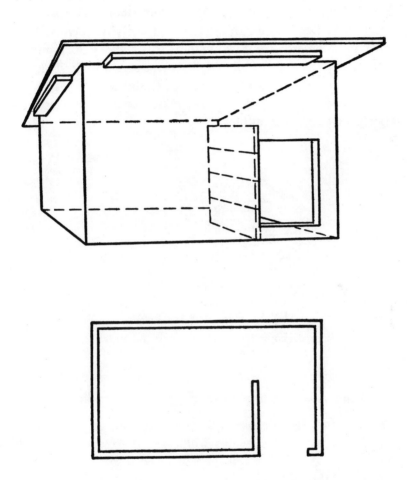

DIAGRAMS OF A DRAFTPROOF HOUSE

Cut-away view and floor plan of a doghouse with an inner partition. The dog enters through the doorway in front, then passes through another doorway (between rear edge of partition and back wall) leading to a snug sleeping compartment where he is well protected from wind and rain.

It will prove a convenience if a section of the roof or one side-wall is hinged. This makes the changing of bedding a simple job. Bedding is important in an outdoor doghouse, both for the warmth it furnishes, the comfort and the protection it affords against the sores and callouses that occur when a dog sleeps on bare boards. Bedding should be changed fairly frequently. When soiled it becomes a paradise for fleas, ticks and lice. It may be straw, cedar shavings or shredded newspapers, but it should be at least four or five inches thick. If the fresh bedding is sprinkled with flea powder, it will help keep the dog free of these pests during the summer months.

IDEAL FOR SUN OR SHADE

This doghouse has a shaded porch and a platform
for use as a sundeck.

Do you approve of using cedar shavings for bedding?

Yes and no. Yes, because cedar has a pleasant smell and a dog who sleeps on cedar shavings will carry the clean odor of his bedding. Also, cedar shavings are believed to discourage a dog's becoming infested with external parasites. No, because the shavings become crumbled and dusty and in a rather short time tend to pack solidly, thus requiring frequent changing. Then, too, cedar shavings are messy for use as bedding for a dog that sleeps in the house, because they will cling to his coat and become scattered throughout the house, besides spilling out of the bed.

Would peat moss or excelsior make good bedding in a doghouse?

Peat moss is messy as dog bedding because it clings to the dog's body and also will stain his coat badly. Excelsior packs down into clumps and wads, and absorbs and holds moisture. Don't use hay for bedding either; it is dusty and irritating. Wheat straw, cedar shavings, or shredded newspapers are best for use during the summer months. A blanket, an old mattress pad or other discarded household bed covering should be provided during the winter months.

Do you think that a smooth-coated dog, such as a Doberman Pinscher or a Whippet, would be all right if he lived outdoors in an unheated kennel or doghouse the year around in a climate like that of New England?

The only dogs which really seem to thrive on an outdoor life in areas where the winters are severe, are those of the heavy-coated breeds such as Chows, Siberian Huskies, or St. Bernards. A smooth-coated dog might survive such treatment but would probably become rheumatic at an early age as a result.

We live in a location where the year-round climate is quite mild. Is it necessary to provide our Great Dane with bedding?

Dogs that sleep on bare floors are liable to develop disfiguring calloused areas on their elbows and hocks, and bare patches on their tails. The calloused places often become so swollen and sore that they need treatment by a veterinarian. If your dog sleeps in a doghouse, give him a thick layer of straw or cedar shavings to sleep on. If he has his bed in the house, provide a mattress or folded blanket for bedding.

Fencing for the Dog Yard

Can single-strand electric fencing, such as is used to fence in cattle be used to enclose a yard for a dog?

No, because dogs learn very quickly to go over or under an electrically charged wire.

What is the best fencing for dog yards?

Chain-link fencing is preferred by most kennel owners. It is not cheap by any means, but lasts almost indefinitely, is easily erected and dismantled, and has a high resale value. The type of wire fencing known as Harvard Mesh or Climax Fence Fabric costs less than chain link. It is usually nailed or stapled to wooden posts. Welded-wire fabric fencing, about the same price as the Harvard or Climax, is obtainable in four-, five- or six-feet heights, and is also erected by fastening to wooden posts. A four-foot fence will be high enough to prevent most small breeds from getting out. Larger dogs will require higher fences, and for individual dogs who are good jumpers or climbers, it will be necessary to have an eighteen-inch-wide wired section supported by brackets bent in toward the pen to prevent escaping. Board fencing has the merit of preventing the dog from seeing and barking at dogs, people, or automobiles that are passing by. It is expensive though, and requires maintenance by painting or staining if it is to endure for any length of time. Some dogs are such diligent diggers that it may be necessary to bury the fencing a foot or a foot-and-a-half in order to prevent tunneling, or to make a concrete barrier five or six inches thick and sunk a foot to a foot-and-a-half deep along the bottom of the fence. If your neighborhood is troubled by stray dogs, you may have to make the fence for the yard high enough to prevent the strays from jumping into it. A double fence with a two-foot space between the inner and outer barriers is a worth-while protection if you are raising puppies, as it keeps strays from poking their noses into the yard and passing along the germs of disease to your dogs.

We have made a fenced yard for the litter of Beagle pups we expect this spring. We have planted a couple of young trees in the yard for shade but they won't be mature enough to provide much protection for another two or three years. What can we use as a temporary sun shelter?

A large beach umbrella makes a good sun shade for puppies. Best of all is a wooden platform, just high enough for the dogs to get under easily, so they may be out of the sun when it is hot. The top of the platform provides a dry place for them to lie when the ground is cold or damp.

Where Fences Are Forbidden

We live in a neighborhood where fences are forbidden. We would like to put our Collie outdoors for a few hours every day but are afraid he might run away. It seems mean to tie him to a tree, as it restricts him so much, but we can't think of any other way to confine him.

Try running a wire about fifty or sixty feet long, seven or eight feet off the ground, between two trees or between the house and a tree. Slip a sliding ring on the wire and attach a chain to it. The chain should be ten or eleven feet long. This will give your dog greater freedom. Be sure he can reach his drinking water at all times, and has a shaded place to rest during hot weather.

Spray for a Doghouse

I understand that if the interior of a doghouse is cleaned and sprayed at regular intervals it will help keep the dog free from fleas. What do you recommend using for a spray?

There are several good sprays on the market which can be purchased at your nearest pet-supply store. Those containing pine oil are favorites with many kennel owners, as the odor is pleasant and the pest exterminating action efficient. Here is the formula for a spray which you can mix yourself:

4 fluid ounces oil of turpentine

2 fluid drams oil of cedar

Add enough kerosene to make one quart of the mixture.

This spray is quite strong smelling, and the doghouse should be aired out for several hours before the tenant is allowed to sleep in it.

A Sleeping Place Indoors

Our dog has a fine comfortable bed which we have placed in a corner of the dining room, but every evening he comes into the living room and lies on the bare floor while we are playing cards or watching television. Why does he do this instead of staying in his nice bed?

Like most dogs, your pet is a gregarious animal and prefers the company of his family to the comfort of his bed. Why don't you move the bed into the living room? Then he can enjoy his bed and be with you at the same time.

It seems to me that I once saw an item about a way to make a dog bed from an old inner tube. My hunting dog is old now and is certainly entitled to any comfort I can give him. Can you tell me how to make him one of these beds?

What you need is a large inner tube, still strong enough to hold air, and two potato sacks (or large cloth feed bags will do). Rip the sacks apart at the seams; then sew them together, making a square pillow slip into which you can slide the inner tube. Inflate the tube until it fills the cover snugly, and then baste shut the open side of the slip. The dog's weight will form a comfortable hollow in the center of the bed and the cover is easily removed for washing.

We bought our Smooth Fox Terrier a lovely wicker dog bed and he has chewed the wicker until it's almost destroyed. What makes him do this and how can we prevent it?

Boredom and loneliness are often the cause of a dog's being destructive. There is no sure way to stop your dog from chewing his bed unless some member of the family would like to sit up all night with him in order to be on hand to scold him when he starts to chew. It may help to let him have a clean, meat-free bone in his bed to use his teeth on. If you buy him another bed, get one with a metal frame. These are virtually indestructible.

How can I be sure that the corner where our dog's bed is placed isn't drafty?

Hold a lighted match at floor level in the spot where you have put the bed. If the flame flickers, it's probably drafty and the bed should be moved.

We have bought a Scottie puppy which we are bringing home next week. The man at the kennel where we purchased the pup asked us if we were interested in buying a secondhand crate to use as a bed for our dog. Are there any advantages in having a dog sleep in a crate or sleeping box?

It is easier to housebreak a young dog that sleeps in a box or crate. He is less likely to soil it during the night, as most dogs will not dirty their sleeping place if they can possibly help it. Another good point about having a dog accustomed to sleeping in a box is that, should it be necessary to put oil, lotion or ointment on his coat or skin, it can be applied just before he is put to bed at night, and by morning will be well absorbed, eliminating the chance of his rubbing it off on your rugs and furniture. Dogs, once they are used to it, seem to like sleeping in a crate and will hop in willingly at bedtime. If you plan to use a sleeping box for your pup, ask the kennel man to have the puppy sleep in the box for five or six nights before you bring him home. In this way he will be at home in his box, and you won't have to listen to any midnight weeping and wailing. Be sure the sleeping box is large enough to allow for his growth. A dog is very uncomfortable in a box or crate which is too small for him.

Our Bulldog is a chronic chewer. He has destroyed two mattresses and a nice blanket we had provided as bedding. What can we try next?

In a case of this kind, use shredded newspaper (newspapers torn into narrow strips).

My dog is quite old and stays in his bed a great deal. A local pet store has foam rubber dog-bed mattresses on sale. They look so thick and comfortable that I've been thinking of getting one for him, even though they are quite expensive. Do you approve of them?

Yes. They are worth the cost, particularly for an old dog, as they don't pack down and become hard, and they last a long time.

Exercise Means Health to Your Dog

My neighbor says that it's cruel to keep dogs in city apartments because they don't get enough exercise. I take our Cocker Spaniel for four or five short brisk walks a day and my husband plays with him for awhile or takes him for a half-hour walk almost every evening. Isn't this enough?

Your dog is luckier than the average city dog and should keep in good condition on the amount of exercise you're giving him. This is enough activity to keep almost any of the smaller breeds in perfectly good shape.

Is there any way to give a dog exercise besides walking him on a leash?

If you can teach your dog to chase and retrieve a ball or stick, you will be able to give him a great deal of exercise without exerting yourself beyond throwing the object he is to bring back to you. He will be going twice the distance that you throw the ball and covering considerable yardage while he's enjoying himself.

My husband thinks that our dog should be taken for a long walk every day, even when the weather is very hot. Is this right?

Exercise during hot weather should be kept to a minimum. Walks should be short and not too brisk. Any romping or other strenuous exertion should take place only during the early hours of the day while it is still cool.

How can I tell if my Boston Terrier is getting a sufficient amount of exercise.

If your dog is overactive and restless in the house, it may mean he isn't getting enough exercise elsewhere. Feel the muscles in his shoulders and thighs. They should be firm rather than soft and flabby. Obesity is another fairly sure sign that your dog is not getting enough exercise for the amount of food you give him.

We spend our summers at a cottage on the beach. Our Springer Spaniel plays in the water practically all day every day, retrieving sticks and balls and swimming with the children. Is this bad for him?

No, swimming is wonderful exercise for a dog. About the only detrimental effect will be that his coat may look rather dried and faded from the salt water, which is not a serious matter except in a show dog.

If a dog passes most of his time in a fenced yard or run, will he get enough exercise?

No, because he will spend most of his time sleeping. Kennel dogs are fairly active when in their runs, either because they have a playmate, or the dogs in the runs adjoining theirs stimulate them to a certain amount of activity. Some of the terrier breeds are so energetic that they exercise themselves. Show dogs, to stay in top condition during their ring careers, usually require long, brisk, daily walks on a leash.

Wardrobes for Dogs

Should I buy a sweater or a coat for my smooth Dachshund to wear during cold weather?

A sweater conforms to a dog's body more closely and gives the chest better protection than a coat. It should be all wool and fairly thick. When you go shopping for his sweater, you had better take your Dachshund with you to be sure of a good fit.

My husband thinks I'm silly because I have bought a sweater and a raincoat for our Boston Terrier, but I think the dog really needs the protection, don't you?

Small, short-haired house dogs should have some sort of covering in cold weather. If they are going to be outdoors for only a few minutes, and will be exercising fairly strenuously during that time, clothing may not be necessary. It is certainly less trouble for you to shake the snow or rain out of a sweater or raincoat, than it would be to have to rub your dog's coat dry after a trip outdoors in bad weather, and there is less chance of the dog's getting the sniffles. A word of caution: don't let your dog go outdoors alone when he's wearing a coat or sweater. He is liable to snag his garment on a projection of some sort and be helplessly hung up until someone rescues him.

WINTER WEAR

A close-fitting wool sweater is the most satisfactory cold-weather garment for the small, short-haired breeds.

Harness, Collar, and Muzzle

For what breeds is a harness considered correct?

None, except those used as sled dogs or draft animals.

Should different breeds wear different types of collars?

Generally speaking, flat collars are used for smooth-coated breeds; rolled round leather collars for dogs with wiry or long coats, though any collar at all will leave a ridge on the neck of a long-coated dog. Some of the toy breeds look rather attractive in fancy-colored patent leather or rhinestone-decorated collars. Old-fashioned, flat, heavy brass-studded collars are becoming to the larger guard-dog breeds, such as Bull Mastiffs and Mastiffs. Chain link training collars are used for all breeds in obedience work, and are suitable for any dog so long as he isn't allowed to run loose when wearing it.

Our dog is inclined to be a fighter. Should we muzzle him when he goes out?

Not if he runs loose, because he will be defenseless in case another dog should attack him. If you take him out on a leash, he might be less obstreperous if he wears a muzzle.

Free Advice From Commercial Sources

Several of the dog-food companies and manufacturers of dog remedies offer free booklets on dog care and feeding. Just how reliable is the information contained in these booklets?

Some of them are very helpful indeed, as they have been written by real dog experts. Others are veritable mines of misinformation. Almost all of these giveaways are gotten up for the special purpose of promoting their sponsor's product. Booklets offered by a dog food company are likely to state that "the only food a dog needs from puppyhood to the grave is Woof-Woof's Complete Dog Meal," and then go on to say that feeding meat, milk, or vitamins is needless trouble and expense—in spite of the recommendations of experienced breeders and veterinarians.

The maker of a special soap for dogs issues a leaflet advocating baths (using their soap, of course) for dogs of all ages, breeds, and states of health, at least once a week, winter and summer. Some of the suggestions put forth in booklets offered by manufacturers of canine medicines are positively dangerous, as they encourage the pet owner to undertake the diagnosis and treatment of ailments which need the attention of a veterinarian.

You will be wiser to get the opinion of an experienced breeder, trainer or veterinarian (depending on your problem), than to rely on advice contained in commercially motivated brochures and booklets.

How to Weigh Your Dog

How can I find out my dog's weight? We have a bathroom scale but the dog can't get all four feet on the platform.

Step on the scales and weigh yourself, then pick up the dog, step on the scales again and see how much the two of you together weigh. Subtracting your weight from the combined weight will give you the dog's poundage. If your dog is too big or too hefty for this method to be feasible, take him to your local Railway Express agency and ask permission to weigh him on the broad-platformed scales which are used for weighing trunks and crates.

Drinking Habits

Our German Shepherd never seems to drink any water. We keep a big pan of clean water in the kitchen for him but none of us ever sees him take a drink from it. Is something wrong with him?

Don't worry about your dog's drinking (or rather nondrinking) habits. He has probably learned, as do so many large dogs, to drink from the toilet bowl, or, if he runs loose, he may know of a brook or pond where he prefers to slake his thirst.

Isn't it a good idea to keep a lump of sulphur in my dog's drinking water pan?

It used to be believed that a block of sulphur in a dog's water pan was a beneficial thing indeed, acting as a preventive for skin ailments, a blood purifier, and general conditioner. It is now known that sulphur is not soluble in water and does not do a dog any more good than would a stone or a piece of wood in his water dish.

Every time our Cocker takes a drink, she gets her ears in the water and then dribbles around the house, making a mess.

We can't very well tie her ears back every time she starts for her drinking bowl. Any suggestions will be appreciated.

Get one of those deep bowls which are wide at the bottom and tapered at the top. When your cocker drinks from it, her ears will be outside the bowl and won't get wet.

Fleas and How to Control Them

Do fleas merely annoy a dog, or can they do him real harm?

Fifty or sixty years ago most people expected their dogs to have fleas. Sir Francis Galton, the English scientist, probably thought he was being very clever when, in 1883, he wrote, "Well washed and combed domestic pets grow dull; they miss the stimulus of fleas." It has been proved that tapeworm eggs are carried in the bodies of fleas and lice and, if a flea-ridden dog bites at himself in an effort to relieve the itching caused by the parasites and swallows a flea while so doing, he will probably become infested with tapeworm. Many veterinarians are now of the opinion that hot-weather skin trouble—called "summer itch" or "summer eczema"—can be avoided if a dog is kept free of fleas during the time of the year when the climate is hot and humid.

We have a book on dog care which states that the way to rid a dog of fleas is to sponge him with a mixture of milk and kerosene, leave it on him for an hour or so and then bathe him. This sounds like a messy procedure to me. Isn't there some easier way to kill fleas?

There certainly is. Flea powder containing 5 to 10 per cent DDT will do an efficient job of eliminating fleas. The simplest way to do this is to stand the dog on spread-out newspapers and, starting just behind his ears, dust the powder into his coat, making sure the powder sifts through his hair right down to the skin. Then turn him on his back and sprinkle his chest and abdomen with the powder. If the weather permits, perform this operation outdoors because the minute you turn Fido loose he is going to shake himself furiously, filling the air with clouds of flea powder. After an hour or so you can give him a good combing and brushing to remove the powder and dead fleas from his coat. If he looks dull and dusty from the powder, go over him with a dampened cloth or chamois after the brushing.

We use a powder containing DDT to keep our Sheltie free of fleas. We have noticed that a few minutes after we powder him, he scratches himself like mad. What causes this?

The DDT in the flea powder causes the fleas to die in spasms, practically turning somersaults and handsprings as the insecticide kills them. These activities produce a tickling sensation, so your dog scratches to relieve it.

Hot Weather Care

What special care should we give our dog during hot weather?

TO KEEP THE
DRINKING WATER
CLEAN AND COOL

Place the water pan in a wooden box. This shades it from the hot sun and helps to keep it free of dust and insects.

During hot weather a dog should have access to cool, clean drinking water at all times. He needs a shady, cool place to lie. His coat should be thoroughly combed and brushed at least once or twice a week during the late spring and early summer, to remove the thick winter undercoat which he sheds at this time of year. He should be powdered with flea powder, containing DDT, once every week or ten days to avoid infestation by these pests. If you live in an area where ticks are a problem, the dog should be frequently examined (don't overlook the inside of the ear flaps, behind the ear and the insides of the legs) and the ticks picked off with tweezers and dropped in a can of kerosene or boiling water.

ALL-YEAR PROTECTION

A wooden platform in the dog's yard provides shade during hot weather and a dry place to sit or lie when the ground is cold or damp.

Violent exercise should be avoided when the temperature is high. Because most dogs are inactive during heat spells, their meals can be slightly reduced in volume, since they do not require so heavy a diet as needed during periods of greater activity. Never, under any circumstances, leave a dog in an automobile parked in the blazing sun. The interior of a car left standing in the summer sun takes on the temperature of an oven in a very short time and becomes hot enough to cause heat prostration or suffocation. The noise of Fourth of July fire-crackers makes that holiday a time of panic for some dogs. If he is nervous, let him stay in a closed room where he will hear as little of the noise as possible. Pet him and talk to him to reassure him that he is in no danger.

Last summer all the goldfish in our garden fishpool died. We replaced them, and a month later all the new fish died. Our Labrador Retriever likes to wade around in the pool, and we are beginning to suspect that perhaps the flea powder we use on him had something to do with the death of the fish. Is this possible?

It is not only possible, it's probable. Rotenone, a common ingredient of flea powder, is very toxic. A small amount of it in a fishpond—as little as one part in ten million parts of water —will kill fish. If you want to keep goldfish in your pool, you will have to fence it off to prevent the dog's wading there during the flea-powder season.

Our dog's coat is a lovely, rich reddish-brown color, but we have noticed that it seems to get lighter in the summer. What causes this?

The bleaching action of the direct rays of the summer sun causes your dog's coat to fade.

Our dog is outdoors a great deal during the summer and his ears get badly bitten by flies. How can we prevent this?

There are several preparations for this purpose, which you will find advertised in the all-breed dog magazines. They contain volatile oils which act as a repellent. If used regularly, these preparations will keep your dog from being bothered by flies.

Our dog seems so uncomfortable during hot weather that I have been wondering if we should shave or clip him for the summer months. He is a large crossbred, with a long heavy coat like a Collie's.

Shaving or clipping a long-haired dog during hot weather is doing him no kindness. Clipping will actually make him feel the heat more, and expose his skin to fly and mosquito bites. A thorough weekly combing and brushing which removes the dead, woolly undercoat will do much more good than clipping. The silky outer coat which will be left serves as a protection against insects and the hot rays of the sun.

Foot Trouble

Is there any preparation available which will help toughen the tender feet of my bird dog?

There is a commercial product which is advertised extensively in such magazines as *The American Field, Field and Stream,* and *Sports Afield.* Bird-dog owners who have used this preparation give favorable reports on it. Here is a home-made remedy for sore or tender feet:

To one pint of slightly warmed pine tar (*not* coal tar) add two cupfuls of tannic acid and mix thoroughly. Paint this mixture on the soles of the dog's feet and sprinkle with dry sand to speed up the drying. Treat the feet in this manner every night for ten days or two weeks. The action of the tannic acid will toughen the soles, until they are as thick and strong as good boot leather.

Every winter we have trouble with our dog's feet becoming sore from walking on the rock salt which so many people use to melt the ice on their sidewalks. Is there any way to avoid this?

Whenever your dog has been on pavements where rock salt has been used, as soon as you bring him into the house fill a pan or basin with lukewarm water and dip his feet in it. Keep each foot in the water long enough to melt away any particles of salt that may be between his toes; then dry his feet.

Problems of Country Life

My Pointer always comes in from a day's hunting with the tip of his tail slashed and bleeding from briars and underbrush. How can this be prevented?

Cut a finger from an old leather glove and slip it over the tip of your dog's tail. Fasten it to the tail with a round or two of adhesive tape.

My Gordon Setter is a wonderful bird dog and gives me great sport in the hunting field. He has an unusually profuse

*coat and after a day of hunting is a mass of briars, burrs
and sticktights that get into his coat. How can this be prevented?*

You can do what many bird-dog owners do—trim his coat.
Cut the fringes off his legs, tail, chest, and underbody. He won't
look so pretty, but the coat will grow back when the hunting
season is over, and you will be spared the nuisance of ridding
him of the debris he accumulates.

What can be done to deodorize a dog that has had an encounter with a skunk?

A time-honored remedy among hunting-dog people is to give
the dog a bath, dry him, and rub tomato juice into his coat and
skin. Allow it to dry on him, then rinse (don't rub) it off with
plain water. A second application of tomato juice will improve
matters still further. Undiluted vinegar (and plenty of it!) sponged
on the dog is recommended by many authorities. A 5 to 10 per
cent solution of ammonia water is usually helpful in neutralizing
skunk odor too.

Is there any painless way of removing porcupine quills from a dog?

A dog that has gotten his face stuck full of porcupine quills
is a sad sight, and the worst of it is that many dogs never seem
to learn that they are always going to be the loser when they get
into a fracas with Mr. Porky. Removing porcupine quills is an
agonizing process because the pointed ends are covered with
tiny reverse barbs which open out like dozens of miniature
harpoon heads when the imbedded quill is pulled from the
flesh. If the quill is twirled once or twice before it is pulled,
the barbs will lie flat against the shaft of the quill, and the
pain of pulling it will be greatly lessened.

Very short quills are harder to handle, but if you can get a
grip on them with pliers or strong tweezers and twist them
before pulling, they can be managed too. Quills that have

gone all the way through the dog's ears, lips, cheeks, or tongue should be gripped by their pointed ends and pulled on through as this will hurt the dog less than pulling from the blunt ends. Dab any places which may be bleeding with an antiseptic, and hope your dog has learned his lesson.

We have a three-year-old dog who normally is fairly clean in his habits, but he has a nasty trick which we cannot understand. Every time we take him to the country with us, for a picnic or other outing, he manages to find a dead, decayed animal or bird, or a cow flop. He rolls himself in these messes and returns to us reeking. We cannot seem to break him of the habit. Why does he do it?

This is an example of atavism—reversion to primitive habits—and it is widespread among dogs. It is unlikely that your dog can ever be broken of it. The strength of the habit seems to vary considerably among dogs. Some never seem to do it, and others do it at every opportunity. It is easy to understand the origin of this instinct, if we think of the dog in his wild state, when he existed by hunting for his food. He discovered that if he rolled in something extremely smelly, his own body scent would no longer be noticeable to his prey. By nature he learned to hunt up wind, but if the wind shifted suddenly, the animal he was stalking would be warned by the dog's scent. Therefore, he used this form of camouflage to make himself safe from detection.

Other common atavistic habits of dogs are the burying of bones, circling several times before settling down to sleep, and tucking the tail between the legs when frightened. The bone-burying is a holdover from the times when the dog in his wild state killed more game than he could consume and buried the leftovers for future consumption. The circling before lying down is believed to be a survival of the wild animal's habit of trampling down the grasses and rushes where he made his bed. The lowered tail, as a sign of fear, is supposedly derived from the fact that, in times gone by, the dog was not always the hunter but was often the hunted. When a larger and more ferocious animal chased him, the dog tucked his long tail between his legs to prevent his pursuer from grabbing it.

Care of Your Dog's Nails

Do dogs need manicures? My dog's nails grow so long that they cause his feet to look spread out, and I've been wondering if they should be trimmed.

Dogs that do not get enough exercise on hard ground to wear their nails down should have their nails shortened about once a month. Nails that are allowed to grow too long can cause sore feet and lameness. The important thing to watch when attending to the dog's nails is not to cut into the quick, which is the live pink flesh within the nail. If the quick is cut, the pain is likely to make the dog touchy about his feet and difficult to handle the next time his nails need attention. To shorten your dog's nails you will need a nail clipper and a heavy, fairly coarse file.

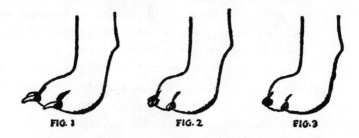

FIG. 1   FIG. 2   FIG. 3

TRIMMING YOUR DOG'S NAILS

FIG. 1: The average nail before cutting, showing the extension of the nail beyond the quick. FIG. 2: Showing how closely the nail should be cut to the quick. If the nail is left like this, it will wear down evenly in a few days. FIG. 3: The nail after filing, with just a thin layer of protecting shell left to shield the tender quick. *Note:* When using the file, it should be drawn only in one direction, that is, from the top of the nail downward in a round stroke to the end of the nail or underneath. Considerable pressure is needed for the first few strokes in order to break through the hard polished surface of the nail. After the first few strokes, the filing is easily accomplished.

Don't use your own manicure scissors; a dog's nails are so tough they will dull them. Special nail clippers for dogs are available at pet-supply counters. You can get a good file at your hardware store. Ask for a "four-way shoe rasp" or a "flat bastard." When using the file, turn the dog over on his back and, holding the foot firmly, take off the nail points. When you have shortened all the nails this way, give each nail a few downward strokes to smooth its edge.

Care of Your Dog's Teeth

Do dog's teeth need attention? My dog has a scaly deposit on his teeth which seems to be causing his gums to recede.

The simile "clean as a hound's tooth" is not any too accurate, for a dog's teeth often require attention. Many dogs needlessly lose their teeth when only five or six years of age, because their owners do not realize this fact. The scaly deposit you mention is tartar, and if this is allowed to accumulate it will eventually push back the gums until the dog's teeth loosen and fall out. The tartar should be removed periodically by your veterinarian, or you can learn to do it yourself. Most good kennel-supply houses can supply tooth-cleaning instruments made specifically for this purpose, or you can get one through your dentist. When using the scraper, remember always to push away from the gum line and toward the end of the tooth. When cleaning the upper teeth, brace a finger against the lower jaw for a fulcrum, and vice versa. Once the tartar has been removed, the teeth can be whitened by brushing with a moist toothbrush dipped in pow- dered pumice or table salt. If the toothbrush seems to bother the dog, almost as good results can be achieved with a piece of soft cloth wrapped around the index finger and dipped in pumice, salt, or peroxide. The ordeal of tooth-scraping can be avoided entirely by proper care, as no tartar will form if the teeth are kept brushed once a week with a toothbrush moistened and dipped in Bon Ami.

My son throws stones for our Shepherd to retrieve. Isn't this liable to damage the dog's teeth?

Picking up and carrying stones in his mouth will wear off the points of your dog's teeth. If the dog enjoys retrieving, throw a ball or a stick for him.

We keep our Setter's coat clean by frequent brushing and baths as they are needed, but he has a most unpleasant odor about him. What could be the cause?

Dirty or decayed teeth, or diseased tonsils can cause a dog to have an offensive breath. Chronic ear troubles and certain urinary ailments are sometimes the reason for an obnoxious smell. If your veterinarian finds none of these causes present, try giving your dog two or three chlorophyll tablets every day.

Care of Your Dog's Coat

In rainy weather, when our dog has been outside, he has a strong "doggy" odor when he comes in the house. Is there any way to prevent this?

A dog that is kept clean should not have any doggy smell about him. Frequent brushing will keep his coat and skin clean and help to prevent this. It will also be a good idea to see that he is well dried off when he comes in from out of the rain. Use an old bath towel, or, what is better yet, a chamois, wet and well wrung out, which will dry a dog far more readily than cloths or a towel. By rubbing well with the chamois and constantly wringing it out, a dog as large and thick-coated as a German Shepherd can be dried in not over five minutes. The rubbing should be vigorous but slow enough to allow the chamois to absorb water.

My long-haired dog is constantly getting tar, burrs, and other troublesome matter stuck in his coat. Sometimes it's difficult to remove these things without either cutting or tearing his coat. Have you any suggestions?

When your dog's coat becomes matted with tar or chewing gum, rubbing a piece of ice into the spot makes the sticky mass brittle and easily removed. Acetone, applied with either a cloth or a piece of cotton, also acts effectively as a dissolving agent on either of these substances. Burrs and sticktights can be removed readily if either petroleum jelly or mineral oil is worked into the tangle with the fingers. By this means the coat can be freed of burrs without being torn.

Combing and Brushing

Is there any way to remove snarls and matted clumps of dead hair from a dog's coat without cutting them out?

Here is one situation in which an ounce of prevention (in the form of frequent combing and brushing) is literally worth a pound of cure. Once a long-haired dog's coat has been so neglected as to develop matted places, it is a tedious job to straighten it out without resorting to the scissors, which will leave the coat ragged and shabby-looking. Mats have to be "teased" out of the coat, that is, first carefully separated into fine strands with the fingers and then worked through with a coarse comb. Grasp the clump of matted hair firmly as close to the skin as possible with the left hand and comb with the right hand so that the pull of the comb will be against the hand; in this way you will avoid painfully yanking the dog's skin. Mats that appear too dense to yield to "teasing" can sometimes be combed out if they are cut into several strands first, using the scissors in cuts parallel to the length of the hair.

Whenever we try to comb or brush our Miniature Poodle, it usually takes two people to hold him while one grooms him. If I try to work on him when I have no one to help me, the only way I can manage is to back him into a corner so he can't get away. This is awkward and difficult. Can you tell me an easier way to handle him?

You will find that your dog will behave 100 per cent better if you put him on a table to groom him, and it will be a good deal less back-breaking for you too. If you groom your dog so seldom that his coat is full of knots and wads of matted hair, it is probably a painful process for him to be combed, and he naturally dreads it. Frequent light groomings will prevent his coat from becoming hard to comb out, will be less unpleasant for him, and easier on you.

How can we make our Cocker's coat more luxuriant? He has almost no feathers and he is dull-looking.

Be sure he is getting enough fat and vitamins in his diet. Groom him regularly. Keep him free of parasites, both external and internal. All this will improve his coat, but remember that if he is from parents who had poor coats that lacked feathering and fringes, even the most careful attention will not produce a beautiful coat, because the hereditary factors for such a coat are lacking.

Oiling the Coat

I have been told that professional handlers sometimes oil their dogs' coats with special preparations in order to make them more beautiful. What is the mixture that is used?

The following recipe is the formula used by the well-known handler Ruth Burnette Sayres. Mrs. Sayres is famous throughout the dog-show world for the magnificent condition of the coats of the dogs in her charge. Here is her skin dressing mixture and directions for its use:

    2 quarts good grade olive oil
    ½ cup kerosene
    1½ tablespoonfuls flowers of sulphur
    3 ounces oil of tar
    Half of a seven-ounce bottle of Glover's Mange Cure
Mix very thoroughly. Never apply until it is extra well mixed.

Method of Use: Rub mixture into coat, making sure you use enough to soak the skin. Leave on for forty-eight hours, then shampoo with castile or Ivory soap. Repeat this treatment weekly for nine weeks.

WHEN YOU BATHE YOUR DOG
It's a good idea to place a rubber mat on the bottom of the tub to give the dog secure footing. And always be sure to keep the soap away from his eyes.

A RUNNING DIVE
A fine hunting dog like this Labrador Retriever does
not hesitate to jump into icy water to retrieve game.

HOLDING A STEADY POINT
This Pointer has found his game and now holds a
steady point, while he waits for his master to arrive.

Messy? Yes, but it does wonders even for problem coats. It is necessary that the dog be free of worms, that he be properly fed, and have extra vitamin A in his diet.

We use a rather oily skin lotion on our Boxer every week or so in order to make his coat shiny. The lotion works very well but applying it is a job none of us likes, as it means soiled wads of cotton or cloths, sticky hands, and (usually) oil-spotted clothing. Is there some easy way to do this?

Try keeping the lotion in a covered bowl or can, and apply it with an ordinary paintbrush.

Ridding the Dog of Lice

Our dog (he's a cross between a Springer Spaniel and a Setter) has no fleas and no sign of skin trouble, but scratches himself violently. What can the trouble be?

It is probably lice. Dogs with long silky coats seem particularly susceptible to the annoyance caused by the nearly invisible pests. Use flea powder containing 5 to 10 per cent DDT to get rid of lice. The powder should be applied at ten-day intervals for three or four treatments.

Clipping and Stripping

What is the difference between clipping a dog's coat and stripping it?

Clipping is cutting the hair with clippers or scissors. Stripping is done with a special grooming instrument which removes dead hair and shortens and evens the remaining coat.

What breeds have coats that are clipped and what breeds are stripped?

Kerry Blue Terriers, Bedlington Terriers, and Poodles are three breeds whose coats are clipped. The terrier breeds having wiry coats are usually stripped. For show purposes, most of the Spaniel breeds and the Setters have their coats thinned out and trimmed to some extent.

Hair Over the Sheepdog's Face

We have an Old English Sheepdog whose shaggy coat com-
pletely covers his face. We are afraid he can't see well with
all that hair over his eyes. Would it do any harm to cut the
hair away from his eyes?

No matter how tempting the idea may be, don't trim the hair on your dog's face. In addition to spoiling the dog's looks, it would injure his eyes to be exposed to the light. Nature has provided this breed with especially long stiff eyelashes which hold the shaggy hair away from his eyes, thus enabling him to see perfectly well.

Using Electric Clippers

The dog beauty shop where we have our Cocker trimmed uses
electric clippers on his coat. Is this an approved procedure?

The use of electric clippers on a Spaniel is frowned on by show fanciers because it spoils the coat. If you have any show aspirations for your dog we would avise you to find a place where his coat will be trimmed by hand. Trimming by electric clippers is a quick process, and is easy on the dog. There is no reason why your dog shouldn't be trimmed with clippers if he is never to be shown.

Any terrier breed having a wiry coat should not be trimmed with clippers either, because the new coat will come in bristly. The job of stripping a terrier coat by hand is a tedious one and the charges for such work are usually rather high. If a dog is a house pet the use of clippers is, for economic reasons, only sensible. The best solution is for the owner to acquire the knack of trimming his terrier himself; not only will the dog look nicer but the owner will be saving money.

Hair on Top of the Poodle's Head

I have noticed that Poodles whose coats are in a show trim usually have the hair on top of their head brushed back and held with a barrette or an elastic band. Why is this?

If the long hair on a Poodle's head is allowed to fall forward it interferes with the dog's vision, besides looking untidy.

One Ear Up, One Down

We have a German Shepherd pup who has one ear up and one ear hanging. Can anything be done about this?

Tape the tips of the ears together in an upright position, using adhesive tape, or the antiseptic liquid adhesive available in tubes may help.

Another method is this: take a large turkey wing or tail feather and trim the tip to conform to the shape of the dog's ear. Cut off the feather at the bottom so that it is just long enough to touch the outer base of the ear when placed against it. Apply a thin coat of shellac to the outside of the ear and to the feather. Press the feather to the ear and hold it there firmly until the shellac sets. Apply strips of adhesive tape along the ear edges to hold the feather firmly. Leave feather in place for ten days. Remove it by soaking with either alcohol or ether.

The ear prop may be reapplied for as many more ten-day periods as are necessary. The treatment will be most effective if it is used as soon as signs of weak ear cartilage are detected. It will not remedy a long-neglected case of lop ears.

Traveling With Your Dog

We are thinking of taking our Cairn Terrier with us on a motor trip this summer. Do you think we will be sorry?

No, your dog will probably enjoy the trip and you'll enjoy having him with you. If he were a large dog it might not be such a good idea, as many hotels and motor courts will accept only small dogs. You will find it a great help to send for a copy of *Touring with Towser,* published by the Gaines Dog Research Center, 250 Park Avenue, New York 17, New York. This is a directory which lists over three thousand hotels, inns and motor courts in this country which will accept guests accompanied by dogs. A single copy costs ten cents.

Can I take my dog to Canada with me?

Yes, there is no quarantine for American dogs entering Canada. You must have a health certificate from your veterinarian and a rabies certificate, stating that your dog has been given rabies immunization within the past six months.

What should we take along for our Boston Terrier when he goes on a trip with us?

You will find it convenient to have a small suitcase or zipper bag for the dog's belongings. It should contain:
1. A blanket or small cushion for him to sleep on.
2. A supply of his favorite canned food, also canned milk and dry cereal, if he likes it.
3. Two pans, one for food, one for water.
4. A can opener.
5. A mixing spoon.
6. A knife.

To vary the canned food diet, you can plan on stopping in the late afternoon to buy him fresh meat for his evening meal. Be sure he has a tag on his collar giving your full name and address.

We always take our dog on auto trips with us but have, once or twice, had trouble with his getting loose bowels. Can we prevent this in the future?

The bowel trouble is probably caused by the water in the localities you have visited. This is particularly liable to happen in certain parts of Florida and Texas. Professional handlers, who take dogs on show circuits in these areas, meet this problem by buying bottled drinking water (available in grocery stores) for their dogs. This water is from very pure sources, usually springs, and using it instead of the local water, when in areas where the supply is of doubtful purity, will prevent intestinal upsets.

Are dogs allowed in the Pullman sections of trains?

Most railroads permit dogs in bedrooms and drawing rooms, but not in the berths of sleeping cars. Many railroads permit small dogs to travel in coaches, but stipulate that the dog be muzzled and occupy no seat space.

My wife and I have invested our life savings in a very modern and well-furnished motor court. We are trying to decide whether to allow dogs or to have a "No Dogs" policy. What is your advice?

If you do decide to take dogs, for your own protection you should insist that guests sign a Guarantee of Indemnity statement, which makes the dog owner fully responsible for any injury the dog may do to other guests or damage to your property. If a guest should refuse to sign such a paper, you had better let him seek lodgings elsewhere, as it might mean that his dog was destructive or not house-trained.

Tell your guests with dogs that they are not to go away and leave the dog alone in their rooms or cabins, as many dogs howl when left by themselves in a strange place and will disturb the other guests greatly. If your community has an annual dog show, watch out for show fanciers with a carload of kennel dogs. Most kennel dogs are completely unhousebroken and will wreck your rugs and furniture. If you do accommodate dog-show people, stipulate that their dogs must be kept in crates or in their cars while staying at your establishment.

Shipping Crate Sizes

Will you please give the approximate dimensions for the sizes for shipping crates for the various breeds?

	Inside Measurements in Inches		
	Length	Width	Height
SMALL TOY BREEDS	10	11	11
SMALL BREEDS	18	15	15
DOGS THE SIZE OF WELSH TERRIERS, DACHSHUNDS, BEAGLES, FOX TERRIERS, ETC.	23	16	18
MEDIUM LARGE DOGS	33	21	24
DOGS THE SIZE OF GERMAN SHEPHERDS	40	26	33
DOGS THE SIZE OF ST. BERNARDS, GREAT DANES	48	30	33

Special Care for Old Dogs

What special care should an old dog receive?

No specialized care is necessary for an old dog that is healthy, but good general care is important. See that his teeth are kept clean and that any abscessed ones are removed by a veterinarian. Be careful about his diet. Don't let him get fat. He will live much longer if he stays in trim condition. He may require less food than he did when he was younger and more active. Give him one or two (depending on his size) all-purpose vitamin capsules every day with his food. Don't let him overexert himself, particularly during hot weather, as some dogs will in their anxiety to please their owners.

In winter, if he is short-coated and seems to feel the cold, provide him with a coat or sweater. Don't let him get wet or chilled. Be patient with him. If he needs a helping hand now and then getting up and down stairs, or into or out of an automobile, give him a lift. Be sure he has a snug place to sleep, with comfortable bedding. Most important of all, if he is ailing and is in pain from an illness for which your veterinarian tells you there is no help, do him the kindness of giving him a painless death. Don't let him suffer.

Can anything be done to prevent failing eyesight in old dogs?

There is vitamin therapy which often helps. It should be started at the first sign of the bluish, filmy look so often seen in the eyes of old dogs. Give daily, two Squibb B-Complex vitamin capsules, one Squibb ascorbic acid tablet (100 mg.) and one 25,000 U.S.P. unit vitamin A capsule.

CHAPTER 6

Thirteen Popular Breeds— How to Trim Their Coats

A comb, a brush, a hound glove and a stripping knife are essential in the proper care of a dog's coat. A steel comb is always preferable, but it should not have sharp teeth.

Dogs carrying a profuse coat and those having long feathering require a comb with heavy teeth set wide apart, while a finer tooth comb is more efficient for dogs having a short coat. Never comb a long-coated dog while the hair is wet, as the comb will tear out live hairs.

The length of bristle on the brush should vary with the length and density of the dog's coat, the long-coated dogs naturally requiring the deeper brush. For those animals carrying a profuse or wire coat, the bristles should be as stiff as it is possible to obtain, while the short-haired or lightly coated dogs may be advantageously groomed with a brush but slightly stiffer than the ordinary human hair brush.

The hound glove gives an incomparable finish where a coat is required to lay flat to the body. It is to be particularly recommended for use on all terriers, setters, spaniels, and smooth-coated dogs. It not only lays the hair in place, but adds greatly to the lustre of the coat.

The stripping knife, or dog dresser, is for the removal of the dead hairs and the trimming of the new ones, to give the finish that conforms with the standard of the breed of dog on which you are working. Hold the handle of the knife in the palm of the hand—the end resting against the heel of the hand and the first finger wrapped around the shank. The hair that is to be removed should be pressed against the knife with the thumb. A slight upward twist of the wrist brings the stripping edge in contact with the hair. Best results can be obtained by removing only a few hairs at a time.

Chalk is advantageously used on any dog having principally a white coat, more specially on the terriers. It should be rubbed in before the dog is stripped, as it prevents the hairs from slipping through the operator's fingers during the stripping. In addition to cleaning and whitening the coat it improves the texture, particularly on those breeds where a hard coat is required.

Dull-pointed scissors are of great assistance in trimming and straightening the lines of the ears, the legs and the belly, also for trimming the feet and between the toes.

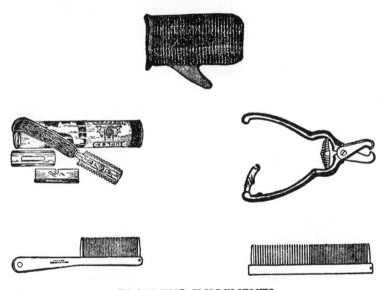

GROOMING IMPLEMENTS

(Top) Hound glove, used for putting a gloss on coats of short-haired breeds. *(Middle row, left)* Stripping knife, for trimming wiry coats. *(Middle row, right)* Nail clippers. *(Bottom)* Two types of steel comb. Not shown but essential is a tooth scraper, for removing tartar.

Wire-Haired Fox Terrier

1. Trim neck closely and evenly down into the back.

2. Trim back level and fine, but not as closely as neck.

3. Front part of neck and brisket to be trimmed very closely, with just a shade more hair left on as one works down to where the front legs join the body.

4. Trim front shoulders evenly and closely.

5. Front legs should be trimmed to straightness. Trim principally on back line. It is often necessary to take out a few hairs on the front and outsides of front legs, where they join the shoulder, to give effect of a straight line from the top of the shoulders down to the feet, from the brisket to the tips of the toes. Trim superfluous hair from edges of feet and between toes, shape feet to roundness.

6. Shape ribs to follow the body conformation, working the hair evenly from a closely trimmed back to a fairly heavy coat on the under part of the chest and ribs. On the under part of the chest only remove those hairs necessary to prevent shagginess. Trim underline of chest to follow body line.

7. Loin is taken out closer than chest but not too fine. Trim underline closely to emphasize tuck up.

8. Do not take all hair off belly, but only those that are snarled or shaggy.

9. In this area trim from a fine back to a fairly heavy coated thigh.

10. From middle of thigh to hock, trim only those hairs that are shaggy.

11. Trim back line of hock straight. Take superfluous hair from feet and between toes, shape to roundness.

12. Trim insides of hind legs clean down to hock joint, taking care to give a clean even line to the hind legs from the rear view.

13. Trim tail evenly but not too closely to a tip toward head. Take out fine in rear where it joins stern.

14. Trim stern very closely where it is joined by the tail, working it heavier toward the hind legs.

DIAGRAM FOR TRIMMING THE WIRE-HAIRED FOX TERRIER

15. Trim skull very closely. Leave eyebrows fairly heavy over the inside corner of the eyes. Leave very little over the outside corner. Trim eyebrows evenly and closely over the outside corner of the eye with plenty of length over inside corner.

16. Trim cheeks closely from outside corner of eye to the corner of the mouth to give proper expression.

17. Trim slightly from inside corner of the eyes downward to corner of mouth to give proper expression.

18. Trim top of muzzle from slightly in between eyebrows to nose to give a straight line from top of skull.

19. Leave chin whiskers and brush forward, but clean under jaw from corners of mouth back to neck.

20. Clean ears closely inside and out. Straighten edges.

Welsh Terrier

1. Trim neck evenly into back.

2. Trim back level but not as closely as the neck.

3. Front part of neck and brisket to be trimmed closely with just a shade more hair left on as one works down to where the front legs join the body.

4. Trim front shoulders evenly and closely.

5. Front legs should be merely trimmed to straightness. Trim principally on the back line. It is often necessary to take out a few hairs from the front and outsides of the front legs where they join the body to give the effect of a straight line from the top of the shoulder to the feet and from the brisket to the tips of the toes. Do not leave any superfluous hair on edges of feet or between toes. Shape to roundness.

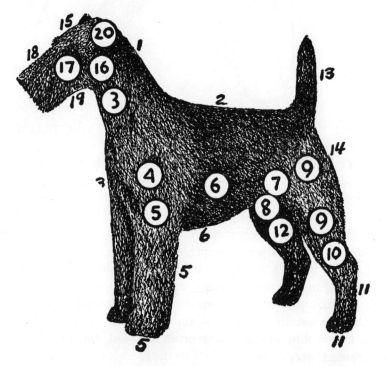

DIAGRAM FOR TRIMMING THE WELSH TERRIER

6. Shape ribs to follow the body conformation, working hair evenly from a closely trimmed back to a fairly heavy coat on the underparts of the ribs and chest. On the underparts of the ribs and chest remove only those hairs necessary to prevent shagginess. Trim chest to follow body line.

7. Loin is taken out cleaner than chest but not too fine and the underline is trimmed closely with scissors to emphasize tuck up.

8. Do not take all the hair off belly, but only those that are shaggy or snarled.

9. In this area trim from finely trimmed back line to fairly heavily coated thigh.

10. From middle of hock to thigh trim only those hairs that are shaggy.

11. Trim back line of hock straight. Trim off superfluous hairs from edges of feet and between toes and shape to roundness.

12. Trim insides of hind legs clean down to the hock joint. Take care to give a clean even line to the hind legs from rear view.

13. Trim tail evenly but not too closely to a tip toward the head. Take out fine in rear where it joins stern.

14. Trim stern very closely where it is joined by tail working the coat heavier toward the hind legs.

15. Trim skull very closely. Leave eyebrows fairly heavy over inside corner of eye. Leave very little over outside corner. Trim eyebrows evenly and closely over the outside corner, with plenty of length over the inside corner.

16. Trim cheeks closely from outside corner of eye to corner of mouth.

17. Trim slightly from in front of eye to corner of mouth.

18. Trim top of muzzle from slighty in between eyebrows to nose to give a straight line from top of skull.

19. Leave chin whiskers, but clean under jaw from corner of mouth back to neck.

20. Clean ears closely inside and out. Straighten edges.

Airedale Terrier

1. Trim neck closely and evenly down into back.
2. Trim back level but not as closely as the neck.
3. Front part of neck and brisket to be trimmed very closely with just a shade more hair left on as one works down to where the front legs join the body.
4. The shoulders to be trimmed evenly and closely.
5. The front legs should be merely trimmed to straightness. Trim principally from rear line. Take out a few hairs from the front and outside of the front legs where they join the shoulder to give a straight line from the top of the shoulder to the feet and from the brisket to the tips of the toes. Trim superfluous

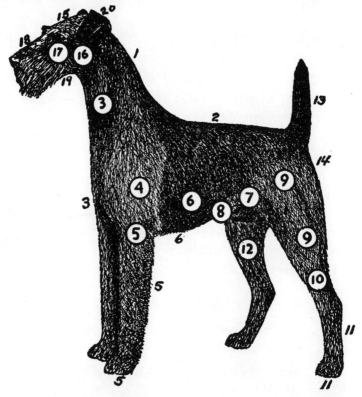

DIAGRAM FOR TRIMMING THE AIREDALE TERRIER

hair from edges of feet and between toes with scissors. Shape feet to roundness.

6. Shape ribs to follow the body conformation, working hair evenly from a closely trimmed back to a fairly heavy coat on the underpart of the ribs and chest. On the underpart of the chest only remove those hairs necessary to prevent shagginess. Trim under line of chest to follow the body line.

7. Take out loin closer than chest but not too fine. The under line is trimmed closely to emphasize tuck up.

8. Do not take all the hair off the belly but only those that are snarled or shaggy.

9. In this area trim from a fine back to a fairly heavily coated thigh.

10. From middle of thigh to hock trim only those hairs that are shaggy.

11. Trim back line of hock straight. Trim superfluous hairs from edges of feet and between toes. Shape to roundness.

12. Trim insides of back legs clean, taking care to give a clean, even line to the hind legs from the rear view.

13. Trim tail closely to a tip toward the head, take out very fine in rear where it joins the stern.

14. Trim stern very closely where it is joined by tail, working it heavier toward the hind legs.

15. Trim skull very closely. Leave eyebrows fairly heavy over the inside corner of the eye. Leave very little over the outside corner. Trim eyebrows evenly and closely at the outside corner of the eye with plenty of length over inside corner.

16. Trim cheeks closely from outside corner of eye to the corner of mouth.

17. Trim very slightly from inside corner of eye downward to corner of mouth to give proper expression.

18. Trim hairs on top of muzzle from slightly between eyebrows to nose to give straight line from top of skull.

19. Leave chin whiskers, brush forward, but clean under jaw from corner of mouth back to neck.

20. Clean off ears closely inside and out. Straighten edges with scissors.

Bedlington Terrier

The Bedlington in his rough state grows a hard, wiry outer coat which is usually quite sparse. Before the trimming actually begins this should be plucked out entirely. After this has been accomplished proceed to work the undercoat.

THE HEAD

The sheep-like appearance of the Bedlington's head is largely obtained by the correct trimming of his pompadour or top-knot. This pompadour should start at the tip of the nose, be slightly and ever increasingly raised as it travels up the top of the muzzle and extravagantly domed on the top of the head, then evenly decreased until it works into the back of the neck slightly below the point where the skull joins the neck.

The flews of the lips, the underpart of the jaw and the cheeks should be trimmed very closely.

The pompadour must be worked into the very closely trimmed muzzle and cheeks very evenly. The actual dividing line between the built up area and the closely trimmed area being from the direct sides of the nostril to very slightly below the outside corner of the eye, to very slightly below the point where the ear joins the head and from there very closely back into the neck.

1. The hair is cleaned closely from the insides and outsides of the ears, but quite a long and ragged but smooth tassel is left on the tip of the ears.

2. Trim back and sides of neck evenly into the back.

3. Trim underpart of neck very closely, leaving slightly more hair as you work down toward the brisket.

4. Trim the back not quite as closely as the neck and try to emphasize the roached appearance of the back over the loin.

5. The sides of the chest and shoulders should be trimmed very closely and flat.

6. As much hair as possible is left on the underpart of the chest to emphasize its depth. The shaggy hairs on this area may be trimmed to follow the desired contour.

7. The loin is trimmed very closely and fine.

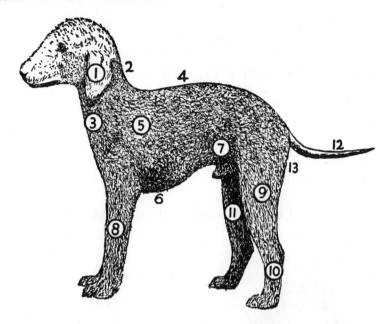

DIAGRAM FOR TRIMMING THE BEDLINGTON TERRIER

8. Trim the very shaggy hairs front the front legs. Trim any hairs from the top outside of the front legs that detract from the dog's straight and narrow appearance when viewed from the front. In trimming around the feet, follow the natural hare foot contour.

9. The rear legs should be trimmed evenly, leaving slightly more hair as you work towards the hocks.

10. Trim only the very shaggy hairs from the hocks.

11. Trim the insides of hind legs closely down to hocks.

12. Trim tail extremely close on under part and sides. Leave a slight amount of hair on top of tail for half its length, the rest of top is trimmed closely.

13. Trim the stern, under the tail, very close and evenly.

Cairn Terrier

Stripping is necessary for the Cairn in order to keep his coat in good healthy condition and emphasize the alert gamey appearance of this breed. His shagginess should be preserved but not to the degree that it hides his virtues and emphasizes his faults.

1. Pluck dead hairs from the neck and trim the new ones slightly. Take off more if your dog is inclined to be heavy or coarse through the neck.

2. Pluck dead hairs and trim the new coat—not closely, but enough to give a level back line.

3. Trim neck and brisket slightly. Too much hair in this area detracts from the dog's quick, active appearance.

4. Trim shoulders of bumpy or patchy places. Leave somewhat shaggy but not profuse.

5. Trim sides of body to follow body conformation.

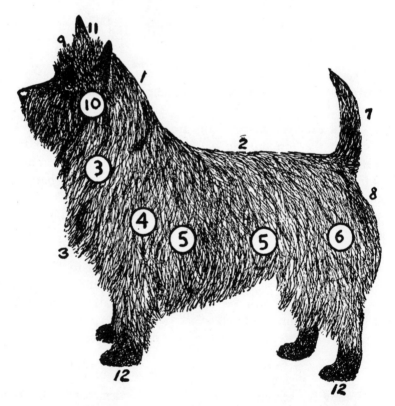

DIAGRAM FOR TRIMMING THE CAIRN TERRIER

6. Trim upper parts of thigh slightly. Leave hair longer and shaggier on lower part, just above the hock joint.

7. The tail should be bushy but not too shaggy. Trim hair, leaving somewhat thick at base and working it slightly finer toward tip. Do not leave any hairs that make the tail appear longer than it is.

8. Trim those hairs from the stern that give a bunchy appearance, but do not remove fringe. Take the hair out closest where the tail joins the stern.

9. Enough hair should be trimmed from the skull so that about one half of the ear stands clear.

10. Hair around cheek should be trimmed slightly to follow the conformation of the head.

11. The backs and sides of the ears should be trimmed absolutely free of long hair. Straighten edges with scissors.

12. Feet should be shaped to roundness with scissors.

Irish Terrier

1. Trim neck very closely and evenly into back.

2. Trim back evenly but not as closely as the neck.

3. Front part of neck and brisket to be trimmed closely, with just a shade more hair left on as one works down to where the front legs join the body.

4. The front shoulders to be trimmed evenly and closely.

5. Front legs should be slightly trimmed to straighten lines. Trim principally on back line; trim superfluous hair from edges of feet and between toes, shaping to roundness.

6. Shape ribs to follow body conformation from a finely trimmed back to a fuller coat on the under part of ribs and chest, but do not leave any on sides or under chest that are in any way shaggy.

7. Trim loin but do not emphasize tuck up.

8. Trim only shaggy or snarled hair from belly.

9. Trim thighs from back line to hock, taking off sufficient hair to show a definite outline of leg.

10. Straighten back line of hock and trim superfluous hair from edges of feet and between toes, shape to roundness.

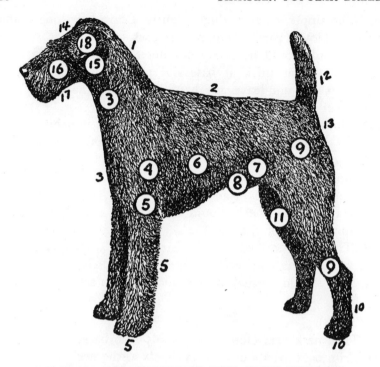

DIAGRAM FOR TRIMMING THE IRISH TERRIER

11. Trim inside of hind legs down to hock joint.

12. Trim tail evenly, but not too closely, to a tip towards head.

13. Trim stern closely and evenly.

14. Trim skull very closely. Leave eyebrows but not too heavy. Leave slightly more over inside corner of eye than outside corner.

15. Trim cheeks clean back from corner of mouth.

16. Trim under eyes to emphasize expression.

17. Clean under jaw from corner of mouth back to neck. Leave chin whiskers and brush forward.

18. Clean off ears inside and out, straighten edges with scissors.

CARE OF THE FEET

Many Irish Terriers are subject to horny or cracked pads. Bad feet are a condition common to both Irish horses and Irish dogs.

The reason for this condition is a matter of speculation. It may be accounted for, perhaps, by the fact that these animals or their forefathers, raised in their native clime, ran on soil which is damper and more boggy than ours. The dryness of our soil and climate dries out their feet, causing this horny and cracked condition.

The loosened horns and edges should be removed with scissors, being very careful not to cut into the live flesh. A thorough massage of the pads each day, with either olive oil or borate of glycerine, is of great help in curing this condition.

While the soreness lasts it is wise to exercise the dog on grass only.

Kerry Blue Terrier

1. Trim neck evenly down into back.

2. Trim back evenly and level top line.

3. Trim under part of neck and brisket closely, leaving a shade more hair on as one approaches the lower part of the brisket, where the front legs join the body.

4. Trim shoulders evenly down into front legs.

5. Leave hair on front legs except for a slight trimming to straighten. Trim on the back line of legs to get the desired effect. It is sometimes necessary to remove a few hairs from the front and sides of the front legs, where they join the body, to give the necessary straight line from the shoulder to the ground and from the brisket to the tips of the toes. Clean hair from between pads and shape foot to roundness.

6. Trim sides from a fairly closely trimmed back to an almost full coat on the under part of the ribs and chest. Trim underline of chest evenly to follow body line.

7. Trim loin sufficiently to show tuck up.

8. Trim from back to middle of thigh evenly, working the hair heavier on the leg.

9. From middle of thigh to hock joint remove only those hairs necessary to avoid excessive shagginess.

10. Trim backline of hock evenly with scissors. Trim hair from between toes and shape feet to roundness.

11. Trim tail evenly but not too closely. Remove all hairs that appear to make the tail look longer than it is.

12. Trim stern of shaggy hairs. Strip closest where the tail joins the body, working the hair slightly heavier toward the bottom of stern and rear of legs.

13. Trim top of skull very closely leaving plenty of eyebrow. Do not trim between eyebrows as with most other terriers.

14. Trim cheeks leaving hair slightly longer than on the skull. Work evenly but quickly into a heavy beard on the foreface.

15. Trim slightly under the eyes to slightly behind the corner of the mouth.

16. Trim ears closely, inside and out. Straighten edges with scissors.

DIAGRAM FOR TRIMMING THE KERRY BLUE TERRIER

Scottish Terrier

1. Trim neck and back evenly.

2. Trim back level but not too fine.

3. Trim front of neck closely, but as one works down to brisket, leave hairs long but not shaggy. Never shorten any hairs that would detract from the appearance that the dog is built close to the ground.

4. The shoulders to be trimmed enough to blend the body of the dog to the front legs with a clean even line.

5. Front legs should not be trimmed. Although they are some-what bent, the hair should be combed to make them appear straight from either front or side view. Trim superfluous hair from feet and between toes and shape to roundness.

6. Trim hair evenly from finely trimmed back to an absolutely full coat on the underpart of the ribs and chest. From the front view the dog should not bulge or look shaggy, but do not take

DIAGRAM FOR TRIMMING THE SCOTTISH TERRIER

so much off as to detract from the appearance of breadth and substance.

7. Only shaggy hair should be taken off thighs. Trim back line of hock straight. Superfluous hair should be trimmed from edges of feet and between toes. Shape feet to roundness with scissors.

8. Trim tail to a point, leaving fairly heavy at base.

9. Stern should be trimmed fairly close where the tail joins but quickly worked into the long hair that helps to make the rear view of the dog heavy and low to the ground.

10. Trim skull very closely, leaving considerable eyebrows.

11. Trim cheeks from outside corner of eye to corner of mouth.

12. Trim very slightly from inside corner of eye to corner of mouth to give expression.

13. Trim backs and edges of ears fine. Leave hair on insides of ears to blend into skull.

14. Trim between eyebrows and part hair over muzzle and comb downward and forward.

15. Leave chin whiskers, but clean hair off under part of jaw from the corner of the mouth back into the neck.

Sealyham Terrier

1. Trim neck from behind ears to back, take out particularly closely at withers.

2. Trim back fine and level.

3. Trim front of neck closely but as one works down to the brisket leave hairs long but not shaggy or bunchy. Never shorten any hairs that would detract from the appearance that the dog is built close to the ground.

4. The shoulders to be trimmed enough to blend the body of the dog to the front legs with a clean even line.

5. Front legs should not be trimmed. Although they are bent, the hair should be combed smooth to make them appear straight from front or side view. Trim superfluous hair from edges of feet and between toes and shape to roundness.

6. Trim hair evenly from a finely trimmed back to an absolutely full coat on the underpart of the ribs and chest. From

DIAGRAM FOR TRIMMING THE SEALYHAM TERRIER

front view the dog should not bulge or look shaggy, but do not take so much off sides as to detract from the appearance of breadth and substance.

7. Only shaggy hairs should be taken off thighs. Trim back line of hock straight. Superfluous hair should be trimmed from edges of feet and between toes. Shape feet to roundness with scissors.

8. Trim tail fine and shape to point tipped toward head.

9. Stern should be trimmed close where it is joined by tail but quickly worked into the long hairs that help to make the rear view of the dog heavy and close to the ground.

10. Trim skull cleanly leaving considerable eyebrows.

11. Trim cheeks fine from outside corner of eye to just back of the corner of the mouth. Carefully blend the long hairs of the whiskers to the entirely cleaned cheek.

12. Trim ears fine outside and inside. Trim edges with scissors.

13. Trim only the very shaggiest hairs from the eyebrows and top of muzzle.

14. Leave chin whiskers, but clean hair closely from slightly behind corner of mouth back into the neck.

Schnauzer

(MINIATURE, STANDARD AND GIANT)

1. Trim neck evenly into back.

2. Sometimes the hair grows against the grain and is unruly on the back, so trimming must be done carefully to obtain the desired results. Trim hairs to even length but not too closely. Avoid a shaggy appearance and make the back line even.

3. Trim neck and brisket closely, leaving a shade more hair as one works down to where the front legs join the body.

4. Trim shoulders closely down into front legs.

5. Trim front legs to straightness. Work principally on the back line. It is sometimes necessary to remove a few hairs from

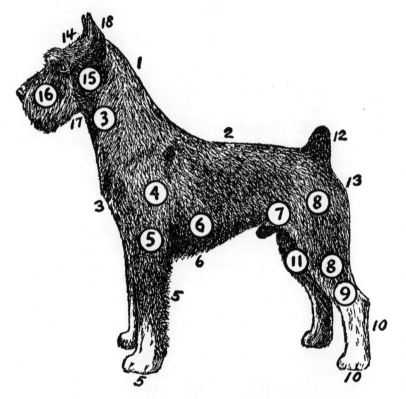

DIAGRAM FOR TRIMMING THE SCHNAUZER

the front and sides of the front legs, where they join the body, to give a clean even line from the shoulder to the sides of the feet and from the brisket to the tips of the toes. Trim superfluous hair from the sides of the feet and between the toes.

6. Trim from back down the ribs, working the hair slightly longer and heavier on the underpart of the ribs and chest. Trim under line of chest to follow body line.

7. Trim loin closer than chest and trim under line to emphasize tuck up.

8. Trim back legs from back to middle of thigh fairly closely.

9. From middle of thigh to hock trim out all shaggy hairs but not too closely.

10. Trim real line of hock to straightness with scissors. Trim superfluous hairs from sides of feet and between toes.

11. Trim insides of rear legs clean.

12. Trim tail of shaggy hairs, but not too closely.

13. Trim stern fairly closely and evenly.

14. Trim skull closely, leaving fairly heavy eyebrows. Leave more eyebrow over the inside corner of eye than the outside corner.

15. Trim cheeks closely from slightly in back of the eye and slightly behind the corner of the mouth.

16. Very little trimming is done on muzzle or chin whiskers except to shorten a few hairs to blend them slightly with the cleanly trimmed cheek.

17. Clean under jaw from slightly behind corner of mouth back into neck.

18. Trim ears clean inside and out. Straighten edges of ears with scissors.

The Setters

(ENGLISH, GORDON AND IRISH)

1. The muzzle should be trimmed of feelers and rasped to perfect smoothness.

2. The skull and cheeks should be smoothed closely and hair taken out where the ear joins the skull. The object is to make

the ear appear to be set as far back on the skull and as low as possible.

3. Trim outside of ears slightly where they join the skull, leaving more hair toward the bottom. Trim insides of ears and the part of the neck which they cover closely to enable the ear to lay closely to the head. Trim edges with scissors, rounding them slightly on the bottom.

4. Clean hair from under part of jaw down the neck evenly.

5. Take sufficient hair from the brisket to avoid bushiness. When the hair is combed down straight it should fall evenly to make a graceful line from the neck into the front legs.

6. Straighten feathering on front legs and very slightly even the hairs growing out over the toes.

7. Clean shoulders sparingly when necessary.

8. Trim a few hairs from loin to show some tuck up but do not emphasize.

9. Trim the fringe on the hocks even.

10. Trim feathering on tail to a graceful even curve tapering to a point toward tip. The tail should never appear bushy. If hair grows too thick it should be thinned out with the stripping knife.

DIAGRAM FOR TRIMMING SETTERS
(English, Gordon, and Irish)

FOR FIELD WORK

The general procedure for trimming the Setter for field work is the same as for the home or show bench, except that some practical hunters find it more comfortable for their dogs and easier for themselves if the long hair on the brisket, ears, legs and underparts of the body is taken off closely, to avoid its being ripped out by the undergrowth and also being tangled and snarled beyond repair by the burrs and ticks.

The Spaniels

(CLUMBER, COCKER AND SPRINGER)

The Spaniel should carry a very dense coat, but in a few cases too abundant a coat is found. When this is true it is necessary to strip out the excess coat over the entire body. This should be done enough so that the coat lays smoothly to the body outline and does not appear bushy or bunchy at any place. After this general thinning process, trim the dog as follows:

1. Trim muzzle of feelers (long coarse hairs) and rasp* to smoothness. Also trim feelers from above the eyes.

2. The skull and cheeks should be smoothed closely, the hair taken out finely where the ears join the skull. The object is to make the ears appear to be set as far back and as low on the skull as possible.

3. Trim outside of the ear slightly at the top where it joins the skull, leaving more hair at the bottom of the ear. Trim the inside of the ear and that part of the neck which it covers fairly close to enable the ear to hang flat and close. Trim the edge of ear evenly with scissors.

4. Trim hair from the underpart of the jaw and down the neck evenly.

5. Trim brisket slightly to avoid a bushy effect.

6. Straighten feathering on front legs with scissors.

7. Clean shoulders if the coat is patchy, bumpy or profuse over this area.

8. Clean feathering from the hocks.

---

* To rasp is to use the stripping knife with a light, scraping action.

DIAGRAM FOR TRIMMING SPANIELS
(Clumber, Cocker, and Springer)

9. Clean feathering from the tail but not too closely.

10. Trim hair to shape of foot, but leave long enough to cover the nails. Do not take any hair from between the toes but trim the excess hair from the bottom of the pads. The effect should be that of a hard, round compact paw.

FOR FIELD WORK

The general procedure for trimming the Spaniel for field work is the same as for the home or the show, except that most hunters find it more comfortable for their dogs and easier for themselves if the long hair on the brisket, ears, legs and the underparts of the body is taken off closely, to avoid its being ripped out by the undergrowth and also being tangled and snarled by burrs and ticks.

GROOMING

Daily brushing with a stiff, long bristle brush (not a wire brush) will greatly improve the appearance of the Spaniel's coat. Always brush in the direction the hair grows as a fairly flat, slightly wavy coat is desired.

A nice sheen can be obtained by finishing off with either a hand rub or by rubbing with a soft towel.

EARS

Spaniel ears being long and heavily coated, cover the aural opening most of the time. This lack of ventilation encourages dirt to collect in the ear and if not cleaned can cause ear canker. It is wise to clean the ears every week or so with cotton slightly moistened with alcohol. As it is never wise to allow water to get down into the ear, avoid using it in cleaning.

Clipping and Grooming of Poodles

Poodle clipping and grooming is a rather specialized art and not easy to describe in a few words. But, as in training a dog, there are basic rules which one can follow to minimize the work and to get results that please the eye and give the satisfaction of a job well done.

There are several styles of Poodle clips with between thirty and forty variations of these styles. It is true, the American show ring permits only three—The English Saddle, the Continental, and the Puppy clip. Other fashions are the popular Royal Dutch, the Terrier Dutch, the Kennel (also referred to as the Working, the Retriever, the Yankee, or the Sporting trim), the Kerry Blue, the Bedlington and the not-so-familiar Shawl Clip.

The variations of the styles of clips are as follows:

Feet—Clipped or unclipped.

Face—Clean; with full whiskers; with French whiskers; bushy.

Ears—Clean; full; with tassels; scissored; bell-shaped.

Tail—With or without pompon.

The Royal Dutch may have high shoulders and high hips, or it may have low shoulders and low hips. The Continental may have rosettes or none at all; it may have two bracelets on the back legs or just one.

Just as no two dogs train alike, not all Poodles look well in the same style clip. Proper trimming will emphasize a Poodle's good points and help disguise whatever faults he may have. No other breed has to such an extent the advantage of artful dressing to cover up poor body structure and major weaknesses. Clever trimming will shorten a long back, give apparent length of leg, disguise weak pasterns, improve a low set tail and manufacture well-bent stifles. The very popular whiskers can minimize an undershot jaw or pronounced snippiness. Unclipped feet hide the fact that they may be flat and have thin pads.

Equipment

Good workmanship in every art depends a lot on the worker's tools. This is especially true in the clipping of Poodles, which, in itself, is no small chore. Buying the best is expensive, but it is money well spent and will pay for itself many times over.

There are a number of small animal clippers available, some better known than others. It will cost about thirty-five dollars for a complete set, which includes the machine, one head, and one clipping blade. The better clippers all cost about the same price, and there is always an advantage in buying a nationally known make. For the purpose of these instructions we will discuss the Oster Small Animal Clipper—Model 2—the one most commonly used. The first point in favor of a good machine is the detachable head, as well as the removable blade. An extra head or two, with different size blades attached, will save time and make clipping more convenient. Extra heads cost about seven dollars each, the extra blades about five dollars each. At first, the different size blades may be confusing to the novice, but not if he will remember that the higher the number the closer the cut. The Oster machine has the blades listed below:

No. 40—Used mostly by veterinarians when preparing a dog for surgery. The No. 40 blade shaves the skin almost as though done with a razor and should never be used for clipping a Poodle.

No. 30—This blade gives a very close cut and should be used more for tidying up the muzzle and trimming around the toenails. It is too fine for use on the average Poodle and is apt to cause skin irritations.

STRIPPING A TERRIER'S COAT — I

Phil Prentice, well-known professional handler, shows how the stripping knife is used in trimming a Terrier. The hair to be removed is held against the side of the knife with the thumb.

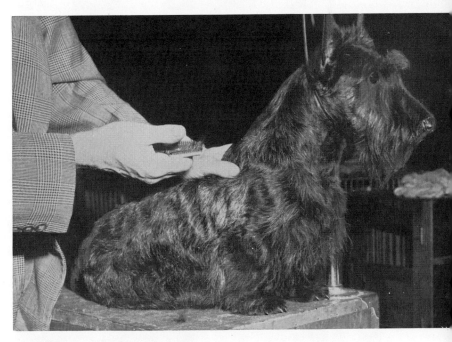

STRIPPING A TERRIER'S COAT — II

With a rolling motion of the hand, the knife is pulled away from the coat, removing the excess hair. It's a good idea to proceed cautiously, removing only a little hair at a time, in order to keep the remaining hair neat and even.

THE SIT-STAY EXERCISE

This group of dogs are competing in an obedience test. They are required to sit this way while their handlers leave them by themselves.

AT THE DOG SHOW

For spectators and dog fanciers, the dog show is a colorful and exciting sports event. For the serious breeder, it provides an opportunity to exhibit stock and compare it with that of other owners.

No. 15—The No. 15 blade is a good all-around general purpose blade. It does a clean job and is less likely to irritate the skin.

No. 10—This is the blade that should be used on the sides of the face and on the Poodle's neck when he is being clipped for the first time. In fact, it should be used on all sensitive parts of the body and on all dogs if clipping bothers them. It leaves enough hair to show the natural color and it gives the clipped parts a smooth silky appearance.

No. 7—This blade leaves a covering of a quarter to one-half inch of hair.

No. 5—This leaves the hair one-half to one inch long and is the coarsest blade.

The high numbered blades, such as the No. 40, No. 30, and No. 15, cut better when used against the way the hair grows naturally. The No. 10 blade cuts well when used either *against* or *with* the hair, but the No. 7 and No. 5 show best results when used *with* the lay of the hair and not against it.

Keep in mind that every blade cuts closer when used against the lay of the hair. In other words, the No. 30 blade *with* gets almost the same results as the No. 15 *against,* the No. 15 *with,* the same as the No. 10 *against.* With the numbers 15, 10 and 5 blades, any style haircut may be given a Poodle, with excellent results.

While on the subject of clippers, this is a good time to mention their care. The oil caps on each side of the machine should be filled with oil at intervals, depending upon how frequently the machine is used. A special oil is provided by the manufacturer for this purpose. The blades should be oiled and a few drops occasionally placed around the motor shaft. All air vents should be kept free of hair and dirt. These are the narrow slits on each side of the clipper and the holes on the cap of the machine. The head should be taken off and packed with grease. The grease is also supplied with the machine. The way to tell if there is enough grease present is to take the head off, after the machine has been running, and wipe the shaft on your finger. If grease comes off on your hand, there is enough. If not, add a little. All these things will help keep the machine from overheating, and will prevent discomfort both for the dog and the person doing the clipping.

When a machine has been used for a long time it may begin to run very slowly. In this case, you should take out the little carbon brushes on each side of the clipper to see if they are worn. An extra set of brushes is usually provided with each clipper set. When the head no longer fits in a snug fashion, the machine should be sent back to the factory to have the worn parts replaced. Vibration caused from a loose-fitting head can ruin the clipper, often beyond repair.

There usually comes a time when, after the clipper is plugged in and the switch turned on, one is greeted by nothing but silence. The chances will be there is a broken wire where the cord fastens to the machine. If one is clever with minor electrical repairs, this can be taken care of in a few minutes. If not, an electrician will have to repair the broken wire. Frequently a blade, even one that has just been replaced, will suddenly stop cutting. When this happens pinch the two cutting blades together, then release them while the machine is still running. This may shift the position of the blades and they will start cutting again. If not, replace with another blade.

All too often Poodles suffer from what are called "clipper burns." These appear when the skin becomes irritated and the dog's constant scratching sets up an infection. Clipper burns are not always caused, as so many people think, from dirty blades. There are different reasons. First, the skin will get sore from a dull blade that pulls the hair instead of cutting it. A second reason, and really the most common, is that too fine a blade may have been used for the dog's first clipping while his skin was still sensitive. Once the skin has become tough from repeated clippings, a fine blade is all right, but care should be taken at first. Other causes may be stretching the skin while clipping or forcing the clippers too hard. Whatever the cause, a soothing skin lotion, applied to all clipped parts after a Poodle has been trimmed, will prevent scratching that may lead to sores on the shaved areas.

In addition to clippers, other necessary equipment for the grooming of the Poodle includes:

Scissors. Regular barber shears with a keen cutting edge. It is wise to have two pairs, so that one or the other may be sent away for sharpening.

Carder. This is a small oblong implement with a short handle. The bent wire teeth, placed close together, are excellent for taking out mats and for loosening the hair before brushing or combing.

Rake. This tool may have either a single or a double line of strong metal teeth. It is used for pulling through the mats of a badly tangled coat.

Combs. Poodle combs come in several sizes—coarse, medium, and fine. The one you will use depends upon the type and condition of the coat. For best results the teeth should be round, and the longer they are the better. Some owners prefer a comb with a handle, others one without.

Brush. Except for the Puppy or the Show Clips, where the coat is left long, a brush is not used very much. It is, however, essential when preparing the Poodle for the show ring. For styles other than Show, the carder and the wide-toothed comb will work better than a brush.

A clipping table that will be comfortable to work at is an important item. One measuring about thirty inches from the floor, or midway between the hip and knee in height, will be less tiring. It should be covered with rubber matting to give the dog secure footing. One that wobbles and shakes will frighten the dog and make him nervous. Good lighting is essential. It is very easy to nip the skin with the scissors when working in a subdued light, especially on dark-colored dogs.

To do a complete job of grooming the Poodle, you should have a tooth-scraper to scale the tartar off the teeth, a file for shortening the nails, and a pair of tweezers to take the hair and wax from inside the ears. There are several excellent nail files on the market, but a favorite is the four-way shoe rasp that may be obtained at most hardware stores. This has the different size files on the same tool, and the speed with which it works makes the chore easy. The sharp points may be snipped off with a nail cutter, but if a file is used for the greater part, the dog will not mind it half as much and there is less chance of cutting the quick. This is the tender part of the nail, and it will bleed profusely if cut too close. A handy ingredient for the medicine chest would be a small bottle of Monsell Solution, kept just for this purpose. Your druggist can supply it, and a drop will stop the bleeding instantly. If the ears are dirty, the wax should be removed with a piece of cotton dipped in alcohol. A little B.F.I. Powder may be dusted in to act as a disinfectant. If the ears have no odor and are clean-looking, dust them with the powder and let well enough alone. An amateur can start ear trouble by probing in the ears too much. To bathe the eyes, an eyewash, such as boracic acid, Alcolol or collyrium may be used.

Clipping the Poodle

We think of Poodle clipping and bathing as being synonymous. The dog is first clipped and the pattern set in the rough stage. He is then combed or brushed out completely, then he is bathed. During the bath, the dog is treated for parasites, dry skin, or skin ailments, after which the Poodle is given the finishing touches. These are a very important part of Poodle grooming. No Poodle should be bathed unless the coat is completely brushed out and all mats removed. This means taking out the matted hair all the way to the skin and not just on the surface. Bathing a Poodle with a knotted coat will only bring disappointment. Wetting the hair tangles the coat more than ever, and when the bath is finished the dog will look dull and dusty and the coat will feel sticky because it is practically impossible to rinse all the soap from a tangled coat.

While being clipped, the Poodle should be trained or held to stand in a position so that he faces straight ahead. Twisting and turning the body will cause the lines to be uneven and the clip thrown off balance. Once the pattern is set, scissors are used to complete the Poodle clip. The natural lines of the body should give the impression of smoothness and symmetry. The hair should first be combed *down* (this is the way the hair falls naturally) and

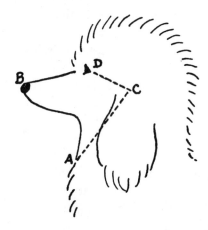

FIG. 1. CLIPPING THE POODLE'S FACE

scissored along the clipped lines. It is then combed *against* the natural growth and the edges again scissored to remove all overlapping hair. Then, by combing the hair out from the body, it can be shaped where necessary—the hollow places filled in and the protruding tufts of hair snipped off.

CLIPPING THE FACE

The English Saddle, the Continental, the Shawl, and the Puppy styles, require a clean face with a V cut on the neck.

With the dog in a sitting position, start the clippers (using a No. 10 blade) about four inches down from the jaw line (A, Fig. 1). Clip up toward the tip of the muzzle (B); then lay the ear back and start the clippers just in front of the ear at point C. First make a straight line to the corner of the eye (point D), then from C down to A on the throat, and from D to the tip of the muzzle again. Remove all the hair in this outlined area by cutting toward the muzzle all the time. The hair is taken from in front of the ears so that they will lie as close to the head as possible, but if the ears are set high, or are placed too far back on the head, some hair left in front of the ears will help to disguise these faults. Keep a firm grip on the muzzle when working around the mouth, because, if the dog is permitted to lick, his tongue may be cut by the clippers. If the dog is not held tight a sudden jerk of the head may also cause the clippers to nip the loose skin along the edge of the lips. No hair is touched over the eyes, but starting at the inside corner of each, a slight reverse V cut is made between the eyes. This gives the short stubby head the appearance of being longer. One that is too flat on top will appear to have more "stop," as it is called, if the cut is made high but straight across rather than with a V.

A clean face with the Kennel, the Royal Dutch, and the Terrier Dutch clips, should have the throat blended into the body length with no definite neckline. This is done by turning the clippers and cutting *with* the hair, then using the next longer blade and cutting against the hair.

If the face is to have full whiskers, the clippers stop when they reach the opening on each side of the mouth. The line from these two points then completely encircles the muzzle. The whiskers, to be even and tidy, are combed forward and scissored, then tapered from the outside edges to the corners of the mouth. Some owners prefer the full whiskers with just the top of the nose clipped.

The true French moustache usually has no hair on the lower jaw and the top of the nose is bare as well. This leaves side whiskers that stick out in a chic fashion. The bushy- or square-type face is done with a No. 5 blade, and the whiskers are scissored to the desired length.

CLIPPING THE EARS

When clipping the ears, start the machine at the head and run it toward the end of the ear. Otherwise, it is easy to cut the ear, and the bleeding will be profuse. When the ears are to be clipped clean, either a No. 15 or No. 10 blade may be used, and the edges of the ears scissored to make them neat and tidy. With tassels, the clippers stop far enough from the end so that an inch to an inch and a half tassel width remains. The tassels are evened and the edges of the ear again trimmed so that there is no raggedness. Other ear styles have a No. 5 blade used on them, or the ears are scissored all over to leave the hair long and bushy without looking stringy. Bell-shaped ears call for close clipping about halfway down and the bottom half cut with a No. 5 blade or scissored to the desired length. For every style of show clip, the ears are not clipped or trimmed at all but show their full natural length.

CLIPPING THE FEET

To clip the Poodle's front feet, the paw is held with the person's thumb on top and the middle or ring finger underside to push the skin up between the toes. The foot is shaved until the dewclaw, or the mark left by the removal of the dewclaw, has just been cleared. In other words, a good inch of pastern should be showing. The back paws may be clipped by pulling them forward as close to the front feet as possible while the dog is sitting, or the dog may stand and the legs be pulled backward similar to that position of shoeing a horse. The back feet should be clipped high enough so that at least one inch of pastern shows when the dog is in a standing position.

When putting bracelets on the front legs for the show clip, the foreleg is clipped toward the elbow. The elbow itself is not uncovered because, if rubbed against hard objects, it will become calloused and sore. On the underside of the forearm it is necessary to turn the clippers and cut toward the paw, as the hair in this particular place grows in the opposite direction. The bracelets on the front legs measure two and a half to three inches in width, depending upon how long the dog's legs are and how much coat he has. A large Poodle carrying a profuse coat needs a large bracelet. The Poodle which is small in size and dainty in make-up looks out of balance if the bracelets are too exaggerated. The bracelets are combed down and scissored evenly along the lower edge. They are then combed up and all overlapping hair removed. Afterwards, while the dog stands, the bracelets are fluffed out and rounded on all sides with the scissors to make them symmetrical.

CLIPPING THE TAIL

The underside of the tail should never be cut close, no matter what style clip is chosen. This part of the Poodle is sensitive, and care must always be taken. If a close-cutting blade is used, the clipping should be done with the hair and not against it. The show styles, such as the English Saddle, the Continental, the Puppy, and the Shawl clips, require that the tail be clipped with a pompon left on the tip. The shaved part of the tail is usually clipped with the same blade used on the face and feet, and there are about three and a half to four inches of skin exposed. If the tail has been docked too short, the pompon is grown out as far as possible on the end. If the tail is too long the hair on the end is cut off, and the pompon is left close to the body. The pompon itself should be nicely rounded.

With all other fashions, such as the Royal Dutch, the Terrier Dutch, the Kennel, etc., it is best to shave the tail the same length as the body, whether there is a pompon or not. This does away with the many different lengths of hair that make the clip look uneven and spotty.

The Puppy Clip

The Puppy Clip has only the face, the tail, and the paws shaved. Dogs exhibited at dog shows in this style clip must be under a year old.

Clean face with a V neck (No. 15 or No. 10 blade).

Ears full.

Feet clipped (No. 15 blade).

Tail clipped (preferably No. 10 blade).

Pompon scissored.

Rest of coat as long as possible, but even.

FIG. 2. THE PUPPY CLIP

The Kennel Clip

(KNOWN AS WORKING, RETRIEVER, AND SPORTING TRIM)

The Kennel Clip is a modified Puppy Clip.
Clean face (No. 15 or No. 10 blade) with throat blended.
Ears full, but even along edges.
Feet (No. 15 blade).
Body (No. 5, No. 7 or No. 10, as preferred).
Tail same length as body with pompon scissored.
Legs scissored to desired length. Should be shaped to give
balance to the body.
This is the ideal clip for the average pet Poodle and can be neatly
administered with scissors alone, or with scissors and a pair of
hand-operated clippers.

FIG. 3.   THE KENNEL CLIP

The English Saddle Clip

To prepare for setting the pattern on the English Saddle
style clip, a No. 5 blade is run over the hindquarters toward the
tail but tapers off over the sides and down the legs (Fig. 4). If
no No. 5 blade is available, this may be done with scissors, but

Fig. 4. FIRST STEP IN THE ENGLISH SADDLE CLIP

it is much slower work. The rump and legs should be done first; then gradually work toward the long coat. You can always take off more hair but, once removed, it can't be put back, so the cutting should be done in stages. To decide where the line should be between the long and the short hair, the side of the hand may be placed on the dog's back and moved backward and forward until you find the spot most pleasing to the eye. This is usually at the last rib but it will vary. Experience will soon tell you at which point it is most suited to your own dog. Once the line is decided upon, complete the circle by clipping under the body as well as on top.

Next come the bracelets on the back legs. To make the lower one, feel for the hock joint with the thumb and index finger (E, Fig. 5). Start the clippers at this point and clip upward. The band should be one to one and three-quarters inches wide and completely circle the leg. The second band is from the stifle joint (F, Fig. 5) to the back part of the leg. This band measures three-quarters to one inch in width, goes completely around the leg, and is cut at a slight angle so it slopes toward the front. The

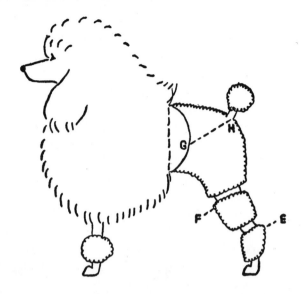

FIG. 5

THE FINISHED PATTERN FOR THE ENGLISH SADDLE CLIP

clippers with a No. 15 blade may be turned over and used to mark this line from the stifle joint to the natural bend in the leg, to give an idea of what the bracelet will look like when finished. This will leave enough hair so that the band can be widened on either the top or the bottom as desired. Most beginners have a tendency to make both bands too wide.

Clean face (No. 15 or No. 10) with V neck.
Ears full.
Feet (No. 15).
Tail (No. 15 or No. 10).
Pompon scissored.
Crescent half-circles (No. 15).
Bands on back legs (No. 15).
Forelegs (No. 15).
Top of saddle (No. 5 *with* the hair).
Sides of saddle scissored.
Bracelets scissored.
Lion ruff long but even.

The double-crescent-shaped saddle comes last, and again it is wise to take off a little at a time. Start by doing a complete strip around the body with a No. 10 or No. 15 blade, to separate the short hair from the long. The strip should be at least one inch wide. Gradually work the clippers backward toward the rump and take out the hair over the loin by making circular or half-moon cuts. These curves should be symmetrical with plenty of depth to make the lower line of the side points even with the natural line of the body. On the Standard Poodle the loin may be shaved back until the center (G) measures approximately seven inches from the base of the tail (H). A common mistake is to take this back too far, which gives the impression of narrow, weak quarters. The point on the center of the back—which is a reversed V—may be widened to make the quarters look heavier, or it may be narrowed to make a dog look thin. Sometimes the saddle is not separated from the long coat at these three points, but this is a matter of personal choice. Breaking the center line usually helps to shorten a long back. Naturally, both sides must be the same. A top view, with the dog standing on the floor and his nose held forward, will soon show if the lines are even. Scissors are used to finish trimming the saddle and bracelets.

The brushing of the long coat known as the mane or ruff is an important part of show-ring grooming. From puppyhood, the dog should be trained to lie flat on his side while being groomed. He will be more comfortable, and it will be more convenient for the person doing the brushing. It may be necessary to force the dog to be quiet at first, but once a Poodle becomes accustomed to it he will enjoy his grooming. Use a stiff bristle brush or a soft wire one. Light combing with a wide-toothed comb is safe when done by an expert but it is not recommended for the novice. The mats should be pulled apart with the fingers then brushed out gradually. With the dog on his side, start at the head and brush toward the muzzle. Hold the unbrushed hair down with the free hand and brush out a little hair at a time. You may start at the saddle and brush toward the tail, or on the side and brush toward the legs, but in all cases, the finish is done by fluffing the hair in the opposite direction. Brushing against the natural growth is what makes the hair stand out from the body and gives the impression of a long, dense coat. The stomach and chest are done while the dog lies on his side, but the top of the head, the back of the neck, and the back itself, are easier to brush when the dog is lying on his stomach with his head between his paws. Last, but not least, the dog should sit quietly while the chest, topknot, and ears receive attention. After a thorough brushing out, the dog should stand while the ragged edges of the long coat are evened off. This makes the coat look thicker, and by trimming it between the front legs and under the stomach, the "lion ruff" tapers toward the hindquarters and gives a more pleasing effect. With the hair fastened back from the eyes with a ribbon, a barret or an elastic, the Poodle is ready for the show ring.

If the Poodle's back is long the chest hair should be combed *down* instead of fluffed out, and cut rather short to make the body appear more compact. At the same time, the hair over the rump and under the tail should be as close as possible. A Poodle with short front legs should have the underside of the long hair cut even with the elbows, and bracelets should be low down on the legs. The leggy, rangy type dog should have the reverse—a long mane and high bracelets. Narrow hindquarters that lack depth of loin look better when the saddle is heavy, with the side points left lower than the natural line of the body. To give the dog a longer neck, the V should be shaved lower down and some of the long coat over the back taken off.

Two or three thorough brushings a week are all that is necessary, except when the dog is changing from his puppy coat to his adult one. Daily grooming is then necessary until the change has been completed.

The Continental Clip

The Continental Clip is different from the English Saddle in that all the hair is shaved from the hindquarters, leaving the bottom bracelets and a rosette on each hip. These rosettes are about three inches in diameter and are scissored so that they will look neat. The width between them is equal to the width of the clippers. The bracelets on the back legs are placed higher than those of the English Saddle so that more pastern shows (Fig. 6).

Clean face (No. 15 or No. 10) with V neck.

Ears full.

Feet (No. 15).

Forelegs (No. 15)`.

Tail (No. 15 or No. **10).**

Pompon scissored.

Hindquarters (No. 15 *with* or No. 10 *against*).

Bracelets scissored.

Rosettes scissored.

Lion ruff long but even.

F<small>IG</small>. 6.   THE CONTINENTAL CLIP

The Shawl Clip

Clean face (No. 15 or No. 10) with V neck.
Ears full.
Feet (No. 15).
Tail (No. 15 or No. 10).
Pompon scissored.
Hindquarters (No. 15 *with* or No. 10 *against*).
Bracelets and rosettes scissored.
Shawl ruff long but even.

Fig. 7. THE SHAWL CLIP

The Royal Dutch Clip

In the Royal Dutch Clip the body is clipped closely from the back of the neck to the pompon on the tail, or to the tip of the tail if no pompon is left. This band over the shoulder blades and between the hips is a little wider than the width of the clipper. The placement of this line of demarcation is optional. It may be high on the shoulders and hips or low, depending on which is more becoming to the dog. The leg hair is left long, and the

scissored pantaloons form ovals on each shoulder and over each
hip, very similar to Victorian leg-of-mutton sleeves in women's
dresses. The Royal Dutch has full whiskers, and the front throat
line is blended. The clipped line on the neck that distinguishes
the fullness of the front legs from the close clipped hair of the
body is half way between the breastbone and the "Adam's apple."
The effect is very much like that of a necklace. The topknot (the
cap of hair that is left on the dog's head) may be squared or
rounded, as preferred. The lines run from the corner of each
eye to where the front edge of the ear joins the head, then around
from in back of each ear along the base of the skull. This line,
at the back of the topknot, may be definite or it may be blended
into the body length.

  Body (No. 15, No. 10, No. 7 or No. 5).
  Tail same length as the body.
  Pompon scissored.
  Feet (No. 15).
  Face (No. 15 or No. 10).

FIG. 8. THE ROYAL DUTCH CLIP

The drawing shows the Royal Dutch Clip with high shoulders and high hips.
The dotted lines indicate the placement of low shoulders and low hips.

Full whiskers, throat blended.

Ears (No. 15 or No. 10). Leave tassels.

Legs may have high shoulders and high hips, or low shoulders and low hips.

Other variations: Clean face, clean ears, French whiskers, full ears or ears scissored or shaped, feet unclipped, tail without pompon.

The Terrier Dutch Clip

Body (No. 10, No. 7 or No. 5). No definite leg line, legs blended into the body length.

Tail without a pompon (may have one).

Feet unclipped (may be clipped).

Ears clean (may have tassels, may be full or same length as body).

Face (No. 15 or No. 10) with throat blended.

Full whiskers (face may be clean).

Fig. 9. THE TERRIER DUTCH CLIP

The Kerry Blue Clip

(TO LOOK LIKE THE KERRY BLUE TERRIER)

Body (No. 5).
Feet unclipped.
Tail (No. 5). No pompon.
Ears (No. 15 or No. 10).
Cheeks (No. 10). Full whiskers, throat blended.
Top of head flat, eyebrows heavy, and hair left long on
top of muzzle and brushed forward.

FIG. 10.   THE KERRY BLUE CLIP

The Bedlington Clip

(TO LOOK LIKE A BEDLINGTON TERRIER)

Body (No. 5).
Feet unclipped.
Tail (No. 5). No pompon.
Ears (No. 15). With tassels.
Face and head shaped like a Bedlington's.
Throat blended.

Note: Wherever specific measurements are given, such as the width of bands or bracelets on legs, they apply to the *Standard* Poodle. The same general rules and technique are employed for clipping and grooming Toy and Miniature Poodles, but the lines of the pattern must be appropriately scaled down to fit the proportions of the individual dog.

Fig. 11. THE BEDLINGTON CLIP

CHAPTER 7

How to Care for the Sick Dog

Veterinary medicine has come a long way from the time when the local vet was likely to be a slightly boozy, tobacco-chewing horse doctor usually to be found passing the time of day with the "boys" at the livery stable. Today's veterinarian spends a minimum of six years earning the degree which gives him or her the right to have the letters D.V.M., or V.M.D., after his name. The better animal hospitals are housed in up-to-date, especially planned buildings equipped with the finest apparatus. X rays, intricate surgery, blood transfusions, the use of sulfa drugs and antibiotics are all taken-for-granted procedures in the practice of modern veterinary medicine. Canine diseases which were considered incurable or fatal as recently as twenty or thirty years ago are now treated successfully. As a result of these advances, and the increased knowledge of proper canine nutrition, the number of years of healthy, happy life which an owner can expect for his pet has increased remarkably.

In spite of the splendid veterinary care which is now available, there are two serious errors which dog owners are likely to make in regard to their pets' health. Some of the very sickest dogs that veterinarians ever see are those which their owners have attempted to treat with home remedies or patent medicines. Many of the nostrums for dogs which are obtainable at drugstores or pet-supply counters are worthless. Some are really dangerous. There are laxatives intended for human use which will kill a dog, even when given in small quantities. Remember these facts when tempted to dose your pet with the odds and ends in the family medicine cabinet. You may save a veterinary bill, but you may lose your dog.

The other common failing is to postpone seeking help when a pet is ailing, thinking, "He'll probably be all right by tomorrow." Some owners put off a visit to the veterinarian until poor Fido is more dead than alive and may require long and expensive treatment, or worse, is past saving. This is not to say that a dog owner should not undertake such simple first aid as removing a thorn from his dog's foot or dabbing a minor cut with metaphen, but the person who really loves his dog should bear in mind that the dog may be man's best friend, but the best friend of a sick or injured dog is a good veterinarian.

The reader who is hoping to find in this chapter a cure-all for distemper, or a guaranteed mange remedy which he can whip up in his own kitchen, is going to be disappointed. What we *do* want to do is to describe the symptoms that should enable the owner to distinguish between a really sick dog and one who is merely paying the penalty of a foraging expedition in a neighbor's garbage can; to describe the indications of worms, skin trouble, and other common ailments; and to supply the knowledge which every pet owner should have of simple first aid and canine medical supplies.

Your Dog's Medicine Cabinet

What medical supplies and remedies should a dog owner keep in the house for home treatment of his pet?

Rectal thermometer.

Petroleum jelly, for lubricating the thermometer.

Boric acid solution, to be used as an eyewash. (If used frequently, take care that it does not run down the face and into the mouth, as often happens with short-nosed breeds.)

Bicarbonate of soda, to be used in enemas. (One teaspoonful to eight ounces of warm water.)

Peroxide, tincture of iodine or tincture of metaphen, to be used in dressing wounds.

Aspirin, for use as a sedative and for fever.

Yellow oxide of mercury opthalmic ointment, for minor eye troubles.

Mineral oil, for use as a laxative or in enemas.

Tweezers.

Milk of magnesia, to be used as a laxative.

Pepto-Bismol, for minor stomach upsets and intestinal disturbances.

Milk of bismuth or bismuth tablets, to be used for diarrhea.

Tannic acid ointment, for treating burns.

Gauze, cotton and adhesive, for dressings.

Signs of Serious Illness

What are the signals of serious illness in dogs?

Abnormally high or low temperatures, listlessness, loss of appetite, persistent vomiting, persistent diarrhea, fits, bloody urine or bloody stools.

Checking Up on Your Dog

How do I take my dog's temperature?

If possible, place the dog on a table. Coat the bulb end of a rectal thermometer with petroleum jelly. Raise the dog's tail and insert the thermometer for one half of its length into the rectum. Hold the thermometer in this position for the required time indicated on the thermometer, usually one or two minutes. The normal temperature range is from 100 to 102 degrees. If you take the temperature following strenuous exercise or excitement and find that it is above normal, wait about half an hour, keeping the dog quiet during this period, and recheck it. It will often return to normal. After using the thermometer, clean it with rubbing alcohol or a similar disinfectant, shake it down, and it will then be ready for use the next time you need it.

What may be wrong with a dog that is listless?

Listlessness in a usually peppy dog is often the owner's first warning of illness. It may be an indication of fever. The temperature should be taken, and if fever is present, the dog should be examined further in an effort to locate the site of the trouble. If the fever persists, professional help will be needed.

Sometimes a dog whose activity is usually confined to leisurely walks on a leash, if taken to the country and allowed to race about, will be inclined to lie around the next day, resting his lame muscles, and is not sick, just tired.

What is wrong with a dog who loses his appetite? Our dog just picks at his food and isn't at all anxious to eat.

This may be an indication of fever, and the dog's temperature should be taken. Loss of appetite accompanies most of the serious infections of the body.

In a puppy, a sore mouth during the time the permanent teeth are being cut will interfere with eating. Inspect the teeth, especially the molars. You may find baby teeth which are partially loosened, and these can often be easily removed. In an old dog, diseased teeth will make eating difficult and unpleasant for him. Heavy tartar deposits open the way to inflamed and infected gums, followed by loosening of the teeth and their eventual loss.

Foreign objects, such as string, thread, tacks, needles or pins, or pieces of bone, may be caught between the teeth, in the tongue or the soft tissues of the mouth and throat. In such cases the loss of appetite is sudden, and is usually accompanied by drooling, gagging, or pawing at the mouth.

Is the old belief true, that as long as a dog has a cool, moist nose he is in good health?

No, although there is some foundation for it, because a dog with a fever often has a hot, dry nose. But don't ever depend on this theory if you have any reason to think that your dog may be running a temperature. Use a thermometer and believe what it tells you. A dog with three feet in the grave can have a cold, wet nose.

External Pests

What is meant by the term "external parasites"?

The commonest is the flea, which comes with the summer and is especially active towards the end of the warm-weather season with the first hint of cooler nights. Fleas do not lay their eggs on the dog, but in the dog's bedding, so that treatment of the dog by powders containing DDT or rotenone, or creosote baths, should be supplemented by cleaning up his sleeping quarters. The dark brown or black gritty material found in the dog's coat is the feces of the flea. Fleas may cause skin trouble by the scratching they induce. They are also one of the intermediate hosts for the tapeworm.

The louse is usually found on the face and ears of the dog, but may be found almost anywhere on the dog's body. They may be present in great numbers before being discovered. The louse is a soft-bodied gray bug which does not move with the speed of the flea. It is easily picked off, and the tan-colored head end with its moving legs is easy to see with a magnifying glass. The eggs of the louse are silvery and firmly attached to the hair. They are difficult to dislodge, and, even after the egg has hatched, the nit case adheres to the hair for some time. This type of reproduction makes it necessary to administer lice-killing dips containing creosote, rotenone, or DDT several times, at about one-week intervals. Fine-combing the dog afterwards will help to remove the dead lice and any which may be merely stunned by the dip. A powder containing DDT may be used when baths are inadvisable.

Ticks are the hardiest external parasites. They can survive in an empty house or apartment for months, waiting for a dog or other animal to appear to provide a meal. Ticks are often found on the dog after a visit to the country or the park. If there are ticks in your area, your dog should be looked over frequently during the summer.

The female tick is gray and soft-bodied. After mating, she feeds until she reaches the size of the end of your little finger. The male is small and dark brown. The young are also small, and go through several stages—depending on the species—before reaching maturity. When the female becomes engorged with the dog's blood, she detaches herself, falls off, and seeks a place to lay her crop of eggs. If she lays them in the house, you may find your dog continually carrying ticks, although he has not revisited the country. If this happens, it may be necessary to have the dipping of the dog coincide with an extermination process in your home.

If only a few ticks are present, they can be picked off, using tweezers, and be disposed of in kerosene, boiling water, or down the toilet.

Ticks may be the carriers of filaria (heartworm) and fever. When present in large numbers they frequently produce anemia.

Is it possible for a dog to have external parasites which the owner cannot see?

Ear mites are visible only in the light and when magnified. These small, active, silver-white mites live in the ear canal, producing itching and a brownish-black dry type of discharge. If allowed to remain, the ear canal will become inflamed, and chronic ear trouble will result. They are passed from dog to dog, as are other external parasites, so that if they are found in one dog of a group that live together, the others should be examined to prevent reinfestation.

The ear is a delicate organ, easily injured, so it is better to have it treated by a veterinarian rather than by the owner. If professional attention is not obtainable, clean the canal with peroxide or mineral oil, floating up the debris. Gently wipe the canal dry with absorbent cotton, then apply 2 per cent yellow oxide of mercury with a cotton-tipped applicator. Repeat the process every five days for three treatments. If the canal continues to secrete excessively it must be examined for other trouble.

Skin Ailments

If my dog should get mange, how would I be able to recognize it?

It may look like the common forms of eczema. There are two forms of mange, sarcoptic and follicular. Follicular mange is also called red mange or demodectic mange. In some cases the experienced dog owner can determine which form is present by the location and the appearance of the lesions. A microscopic examination of a scraping of the skin is often needed to make a positive diagnosis. As a rule, sarcoptic mange produces intense itching, and appears on the backs of the hind legs, in the armpits, and on the feet. The head and neck may also be involved. It may be accompanied by a musty smell, especially in advanced cases.

Follicular mange appears as moth-eaten-looking patches, especially on the face, head, and along the back. Generally there is no itching. It commonly reveals itself about the time that teething is in progress.

Both types of mange can be contracted by human beings, with sarcoptic being more freely transmitted than follicular, but in most cases the former is the easier to correct.

Can mange be cured by the remedies available in drugstores and pet-supply shops?

If you are dealing with sarcoptic mange, such remedies will probably be effective. If follicular mange is suspected, it is better to have the diagnosis confirmed by a veterinarian, and have him outline a course of treatment. The general health of the animal may need to be improved, and in some stubborn cases treatments by injection may be necessary.

My Scottie develops skin trouble every summer. Can I prevent it?

It is hard to say, for summer skin trouble assumes various forms. It may be produced by various causes such as warm, humid weather and its accompanying fleas, ticks and flies, too frequent bathing, and faulty feeding. Singly, or in combination, these conditions produce an itchy skin from which the hair falls or is pulled.

In the prevention of summer skin troubles it is important that the dog be kept absolutely free of external parasites. The use of flea powder or, even better, a powder containing both insecticide and fungicide is recommended.

After correcting any of the known causes, the dry type of skin may be treated with baby oil or lanolin-base hair tonics. Cases of long standing may need a more stimulating type of application, such as a balsam of Peru mixture or one of the mange mixtures prepared for human use.

For the moist type of summer itch, in which the skin is red and wet and the sparse hair is left standing stiffly in the sore areas, B.F.I. powder may be dusted on the area, or a solution of 5 per cent tannic acid and 5 per cent salicylic in alcohol may be applied.

Putting a Queen Elizabeth collar (a circle of stiff cardboard) around the dog's neck will help to prevent his doing further damage to himself by chewing. A sedative is often necessary until the intense itching subsides.

What is a fungus infection?

A microscopic plant infection, which may range from the familiar brown scaly patches on the skin in summer, to the highly contagious ringworm.

Isn't it possible that the summer skin trouble which so many dogs get every year is poison ivy?

No, because most dogs are immune to poison ivy and are not affected even

ELIZABETHAN COLLAR

This collar, consisting of two semi-circles of cardboard laced together with strong string or shoelaces, will prevent a dog with a skin ailment from biting and further irritating the affected area.

if they should choose to take a nap in a bed of it. However, some dogs are sensitive to grasses and plants, and may develop redness of the skin through contact with them.

If a dog keeps biting and licking at patches of skin trouble on his sides how can he be stopped?

The cone-shaped collar used to prevent a dog's scratching his head and ears will usually work. If not, an Elizabethan collar fastened around the neck will do the trick. The simplest way to make the collar is to cut two semicircles, the inner circumference

CONE COLLAR

A cone of cardboard, secured to the dog's collar with string or shoelaces, will keep the dog from pawing at irritated skin around the head and ears.

conforming to the dog's neck measurement, then punch holes along the four straight edges and lace the two pieces together with strong brown string or shoelaces. Still another way to stop biting or scratching at healing body lesions is this: Take a turkish towel long enough to go around the dog's chest and rib cage and overlap on top. Cut two properly spaced holes in it for the dog's front legs. Put it on the dog, the longer measurement of the towel going around the dog's body, and fasten the edges at the scruff of his neck and along his back with strong safety pins.

What does ringworm look like?

In the dog it appears as a raised circular or oval area, the surface of which has little or no hair, and is marked with small craters which discharge blood and pus. It spreads quickly from place to place on the dog, to other dogs and to people.

In treating ringworm try to keep the dog confined to prevent the ailment's being spread by his sitting on beds and chairs. In most cases tincture of iodine may be applied daily for two or three days, later followed by daily treatments of Iodex rubbed in well. If the lesions are widespread, the dog will have to be treated all over the body and he should be examined before you undertake such a task. The treatment may consist of sulfur dips, oil-and-sulfur applications or even X-ray treatments.

Distemper, the Killer

What are the salient facts on distemper?

This is a contagious disease of dogs caused by a virus. It affects chiefly dogs in their first year, though is not by any means unknown in older dogs. It assumes one or more of several forms, and any of the signals of illness may mean distemper. The digestive, the respiratory, and the nervous systems may be involved. A form involving the skin is less frequently seen. This will give you an idea of the difficulty that may be encountered in making a diagnosis. Although dogs frequently survive distemper—but seldom without treatment by a veterinarian—many of these survivors are left with chorea (chronic twitching and jerking of the muscles), while others will show damage of the heart, intestines, eyes or other parts. A common aftermath of distemper is teeth with pitted and scarred enamel.

Can I protect my dog against distemper?

Yes. Although inoculations are not guaranteed to be 100 per cent effective, it is certainly worth taking advantage of this help. The few inoculated dogs that do contract distemper usually have light cases and recover from the disease.

Young puppies may be given protection by injections of anti-canine distemper serum. This temporary protection lasts about two to three weeks, and should be repeated at such intervals until the puppy is old enough for his permanent inoculations. The permanent shots are given to healthy pups at about three to four months of age. There are several methods of producing this lasting immunity and your own veterinarian is the one to advise you, as he is familiar with local conditions.

What can be done for a puppy with distemper?

If given early, serum is effective. The sulfa drugs and the antibiotics, such as penicillin and aureomycin, help to overcome the secondary infections which are usually present. It is important that the puppy be kept as strong as possible with vitamins and good food. General nursing care, such as keeping the eyes and nose free from discharges and keeping the rear end clean of fecal material, is necessary for the comfort of the dog. If the puppy is eating well and you are able to follow the directions of your veterinarian, the puppy may be cared for at home. His being in familiar surroundings may help to keep his spirits up and encourage him. If he stops eating, however, and you are unable to feed him by force, hospitalization may be necessary in order that intravenous feeding can be carried out. Because of the complex nature of this disease, it is impossible to outline a treatment to apply to all cases.

Are distemper and pneumonia the same disease?

No, they are different. The usual pneumonia symptoms are loss of appetite, fever, and shallow respiration. A rasping sort of noise can usually be heard in the dog's lungs if one's ear is held against his ribs. Prompt treatment by a veterinarian is indicated.

What after-effects are liable to occur in a dog that has had a severe case of distemper?

Pneumonia sometimes follows distemper, so does the inflammation of the brain known as encephalitis. Convulsions are a fairly frequent aftermath. Chorea is quite common. Loss of sight in one or both eyes, destruction of the scenting powers, and impaired hearing are other possible results.

Is it possible for a dog to catch distemper in the summer?

A dog can come down with distemper at any time, though the disease is usually more prevalent during winter months.

Other Serious Ailments

Is there any disease besides distemper against which dogs should be inoculated?

Yes, infectious hepatitis, a serious virus that attacks dogs of all ages but mostly kills young dogs and puppies. Serum and vaccine are available to give protection against both distemper and infectious hepatitis. This is so deadly a disease, it is important that puppies be immunized against it as well as against distemper.

Can a human being catch hepatitis from a dog suffering from it?

No. The virus that causes this dog disease does not affect humans but is highly contagious to other dogs. Dogs that have had hepatitis and gotten over it often carry the disease and shed the virus in their urine for long periods after their recovery.

Would I know something was wrong with my dog if he had infectious hepatitis?

Yes. The disease usually strikes suddenly. Its symptoms are loss of appetite, great thirst, vomiting, diarrhea and fever. Often an afflicted dog will grunt or groan with pain. Immediate medical attention is essential as this disease progresses with such speed that it has been known to kill in a matter of hours. In past years this malady was often mistakenly diagnosed as distemper. Now it is recognized as a separate and distinct disease.

What is hardpad disease?

There is a good deal of argument among veterinarians as to whether this ailment is a variation of distemper or a separate disease. Whichever it is, hardpad is a debilitating and frequently fatal illness. Its symptoms are a high fever (around 104° F.), poor appetite and moderate discharge from the eyes and nose. As the disease runs its course the pads of the dog's feet harden and will eventually peel. The chances of recovery from this ailment are poor unless prompt and efficient veterinary treatment is secured.

Dental Problems

An abscess appeared on our dog's face below his eye. It almost healed then opened and drained again. What causes this?

A diseased upper molar is the commonest cause of this condition. Removal of the infected tooth is usually necessary.

A few days ago we noticed that our young Collie has cut all of his second teeth but still has his baby upper canine teeth alongside the new ones. Should anything be done about this?

The long roots of the baby canine teeth have not been reabsorbed, so they will not loosen and fall out. They should be removed by a veterinarian. Don't try doing this job yourself, as the tooth may shatter and fragments will be left in the jaw.

Is it true that bones are bad for dogs because they cause wearing down of the teeth?

A weekly rib bone, knuckle or marrow bone is beneficial to a dog's teeth, as it helps to keep them free of tartar. Too many bones can cause constipation, but fed in moderation are a great source of enjoyment and act as a natural toothbrush.

Is dentistry, such as the filling of cavities or the straightening of crooked teeth, ever practiced on dogs?

Canine dentistry is not unknown, but the practice is not common. In a few instances pits in the enamel caused by fever diseases have been filled, or attempts have been made to align crooked teeth if the dog was an especially promising show specimen. Dental cavities are quite rare in dogs and usually only occur in teeth with damaged enamel, or those from which the gums have receded because of heavy accumulation of tartar. Teeth with pitted enamel usually last as long as those which are unblemished, if they are kept clean. The straightening of irregular teeth is too expensive and tedious an affair to be practical for the average household pet.

Does a dog's diet have much effect on his teeth?

Adequate calcium, phosphorus and vitamin D are necessary for the development of strong, well-formed teeth. Malformed or structurally faulty teeth usually result from dietary inadequacies.

My Coonhound puppy's milk teeth are quite loose but refuse to fall out. Shall I try to pull them?

If the teeth are so loose that you can take them out with your fingers, go ahead. If you feel squeamish about doing this, give the puppy a large rib bone to chew. The process of gnawing will often cause the loose milk teeth to drop out.

What is wrong with a dog that drools a great deal?

If the dog drools when he watches his dinner being prepared, or when he sees a tidbit he knows is for him, it means nothing except that the anticipation of food is causing heavy salivation. Continual drooling at other times may indicate that the dog has a fragment of bone, a stick, a pin or other foreign body stuck between his teeth.

Nursing the Sick Dog

How do I give medicine to my dog?

Small and medium-sized dogs are best treated on a table. Large dogs should be seated in a corner so they are unable to back away.

The easiest way to give pills or capsules is to open the dog's mouth and push the pill as far as possible down his throat, then hold his mouth closed until he swallows. This method is the only one to be used with certain worm capsules which contain fluids that will burn the mouth and throat if the capsule is punctured.

Some dogs can be fooled into taking pills if the medicine is concealed in chopped meat, liverwurst, or soft candy. In this case, it is not necessary to put the dog on a table or in a corner.

Some tablets can be broken into small pieces and put into honey, chocolate, maple, or Karo syrup, and administered as liquids. Others, with little or no taste, may be dissolved in water and administered.

When giving liquid medicines, never open the dog's mouth. Pull out the corner of his lip on one side and, tilting his head upward, place the liquid in the pocket formed between the lips and the teeth. A small bottle, test tube or vial is easier to handle than a spoon. Give small amounts at a time, allowing him to swallow comfortably. If the dog holds the medicine in his mouth, refusing to swallow, keep his head tilted up with one hand and tickle his throat with the fingers of the other to make him gulp.

GIVING YOUR DOG
LIQUID MEDICINE

To give your dog liquid medicine, pull out the corner of his lip on one side, making a pocket between the lips and the teeth. Tilting his head upward, pour the liquid into the pocket. Hold his head in this position until the medicine has trickled between his teeth and been swallowed.

How can a sick dog that has lost his appetite be tempted to eat?

It is vitally important that an ailing dog not become weakened through lack of nourishment, so almost any means must be resorted to in order to tempt his appetite. Try any type of food at all. Some sick dogs will like sweets such as malted-milk tablets or ice cream. Others will like liverwurst. Sometimes it is necessary to go as far astray from regulation dog diets as to offer him cooked shrimp, boiled custard, cream of mushroom soup, arrowroot pudding, French toast. In other words, try anything that you think he might find enticing. Many dogs will become interested in something you are eating.

Try feeding him in a different place from where he usually has his meals. Sometimes he will eat from your fingers. Offering a small portion at a time seems to increase the dog's interest in food. Occasionally an ailing dog can be induced to eat if he is hand-fed and the owner persuades him by a little "sweet talk."

If necessary, a dog can be kept alive by forced feedings. The food must be of a mushy consistency and put in the dog's mouth spoonful by spoonful and the dog made to swallow. This is an untidy and tedious procedure but it has saved many a dog's life. It will help if the dog has a towel or bib around his neck and the person doing the feeding wears an apron to protect clothing.

I have heard it said that it is helpful if a certain amount of "canine psychology" is employed in nursing a sick dog. What is meant by that?

Dogs that are critically ill sometimes become so low in the mind that they apparently give themselves up in despair, making no attempt to fight their illness. When a dog gets into this state of mind, petting and encouragement seem almost more important than medication. The owner who has an understanding of canine mentality can often lift his dog out of the dumps by talking to him and fondling him.

We once saw an impressive demonstration of this mental therapy. It was on a circuit of Southern shows, where a certain champion had had a spectacular winning streak. The dog was entered but absent at the fifth show of the series, and the story went around that he had contracted a serious ailment and was in poor, if not hopeless, condition. The day following the show we saw the sick dog and his handler in a small city park. The handler was walking the dog slowly along a sun-dappled path, stopping occasionally to pet him and croon to him in a coaxing tone.

"It was around the show yesterday that your dog was all but dead, and here he is up and walking around. What happened?"

"He's sick, real sick," the handler answered, "but I'm trying to keep him from finding it out."

It worked, too. The dog made a quick recovery, regained the weight he had lost while ailing, and was being shown and winning again in a month.

This is not to be taken to mean that you can talk your dog back into health if he is stricken with a virulent disease. Competent veterinary advice, proper medication, and careful nursing are extremely important. But when you consider how much his owner's presence can mean to a dog in the best of health, it is not surprising that the constant, affectionate attention of someone he loves is often a potent factor in the recovery of a sick dog.

How can a dog be prevented from scratching at a sore ear?

There are two methods. The first consists of making a cone-shaped arrangement of heavy cardboard or a sheet of stiff, light-weight plastic material. The cone is made deep enough to reach from behind the dog's ears to about an inch past the tip of his nose. The narrow end should fit around his neck (not too tightly) and can be laced to his collar. The seam of the cone may be closed with double thicknesses of Scotch tape or laced with heavy string, passed through holes punched in the edges. The second method is to cover the dogs paws with pads of cotton bound on with adhesive tape. Needless to say, the mittens made in this manner become filthy in no time at all but are an effective means of preventing self-injury by scratching.

Do you think it possible for a dog to be a hypochondriac?

It is rather doubtful that dogs are able to conjure up imaginary ailments, but many of them are capable of faking pain if they know their owners will make a great fuss over them. We know of a young Collie whose right foreleg was broken in an accident. Long after the break was completely healed, he would hold the leg off the ground and limp pitifully when in the presence of his owners, because it was a sure means of being kissed and petted. If the dog thought no one was watching he would gallop freely on all fours without a sign of pain. His owners put an end to the masquerade by attaching an elaborate bandage to the *left* foreleg. The pup, confounded by this device, carefully held the left front foot off the ground for a day or so and then gave up the whole business. Such behavior may not be true hypochondria, but it is certainly the next thing to it.

Stomach Upsets and Intestinal Troubles

What is wrong with a dog that begins to vomit and keeps it up, is very thirsty, but vomits the water soon after he drinks it? What should be done?

Take away his water bowl. Give him water a few spoonfuls at a time. Give him milk of bismuth or bismuth tablets in doses of from one teaspoonful to one tablespoonful, depending on his size, and repeat the dose every hour for several doses. If the dog vomits the bismuth, he should be taken to the veterinarian without delay. It may be necessary to treat him by injections if his stomach refuses to retain medicine, as persistent vomiting soon makes a dog dehydrated and weak.

Occasionally our dog will eat his dinner and then in a little while will vomit it. He doesn't seem to be sick when this happens, but the disgusting part of it is that he usually begins to eat what he has vomited before we can get it cleaned up. Why does he do this?

This habit of dogs is revolting to most people. When a dog does this he may have overeaten, or eaten too rapidly, or he may wish to empty his stomach for some other reason. It is not anything to be alarmed about unless it is repeated at each meal. In that case, further examination should be made, especially for foreign bodies in the stomach or for an obstruction in the digestive tract.

Our dog goes out in the yard and eats grass. Afterwards, he often vomits. Can you explain why he eats grass?

Some dogs eat grass because they appear to like it. Many dogs eat it when they want to empty their stomachs for some reason. It may be a sign of indigestion, and if the dog seems to vomit more than occasionally, he should be examined by a veterinarian to determine the cause.

What is wrong with a dog that vomits yellow foam or froth? Our dog does this sometimes, always in the morning.

This may happen to dogs that are fed once a day, getting their meal in the late afternoon or evening. It usually indicates that the dog is hungry and empty. Try feeding a few dog biscuits or a couple of pieces of toast in the morning. It may also be produced by intestinal parasites, so the dog's stool should be examined microscopically for worm eggs.

What is enteritis and how is it caused?

Enteritis is inflammation of the bowels. When the stomach and intestinal tract are involved the condition is known as gastroenteritis. Inflammation of this sort is not a disease in itself but is a *symptom* of the presence of some other trouble. The causes may be any of several: a foreign body in the alimentary canal, distemper, severe worm infestation, coccidiosis, poisoning, toxemia, telescoping of the bowel.

What causes diarrhea in dogs?

Simple causes, such as excitement or an abrupt change of diet, should be recognized by the owner. An unaccustomed meal of liver or kidneys can have a laxative effect. Dry food bought in large quantities may become infested with feed mites in warm weather. In small numbers, these mites do not appear to cause trouble, but cases of diarrhea have been traced to such feed.

Worms could be eliminated as a possible cause of diarrhea by having an examination of the stool made by a veterinarian.

The presence of a foreign body in the intestines may be the cause. Persistent diarrhea in an older dog is often associated with kidney trouble or with tumorous growths in the intestinal tract. In a younger dog, diarrhea may be a symptom of the infectious diseases, especially distemper.

Straining, with the passage of frequent small stools, may accompany both prostate trouble and stones in the urinary tract of the male dog. Difficulty with the voiding of urine is also present.

Why does my dog have a bowel movement only every second or third day? The stool is very hard and it seems to be difficult for him to pass it.

Too many bones will produce a very hard dry stool which crumbles when touched. If the dog is having trouble with such stools, reduce or eliminate the bones in his diet. Mineral oil added to his food will help to make the passage of such a stool easier. If the dog is in great distress, a few ounces of mineral oil may be injected into the rectum using a rubber ear or ulcer syringe.

The number of stools and the size of the stool can be increased by feeding additional bulk in the form of mashed vegetables, or one of the cereals, biscuits or canned foods made especially for dogs.

What is false constipation?

This is interference with the passage of the stool produced by a mat of hair and stool plastered across the opening of the rectum. Treatment for this condition is to clip away the hair which is holding the mass, and bathe the soiled area. If the tissues are sore, apply petroleum jelly.

Fits and Their Causes

My five-month-old puppy had a fit today. What caused it?

The cause may be one of many. In a puppy of this age, the cutting of the permanent teeth may be the exciting cause. A deficiency of calcium may have developed. Young dogs are nitwits about what they eat. Sand, dirt, wood or other foreign matter will cause digestive pain which may produce a fit. A heavy infestation of worms will also cause them. Puppies suffering from vitamin deficiencies, either because of faulty feeding or from parasitism, are subject to fits. Those of a nervous temperament may have hysterical fits from overexcitement, particularly on a hot day. This is the type of fit seen in the crowded park on a summer Sunday after the puppy has been romping with a group of excited children. Fits are often part of the distemper picture. A puppy which has had a fit should be examined as soon as possible.

What should the owner do when his dog has a fit?

Try to be calm, though this is not easy advice to follow, as most owners are so horrified when their dogs have fits that they all but have one themselves. Cover the dog with a blanket or coat to prevent his injuring himself and you. If possible, get him into a dark quiet place. If he is having the type of fit in which he is running about banging into things and trying to climb the walls, and is too strong for you to hold him down, leave him alone until it is over. When the fit has passed he may appear normal, very tired or still nervous. If he is nervous, a sedative may be given before taking him to be examined.

The Why and Wherefore of Worms

How can I tell if my dog has worms?

Unless the dog has vomited worms, as sometimes happens in the case of roundworms, or has passed worms--roundworms or segments of tapeworm—a microscopic examination of the stool is the only way to determine the presence of worms and the type present.

A teaspoonful or two of the dog's stool, well-formed if possible, should be taken or mailed to your veterinarian. It should be placed in a small jar with a tight cap. An empty mustard jar or an old cleansing cream jar are good containers for this purpose. The specimen does not have to be rushed to the veterinarian in a matter of hours. If you live in a rural area and are far away from professional help, write to the American Veterinary Medical Association, 600 So. Michigan Avenue, Chicago, Illinois, and ask for the name and address of the nearest veterinarian who would make an examination for you. Write him the full particulars of your case, being sure to mention your dog's age and weight, and make arrangements with him to send a specimen for testing.

How do dogs get worms?

Except for tapeworms, puppies can get worms directly from their mothers, or from bedding or yards soiled by a dog with worms. Dirt yards are difficult to keep worm-free. Stools must not be allowed to remain on the ground for any time at all. A thorough soaking of the dirt with a saturated salt solution will help destroy the worms and worm eggs in the soil. The brine solution should be used hot, and the proportions should be about three pounds of salt to two gallons of water. The tapeworm is carried by the flea or louse as the intermediate host. Another type is carried in cyst form in wild rabbits, birds, and fish.

Can I worm my dog at home?

Yes, if you are able to follow accurately directions given by the veterinarian who prescribed medicine after making a diagnosis.

Will feeding a dog plenty of onions or garlic keep him free of worms?

This belief is as much of a fallacy as the idea that milk makes worms, or potatoes will cause skin trouble. It's just not so.

Why did my neighbor's dog die after she wormed him? The medicine she used was from a reputable pharmacy, and it contained the same drugs as the remedy the veterinarian prescribed last year for her other dog.

Many dogs die following unsupervised home worming treatments because they were not suffering from worms alone. Worm medicine is toxic; therefore, it is always advisable to have it prescribed by a veterinarian who has examined the dog for other possible complications as well as worms.

What are the different kinds of worms that dogs get, and what do they look like?

Roundworms are the commonest, and they are found most often in puppies. They are white, firm-bodied worms from two inches to eight or ten inches long. They may be vomited or passed with the stool, and they tend to curl. Pups with roundworms usually have distended, bloated-looking abdomens, especially after eating. Their eyes may be dull and watery, and they often have a cough.

Tapeworms are the other worms which are visible to the naked eye. The segments are found either clinging to the stool or on the hair around the rectum or in the dog's bed. When fresh they are flat and fleshy, one-half to three-quarters of an inch long, pinkish in color, and have a stretching motion. When dead and dry, they are smaller, tan in color, and look like grains of rice. Segments are most often found in the late fall or early winter, after the flea season has passed. These small pieces may appear in great numbers every few days or as an occasional segment at greater intervals, depending upon how many individual worms have their heads buried in the wall of the intestine. These heads stay fixed, producing a chain of segments. As the segment at the far end of the chain is mature, it breaks away and passes with a stool or independently. A fecal examination will not expose the tapeworm unless a segment happens to be with the specimen. The passing of a segment often causes a dog to suddenly leap up and inspect or bite at his rear. A dog harboring tapeworms may have a ravenous appetite but will remain thin and have a dull, lifeless coat.

Hookworms are not visible in the stool without a microscope. They are small, about one-half inch in length. They burrow into the intestinal lining and live on the blood of the dog. They produce anemia, emaciation, and diarrhea, often bloody. The whipworm also remains in the intestinal tract, preferring the blind pocket known as the caecum. A small worm, shaped like a buggy whip, it produces intestinal disturbances such as gas formation, bloating, and intermittent diarrhea and vomiting. The location of the caecum makes the removal of whipworms difficult, and several methods of worming may be tried by your veterinarian if he feels they are causing difficulty. Removal of the caecum by surgery has been resorted to in order to get rid of these parasites.

A worm, several inches long, living in the dog's heart, its blood vessels, and the large vessels of the lungs, is the filaria or heartworm. The young are found in the blood stream, and diagnosis is made by examining a blood sample to determine the presence of these microfilaria. They are transmitted by the bite of mosquitoes and ticks, especially in the warmer climates. They are, however, found as far north as the New York City area. Because of their interference with the circulation, they produce coughing, weakness, and swelling of the legs and feet. Treatment for filaria is usually by injections.

Are there other parasites besides worms which may cause trouble in the intestinal tract?

Coccidia, which are microscopic, may invade the wall of the intestine. They produce diarrhea, and if the dog—especially a puppy—is infested by contact with the loose, parasite-laden stool, he is soon a thin, sad-looking specimen with a persistent case of diarrhea. Even fits may result. This parasite is a problem in puppies obtained from sources where they have been confined in crowded, unsanitary conditions, such as exist in most pet shops.

My dog scoots himself along the floor on his haunches. Does this mean he has tapeworm?

It might, but more often it is caused by overfilled or infected anal glands. These scent glands, located on each side of the anus, may be emptied into a handful of cotton by gentle pressure of the thumb on one side and the forefinger on the opposite side. The normal secretion is brown. If pus or blood is obtained, the glands require treatment by a veterinarian. Abscess formation of the glands is common if they are neglected.

Various and Sundry Ailments

I have heard that dogs get a disease called "blacktongue." What can be done to avoid it?

As long as your dog is getting a well-balanced vitamin-supplemented diet you need not worry much about his contracting this ailment. It is caused by lack of niacin, found in vitamin B complex. The name of the disease is derived from the fact that the tongue of a dog with this ailment turns black after death.

Is there a disease which dogs can get from rats?

The disease is called leptospirosis. It is caused by a spirochete carried by rats. Dogs can contract the disease by eating garbage or bones soiled by rat urine, or by killing and eating rats. The disease manifests itself in two forms and only an experienced veterinarian is able to make an accurate diagnosis. The dog owner whose pet has contracted either form of the ailment will soon realize that his dog is in serious trouble. The common symptoms are loss of appetite, intermittent fever, vomiting, rapid loss of weight and a craving to drink enormous quantities of water. Massive doses of penicillin will usually arrest the disease if given

soon enough. Death may occur within eight or ten days if treatment is delayed.

*When we are at our fishing camp, our Pointer often hangs
around when I am cleaning fish and eats the leavings. We
are afraid we shouldn't let him do this because we have
read that dogs get a terrible sickness from eating raw fish.
What is the disease and how do dogs get it from fish?*

Almost all fish found in fresh water on the west coast of this
country and Canada are carriers of a minute fluke (a parasitic
trematode worm). If a dog finds and eats a dead fish, or gets hold
of fish entrails, he is liable to become infected with a highly fatal
disease caused by the fluke. It is commonly known as salmon
poisoning. The symptoms are similar to those of distemper—
high fever, running eyes, no appetite, great thirst, bloody diarrhea.
It is reported that immediate treatment with sulfa drugs has
proved effective against the ailment. Untreated cases usually die
in eight or ten days. The danger of the disease can be avoided by
never allowing your dog to have any fish unless it has been
thoroughly cooked, as the flukes are destroyed by heat.

Do dogs ever have cancer?

Yes, and in many different forms. If a dog develops a suspicious
lump or swelling, a biopsy can be performed, and an examination made by a pathologist will determine whether or not the
growth is malignant. It is entirely possible, if the condition is discovered and treated in time, that the dog may recover and enjoy
good health for many years afterward.

*Our Beagle has a slightly raised bulge on the inside of one
ear flap. It seems to hurt her when we touch it. What should
be done about it?*

The condition you describe is known as hematoma (or haema-
toma). It is fairly common in long-eared dogs whose ear flaps
are easily bruised, causing bleeding between the layers of skin
and cartilage. Don't ignore this condition and don't attempt to

treat it yourself. If neglected or improperly treated, the result will be a disfiguring, thickened, puckered-up condition, something like a "cauliflower" ear. It requires professional skill to drain off the imprisoned fluids and to keep the ear dressed until the skin and the cartilage have united smoothly.

Can a dog catch a cold from his owner?

Many veterinarians believe that certain respiratory ailments can be transmitted to dogs by human beings. It is a generally sound idea to be careful always not to cough or sneeze in your dog's face and to keep him away from your own face if you are suffering from the sniffles.

What is wrong with a dog that staggers when he walks?

Staggering is usually a symptom of the brain or spinal cord being damaged or diseased. It is often seen as an aftermath of acute virus ailments. Injuries (such as being hit by an automobile), some poisons and certain narcotics can also cause a dog to have a weaving or unsteady gait.

Rickets in Dogs

How can rickets be recognized?

Rickets may first appear in a pup of about two months. The puppy often shows lameness, first in one leg and then in another. He may cry out and be reluctant to walk. The toes of the feet often spread and appear to flatten, or the pup will walk on the underside of his wrists (pasterns) instead of the pads of his forefeet. He may go down on his hind legs so that his hocks are touching the floor. The back is arched and he is potbellied. In some pups the forelegs are bowed and the hind legs cow-hocked. A row of beadlike enlargements may be felt along the ribs.

What is the treatment for rickets?

Prevention is most important. Proper feeding of meat, eggs, and milk is necessary. The puppy which is not a good milk-drinker should get calcium, phosphorous, and vitamin A and D supplements early. All pups should have cod-liver oil and plenty of sunshine. Treatment consists of increased doses of the above minerals and vitamins, and is effective only in the early stages.

Confinement in a small cage or pen at the time of growth will contribute to poor feet and legs. However, overexercise of a puppy with rickets is dangerous because of the ease with which his bones will fracture.

Accidents and Emergencies

What is the best way to handle a dog hit by a car?

If the dog is unable to get up, or won't try to, ease him onto a blanket, a small rug or other improvised stretcher. Do everything possible to avoid changing the position in which he is lying and jiggle him as little as possible. Then rush him to the veterinarian. If you can, have someone telephone the veterinarian to let him know you are on your way with an emergency case.

How should burns be treated?

If the burns are not extensive or serious, apply tannic acid ointment or Unguentine. In case neither of these remedies is on hand, make a pot of very strong tea, cool it, and apply it liberally. A quick cooling method for the tea is to pour it in a bowl or pan which is placed in a larger container filled with cracked ice.

What can be done for a dog bitten by a snake?

Because such accidents usually occur in areas where professional help is remote, the owner should lose no time in taking what measure he can to cope with the crisis. Using a sharp knife, or a razor blade, several cuts should be made through the bite wound. The wound must be pressed to bleed freely, or sucked, if the person treating the dog has no open cuts or sores in his mouth. After the pressing or sucking, whatever antiseptic may be available should be used to wash the wound thoroughly.

Always carry a dog that has been bitten by a snake. If he walks it will speed the circulation of poison through his system. In most poisonous snake areas, veterinarians and physicians have on hand a supply of serum for use as an antivenom for the snakes found in their locality. Try to obtain the services of someone who can administer this serum, as it is the only sure antidote for the venom of poisonous snakes.

I managed to release a large farm dog caught in an animal trap, but was badly bitten in the process. Is there any safe way to handle a dog in such a predicament?

Even the gentlest of dogs often bite when held in a trap, as they are frantic with pain and fright. Should you encounter a situation of this sort, if possible muzzle the dog before attempting to free him. If you have nothing with which to make a muzzle, a forked stick or the tines of a pitchfork placed over his neck at the back of his head will pin his head to the ground and prevent his biting the person trying to help him.

Directions for handling dogs often mention using an emergency muzzle. How is this done?

A length of gauze bandage, heavy cloth tape or a strip of strong fabric are the easiest to use. A loop is made by making the first hitch of a knot. This loop is slipped over the dog's nose, well back of the soft nostril portion, with the knot on top of the nose. The ends are drawn down under the jaws and crossed again, then brought back and tied in a firm bowknot at the back of the dog's head, passing behind the base of the ears.

What do I do if my dog eats something tainted or poisonous?

Induce vomiting by placing a teaspoonful or more of salt on the back of the dog's tongue. If this fails to produce vomiting, mix water and peroxide half-and-half and force it down. When the vomiting has stopped, egg white may be given. *Immediate* action is vitally important when a dog has poison in his stomach. Even a very few minutes can make the difference between life and death under such circumstances.

How are cuts or wounds from fights usually treated?

If the dog is in pain, he should be muzzled before his wounds are examined. Then trim away the hair from the edges of the cuts, clean them with peroxide and apply tincture of iodine or tincture of metaphen. If the wound is bleeding profusely, use a large pad of gauze and cotton as a bandage, applying as much pressure as possible against the wound. For deep bleeding gashes on the legs, a tourniquet may be used, but remember the danger of leaving it on too long. It should be released every few minutes. Wounds that are hemorrhaging should be treated by a veterinarian, as they usually require suturing.

If a dog is accidentally given an overdose of sedatives, what antidote should be used?

If detected immediately, induce vomiting. If some time has elapsed, but the dog is still conscious, give him strong coffee, about four or five tablespoonfuls for a twenty-pound dog. For larger dogs, give one ounce for every ten pounds of body weight. Should the dog be found in a deep sleep, professional help should be obtained in a hurry.

Is it true that a dog can heal wounds and cuts by licking them?

Because the surface of his tongue is rough, a dog can, to some extent, clean cuts and wounds of dirt and dead flesh. Deep bleeding wounds, puncture wounds, and those which the dog cannot reach with his tongue, should be treated, either by the owner or a veterinarian, depending on the severity of the wound.

Can artificial respiration be employed to revive a dog that is suffering from immersion?

Dogs that have almost drowned have been saved when taken out of the water before their hearts stopped beating. To give artificial respiration to a dog, put him on his side and apply pressure to his ribs with your flattened hand. Release the pressure quickly. Keep repeating the pressure and release at two or three second intervals and *keep it up* as long as there is any discernible heartbeat.

Our Setter pup gnawed through an electric cord and was knocked out. Is there any approved treatment for an accident of this kind?

Be careful when handling a dog that has had an electric shock. Sometimes the charge of the electricity will cause him to clamp his jaws on the wire and he is unable to let it go. If possible, disconnect the wire, or, if this cannot be done, yank the wire out of his mouth, protecting your hand with a thick potholder or several folds of heavy cloth. If the dog is unconscious, use artificial respiration and massage. Get him to a veterinarian with all speed for the administration of stimulants.

Is there any way to tell if an injured dog is bleeding internally?

Usually when a dog is losing blood rapidly, his gums will appear bleached, looking gray or whitish. Medical attention must be secured immediately if a dog in this condition is to be saved.

How long should it take for the bone to unite when a dog has suffered a fracture?

In cases where a simple fracture has been properly set within the least possible time after the break has occurred, the bone will knit in about twenty days if the patient is a puppy or still quite young. The bones of older dogs seem to require a little more time to heal, usually twenty-five to thirty days.

What should be done for a dog that has been stung by a bee or hornet?

If it is obtainable, wrap a cube of laundry bluing in a small piece of cloth, dip it in cold water and apply it to the swelling. Watch that the liquid doesn't run into the dog's mouth or get in his eyes. If nothing else is at hand, make a small mud pie and plaster it on the sting. Dogs that have been severely stung often go into shock and will require treatment by a veterinarian.

The Facts About Rabies

What can be done for a dog bitten by a rabid dog?

If the bite is not too near the brain, the dog can be saved by the series of injections known as the Pasteur treatment. The injections must be started as soon as possible after the dog has been bitten. Most dogs attacked by an animal known to be rabid are destroyed, as few people will take the risk of exposing themselves to a dog that may be infected with such a dreaded disease.

What should a dog owner do if he thinks his pet may have been bitten by a dog which is rabid?

The dog should be confined in a place where he can have no contact with either people or other animals. Then call your veterinarian who will tell you what further steps are necessary, for in some communities a case of this sort is handled by the health authorities.

How do dogs get rabies?

This disease is caused by a virus which is carried in the saliva and is usually transmitted by a bite. The virus may also enter the body through cuts or scratches which have come in contact with saliva containing the virus. The virus travels along the nerves to the brain and causes death. Rabies does not affect dogs and human beings only, for farm animals are subject to it too, often contracting it from the bite of a rabid fox or other wild animal. The dog that runs at large is in much more danger of being bitten by a rabid animal than is the dog under careful control at all times.

Is rabies fatal?

Always.

Do all animals which are bitten by another animal which is rabid develop rabies?

No. Investigation has shown that not all animals bitten by dogs which were proved to have rabies, develop the disease.

How long does it take for rabies to develop after the bite that caused it?

The incubation period may be a matter of several days or it may be as long as six months. The length of time varies with the location of the bite. The closer the bite is to the brain, the more rapidly the symptoms will develop.

How does a dog with rabies behave?

The disease assumes one of two forms. In the "dumb" or paralytic form, the dog is mentally depressed. The lower jaw droops, the dog drools, and he doesn't bark. The paralysis spreads and death follows in about a week. In the furious form, the dog bites at any passing object or animal. There is a tendency for the dog to roam, biting as he goes, and this accounts for the spread of the disease. The biting stage may be preceded by a change in personality, the shy dog becoming friendly, or the friendly one becoming standoffish. There is also a change in voice that is well-known to those familiar with the disease. In the late stages of rabies, the dog is unable to eat or drink. Paralysis and then death follow in about a week to ten days from the time the biting stage was reached.

How can dogs be protected against rabies?

Rabies inoculations are available, and, as in the case of other inoculations, while not 100 per cent effective, they offer protection against this fatal disease. In the city, where the dog is confined to a leash by law, the danger of his being bitten by a rabid dog is very slight. In the country, where the dog roams at will, chasing wild game or running with strange dogs, the danger of his receiving an unnoticed bite is great.

Certain states and countries have strict laws covering rabies inoculation, and unless your dog complies with these laws he will not be permitted entry. To avoid trouble in traveling abroad, check first with the consulate or information service of the countries you plan to visit.

The Railway Express Company has compiled a list of the various state laws regarding the interstate shipment of animals. A call to them before shipping your dog will get the answer as to the requirements of the state in which you are interested. If you are motoring through several states with your dog, it may avoid a lot of trouble if you are able to show a rabies inoculation certificate and a health certificate issued by your veterinarian just before you started the trip.

Female Difficulties

When a female dog is operated on to prevent her from ever having puppies, is it "spaying" or "spading" her?

The term is spaying. The past tense is spayed.

At what age should a bitch be spayed?

Most veterinarians prefer to perform the operation before the bitch has come in season for the first time, that is, when she is about five or six months of age. If such an operation is planned, have your veterinarian examine the pup when about four months of age and ask his advice about when to have the job done.

There is a female dog in our neighborhood that is a constant source of trouble. She seems to have some sort of a continual slight discharge and she attracts male dogs at all times as though she were in season. What's the matter with her?

She has a disturbance of her reproductive organs. It may be a hormone upset, growth, or infection. In some cases, removal of the organs by surgery is the only way to correct the condition.

We have an old spayed Retriever bitch who seems to have lost control of her bladder. She has, since the time she was a puppy, been a clean dog, but now she even wets her bed, the floor, or anywhere in the house without being able to help it. Can we do anything to correct this condition?

This trouble is not particularly uncommon. If a veterinary examination shows it is not kidney or bladder difficulty, the chances are that a hormone imbalance is the cause. Female hormones administered at proper intervals will correct the lack of control.

My Pointer bitch has never had puppies, but about two months after she is in season her breasts fill with milk, her appetite increases, and she makes "nests" all over the house. The last time this happened she was really pathetic. She made a bed in the hall closet and then adopted an old fur slipper and mothered it as tenderly as though it were her own puppy. Is there something wrong with her?

The trouble with your bitch is frustrated motherhood. The condition is known as false pregnancy. All the symptoms of normal pregnancy are displayed, including abdominal swelling and lactation. Some bitches take this so hard the only kind thing to do is to allow them to have a litter of puppies. If the swelling of the breasts does not subside normally in two or three weeks, rub them twice a day with camphorated oil until they flatten out again.

Diet and Long Life

Is correct diet the best way to prolong a dog's life?

Optimum nutrition plus periodic check-ups by a veterinarian will contribute greatly to a dog's longevity. Health examinations at six-month intervals will discover conditions which need treatment, such as worm infestation, diseased teeth, canker of the ear, and so on. Blood tests, the examination of specimens of urine and feces, enable the veterinarian to discover a number of ailments while still in the early stages and easily nipped in the bud.

About Veterinarians

Which is the correct term for a person trained in animal surgery and medicine, veterinary or veterinarian?

Both are correct. However, veterinary is more common as an adjective. For example, one speaks of the practice of veterinary medicine or veterinary surgery.

I always hesitate to leave my dog at the veterinarian's to be wormed, for fear that he may catch a serious disease from some other dog. Isn't this liable to happen?

A well-run veterinary hospital is more conscious than the average dog owner of the danger of contagion. Hospitals with small staff or limited space often refuse to take animals with contagious diseases, because it is impossible to allot a portion of the hospital personnel and a section of the building to the necessary isolation. The better hospitals equipped to care for contagious disease have a rigid routine of cleanliness and segregation.

Any dog which is to be left at an animal hospital should have had distemper immunization. If the dog is too young to have had permanent inoculation, or there is any doubt about whether or not he has been vaccinated, he can be given a shot which will provide temporary protection at the time he is left at the hospital.

Isn't a sick dog likely to be happier and better off at home with his owner than in a dog hospital?

It depends how serious the illness and how capable the owner is of following instructions and administering treatments and medication. Surgical and accident cases that require blood transfusions or intravenous feeding must be hospitalized, so must cases which demand careful observation by trained personnel, in order that diet, therapy, or medicines may be adjusted to any changes in the dog's condition. Dogs with broken bones or internal injuries are benefited by confinement and quiet environment, conditions not easily achieved in the average home.

Almost everyone has heard of or read about the American Medical Association, the organization of physicians and surgeons. Is there a similar organization for veterinarians?

Yes, it is the American Veterinary Medical Association. It is concerned with the educational standards of veterinary colleges and the ethics of practicing veterinarians. It has been estimated that there are about fifteen thousand practicing veterinarians in this country at the present time. Of this number, ten thousand are members of the A.V.M.A., which means that they are adhering to the rather rigid code of ethics of the association. It publishes a monthly journal for its members, containing scientific articles pertaining to the various branches of veterinary medicine, and a journal of research.

On the wall of the reception room of the animal hospital where we take our dog there is a framed certificate stating that the hospital is a member of the American Animal Hospital Association. Is this a branch of the A. V. M. A.?

No, it is a separate national organization composed of veterinarians who run hospitals for small animals. The members of this group have set standards which they feel are necessary for the proper management of a dog and cat hospital. These rules cover the physical equipment of the hospital, and the methods of treatment employed. Hospitals belonging to the group are inspected for adherence to the association's standards. Hospitals desiring membership must be able to meet the organization's requirements before they are permitted to join.

The Sickly Dog

About a year and a half ago we bought a Terrier pup from a pet dealer. Although he is a full-grown, fairly healthy dog now, we have had to pay about five times his original purchase price for vet bills. Dog-raising must be a terribly expensive hobby, and as far as professional kennels are concerned, I don't see how they stay in business at all. What is the explanation?

The chances are that your pet-shop puppy was infested with worms or coccidia when you bought him, perhaps had had no immunization against distemper, and may have been badly undernourished. Raising a puppy with any or all of these troubles is bound to be costly and is frequently heartbreaking, for it often happens that no sooner is he over one ailment, than something else goes wrong with him.

The intelligent breeder, whether professional or amateur, keeps his stock scrupulously free of parasites, feeds the best possible diet, supplemented by minerals and vitamins, and provides maximum immunization against contagious diseases. His experience enables him to detect the first signs of any illness in his kennel and to obtain professional advice in dealing with it at the onset. Kennels which follow these practices (and if they don't, they seldom last very long) generally have annual veterinary bills which are negligible compared to those of many pet owners having only one or two dogs.

Post-mortem Examinations

Are post-mortem examinations ever performed on bodies of dogs that have died from unknown causes?

Frequently. It is only sensible for the owner of a dog that has died of an undiagnosed ailment to permit a post-mortem examination when the veterinarian asks permission. It is not impossible that the dog may have died of an ailment which humans can contract, in which case an autopsy may prove a protection to the owner.

Sometimes the dog population of a whole town or county is endangered by a highly contagious canine disease. If the owners of the dogs that succumb will permit the bodies of their dogs to be examined, it may be that knowledge will be gained that would be useful in treating other dogs.

ELIZABETH J. COLLINS, V.M.D.

Part Two

●

HOW TO TRAIN YOUR DOG

CHAPTER *8*

Teaching Your Dog Good Habits

There was once a dog lover who went to a nearby kennel, picked out a plump, healthy, friendly, four-month-old puppy, and proudly drove home with the puppy cuddled beside him on the front seat of the car. The puppy was not carsick during the ride and upon arriving home showed himself to be perfectly house-trained. Not once did he soil a carpet or floor, he didn't let out so much as a whimper after being put to bed at night, and he never chewed a chair leg, shoe, rug, or drapery. End of fairy tale.

You can be reasonably sure that nothing like this will happen to you. Your new puppy may be violently carsick during the drive home from the kennel; he will relieve himself freely wherever he happens to be in the house; he will wail piteously during the first few nights; and he will try his teeth on anything he can get hold of, the more expensive the better. Sounds discouraging, doesn't it? Well, it's not that bad. Puppies have been behaving like this for a long time. A good many easy and effective methods have been worked out to cope with all of these problems and most of the others you are likely to encounter, too.

During the short period when a puppy may be troublesome, you will find that he will atone for his sins by being one of the most amusing, lovable, and beguiling animals on the face of the earth. The puppyish phase is brief indeed compared to the many years of devotion and companionship which your dog will give you during his maturity. You will look at him one day and suddenly realize that he's no longer a puppy—he's a half-grown young dog, and it's been days since you've mopped up a puddle!

251

Bringing Your New Puppy Home

What preparations should we make before bringing a new puppy home?

First, decide where the puppy is to sleep and fix up some sort of bed for him. He probably won't be house-trained, so a room with an easily washed floor, such as the kitchen or bathroom, is a good choice. Avoid places which are drafty or damp. The bed can be anything from a heavy corrugated cardboard carton, obtainable from your grocer, to a luxurious bedstead with a foam rubber mattress. Whatever the bed may be, it should have some sort of comfortable bedding—a cushion (preferably with a washable cover), a piece of old blanket, or a thick layer of newspapers torn into strips.

Then find out from the person who sold you the pup what his diet has been, and make sure you have the necessary supplies on hand for giving the newcomer the food to which he is accustomed. You can change his diet later on if you wish, but right at first is not the time to do it.

Next, provide yourself with a rectal thermometer, such as is used for human infants. This is so important that we wish we could print it here in large red letters. Use it at the first sign of listlessness or loss of appetite on the part of the puppy. Deviations from the normal canine temperature of 101.5° are usually the first indications of any serious ailment.

Finally, decide what you are going to call the pup and plan to use that name from the start. If he is not already registered, and it is up to you to think of a formal name for him, let that go for the time being. What you want to select now is his call name. It should be short, not more than two syllables. *Polly, Sammy, Kip, Cookie, Sister, Bing* are examples of the right sort of name. If the name chosen is used consistently, the pup will soon realize that that sound means *him* and he will have learned the first of the many lessons ahead of him.

*What is the best way to treat a puppy when he first arrives
in his new home? Should he have lots of petting and attention or should he be left on his own to look things over?*

It depends on the puppy. If he is a little timid and seems
awed by his new surroundings, petting and cuddling will reassure
him. If he is the bold type, let him do a little investigating on
his own. This does not mean he should be given the run of
the house, for at this stage his house manners won't entitle him
to much freedom.

Don't offer him food within the first few minutes of his arrival
as he will probably be too confused or excited to accept it. Give
him his first meal after he has had a chance to settle down a
bit. If there are children in the family don't let them all pounce
on the puppy at once and pull him around and maul him. Explain
that they will have to go slow and easy and be very gentle,
otherwise they may frighten the pup and he won't like or trust
them.

The Beginning of Training

What are the first things a puppy should be taught?

It is important that a puppy know his name, for in this way you
can get his attention. His learning of this will be automatic if
you use the name consistently when calling him or talking to
him. The next steps are house-training; learning to spend the
night quietly in his bed with no yowling or howling; and coming
to understand that he must not chew furniture, clothing, or anything else except his own toys and bones.

*I have just purchased a purebred Irish Setter puppy for which
I paid a good price. I want him to be a well-trained dog. At
what age should I begin this training?*

If the puppy is under four months you can paper-break him,
teach him to stay alone without howling, and train him in regular
habits. He should learn what the word "No" means when he
does wrong. If the puppy is four to ten months of age he can be
housebroken, taught not to steal and not to destroy things, and

to stay off the furniture. He may be given simple obedience training for house manners, which means to walk on the leash without pulling, to sit and lie down on command, to stay in one place when told, and he should be trained to come when called. Obedience training in the competitive sense should not be taken seriously until the dog is almost a year old.

Is discipline at too early an age liable to have a bad effect on a dog's disposition?

Yes. Many dogs have become permanently nervous or cowed because their owners have attempted intensive training when they were still very small puppies.

Why is it that puppies so often "go off their feed" when they first go to a new home?

The strangeness of a new environment is sometimes so disconcerting to a puppy that he loses his appetite, or the food may be so different from the diet to which he is accustomed that he does not like it. Most litters of puppies in a kennel are fed together, all eating from the same pan. A puppy eating alone for the first time seems to miss the competition of his brothers and sisters and frequently, even though he is perfectly healthy, will pick at his food or refuse it. This phase is usually a fleeting one and nothing to cause worry on the part of the owner.

How long should it take for a puppy to become acquainted in a new home and not act frightened of his strange surroundings?

The friendly, not-a-nerve-in-his-body type of puppy will make himself at home the moment he enters his owner's house, but with the reserved, retiring pup it may take ten days or two weeks for his better qualities to assert themselves. One should give a puppy at least two weeks to a month before passing judgment on his disposition. The younger the puppy the more quickly he will forget the past, but it should be remembered also that the younger he is the more attention he will require and the more difficult it will be to train him.

Collar and Leash

Should my three-month-old puppy wear a collar?

It will be much easier to teach your puppy to walk nicely when on a leash if he is first accustomed to the feel of a collar on his neck. Use a plain, narrow leather collar while your pup is little. If you want to start him in obedience training when he is older, about nine or ten months of age, then get a chain-slip collar.

My new puppy is ten weeks old and, until I got him, never had a collar and leash on. When I try to take him for a walk, he lies down and won't budge. How can I cure him from being so balky?

The puppy is not really balky. He is probably a little afraid of the collar and leash, and doesn't understand what it is all about. First, get him accustomed to wearing a collar. Then, holding the end of the leash, play with him and coax him to come to you. If he tries to go in the opposite direction, go with him until he finds he has nothing to fear from the leash.

What should I get for my Boston Terrier pup, a collar or a harness?

Get a plain, flat narrow leather collar. With a harness it is impossible to teach a dog to walk on a leash properly. A harness encourages pulling and tugging and many of them are put together with rivets which scratch the skin and cause sores.

The Basic Rules of Dog Education

Is it advisable to have one's dog trained by a professional?

When a person does not have time to train his dog, a professional trainer should do the actual training, and the lessons can be continued by the owner, after he has learned how to handle a trained dog. If bad habits are to be broken, the advice of a professional may be necessary. The average person does not have the knowledge of how to overcome bad traits, but for all-around obedience it is better for the owner to train, because the dog will have more respect for him.

Are there any general fundamentals of dog training that a person should know in order to raise a dog to be a well-behaved pet?

There are, and they are quite simple:

1. Discipline must be consistent. *Example:* If you want your dog to keep off the furniture you must make him stay out of that comfortable wing chair he likes so much, *all* the time. If you chase him out of it one day and allow him to take his morning nap in it the next, you won't get anywhere with him.

2. Correction must always be simultaneous with offense. It is useless and unjust to punish a dog today for what he did yesterday afternoon or even an hour ago.

3. Always, if it is humanly possible, prevent your dog from making a mistake in the first place. The answer to this is *watchfulness* while he is young and has no idea of what is right and wrong. If you can stop him before he ever starts any wrongdoing you'll be away ahead of the game.

4. Be patient. Teach your dog one thing at a time. A dog's education should be a step by step process. Don't let your children or anyone else in the family bedevil an unhousebroken puppy by trying to teach him tricks.

5. Be fair. Be sure your dog understands what you want him to do. Remember, your dog is anxious to please you and, if he misbehaves, it may be that he simply hasn't gotten the idea you're trying to put across to him.

6. Severity of corrections must be tempered in accordance with the individual dog's disposition. Don't risk cowing a sensitive puppy by being overfirm with him.

7. Don't expect too much of a dog while he is still very young. Postpone teaching serious obedience work or difficult tricks until he is about one year of age.

8. Be gentle. Don't lose your temper. Successful dog trainers don't shriek, stamp their feet, and wave their arms. A human being who has lost control of his temper is a frightening spectacle, and if you let your exasperation get the better of you in handling your dog he will become afraid of you.

9. Remember that a dog learns by the association of pleasant or unpleasant results in connection with various acts. *Example:* He will learn that it's a poor idea to bark whenever the doorbell rings because every time he does it he gets a scolding or a whack on the backside or, conversely, he finds out that if he sits up when so commanded he will be rewarded with a luscious tidbit of dog candy.

10. Always use the same words of command and always use his name first in order to get the dog's attention. *Example:* If you want him to sit, say, "Sandy, *sit!*"

11. Never tease your dog, play tricks on him just for your own amusement, or humiliate him by laughing at him if he is frightened or bewildered. He will lose confidence in you.

12. Keep in mind that the most important qualifications for training a dog are kindness, persistence, consistency, and above all patience and patience and patience.

Basic Training Commands

What words should be used for the various commands?

You can make up your own vocabulary of dog language. Here are some of the words used most often. The shorter a command, the more effective it is.

> To call the dog to you: "Rowdy, come!" or "Rowdy, come here!"
> To make the dog sit down: "Rowdy, sit!"
> To make the dog lie down: "Rowdy, down!"
> To make him stay put: "Rowdy, stay!" or "Rowdy, hold it!"

To show disapproval: "Bad, Rowdy!" or "Phooey on Rowdy!"

To speed him in carrying out an order: "Hurry, Rowdy!" or "Quick, Rowdy!"

To order him to jump: "Rowdy, hup!" "Rowdy, jump!" or "Rowdy, over!"

To order the dog to retrieve: "Rowdy, fetch!" "Rowdy, get it!" or "Rowdy, take it!"

To silence him: "Hush, Rowdy!" or "Quiet, Rowdy!"

To show approval: "Good boy, Rowdy!" or "Smart fella, Rowdy!"

To make him desist from bad behavior: "Rowdy, *No!*" or "Rowdy, stop that!"

To make the dog give you an object retrieved: "Rowdy, out!" or "Rowdy, drop it!"

The list could be much longer but you will probably, as most trainers do, compose your own special terms for the various commands. The main thing is to be sure no two commands sound too similar. Be sure to always phrase the command in exactly the same way. Do not say "Rowdy, come" then "Rowdy, come over here" and then "Rowdy, here."

Do dogs recognize words?

They certainly do. That is why it's so important that you always use the same words of command and that the various commands should not sound too much alike.

Housebreaking Your Puppy

Why do most people have such a terrible time teaching puppies to be clean in the house?

Usually because they undertake the hopeless task of trying to house-train puppies that are only six or eight weeks of age. Almost no puppy has the bodily control or the necessary mental powers to learn house manners before he is four or five months old. Another reason for difficulties in housebreaking is that owners apply corrective methods instead of preventive methods in their training. That is, they let the puppy wander around the house making messes and *then* scold or spank him instead of seeing to it that the puppy has no opportunity to make a mistake in the first place.

About what length of time should it take to housebreak a puppy?

The length of time will differ with individual dogs and also with the various breeds. Generally speaking, puppies of the large breeds (and a good thing it is, too) will learn house manners faster than those of the small breeds. The age of the dog is also a factor and so is the skill of the trainer and the amount of time he spends on the puppy's education. If the puppy is old enough for training, and the trainer consistently applies the proper methods, housebreaking can be taught in a week or ten days.

Are there professional trainers who will undertake to house-train puppies?

Yes. Many kennels that specialize in obedience training will teach puppies house manners. The breeder from whom you buy your pup may do this kind of training or, if he doesn't, will probably know of someone who does.

How long would a puppy have to stay with a professional trainer to be housebroken?

Because he must be able to guarantee his work, a professional dog trainer usually requires at least three or four weeks to house-break a dog.

We bought our Beagle pup when he was five months old and sent him to a trainer to be housebroken. After three weeks the trainer said we could take him home and the first thing the puppy did when he got into our house was to make a mess on the living-room rug. Who is at fault?

You are, if you did not give the puppy an opportunity to relieve himself before you brought him into the house. Even though your Beagle may have been perfectly clean in the trainer's house, he should have been carefully watched until you were sure he understood that the same rules held in *your* house.

What definite rules should be followed when housebreaking a puppy?

The first and most important rule is not to give the puppy the run of the house. Whenever the household is busy and no one can take the time to keep an eye on young Sir Leaky he should be tied to a table leg, a radiator, his bed, or confined in a pen or crate. Never should he be permitted to roam from room to room, unchaperoned.

He should be taken out (or to his papers, if you are paper-training him), the first thing in the morning, after each meal, after a hard romp, always after a nap, and the last thing at night. Every time the puppy performs properly when he is put outdoors he must be petted and told what a good, smart, wonderful fellow he is. Housebreaking is an excellent example of preventive training because the puppy is taught to do the right thing by giving him no opportunity to do the wrong.

My next-door neighbor claims that the only sure way to house-train a puppy is to rub his nose in any messes he makes. Will this really teach a dog to be clean in the house?

Rubbing a dog's nose in one of his messes is more disgusting than the mistake made by the dog. It is usually done in temper, serves only to terrify and perhaps sicken the puppy, and nothing at all is to be gained by such a mean and dirty practice.

When an unhousebroken puppy circles around and begins to squat down to relieve himself should he be allowed to go ahead and finish and then be scolded?

No. The minute he shows the danger signals of restlessness, circling or squatting, snatch him up and whisk him outdoors (or to his papers, if paper-training). This requires careful watching, patience and a certain degree of agility, but every time you can catch a puppy *before* he has made a mistake you may rightfully regard it as a triumph, and a long step forward on the way to complete truthworthiness in the house.

Does it do any good to scold a puppy after he has made a puddle or a mess?

Yes, if you do it *immediately after* he has made the mistake. Don't ever scold or spank a puppy if you find the evidence an hour or so after the crime was committed. The puppy won't know what he is being punished for and will only be bewildered and frightened by what seems to him an injustice. The only time that discipline will make the correct impression is when it is administered either at the time of the mistake or within a very few minutes afterward.

When a not-yet-housebroken puppy wets on a rug, is there any way to prevent a stain or bleached spot?

If the puddle is in a convenient location for such treatment, slide a pan or basin under it and pour two or three quarts of plain cold water through the rug. When you remove the pan, shove a thick layer of newspaper under the wet place to sop up the moisture that is still in the rug. If your carpeting is of the wall-to-wall type, or the spot is in the center of a large rug and difficult to get a pan under, make a solution of one-half cup of white vinegar in a quart of water and saturate the spot with this mixture. Let it stand for five minutes, then sponge up the moisture and repeat the process.

Puppy urine is not as acid as that of grown dogs and is therefore not liable to cause as bad a stain or bleached area. There are several commercial products on the market which will prevent urine stains on rugs. They are effective but not particularly reasonable in price.

How long a time should a dog be kept outside to relieve himself during the housebreaking period?

Not more than ten or fifteen minutes at a spell. If the weather is bad, the period should be cut even shorter, for if he is left

out in the cold or rain for long periods it will discourage him
from asking to be let outdoors the next time. He would rather
risk a scolding for soiling the house than be forced to remain
exposed to chilly or wet weather for what seems like hours to him.

Paper-training Your Dog

What is meant by paper-training a puppy?

Teaching him to go to the spread-out newspapers to relieve
himself, instead of training him to go outdoors for such purposes.

*What is the point of paper-training a puppy instead of teach-
ing him to go outdoors?*

Putting a young puppy (especially a pup of any of the smooth-
coated breeds) outdoors is a risky business during severe winter
weather. The sudden change from a heated house to the chilly
outside can cause illness. Rather than expose a puppy to snow,
rain or low temperatures, many owners prefer to teach their
puppies to use a patch of flat spread newspapers. This method is
considerably less trouble than taking a puppy outdoors every
couple of hours, (an important point to apartment-house dwell-
ers) as the only labor involved is that of picking up the soiled
papers and putting down fresh ones.

*How should I go about paper-training my Boston Terrier
puppy?*

First lay out a double or triple thickness of newspapers, consisting of four double sheets laid flat and slightly overlapping at
the edges. Put the papers where the puppy will *always* be able to
get to them. Then keep an eagle eye on the puppy and the
moment he gives any indication of wanting to wet or move his
bowels, rush him to the papers and keep him there until he has
performed. It may require several days of vigilance and quick
action before he will go to the papers of his own accord, but
when he does, extravagant praise and petting are in order

We are trying to paper-train our puppy and so far have been able to hustle him to his papers almost every time it was necessary, but once we get him there we have trouble making him stay on the papers until he performs. Have you any suggestions?

Putting some sort of an enclosure around the newspaper area would help. There is a type of stiff wire edging about fourteen or sixteen inches in height, commonly used for protecting flower beds, which would serve for this purpose. It is obtainable at hardware stores and garden-supply firms. It should be bent into shape to surround the papers with a narrow gap left open for an entrance. Shove the pup onto the newspapers through the entrance way, then close the gap with a piece of plywood or heavy cardboard and leave him in the pen until he has performed.

My Terrier puppy is getting the idea of being paper-trained but he only puts his front paws on the paper and the puddle goes on the floor. Is there some way to make him understand that he must get all four feet on the papers?

If possible, catch him in the act and push him completely on to the papers, then praise him when he hits the mark. An enclosure such as that described in the answer preceding this one would help too.

How large an area should be covered with newspapers when paper-training a puppy?

The best way is to cover the entire floor of a small room, such as a bathroom or laundry room, with the spread-out papers. If this arrangement is not practical, use from four to six double sheets, two or three layers thick. When the puppy has become reliable about using the papers, the area covered can be gradually decreased until just one or two double sheets will be enough.

Our four-month-old Cocker Spaniel is almost paper-trained, but now and then, he seems to forget all about the papers and just lets go wherever he happens to be. How can I make him understand that he must use the papers every time?

You may have decreased the size of the newspaper-covered area too rapidly. Cover a larger area with papers and refresh your puppy's memory by treating him as if you were just starting to train him, then gradually reduce the size of the papered area. If he gets careless after this, scolding or spanking will be justified.

Since I work very late hours and consequently do not arise early, I want my Corgi to be paper-broken as well as housebroken. Will it confuse the dog if I try to train him to either use the papers or to go outdoors?

Not necessarily. Paper-train him first; then, at the time you change him from paper-breaking to housebreaking, pick up all the papers during the day but leave them down at night. A few days of watchfulness on your part should make it clear to him that it's all right for him to use the papers any time they are spread down for him.

We have paper-trained our Pomeranian and she is very good about going to the papers whenever it is necessary. Once in a while the door to the room where the papers are spread down is left closed by mistake and then there is a puddle on the floor. Should we spank her when this happens?

No. It would be most unfair. If there is any spanking to be done, spank the person who leaves the door closed.

Special Training for Special Problems

The city where I live has an ordinance which makes it an offense for a dog owner to permit his dog to soil the sidewalk. How can I teach my dog to use the gutter?

Curb training is easy. Walk your dog in the gutter or on the very edge of the sidewalk. The fact that other dogs have used the gutter will stimulate him to go there too. Until he catches on, keep him away from the middle of the sidewalk and praise him when he performs in the gutter. Before long he will pull you across the sidewalk in his haste to reach the gutter when he wants to relieve himself.

My Welsh Terrier is a smart puppy and I had no trouble getting him to use papers, but I can't get him to do anything when he is outside. He waits until he comes back into the house and then rushes to his papers.

You must pick up the papers. Housebreaking and performing outside (whether on or off leash) go hand in hand. Your Terrier should go out the very first thing in the morning, but not for more than ten minutes. If at the end of this time there are no results, bring him in the house and confine him by tying him to his bed or the leg of a table or a radiator. Better yet, if you have one, put him in a crate. This will force him to control himself until he is given another chance.

Take him out again in about half or three-quarters of an hour. If he performs properly, praise him and give him his freedom in the house for as long as you are able to keep an eye on him. If he does not relieve himself, confine him again when you bring him indoors. Stick to this routine until the puppy gives in and you get the desired results outside. If you wish, when you know it is time for him to move his bowels, use an infant's size glycerine suppository just before you take him out in order to hurry things up.

What causes a puppy to wet the floor when we reach to pat him? This annoying habit has caused my mother to threaten to get rid of my Cocker Spaniel. Can something be done about it?

The wetting occurs because the puppy is nervous or excited. It is a fairly common reaction of young dogs and they almost always outgrow it. Whatever you do, don't scold or spank him when this happens, as he really can't help himself and any harshness will only increase the emotional stress which causes the wetting. The best thing to do is to ignore the puppy as much as possible, especially during the first few minutes of welcome when you have been away from him. Let the pup make the advances, and when you do pat him, do it slowly and nonchalantly. Avoid making any quick grabs or passes at him with your hands.

During the day our dog has perfect house manners but almost every night he dirties the floor of the kitchen where he sleeps. How can we get him over this?

The best solution would be to obtain a crate and make him sleep in it. A dog will do almost anything to avoid soiling his sleeping place, and confinement in a crate would make him control himself. Be sure the crate is large enough for him to be able to stretch out comfortably and has a cushion or thickly folded blanket for bedding. He should always be given a good run before you shut him up for the night and be let out as soon as anyone in the house is up in the morning. If you feel a crate is too expensive or, for some reason, impractical, try tying him closely to his bed every night. The less he can roam around the less likely he is to forget his house manners.

Fritz, our Boxer, is a perfect gentleman at home but when I take him in a store with me, or to a friend's house, he seems to forget he ever heard of housebreaking and is apt to lift his leg anywhere he chooses. How can we teach him better visiting manners?

Fritz, in common with many other dogs, doesn't understand that the same rules about being clean in his own house hold good any place else where he happens to be indoors. Whenever you take him in a store or to the home of a friend, keep a short firm hold on his leash, and the moment he starts sniffing around or indicates he is about to wet give a hard jerk on the leash pulling up his head sharply and say "No!" in deeply disgusted tones. Do this consistently and he will get the idea.

Our Bull Terrier is housebroken but he doesn't like going out in the rain. On rainy days he just stands around looking

forlorn while he is out in the yard and refuses to do any-
thing. Then, of course, sooner or later, because he hasn't
relieved himself while he was out, there is a mess in the
house. How can we get him to function as he should, rain
or no rain?

Some short-haired dogs have a great dislike for cold and wet
weather. Except in extreme cold, put your dog out and watch
him until he does what he should, then bring him inside immediately. If, after ten or fifteen minutes, he has not relieved himself,
bring him inside, but treat him as an unhousebroken puppy and
tie or confine him to avoid a mistake in the house.

When the Older Dog Misbehaves

I have a three-year-old German Shepherd. He is completely
house-trained but misbehaves if we go out and leave him
alone even if it is only for fifteen or twenty minutes. Why
does he do this, and how can we cure him of this bad habit?

When a mature, house-trained dog behaves as your Shepherd
does, he is doing it for spite. He resents being left behind, and
soiling the house is his way of getting even. Try leaving him alone
for a short period, say ten minutes, first giving him an ample
exercise period before you go out, so there is no possible excuse
for him to make a mess. If, when you return, he has dirtied the
house, take him by the collar, show him the mess he's made and
give him a hard spanking, scolding him severely at the same time.
After you have punished him don't make up with him right
away. Give him the silent treatment for two or three hours to
make your displeasure sink in more deeply. Another thing you
can do is to let him think you have gone out and then sneak
back into the house and try to catch him in the act. The element
of surprise will have a lasting effect.

My dog is seven months old now and is well house-trained.
However, he will only perform when he is running loose.
When I take him for a walk with his collar and leash he

*refuses to do anything. We plan to move to the city soon and
when we live there he will always have to be on a leash
when he goes out. What can we do?*

Dogs that are used to running loose often seem self-conscious
about performing when they are on a leash. Use the collar and
leash every time you take your dog out and he will soon become
so accustomed to it that he will relieve himself as freely as though
he were at liberty. It will help if you keep his collar on him all
the time too, then the weight of it on his neck will not feel strange
to him. Two leashes tied together will give the dog more freedom.

*One day recently I went out, leaving Bunky, our Setter, alone
in the house. I was gone much longer than I had expected
to be—five or six hours altogether—and when I returned it
appeared that Bunky hadn't been able to wait that long. He
was so ashamed of himself and unhappy about what he had
done that I didn't have the heart to scold or punish him. I
just mopped up the mess and said nothing. Did I do the
right thing?*

You did the only fair thing under the circumstances. Any time
that a dog is left shut up in the house for an unreasonable length
of time, he is liable to be unable to contain himself, and it would
be a great injustice were he to be punished. Another time when
a dog should not be chastised is if he has an intestinal upset and
is "caught short" in the house. A house-trained dog is usually
so distressed over an incident of this sort that it would be heartless
to punish him for it.

*We have about decided that our Collie must be mentally
retarded. He is a big dog now, eight months old and he still
squats down when he wets instead of lifting his leg. At what
age do dogs start lifting their legs?*

Most male dogs start the leg-lifting habit at five or six months
of age, but many are a year old before they do this, especially if
they are not around an older male from whom to learn the trick.

CHAPTER 9

How to Correct
Your Dog's Bad Habits

Dogs are not angels. Even the best of dogs will develop a few bad habits. Often, they grow up as stealthily as weeds in a flower bed—unless you are constantly on the lookout, you may not notice them before they overwhelm you. Here, as elsewhere, an ounce of prevention will go a long way, and our last chapter was devoted to showing you how to apply it. This one suggests how to administer a pound of cure when necessary—when your dog sleeps on the furniture, begs at table, barks incessantly, chews up the rug, chases cars, attacks people and animals, or falls into the clutches of other vices that dogflesh is heir to.

We hope you will never have to punish your dog. For some bad habits, there are other ways of correction. If you must practice the sterner measures of discipline, it is wise to start your reprovals gently. Some dogs do not tolerate punishment as well as others, and you will have to gauge how much yours can take. Each time it is necessary to reprimand a puppy for the same mistake, the correction should be progressively more severe. When he ignores your commands and goes cheerfully on his way, you are not being firm enough with him. If he acts uncertain and backs away from you, you are being too severe with him, and must ease up a bit. But one good correction is worth a dozen half-hearted attempts in all training.

Correcting Bad Habits in the House

What is the best way to teach a dog to keep off the furniture?

By starting right from the time he is a puppy. Never allow
him to get up on a chair or sofa. If he does get up, push him
down. If he does it again give him a cuff and shove him down,
not so gently as the first time. As long as you make your dog stay
on the floor, give him something comfortable to lie on in a non-
drafty corner or nook.

*Our Irish Terrier knows better than to sleep on the furniture
when we are around, but when we are out he makes himself
comfortable on our newly reupholstered sofa. What can we
do about it?*

You'll have to trick him. The next time you are going to leave
him alone place a set mousetrap on his favorite spot on the sofa.
There is no need of concealment; put the trap right out in the
open on the seat. When the dog jumps up on the sofa, his weight
hitting the cushion will spring the trap, making a startling but
harmless noise.

It is the association of something unpleasant that does it. The
dog will wonder why his favorite sofa (or chair) suddenly snapped
at him and will give it a wide berth for a long time. Never use
a rattrap for this purpose. Rattraps are too powerful in action
and might injure a paw or tail. If your dog is so small that even a
mousetrap might hurt him, cover it with a thin towel.

*Our Schnauzer has become a terrible beggar. She hangs around
the table, gets in the way of whoever is serving, and even
barks at us if we don't give her a handout. It's so embarrassing when we have guests. What is the remedy?*

The remedy is never to give her, under any circumstances, one
scrap of food from the dining table, and make the whole family
promise to do the same. If someone hadn't fed her at the table
in the first place she wouldn't have become such a shameless
beggar. Don't permit her even to stay in the same room when

the family is dining. Chase her out every time she tries to come in and, if necessary, give her a whack on the backside to show that you mean business.

We have a male dog who has the embarrassing habit of climbing on people and going through the motions of mating, especially if he has been romping and is rather excited. I'd like to know how to break this distressing habit.

Dogs with this particular habit must be given severe punishment at the first sign of such action. A sharp and unexpected whack on the rear end, sufficiently hard to knock him off balance is about the best correction.

Crying and Barking

Why is it that when a puppy goes to a new home he usually keeps the whole family awake for the first few nights by crying?

When a puppy is put to bed in his new home it is usually the first time in his life that he has ever been alone. He misses the comforting warmth of his litter-mates sleeping with him, he is in a completely strange place, he is lonesome, he is probably a little scared, and he is still very much of a baby. Under the same circumstances most human infants would yell their heads off too.

We are getting a Pointer puppy soon and we are dreading those unwelcome midnight serenades we'll hear for the first week. Is there any way to prevent them?

If you have ever watched a litter of slumbering puppies you have probably noticed that they do their sleeping in a heap. The thing a puppy misses most when he is separated from his brothers and sisters is their cosy body warmth. When you put your puppy to bed at night, fill a rubber hot-water bottle about two-thirds full of water just a little hotter than luke-warm. Don't fill the bottle all the way, it should have some "give." Cover it with a piece of old wool blanket or a turkish towel, fastening the cover-

A SLEEPING PLACE FOR THE NEW PUPPY

A cozy bed placed in a warm, draft-free spot, and the
comforting tick of an alarm clock often keep a new
puppy quiet and contented through the night.

ing with safety pins. Tuck this in the puppy's bed as a substitute
for his so-sadly-missed family and he will snuggle contentedly
against it, treating himself (and you) to a restful night.

It will also help if you give him a light warm meal just at
bedtime, as a full stomach makes a puppy sleepy. Some owners
claim they have kept puppies from wailing at night by placing an
old-fashioned windup-type alarm clock with a loud tick in the
room near the puppy. The ticking sound seems to sound like
something alive to the puppy and makes him think he is not
alone. The alarm clock trick will not work with all puppies but
is worth trying if you have a clock of this type.

We have had our puppy two months and she still barks and
howls every night after we put her to bed. We usually go and
pet her and try to calm her down but she keeps yowling.
She is seven months old now. Isn't it about time she stopped
this babyish behavior?

As long as she knows that by howling she can get someone to
come to her and pet her, your dog will make a fuss every night.
She is spoiled and you will have to be a little tough with her
before she will behave like a lady. The next time you put her to
bed and she starts yowling, bang sharply on the door of the room
where she is and tell her in a loud stern voice to stop that racket.

If the noise continues, go to her but don't do any petting. Take her by the scruff of the neck with one hand and give her three or four sharp slaps on the rump with the other, scolding her severely.

Leave her, and if there is any further noise, don't go back again, even to punish her, for incredible as it seems there are dogs (and yours may be one of them) who will make a commotion just to get someone to come to them, even though it means a spanking. If you follow this treatment faithfully and don't weaken and do any petting or consoling, your dog should be over her bad habit in a few days.

My dog is good during the day but yowls when I put him to bed at night. He doesn't sleep in my room, but is with me the rest of the time. How can I get him to be quiet at night?

Since you permit your dog to be with you all day long, he naturally doesn't like it when he is left alone at night. If you will shut him in a room by himself for short intervals during the day, he will become accustomed to being away from you and won't feel so abused when he is alone at night.

My Spitz is obedient in most ways, but I can't cure him of barking when the doorbell rings. Do you have any suggestions?

The moment the dog barks throw something at him that will make a noise when it hits the floor and startle him. At the same time command him to hush. You can use a rolled-up magazine, an old book, or a foot-long length of chain made of links about the size used for dog chains. Just be sure it is something that will make plenty of noise yet not injure the dog. Since you are correcting a habit that has already been formed, you will have to be very persistent in your discipline. If just throwing the object at the dog does not distract him, try tossing it lightly at his heels.

What can I do about my dog's incessant barking? We have a nice yard for him and a comfortable house, but after he's

been out for a few minutes, he gets bored and barks con-
tinuously until we bring him in the house again for the
sake of peace?

Certain dogs will never learn to be quiet. However, through
training, the barking can be controlled to a certain degree. Every
bark should bring unpleasant results. Throw something and
startle him, or make a loud noise. If the dog is given obedience
training, he will have more respect for his owner's voice, and will
not be so apt to ignore the command to keep quiet.

We are the owners of a male Dachshund and at present are
living in an apartment. When we go out the dog howls all
the time we are gone. Naturally, this is terribly annoying
to the other tenants, and we must find some way to put a
stop to it. We have tried exercising him hard before we go
out in an effort to tire him, but that hasn't worked. He has
a cozy bed in the kitchen so we know he isn't cold or uncom-
fortable. Can you offer any suggestions?

First, don't let your dog be with you every minute of the time
when you are at home. Keep him away from you for short intervals leaving him in one room and then another. In this way you
will be nearby to make the necessary corrections when the rumpus
starts. When he starts yowling a bang on the door and a sharp
word may be enough to quiet him. If not, a spanking is in order,
and when you spank, always hold him firmly by the scruff of
the neck or collar.

If he is quiet during the day when left alone, pretend to go out
some evening, letting him see you leave. Close the door by which
you make your exit with a definite slam, and then wait outside.
As soon as any hubbub starts, dash back in and make it tough for
him. You may have to do this more than once and it will take a
good deal of patience, but this procedure should put an end to
the yodeling concerts, for your dog will never be sure you have
really gone away, and will think twice before letting himself in for
a trouncing.

Damage By Chewing is Avoidable

It seems that every puppy we have ever owned has been a terror for chewing things. Shoes, furniture, clothing, rugs, in fact everything in the house has been damaged. Is there any way to keep a puppy from using his teeth on his owner's belongings?

A puppy's urge to chew is powerful, especially at the time that he is losing his needle-sharp milk teeth and the second teeth are coming through the gums. It will serve as a protection to your belongings if the puppy has three or four toys or bones of his own upon which he can vent his desire to gnaw. Dog supply shops have plenty of fine toys which are both safe and amusing for a puppy. Leather and solid rubber toys are safest, and most puppies love those polished bones which are made from real animal bones. Don't give a puppy anything made of wood to chew and avoid hollow rubber toys and those containing squeaking devices.

Because he has chewing items of his own doesn't mean a puppy won't ever take it into his head to gnaw the leg of a chair or one of your galoshes for he probably will. You will just have to watch him a bit while he is in the midst of the "chewing age." Whenever he does start to use his teeth on a forbidden article, give him a light rap on the muzzle and a sharp "No!" Then give him one of his own belongings.

If I give my Retriever pup an old shoe or glove to play with and chew, won't it help to keep him from destroying my good things?

Definitely not. A puppy has no sense of value. You can't expect him to know the difference between a pair of shoes that are ready for the trash can and the newest and best you own. For this reason, rags, old stockings and socks, wornout shoes, slippers, and gloves, or any other discarded articles of wearing apparel are not sensible playthings for young dogs.

Sammy, my Scottie, is a well-behaved little dog, but at the age of three he has developed the naughty habit of chewing the corners of the scatter rugs in the hallway. We have scolded, spanked and threatened, but the minute we turn our backs he is at it again. How can we reform him?

Sprinkle the rug corners with red hot Cayenne pepper (not paprika). One sniff or taste of this fiery seasoning will probably cause Sammy to lose all interest in your scatter rugs, or at least in the ones you sprinkle. If you catch him in the act, throw something to startle him.

When a grown-up dog starts destroying rugs, furniture, or clothing he usually does it from boredom or loneliness. It might prevent Sammy from damaging other household items if you brought him a toy or two for his entertainment and chewing pleasure.

Is playing tug of war with a puppy apt to injure his teeth?

Pulling on an object that a puppy is holding in his mouth is not only harmful to his teeth, but may have a bad effect on his disposition. It teaches him how powerful his teeth can be and later, if you should want him to learn to retrieve, he would be stubborn about giving up the object he had fetched. This sort of roughhousing is likely to make him overrough in play and inclined to grab and snatch with his teeth. No tug-of-war games, please.

More Bad Habits Around the House

What can be done about the overfriendly dog who insists on jumping on people?

Every time he starts to jump on you, take a step forward and raise your knee so as to hit the dog's chest, saying "Down!" at the same time. You'll have to do this every time the dog jumps on you and don't *ever* pet him when he has jumped up and is resting his paws against you. If the shock of hitting your knee knocks him over, it won't hurt him, so don't offer him sympathy. Get the other members of your family and your friends to give him the same treatment. It will presently dawn on him that something decidedly disagreeable happens to him every time he jumps on someone.

Another way to correct this annoying habit is to hold the dog's front paws in your hands when he jumps on you and, while talking to him perfectly pleasantly, to step on his back feet just hard enough to hurt them a little. The knee method is faster though and seems, somehow, a bit less cruel. It is important that dogs of the large breeds learn this lesson early in life. By the time they are full-grown, they are strong enough to knock the average person down flat before the victim can raise a knee in self-defense.

We have a Kerry who exhibits real skill in removing the lid of the garbage can and scattering the contents all over the yard. Is there some way we can stop this scavenging?

Sprinkle the top layer of the contents of the garbage can with Cayenne pepper. It will probably be necessary to do this for a week or so, but it should do the trick. If you ever catch the dog in the act, be severe with him, as the habit is a menace to his health because of the danger of his getting hold of spoiled food.

Our Doberman Pinscher has become an accomplished thief. He steals food from the kitchen and dining-room tables every chance he gets. Recently I was called to the telephone while I was getting dinner and he stole and ate a whole pound of butter. How can we reform him?

You will have to catch him in the act to make any lasting impression, and, in view of the fact that he is by now an experienced pilferer, it may be necessary to do it more than once. Have the dog in the kitchen with you and put some food in an easily reached position on the kitchen table, then leave the room. As stealthily as possible, spy on your dog through the crack in the door and, the moment he starts to help himself to the food, dash into the room, give him a thorough trouncing and a bitter scolding. Catching him once may do the trick. If not, you will have to set the trap again and let him fall into it and be punished accordingly.

Our Setter always scratches to be let in the house and every summer he tears holes in the screen door. What can we do about this?

First, teach him to "speak" on command. You will find instructions for this in another chapter. Once he has learned this lesson, stay near the door when he goes out and watch for him when you think he's ready to come into the house. As he approaches the entrance, command him to "Speak!" As soon as he does, open the door for him. Repeat about fifty times and then maybe he'll bark instead of clawing the door down for admission.

If you think this procedure would be more trouble than it would be worth, here is how to protect the screen door from any further damage. Fasten two ordinary round brass curtain rods, in holders, across the lower section of the outside of the door. Put one near the bottom and the other halfway up. Between them fasten a piece of heavy, square mesh wire netting, attaching it with wire to both rods. Your dog's nails will not be able to reach and tear the screening, but he will still be able to make enough racket to summon some member of the household to let him in.

We live on a busy thoroughfare and I am afraid my dog may get run over. Is there any way I can teach my dog to stay in the yard even when the gate is open?

If this is a young puppy and he is paddled and put back every time he goes through the gate, he may gradually learn to stay in the yard. If he is older, and already knows the meaning of freedom, you won't have an easy time training him. Leave the dog in the house and have someone hide outside the gate. Let the dog out, and when he starts through the gate have the person outside throw a large stick on the ground in front of the dog and command "Get back!"

It will take much repetition to teach your dog that he mustn't go through the gate, and there is no way of guaranteeing that he won't some day be tempted too far by the sight of another dog or a cat out in the street. You could never really be sure he was safe. If he were our dog, we'd see to it that the gate was kept closed and that he had no opportunity to go out and risk possible injury.

When we got our Great Dane pup he was four months old and he didn't know how to go up and down stairs so we carried him. Now he's six months old and it's getting to be like carrying an ox. How can we teach him to get up and down the steps of the porch by himself? It is a rather long flight and he seems afraid to try it.

Most puppies are afraid of stairs because they were raised in kennels where everything is on ground level, but your Dane will never learn to get up and down stairs as long as you continue to be a pack horse for him. Assuming that he will go on a leash by now, give him a few starter lessons by taking him to a building entrance that has a gently sloping flight of just three or four steps. If he balks at going up, force him along by his collar. Do the same thing going down, placing a hand on his shoulders to steady him and telling him to come along and be a brave fellow.

Do this three or four times, and the next day try him on a longer flight of stairs, being careful to give him enough physical and verbal support to prevent his scaring himself by falling. As soon as he is negotiating these kindergarten flights without fear or awkwardness, try him on your own stairs. He may balk at this because he's learned by now what fun it is to be carried, so urge him along by his collar and give him a slap on the rump, if he gets too stubborn. It shouldn't take more than two or three lessons for him to realize he can manage the stairs by himself.

Punishing Your Dog

Do you think there are circumstances which justify giving a dog a thrashing?

With mature dogs, yes. There are times when a full-grown dog, who knows better, will deliberately indulge in actions which he knows are wrong or forbidden. In a case of this sort a trouncing is certainly in order. In regard to puppies, it depends on the individual. Some puppies are so sensitive that a single scolding word is enough to crush them completely, others are such thick-skinned individuals that nothing short of a whack makes any impression.

Does spanking a puppy with the bare hand cause hand-shyness?

Absolutely not. If a puppy deserves a spanking, the bare hand may be used to paddle him as long as he is held firmly by the collar, the scruff of the neck, or by the flap of loose skin under his throat. Hand-shyness is caused by swinging at the puppy as he darts away, sometimes connecting, yet more often not. No dog, puppy or grownup, should ever be hit anywhere near the head. That will make him hand-shy and is dangerous because a blow on the head is so liable to injure an ear or an eye. The place to spank a dog is on the rump.

Why do most books and articles on dog training suggest using a folded newspaper or light magazine for spanking a dog?

Because either of these objects produces a loud noise when the dog is smacked. It is believed that this procedure makes a lasting impression on the culprit without really hurting him. If you ever whack a well-muscled adult dog with your bare hand you will find out that it is much more painful to your hand than it is to the dog. The only trouble with the folded newspaper or magazine advice is that neither of those articles ever seems to be handy when one's dog is in need of physical proof of one's displeasure.

I am the owner of a ten-month-old Pekingese who is just as sinful as he can be. He isn't unintelligent, he's just plain naughty and no amount of scolding does any good at all. He is so small that I don't dare spank him for fear of causing an injury but I must admit that I'm sorely tempted at times. What can I do that will instill a sense of discipline without really hurting him?

The next time your Peke is disobedient or bad in any other way, pick him up and give him a hard shaking. This will be just as unpleasant as a spanking and there is no risk of hurting him.

If a dog has misbehaved and is due for a spanking, should he be called to the trainer and then punished?

No. *Never, never* call a dog to you and then punish him. If he has committed a misdemeanor which merits a paddling, *you* go to *him*. If he has, for instance, chewed up a sofa cushion, take him by the collar and lead him to the site of the crime. Show him the torn-up cushion, tell him in no uncertain terms that he's a menace to society, and then give him a smack or two.

The Dog That Wanders Off

My old Retriever is known as the village bum, as he never stays home. How can I prevent his young son from following in his father's footsteps?

Usually dogs prefer to travel in pairs. You might avoid letting the two out together, especially since one is an older dog, and already has the habit of straying. The young Retriever should be confined in an enclosure until he is old enough to be trained, at which time a course in general obedience is recommended. The training, when completed, will give you control over the dog, so that any attempt to leave the premises can be halted and any forthcoming training fully understood.

How should a runaway dog be treated when he finally decides to come home after hours or days of roving?

If your dog has an inclination to wander, the one thing *not* to do is to give him a spanking when he returns. If you do this he will only stay away that much longer to postpone the punishment he knows he's in for, like the drunken husband who stays out till 4:00 A. M. trying to get up his courage to go home and face an irate spouse. This doesn't mean that you should roll out the red carpet for the returning truant. Treat him rather coolly and let him worry a little about whether you still love him or not. After an hour or so, feed him and resume friendly relations.

To get a dog hobo over his taste for wandering is a long, time-consuming affair requiring much patience and great persistence. First, you'll need to teach him some basic obedience—to come on command, to stop in his tracks when told, and generally to respect all orders. Once he has grasped these rudiments you will have to keep an eagle eye on him every time he goes outside and the moment he starts to wander off, call him back. After you have done this a few hundred times he may get the idea and decide to stay in his own yard.

On the other hand, if he is a big dog requiring much exercise for his health and well-being, he may still go off on hikes by himself because he really needs them. If your dog is one of the hunting breeds and you live in an area where there is much game, it will be an almost impossible task to keep him home unless you fence him in, because the urge to seek game is so much a part of such a dog's heritage and nature that he can't resist it. Many dogs become tramps because they don't get enough attention at home. Just being well-fed will not keep a dog around his owner's residence if no one ever has time to take him for a walk or talk to him or pet him. The problem of the wandering dog is not an easy one to solve. It is up to the owner to try first to figure out *why* the dog is a rover and then to do what he can to remedy the underlying cause.

For a number of years there lived in the town of Glen Cove, Long Island, New York, an enormous St. Bernard known as Butch. Butch was such a bum that he became celebrated. *Life* magazine printed his picture and many newspapers devoted feature articles to him. Butch had a perfectly good home where he was well fed and treated with kindness—when he was there. The trouble with Butch was he was so gregarious that home life seemed very dull to him. He preferred the social life of the village streets where he could fraternize with his hundreds of human friends.

His days were spent stretched across a busy sidewalk where his enormous bulk forced the passers-by to walk in the gutter to get around him—an inconvenience they accepted cheerfully, for Butch was a town character and widely loved. His evenings he spent in the lobby of the Cove Theatre. He seldom went home to dine, for any butcher in town would give him a handout.

Occasionally he boarded one of the Long Island Railroad trains and enjoyed a free excursion to Oyster Bay and back. He often slept in the railroad station, and on two occasions had to be rescued from the ladies' room in the dead of night where he had been locked in by mistake. Though Butch had a fine life it is doubtful that his owner derived much enjoyment from him, unless there is a certain pride in owning a famous bum. When your dog shows an infuriating preference for the company of the neighbors, remember Butch. Perhaps your errant pet is just oversociable.

Dogs and Automobiles

Why do dogs chase cars and how can this be stopped?

The dog's natural instinct is to chase anything that runs away from him. Most dogs are bluffing when they do this and if whatever they are chasing should turn and chase them, they would run for their lives. Observe what happens when a furiously barking puppy approaches a stranger. If the person suddenly chases the puppy, the tail goes down and the pup runs as fast as he can. This holds true when a dog runs after automobiles. For this reason the correction must come from within the car.

One system is as follows (for this method the trainer needs an assistant, a car, and a long carriage or buggy whip—not an easy object to find in this machine age): While one person drives, the other sits by an open window of the car with the whip ready for action. When the dog charges toward the car the whip must be used with full force on him and he should be told in an angry voice to "Go home!" If a whip is unobtainable, have several old magazines (about the size of *Time* or *The New Yorker*) tightly rolled and tied with string. Throw these at the dog as he approaches the car, hitting him if possible.

Another method is to follow the same general procedure but instead of a whip or magazines, the trainer uses a powerful squirt gun or water pistol loaded with a weak solution of ammonia and water (one-half tablespoon of ammonia to one quart of water). Dogs detest the odor of ammonia and if the squirt gun is well aimed, the lesson is usually learned after one or two experiences with it. The idea, of course, is to cause the dog to associate an unpleasant experience with the act of running after a car, to which is added his utter astonishment at having an automobile "attack" him. If you use the squirt-gun method, be sure the ammonia solution is *weak*. If strong, it can blind a dog.

The methods we have suggested for curing a dog of car chasing are stern, but the habit is too dangerous to be tolerated. Most motorists will do everything short of wrecking their cars to avoid hitting a dog, but in heavy, fast-moving traffic a driver usually can't swerve out of the way of a dog that leaps out from the roadside. The life of a car-chasing dog is usually a short one.

I have read that a good way of stopping a dog from chasing cars is to tie an empty five-gallon tin can to his collar by a long rope. Does this really work?

It will work only as long as the tin is attached to the dog's collar. As soon as it is removed he will go right back to car chasing. No one would want his dog to go around with a huge rattling tin can tied to him all the time. The method of making the dog think the car has attacked him is really more efficacious.

My Golden Retriever is a pest when I take him out in the car. He keeps jumping from the back seat to the front and knocking into me while I'm driving. How can I teach him better motoring manners?

If your dog had a course in basic obedience training he would be a pleasanter motoring companion. Once he learned "to sit" and "stay" on command, you could make him sit down and remain quietly on either the front or back seat of the car.

Is there a cure for car sickness? Our dog is a year and a half old and she still gets sick when I take her driving.

If your dog had been accustomed to riding in a car from the time she was a small puppy, you probably could have avoided the trouble you're having now. Your veterinarian can supply you with a sedative which will prevent the nausea caused by auto rides.

One of the best of these is a product which was used with great success during World War II to prevent seasickness on troop transport ships. It should be given to the dog on an empty stomach about half an hour before taking her in the car. After a few trips with the use of the sedative you will most likely find that your dog has such a relaxed attitude toward motoring that you can discontinue its use.

Our Springer Spaniel insists on sleeping right in the middle of the road in front of our house. So far, he has been lucky, or else the drivers have been considerate, but we know that he is liable to be hurt or killed if he persists in his casual sleeping habits. How can we teach him to not do this?

The best way to make your dog understand that the middle of the road is not the place for naps is to watch him, from a place of concealment, and the moment he settles down for a snooze, throw some object such as a rolled-up magazine or a small piece of kindling wood to startle him and cause him discomfort. If it isn't possible to hide within throwing distance, use a BB gun to sting him out of his repose. If he is disturbed frequently enough, he will soon find a more peaceful and safer spot for sleeping.

Our big Poodle refuses to get in the car. In fact, every time he even sees it, he starts drooling and tries to get away. I'd

like to get him over this because it is not always convenient
to leave him at home.

Your dog has evidently had an unpleasant experience of some kind in a car, and you will have to erase this from his memory. Try to introduce some pleasant associations with the car such as feeding and petting. With the car motionless, put his dinner on the floor and then lead him up to it and let him eat there a few times. Sit in the car with him and pet him and talk to him.

When his fear of the car has been overcome, take him for a few short rides. Be sure always, when you take him riding, that he has not had food or water for a couple of hours beforehand. If he acts nervous, stop the car and give him a few pats and some reassuring conversation.

If Your Dog Attacks Other Animals

Is the statement true, "Once a chicken killer, always a chicken killer"?

No. Certain dogs' instinct to chase anything that moves often gets them in trouble. If the chickens were to take a few lessons from the feline family, and return the attack, the dog would undoubtedly call a halt. Since they don't, the owner must do the punishing. Old-timers claim that the way to cure a dog of chicken-killing is to beat him over the head with the slain chicken, and then tie the dead bird around his neck till it rots off. This is a drastic cure and almost as hard on the owner as it is on the dog.

A better method is to turn a chicken loose while the trainer, armed with a BB gun, watches from a place of concealment. When the dog makes a dash for the chicken the trainer brings the air rifle into play, aiming for the dog's rear. The pellet will not have enough power to really injure the dog but causes an effective sting. One lesson may suffice. If not, you will have to set the stage again and let the dog find out once more that chicken chasing has painful consequences.

There are two old-fashioned but often effective ways of reforming a chicken killer. One is to let him into a pen where there is a mother hen with small chicks. The old biddy will give the dog a pecking and a beating with her wings that should make him lose interest in anything with feathers on it, for keeps. The other is to tie the chicken killer in the henhouse on a short chain for one week. During this period his meals are made purposely skimpy so that his imprisonment will be that much more unpleasant. The theory is that by the end of the week he will be so utterly sick of the sight, sound, and smell of chickens he will never look at one again.

How can a dog be cured of chasing cats?

Many dogs will chase a cat that runs, but lose interest when kitty takes a stand in self-defense. Perhaps they have already learned the power of those sharp claws and respect them. It is dangerous to let a dog learn his lesson through such an experience, as often he is not fortunate enough to come out of the battle with both eyes intact. Using a BB gun in the same manner as recommended for curing a chicken killer will often help. Sometimes an inveterate cat chaser gets over his hatred for cats if he lives in the same house with one. The constant association with the cat seems to develop a tolerance, even though at first there will be plenty of hissing and growling and many scoldings may be necessary.

It must be admitted that it's an intrinsic part of dog nature to chase cats, and there are dogs that can *never* be taught not to attack on sight any feline they may encounter. This is particularly true of the terrier breeds. We once owned an Airedale who made war on cats with great energy for many years. An improvement in his attitude was brought about by a large, tough tomcat that he treed injudiciously one day. The cat jumped down on him and gave him a clawing and biting that left one ear all but torn off and numerous minor wounds all over the dog's body. That did it. A veterinarian sewed the torn ear and doctored the cuts and scratches. The lacerations healed nicely, but that Airedale never appeared to so much as notice a cat again as long as he lived. If you own a dog like this, about all you can do is to discourage

him as much as possible and hope that he will learn his lesson
without losing an eye.

*Our German Shepherd has fallen into bad company. He has
taken to roaming with a pack of dogs that get together and
go hunting. Lately they have been chasing and killing deer.
The game warden in this area has issued a warning to dog
owners that he will shoot on sight any dog that he discovers
chasing deer. We don't want our dog to be killed. What
should we do?*

Once a dog has acquired a taste for hunting it is liable to be
quite difficult to reform him. The safest course would be to fence
in your yard (or part of it) and keep the dog confined in it. Never
let him loose unless someone is around to call him back should
he start to wander away from your own property.

Hunters break dogs from chasing deer by the use of liquid animal musk. This substance is usually advertised in sportsmen's pub-
lications and magazines devoted to coon hunting. The musk is
rubbed on the dog's front legs and paws so the scent will be under
his nose continually. The constant odor of the musk usually makes
the dog so fed up and disgusted with the scent of deer that he will
no longer take any interest in them. The musk of rabbit, fox,
coyote, and skunk are also available and can be used to break a
dog of chasing these animals, if it is so desired.

*Some people down the road from us have bought a small flock
of sheep and are keeping them in a pasture between their
place and ours. Our dog has taken a decidedly unwholesome
attitude toward the sheep and has been seen chasing them.
We are worried, because he is big and strong enough to kill
a sheep. How can we make him stop chasing them?*

You can try the BB gun method suggested for curing chicken
killers. If your neighbor has a ram in his flock you could try the
old-time remedy of penning up the dog with the ram. By the time
a ram is four or five years old his disposition is usually anything

but sweet, and he is capable of giving a sheep-killing dog enough of a pushing around to instill a distaste for wool-bearing animals.

Sheep killing is a very serious offense, and in most states the owner of a flock is perfectly within his rights if he kills a dog that attacks his sheep. Any tendency toward sheep chasing should be sternly discouraged, for once your dog has actually killed a sheep he may be incorrigible.

How to Handle the Aggressive Dog

My husband keeps his hunting dog in a fenced-in yard. We have always been kind to the dog and, until recently, he has always been good-natured. Now, he growls when I try to take his water dish to refill it, or remove his empty food pan. I am afraid he will bite someday. What can I do to get him over this meanness?

When going into the pen to pick up his empty food dish take a deep pan or small bucket of water with you. If the dog growls or approaches you menacingly when you start to pick up his dish, dash the water in his face. Do this for a few days every time you go in the pen until he ceases his threatening behavior. The dog's actions probably are not caused by real viciousness. He probably has adopted a possessive feeling towards his food and water pans, resents having them removed, and is trying to bluff you out of taking them. Whatever his motives, don't let him get away with such actions.

Our Chow dog, Ching, has developed a great dislike for the mail carrier. We can't understand it, because the dog ignores other people who come to the house, and we are certain the mailman, whom we know and like, has never harmed him in any way. We don't want to buy the mail carrier a new pair of pants, but it looks as though we might have to if we can't make Ching behave himself. How can we get him to be less hostile toward the mailman?

If your Chow could talk, perhaps he could explain why he acts the way he does. The mailbag across the postman's shoulder may have some meaning. Ching may feel he is protecting the house from robbery, since the postman sometimes takes mail away with him. Perhaps it is the uniform he is wearing. The uniform may recall some previous unpleasant association.

We would suggest that a member of your family be on hand every morning when the mailman arrives. Greet him in a friendly manner, and, at the same time, have the mailman greet the dog, using his name. It would help if the postman would sit down on the porch steps for a few minutes and offer the dog something special to eat. Later, watch for the mailman, and when he arrives, warn Ching to behave. This training cannot be done spasmodically, but must be done every day for as long as necessary until the dog has learned to accept the postman's visits.

My Dalmatian has an aggressive nature. There is one special dog in the neighborhood that he always picks a fight with. Will he ever get over this?

One suggestion worth trying is to muzzle both dogs, and turn them loose together in an enclosed area. In this way, their feelings toward one another would be freely aired, and the physical damage to each dog would be at a minimum. After a few such encounters, their animosity may be cured and you could try them together without their muzzles.

My Shepherd is friendly toward people, but his one aim in life is to attack every other dog he sees, when he is on a leash. How can I cure him of this?

You may never completely overcome this tendency to where the dog will be trustworthy at all times. He can only be kept under control through obedience training, so that future flights may be avoided. If the dog is not on leash, a warning or command will often cause a dog to cease jockeying into a fighting position.

It is common knowledge that trouble frequently occurs when dogs are restrained by the leash, although they will be friendly when allowed to run free. If an attack is made when the dog is on leash, the end of the leash or a small stick should be brought down sharply across the dog's nose just as he lunges forward. The correction must be severe in order to overcome the dog's momentary hysteria.

My two-year-old Kerry Blue Terrier is becoming belligerent toward people—even towards me. I have raised him from a puppy. The attitude is mostly in play, as we have always had games together, but lately he is becoming more serious and frequently bites quite hard. What has caused this change?

Playing with a young puppy in a roughhouse manner is a form of teasing from which the puppy must either run or stand ground for protection. A dog's only defensive weapon is his teeth. During your Kerry Blue's puppyhood, the playful nips were not serious, but they have become more painful because he has learned the power of his teeth and is using them to his advantage. All playing should stop at once and the dog must be reprimanded sharply the moment he becomes the least bit rough. A course in obedience training would help to make the dog respect your commands.

Every day when I take my dog for a walk we pass a house where a huge dog rushes out and barks furiously. What should I do? I am quite afraid of him because he is so big.

The next time stand perfectly still and in a quiet yet firm tone of voice demand that he "get out of here." If the tone of your voice makes him stop, repeat the command and take a step or two toward him. Once he has turned, you can quickly pick up a stick or a stone and throw it at his heels. Never threaten a dog, especially a big one, with a stick when he is close by and facing you. Such action will frequently cause him to attack more seriously.

We have had a dog ever since my husband and I were married. I am afraid we have been overloving with the dog and he is a little spoiled. Now that we are expecting a baby, do you think the dog will be jealous of the baby?

Probably not. It might make the dog resentful if the family pushed him so far in the background that no one ever gave him a pat or a kind word after the arrival of the baby, but if you continue to give him a reasonable amount of attention he won't be jealous. Most dogs accept a baby as a member of the family and adopt an affectionate and protective attitude.

However, if your dog should turn out to be unusually jealous and display resentment toward the baby it would be only sensible to try to find him another home without delay. This is doubly important if he is a large dog.

Is it true that a barking dog never bites?

We wouldn't advise you to count on it. Usually a dog who intends to bite will approach with his head carried rather low, growling. If you ever find yourself in a position where you think a dog may be about to attack you, don't run from him. Stand your ground until he turns away or is called off.

The Shy Dog

My Wire-haired Terrier is a year and a half old. Although I bought her at six months of age, she is shy and I can't do much with her. Would it have helped if I had taken the puppy away from the kennel when she was younger?

Perhaps, but in this case the shyness is probably inherited and not acquired. It is doubtful if your Wirehair will ever have the vivacious attitude that is typical of her breed. A little obedience training will give her confidence. Breeding her may also help.

The people who owned our English Setter before we did must have been cruel to her, because she trembles and cowers if anyone so much as raises his voice when he speaks to her. She ducks away from our hands if we make a quick move, although we've never spanked her. Do you think we can gain her confidence, and restore her spirit? She is just eleven months old and we have had her for about three weeks now.

Since your Setter's attitude may stem from rough treatment and not inheritance, and because she is still very young, she will probably overcome her timidity through kind and gentle handling. All motions should be slow, and she should always be spoken to in a quiet voice; praised and petted a great deal. Good-natured tousling when playing with her will help to get her over her hand shyness and her fear of sudden motions. Obedience training, if carried out gently, would give her more self-confidence.

CHAPTER *10*

Obedience Training
Made Easy—*1*

If you have had any experience with a dog that willfully went forward after you had emphatically instructed him to stand still, and stood still as a rock after you had clearly told him to go forward; if you have ever been led by a dog on a leash when you wanted him to follow—then you don't need much convincing about the desirability of an obedient pet. Teaching a dog to obey your commands immediately and willingly is what we call obedience training.

Basic obedience training consists of simple exercises, such as sitting, lying down, staying when told, and coming when called. These are the fundamental lessons in good dog-manners. In advanced training, dogs are taught to retrieve articles, jump, seek lost objects, trail, and tell one scent from another. Advanced training also prepares dogs to do police work, lead the blind, and perform other highly specialized jobs. But the primary purpose of obedience training, so far as the average dog owner is concerned, is to make a dog a well-behaved companion.

Canine courtesy got its first real start in America in 1933, when Mrs. Whitehouse Walker, former owner of the Carillon Kennels, brought the idea of obedience training to this country from England. Obedience training had long been known and practiced in Europe, where it was used to school dogs for police and army work, and for acting as guide-dogs for the blind. The European training methods, however, were primarily designed for the education of the larger, stronger breeds, and tended to emphasize their aggressiveness in the line of duty—a most unwelcome characteristic from the viewpoint of the average American dog owner. Thanks to Mrs. Walker, obedience training, as she introduced it, and as it has been carried on in this country, is suitable for any breed, regardless of size or muscle power, and points entirely toward enhancing the intelligence, attractiveness, and natural good manners of the dog.

Many a dog owner who witnessed early exhibitions of trained dogs immediately got the urge to go home and "try it on his own piano." This led to the formation of training clubs and classes, for the purpose of schooling both owners and dogs.

Today there are over two hundred active organizations in the United States which are devoted to the purpose of showing dog owners how to transform canine hooligans into four-footed ladies and gentlemen. Trials for obedience-trained dogs are held at most of the larger dog shows, and the American Kennel Club awards titles to dogs that satisfactorily pass these tests. Hundreds of dogs whose owners have no interest whatsoever in the winning of obedience degrees are completing training courses. The owners know that a trained dog is simply a better pet, a greater source of pride to his master, and a happier dog than the poor untaught creature whose misbehavior brings on continual scolding and spanking.

Starting Obedience Training

What commands should a dog understand in order to be considered a well-behaved companion?

Before any dog can rightfully be considered a four-footed gentleman, he should have learned to:

1. Walk at heel, that is, at your side.
2. Come promptly when called.
3. Sit on command.
4. Lie down on command.
5. Stay where told (either sitting or lying down).

6. Respond instantly to the command "stop," "no," or "phooey."

This is called basic obedience training and may be started when the puppy is four or five months old, if the training is gentle and the corrections not severe. The older dog, whose education has been neglected, will have to be handled more firmly. Owing to his age, he may have formed bad habits that must be broken. While the young puppy may often be trained with a leather collar and an ordinary leash, the older dog, whose mature strength makes him more difficult to control, must have a training collar and a good strong leash.

I have two Setters and they both need training. I want them to work together on leash. Should I train them both at the same time right from the start?

Each dog should be trained separately until he knows all the commands. Later, when the dogs are worked together, it will not be so difficult, and they will be under better control.

You Can Train Your Dog

Is obedience training difficult for the amateur who knows little about dogs and their training?

Dogs learn through pleasing or displeasing results. They do things that bring a pleasant reward and quickly discontinue the ones that bring the opposite. When a dog's good behavior is repeated until it becomes a habit, we have what is known as *obedience*. Even an amateur is capable of commanding a certain degree of obedience from his pet.

Can anybody learn to be a good trainer?

Almost anybody can learn the technique of training, but that does not necessarily make him a good trainer. Good trainers, it seems, are born with the necessary qualities. They sense how a dog's mind works. They have the natural ability to coordinate their body motions with every move the dog makes. The result is perfect timing. Not everyone has these capabilities. The best trainers usually have rather definite, self-assured personalities, too.

Are there differences in training techniques?

There are really two kinds of training. One method is to teach the dog to do the right things by avoiding the wrong; the other to correct bad habits that have already been formed. By using the preventive method when possible, there will be less need of the other which is always more drastic. Training is an art, and as in all arts the technique will vary with the individual.

My friends say that since I am very patient, I would make a good dog trainer. Do you think they are right?

To make a good trainer, you must indeed have patience, but there are other things you must have as well. You must be able to understand how a dog's mind works, and to be able to transmit your wishes to the dog. You must know the dog's temperament, and be able to anticipate his next move. You must know when to be gentle, when to be firm, when to scold, and when to pet. You must also judge at what point to let up on the training.

How can a person judge if he would make a good trainer?

When directing a dog's training, the responsibility of the owner must be fully realized. Since all corrections must be simultaneous with the act, the person must have an excellent sense of timing and coordination. He must be consistent and must correct all mistakes regularly. The forcefulness with which the corrections are made depends upon the dog's disposition, so the trainer must have knowledge of the different breeds. And last, but not least, he must be versatile, as he will have to try out different methods to meet different problems.

Do men make better trainers than women?

Men usually get quicker results because they handle the dog more firmly, and they give commands with authority and in a low tone of voice. The dog knows better than to take advantage and, instead, soon has respect for the trainer. Women who are firm and have definite, positive personalities get good results in training.

Is it true that the personality of the owner will be reflected in his dog?

Yes. Dogs are generally a mirror for the character and personality of the human beings with whom they are associated. Dogs belonging to neurotic people are often neurotic too. The calm individual usually has a calm, placid dog. The gay, energetic person's dog is liable to be a peppy, lively pet. A surly, disagreeable dog may serve as a tip-off to the true nature of his owner. Perhaps if more owners realized how revealing a pet's behavior can be, they would take more care that their dog's conduct should be a credit to them.

The Best Age for Education

What is the best age to start obedience training?

Simple training may start at six months, provided the training is not too intensive. Training clubs and classes usually accept dogs for registration at eight months, but professional trainers like an older dog to work with. Of course, much depends upon the breed of dog and upon his disposition. Boxers, for instance, do well when started in training at six months of age, if they are handled in a firm but quiet manner, and discipline is not too severe.

What effect does too early training have on a dog, if any?

The effect of too consistent obedience training at an early age is similar to a nervous breakdown in a human. The dog becomes overexcited at the least provocation; is never relaxed; his work is inconsistent; and he may have hysterical outbreaks. Such a dog should be given a complete vacation from training for several months, and when training is resumed, he should be handled in a kind, quiet, and gentle manner.

Is a dog two years of age too old to start in obedience training?

No, it is a very favorable age to commence training.

Are there many instances in which old dogs have been success-fully trained?

There are a great many cases in which the theory that, 'You can't teach an old dog new tricks," has been resoundingly exploded. A shining example of an old dog learning a multitude of new tricks is the Dalmatian bitch Io. Mr. and Mrs. Harland Meistrell of Great Neck, Long Island, were given Io when she was ten years old. Io's previous education consisted of being housebroken and no more. The Meistrells took Io to the training classes held by a local dog-training club, and in spite of the fact that her owners had never trained a dog before, within twelve months from the start of her schooling, Io had won the most advanced obedience degree attainable, that of U. D. T. (Utility Dog Tracker). She was the third dog in the history of obedience to win this degree within such a short period of time.

How can I tell if my dog is ready for training?

First, the dog must be physically fit. His sight and hearing must be good and he should be neither under- nor overweight. Training requires stamina. A rundown or ailing dog will not be able to absorb schooling.

Second, the dog must be sufficiently mature and calm to be able to concentrate. You can test your dog's ability in this line by watching his reaction to an unusual sound which continues for a minute or two. His reaction should be one of curiosity and sharp interest. He should not shy away, ignore the sound or lose interest in it after the first two or three seconds.

Third, and most important, the dog must have complete trust and confidence in you, his trainer. He should have respect for his trainer, but not fear him. He should not flinch at the sound of your voice or the touch of your hand. If he does, you will have to regain his trust before training can be successfully undertaken.

At what age is a dog considered to be in his prime when competing in obedience trials?

The age will vary with the individual dog but the consistent winners at obedience trials average five to six years of age or older. During one recent exhibition at Madison Square Garden several dogs that were eight and nine years of age were featured.

Training and Intelligence

Do dogs reason?

Dogs do not have the deductive reasoning power that man and some of the great apes have. Dogs learn through association and though repetition. They perform acts that bring pleasing results and discontinue those that bring displeasing ones. When left to their own resources, they act through instinct as well.

Is it true that crossbred dogs are smarter than purebreds?

Definitely not! Mongrels give the impression of being smart because through their wanderings they have taught themselves to do the things we must train our more restricted purebred dogs to do. Don't misunderstand! There are plenty of intelligent mongrel dogs but, generally speaking, they are not easy to train. Their temperaments follow no special pattern, while the purebred usually runs true to form and behaves in a predictable way that is characteristic of his breed.

Can every dog be trained?

Every dog will improve through training. How well the training progresses depends upon the breed of dog, the age, the disposition, and, most of all, *the owner's ability as a trainer.*

Is a female dog more desirable for training than a male dog?

It depends upon the individual dog. The trainer can hold the attention of a female easier than he can a male, because the male is usually more interested in other dogs and in what is happening around him, but there is the disadvantage of having the female's training interrupted and obedience competition postponed when she comes in season twice a year. There have been excellent obedience workers in both sexes, so no definite rule can apply in this case.

Is it possible to train a dog that is blind?

Yes. Blind dogs have been trained successfully, and there are cases where such dogs have received the C. D. title in competition at dog show obedience trials.

Is it possible to train a dog that is deaf?

A deaf dog can learn to be obedient by the use of manual signals, just as the blind dog will obey entirely by voice commands.

Training and Temperament

Will training change a dog's temperament?

Training will not change a dog's natural temperament but will bring about a better understanding between the master and his dog. In other words, a dog that is, by nature, shy and retiring will never make a good guard or attack dog, nor would one of a vicious strain ever be completely trustworthy.

If training is such a good idea, why do so many obedience-trained dogs lack spirit and act unhappy about the whole thing?

Training that has been too severe or of a nagging nature will make a dog sulky and indifferent. *When properly done,* training does not affect the dog's spirit. It will help to overcome shyness, develop his personality, and bring out his best qualities. The lazy type of dog sometimes gives the impression of lacking spirit, but this is the dog's natural temperament, and cannot be blamed on the training.

*I live in New York City and own an obstreperous Boxer. When
I remarked on his behavior to an acquaintance I was told
that it was to be expected, as all Boxers act more or less
the same way. In Europe this is not the case, as often two
or three dogs of this breed are in a home together, and they
always have good manners. What is the explanation of this?*

The dogs in Europe are raised as house pets from puppyhood.
Their training is started early, and their lessons learned gradually
over a period of time. In the United States the kennels are large,
and the dogs do not receive so much individual attention. Frequently dogs are not sold until they are several months of age,
when it is more difficult for them to readjust themselves to their
new life outside the kennel. That is perhaps why Boxers have the
reputation of being hoodlums.

*What kind of temperament should the ideal dog for training
have?*

The ideal type of dog for training is on the friendly side. He
is anxious to please, he is not too sensitive and not too playful.
He has a happy disposition, and is interested in the trainer and
what the trainer is doing. Dogs that are shy, those that are
aggressive, the lazy ones, and the clowns usually present training
problems.

*Is it possible to pick the right training temperament in a
young puppy? What does one look for?*

A good choice would be to select an alert puppy with bright
eyes and a keen expression, one that is curious, active, interested
in people, and not afraid of sudden noises. He must, of course,
be free of worms, be in good health and in high spirits, because
it is impossible to get good training results from a sickly dog.

Must a shy dog be handled in any special way?

Even if a dog is shy he must not be given his own way nor be
permitted to take advantage of the trainer. If given exaggerated

praise and patting when he does right, and gentle yet firm correction when he does wrong, the shy dog will learn to obey and will even gain confidence in himself.

The Dog That Fights

We have two dogs that fight whenever they get together. Will obedience training stop them from fighting?

Not to the point where the dogs will ever be completely reliable. Obedience training teaches a dog to respect the owner sufficiently so that a command or a word of warning may avoid a possible fight, or it may stop one that has already begun.

Will training overcome viciousness?

No, not if a dog is innately savage.

We have a large dog who started getting mean when he was about three years old. We have taken him to two professional trainers and they both gave him up as hopelessly ferocious. What shall we do now? He is big enough to be dangerous.

This may seem cruel advice, but the truth is that the only solution is to destroy the dog. You will never have peace of mind otherwise. You are inviting tragedy as long as you harbor a dog which even professionals admit is too tough for them.

My Dalmatian is an inveterate cat chaser. If I train him in obedience and teach him to stay within a certain area, will he stop darting through the gate to chase every cat he sees?

Dogs, the same as human beings, are not always able to resist temptation, and the obedience-trained dog is no exception. The training, as you have outlined it, would give you more control over the dog, and he could be more easily discouraged from taking part in such adventures, but he probably will still chase an occasional cat or two.

The Effect of Training on Hunting Dogs

I have recently purchased a young dog for the purpose of hunting. If I have this dog obedience-trained, will it ruin him as a hunting dog?

Even though all hunting dogs receive a certain amount of obedience training prior to the actual field work, this is done for the purpose of getting the dog under control. Obedience trials require perfection. Such exactness could easily interfere with your dog's natural hunting instincts. It would probably be better to train him for hunting first, then later train him for obedience work.

The Effect of Training on Show Dogs

It it true that a dog should not be trained for obedience if he is to be shown in breed competition?

There are both advantages and disadvantages to this. The training for close heel work required in obedience trials may cause a dog to crowd the handler in the breed ring, which is not in the dog's favor, but most dogs seem to understand when they are working in obedience competition and when they are not. It would be advisable to replace the training collar with a leather one or a show lead, while the dog is being shown for breed competition, since he associates the chain collar with the obedience ring. The advantage in having the dog obedience-trained is that he will stand firmly while being examined and will gait in a straight line and not pull on the leash.

If I train my Collie to sit at heel as required in Novice Obedience Classes, won't this interfere with showing him in breed competition at dog shows?

Not if you train your dog to stand at heel on command. By alternating the "sit," the "stand," and the "down," the dog will soon learn the difference between these three positions if the commands are given clearly and distinctly.

Because my dog is a terrier, I was told he should not be obedience-trained before he is shown in breed classes at dog shows. Is this especially true of the terrier breeds?

Terriers show to advantage when they are on their toes and ready for adventure. One that has been too strictly trained often lacks this spirit. If such a dog is obedience-trained, great care should be taken that his pep and fire are not dampened.

Training Takes Time

How long does it take to train a dog in novice work? How long for advanced?

The professional trainer usually likes to keep a dog six to eight weeks for novice training in order to make him steady under all conditions. The advanced work requires three months or longer, depending upon the number of exercises taught and upon the individual dog. The amateur will need more time all around.

I frequently read in advertisements how a dog can be trained in five weeks' time. Is this possible?

The average dog can be taught the rudiments of obedience in five weeks, but he should in no way be considered a trained dog. To train a dog in the basic work and to make him steady, most professionals require six weeks to two months. Advanced training takes at least three to four months.

How long should a dog be trained each day in routine obedience exercises?

It depends upon the individual dog and upon how much training the dog has had. In the beginning, twenty minutes to half an hour will accomplish a lot. This may be done in two periods of fifteen minutes in the morning and fifteen minutes in the afternoon or evening. The training periods should be even less for those dogs that haven't much stamina and tire quickly. On the other hand, the dog that is being trained in advanced obedience can work three-quarters of an hour to a full hour, as he is well seasoned and accustomed to hard work.

Obedience in America

When was obedience training first introduced into the United States, and by whom?

Obedience training, as it is known today, was brought to this country from England in 1933 by Mrs. Whitehouse Walker. Prior to that, almost all training was done professionally, and the training was used primarily for the working breeds and for those dogs trained in highly specialized fields of activity.

Is it a fact that obedience specialty shows were held before obedience trials were recognized by the American Kennel Club?

Yes, this is a fact. The first all-obedience specialty show was held in the fall of 1933, almost two and one half years before the American Kennel Club accepted these trials. It consisted of only one class and a tracking test. Five dogs competed, and the show was held at Mt. Kisco, New York.

When was obedience recognized and accepted by the American Kennel Club?

In the spring of 1936 the American Kennel Club approved obedience tests. At that time rules and regulations were drawn up governing all trials and the awarding of obedience titles.

What dog shows held obedience competition at their shows prior to the time the American Kennel Club recognized obedience trials?

The North Westchester Kennel Club held the first trial in 1933. In 1934 they held a second trial along with the Somerset Hills Kennel Club at Far Hills, New Jersey. In 1935 there were six trials held at the following shows: North Westchester, Somerset Hills, Philadelphia, Orange, Lenox and Westchester. In 1936, the year the American Kennel Club approved the trials, the number jumped to seventeen.

Is there extensive interest in obedience training in this country?

There is, and it is increasing. In one recent year there were 251 obedience trials held in America. All together, approximately 14,000 dogs participated in these trials.

How can I get some information about the official rules and regulations of obedience trials?

A copy of the latest official rules and standards for obedience trials may be obtained by writing to the American Kennel Club, 51 Madison Avenue, New York, New York. This manual includes detailed information concerning such matters as requirements for various classes, the scoring, penalties, and proper execution of the exercises.

Does a dog have to be registered to compete in obedience trials?

No, but it must be obviously a purebred.

Are mongrels excluded from A.K.C. licensed obedience trials?

Yes, but they can attend some obedience classes and receive diplomas if they successfully complete the course of training.

I understand that a spayed bitch or a castrated dog cannot be exhibited in bench show competition. Can an altered animal compete in obedience trials?

Yes.

Obedience Titles

Will you explain the meaning of the letters C.D., C.D.X., U.D., and U.D.T. used after a dog's name?

The letters stand for obedience titles awarded by the American Kennel Club and won in competition at dog show obedience trials. C.D. means "Companion Dog" and it is the first title to be awarded. C.D.X. means "Companion Dog Excellent," U.D. means "Utility Dog." The final title of U.D.T. means "Utility Dog Tracker."

Who was the first dog to gain all obedience titles in the United States?

The first dog to gain the U.D.T. was a Standard Poodle, Carillon Epreuve from the Carillon Kennels. Glee, as she was known, won her C.D. at the first two shows held under A.K.C. rules in 1936. Her C.D.X. and U.D.T. were completed in 1937.*

Is more than one obedience title ever used after a dog's name at one time?

Since all obedience titles (except tracking) are progressive, when a dog acquires the next highest title the previous ones are usually dropped. Thus the C.D. gives way to the C.D.X., the C.D.X. to the U.D., and the U.D. to the U.D.T. However, a dog that is a C.D. may pass his tracking test before completing the rest of his training. In this case the letters would read C.D., T.D. (Companion Dog—Tracking Dog). If obedience titles are gained in another country the word "International" is used before the title won in the foreign country.

In how many foreign countries must a dog gain a title before he is known as an International champion of obedience?

One other. The same is true in obedience trials as in the breed classes. For instance, any dog that has become a champion in both the United States and Canada is known as an International Champion.

---

* Carillon Epreuve was trained and handled by Blanche Saunders.

CHAPTER 11

Obedience Training
Made Easy—*II*

Now that we are familiar with the basic facts of obedience training, we are ready to get down to practical work. You will need only a little equipment, most of which you can improvise from materials around the house, but you will need lots of patience, for which, at this writing no substitute has yet been developed.

Once you have begun training, you may find that your dog seems to have transferred his affections to other members of the family. Take heart, don't be discouraged—this is a temporary condition. Your dog will simply be seeking protection from being trained. Many dogs go through this stage before they get over the idea that training is work and accept it as an opportunity to show off their accomplishments. If the rest of the family will cooperate by ignoring the dog, you will have nothing to worry about.

You will be eager, naturally, to see your dog progress rapidly, but you mustn't be too severe in putting your dog through his paces. Training that is too severe can depress a dog's happy spirit, and after all, it is not a dispirited canine precisionist that we want, but a responsive and willing companion. Accuracy will come over a period of time—but, again, patience is all.

In this chapter we want to tell you when and how to train your dog. We'll describe the equipment that you'll need and the procedures to follow. We'll show you how to teach your dog to do all the simple exercises, as well as jump, retrieve, and perform a few tricks. And if your dog has a behavior quirk that interferes with his training—slowness, timidity, excitability, etc.—there is something here for him, too.

Any questions?

Do's and Don'ts

What rules—if any—should the trainer keep in mind while teaching a dog obedience?

The following *Do's* and *Don'ts* are important:

DO

Do play with the dog before and after each training period When working, be serious.

Do, if possible, have a regular time and place for training.

Do be consistent. Always use the same signals and the same commands.

Do be patient. The lessons must be repeated over and over.

Do be firm and don't give in just because the dog doesn't like certain parts of his training.

Do keep your hands off the dog as much as possible. Corrections must be made with the collar and leash.

Do remember all training is progressive. Review the previous lessons that lead up to a new exercise.

Do be kind.

Do, if a spanking is necessary, hold the dog firmly by the collar while he is being punished. This will prevent hand shyness.

Do use the correct tone of voice when giving commands.

Do see that the dog is in a happy frame of mind at the close of the training period.

Do use only a plain training collar—not a spike.

DON'T

Don't play and joke with your dog while training. Don't laugh at him.

Don't overtrain. Five to ten minutes a day is enough at first. Later, twenty minutes to half an hour will do.

Don't train after the dog has eaten a hearty meal or during the hot part of the day.

Don't let the dog get bored. Introduce new exercises from time to time to keep him on his toes.

Don't move on to a new step until the dog understands all preceding ones.

Don't finish a lesson with the dog getting his own way. See that he does what you command even though not perfectly.

Don't lose your temper.

Don't expect a miracle. It takes weeks of training to make a dog steady under all conditions.

Don't nag the dog.

Don't grab at the dog with your hands or lift him up by his skin or by his tail.

Don't reward with food all the time. The dog should learn to obey because you ask him.

Don't let the dog blame you for the corrections. Let him take the blame for all mistakes.

Don't punish the dog by striking him in temper.

Don't punish the dog unless he understands why he is being punished.

The Training Routine

Is there any special order in which the obedience exercises are taught? What, for instance, comes after heeling, and are there any advantages in following a certain routine?

Here, age is the deciding factor. A young puppy should be taught to "Come" as one of the very first exercises. By coaxing him to respond for a pleasant reward, such as a pat or a morsel of food, you will get him to obey more readily when serious training begins. The older dog, since he must be trained entirely on leash, must go through a definite routine for a long period of time before he can be expected to obey. Probably the most satisfactory order of the various exercises would be as follows:

1. Heeling and sitting. (This includes sitting in front of the trainer and is known as the "Come-fore." See page 329.)
2. Sit and stay.
3. Going to heel position.
4. Coming when called.
5. Standing at heel position and stand-stay.
6. Lying down on command and down-stay.

Commands and Signals

Do dogs respond better to voice commands or to signals?

When the voice is used, it should have the right intonation and be one of authority. Whining or hysterical commands get poor results. When hand signals are given, the trainer should not be careless, but should make each motion clear and distinct, otherwise the dog will become confused. Since all corrections are made with the hands, motion means more to a dog at first than voice. As the training progresses, voice and hand signals become of equal importance.

If one wishes the dog to obey entirely by signals, why must voice commands be used at all?

It is to the trainer's advantage to give both the command and signal together during the actual training period. When the dog has had enough experience to keep him well in hand by means of signals, the voice commands will no longer be necessary.

Words and How to Use Them

What are the voice commands used in obedience training, and what do they mean?

"Come"—Command used to make the dog run to the handler.
"Come-fore"—Used to bring the dog from the side of the handler to a position in front of and facing the handler.
"Down"—To make the dog drop to the ground in a prone position.
"Go"—To send the dog away from the handler.

"Good dog"—An expression of approval when the dog does the right thing.

"Heel"—(a) Command used to make the dog walk at the handler's side.

(b) Command used to make the dog go to Heel position from the Come-fore position.

"Hup" or "Up"—Command used for jumping.

"Look-for-it"—To make a dog seek an object that he will recognize only by smell, as when seeking a lost article, or tracking, or in scent discrimination.

"No"—To caution the dog or to let him know that he has done wrong.

"Out"—To make the dog release his hold on whatever object he has in his mouth.

"Phooey"—An expression used to correct a dog when he has made a mistake.

"Sit"—To make the dog sit down.

"Stand"—To keep the dog on all four feet.

"Stay"—To make the dog remain by himself in either the sitting, the lying, or the standing positions.

"Take it"—To make the dog take an object either from the handler's hand or off the ground.

Will you explain what is meant by the different tones of voice used when training?

There are three tones of voice used throughout all training. For the dog just starting training, or for the shy dog that lacks confidence, the coaxing voice is used to give all commands. Once the lesson has been learned, the ordinary voice is used to give the command so that the dog will know what is expected of him. When the dog refuses to obey, the trainer *demands* obedience in no uncertain terms. It is surprising how well these different tones of voice work with dogs, just as they do with children.

*Do dogs really understand such words as "Stop," "No," and
"Phooey," or is it the tone of voice that impresses them?*

The tone of voice means more to a dog than actual words,
but the dog soon learns to associate certain words with certain
actions. The negative approach in this case will indicate that the
dog has done or is about to do something wrong. It will check
him at once or serve as a warning to avoid a disgraceful act for
which the dog would have to be punished. Take, for instance, a
young puppy that steals. The first time the puppy takes something he should not, the trainer raps the puppy's muzzle and
uses the word "No" in a very reproachful tone of voice. The
next time the puppy sniffs the table, he will remember his
previous lesson if the trainer quietly says the word "No."

How to Use Hand Signals

Will you describe the hand signals used in obedience training?

Come—A motion across the body from the side toward the opposite
shoulder.

Come-fore—A motion from the side to in front of the handler, to
make the dog come around and sit in front.

Directed jumping—The arm is extended full-length to the side and
parallel to the ground. Right arm indicates right hurdle; left
arm indicates left hurdle.

Down—(a) When facing the dog, raise the arm above the shoulder
in a striking motion.

(b) When the dog is at Heel position, the arm hangs
straight down with wrist bent and fingers parallel
to the floor.

Go—The arm is extended full-length in front of the handler.

Heel—(a) A swinging motion of the arm from in front of the
handler to his side, to make the dog go to Heel.

(b) A forward motion of the arm, to make the dog start
walking at Heel.

Jumping (broad jump)—The arm nearest the dog is raised quickly,
parallel to the hurdle.

Sit—When facing the dog, extend the hand palm upward. Flip the fingers upward with a quick wrist motion. No signal is used to make the dog sit at the handler's side.

Stay—The arm is extended downward, palm back, and held momentarily in front of the dog's muzzle.

Stand-stay—Same as the "Stay" signal.

The Training Equipment You Need

What equipment must be purchased in order to train my dog in obedience?

The two most important items are the correct training collar and the proper kind of leash. The collar should be a slip chain, and, although it will vary with the size of the dog, a heavy chain link is always preferable to a thin one that cuts into the neck.

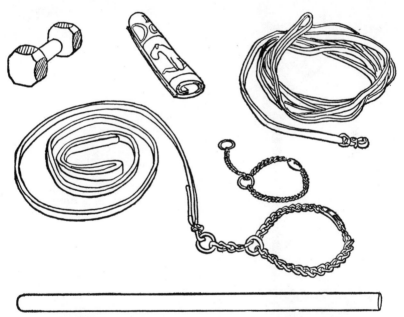

EQUIPMENT FOR BASIC OBEDIENCE TRAINING

For basic obedience training, you will need a dumbbell; a rolled-up magazine; a long line, 25 to 50 feet in length, with a snap on one end and a handle loop on the other; a chain-link training collar of proper size; and a jumping stick made from an old broom or mop handle, painted white for better visibility.

The leash should be about six feet long and of good leather, with a strong snap that will not open by accident. A flat leash is easier to handle than a round one. A chain leash is impractical and should not be used. For advanced training, a regulation dumbbell will be necessary; scent discrimination articles of wood, leather, and metal; a set of hurdles, consisting of the solid, the bar, and the long jumps. Details of the hurdle are published in the American Kennel Club rule book for obedience.

What is a training collar? Does the word apply to any special type collar?

A training collar is any collar used for the purpose of training. It may be made of leather, or of plain metal chain links. It

THE TRAINING COLLAR

To form the training collar, hold one ring above the other, and drop the links through the lower ring.

may be made of prongs that press into the neck, or one so constructed that when the leash is pulled tight the collar closes together and pressure is applied by pinching the dog's neck. The last two are referred to as spike collars. The one commonly used in obedience training and recommended for this purpose is the plain metal chain-link slip collar.

How can I tell what size chain collar to buy?

When the collar is placed on the dog's neck, and pulled tight, there should be two to three inches of overlap, providing this length permits the collar to slip over the dog's head easily. It is better to have the chain too short than too long, to avoid wasted motion.

Is there a correct way to put a training collar on?

Yes! With the dog on your left side, the collar is placed on the dog's neck with the leash fastened to the ring of the chain that passes OVER the neck. If it passes under, it is wrong because this will not let the collar loosen automatically. If there is any

THE WRONG AND RIGHT WAYS TO PUT ON THE TRAINING COLLAR

(Left) The leash here has been fastened to the ring of the chain that passes under the dog's neck, and the collar will not loosen as it should. *(Right)* Here the leash has been properly fastened to the ring of the chain that passes over the dog's neck. The collar will loosen as the leash is slackened.

doubt in your mind, slip the chain in collar form around your left hand and experiment. If it is put on correctly the collar will loosen when the leash is slackened. If not, it will stay tight.

What is a spike collar? This was recommended to me recently for training my Great Dane.

A spike collar has prongs that press into the dog's neck when the leash is pulled tight. Some have the points turned back, so they are not as harmful. Even so, the spike collar is not recommended for the amateur trainer except when he has an unusually strong dog or one of a bad disposition. When used regularly for obedience training, the spike collar may cause the dog to work in a dejected mood, and he will appear cowed and browbeaten.

I have heard arguments both for and against the practice of leaving my training collar on my German Shepherd all the time. I am wondering which is correct.

From a trainer's point of view, there are both advantages and disadvantages to such a practice. The obstreperous type of animal will be kept under control more if he knows the training collar is there ready for use when necessary. On the other hand, the lazy or less enthusiastic animal, that only enjoys showing off at times, may be pepped up if the collar is put on just prior to his working periods.

Is the practice of keeping a slip collar on dangerous?

For hunting breeds or for those dogs that roam a great deal, there is always the possibility of something catching in the ring to cause the collar to tighten and choke the dog. The collar may become lost if it slides over the dog's head when he sniffs along the ground. If your dog has much freedom, it would be advisable to have him wear a plain leather collar rather than the training one.

What kind of leash should I buy for training a dog that weighs about sixty pounds?

The training leash should be about six feet long and made of good flat leather with a strong snap. For large dogs, the leash should be about three-quarters of an inch wide. For small dogs, one that measures one-half inch is heavy enough. A round leash is not satisfactory because it slips through the hands too easily. Neither is a chain leash practical, because it will cut the hands. The flat leather kind is recommended, but avoid buying one with a French snap that may open accidentally.

Will you describe the proper way to hold the training leash?

The loop is placed around the right palm and the leash taken in the left hand a short distance from the dog's collar. The right hand crosses in front of the body and grasps the leash just above the left hand. This hold will give the trainer excellent control over the dog, even when the leash is released momentarily by the left hand for such purposes as patting the dog or for making corrections.

A dog-supply shop recently sold me a leash they said was the proper six-foot training leash. This is awkward to hold because it seems so long. Wouldn't my short one do as well?

The long leash is necessary to permit the trainer to work at a distance, as the training progresses, and still control the dog. If you hold the leash the right way it will not seem awkward.

Is there any reason why the leash should not be held in the left hand while training?

At the start of training, a right-handed person will have better control over the dog if the leash is held short in the right hand, and the left hand is used to make corrections and to control the dog. Later, after the dog has had experience, it is a good idea, during the routine practice, to carry the leash in the left hand occasionally.

Is a chain leash recommended for a strong dog that constantly bites at the leash?

A chain leash is not recommended for the actual training. The chain is hard to hang on to, and when the dog pulls it hurts the hands. The leash should be of good strong leather, and when the dog bites at it, the trainer should give the dog a sharp whack across the nose with the handle of the leash.

Since I started training my Collie, the long hair around his neck has worn down considerably. I don't want to stop training him, so what can I do to prevent damage to his coat?

The training collar certainly is hard on a dog's coat, especially the long-haired ones such as the Collies, Poodles, and Sheepdogs. One thing you can do is to use a leather slip collar instead of a chain one. Training results will be slower, but it will be less harmful to the coat. The alternative is to make up your mind that the coat must be sacrificed during the training period. Once training is completed, you can concentrate on getting the coat into good condition again.

Teaching Your Dog to Walk on a Leash

What is the best way to teach my Boxer to walk nicely on the leash? He pulls and hauls so that none of us ever wants to take him for a walk.

The first thing you will need is a chain-slip collar. Because your dog is a Boxer, the collar should be made of heavy links and not light ones. When you take the dog for a walk, command that he "Heel," and snap the leash hard. When he goes ahead, make an abrupt about-turn, and go in the opposite direction. After you make the turn, jerk the leash again, and repeat the command "Heel." If he lunges ahead, make another quick about-turn, and jerk the leash harder. Practice turning to the right, and snap the leash sharply. Turn to the left, and bump your knee into the dog. Make a continuous circle to the right; then circle around to the left and watch for every opportunity to correct the dog when he steps out of line. Alternate a normal walk with a slow walk and with a running pace. As soon as your Boxer understands that he is more comfortable walking close to your left side, he will go along without pulling.

My three-year-old Boston Terrier refuses to walk on leash. When I jerk his collar, he is more stubborn than ever. Should I continue to jerk him even harder until he obeys?

No. Instead of jerking your Boston Terrier, pull the leash tight and drag him slowly along the floor, until he makes up his mind he would rather walk than be dragged. When he gets on all four feet and starts to walk by himself, slacken the leash to give him more freedom, and praise him a great deal.

Training Your Dog to Heel

What is the easiest way to teach a dog to go to the heel position? This always seems such a difficult exercise.

To make this lesson as easy as possible, with the dog sitting facing the trainer, the trainer walks to the right, past the dog, and continues walking. The dog will turn around to follow the trainer and will swing into the heel position automatically. The command "Heel" is, of course, given. Later the trainer walks backward two or three steps to get the dog on his feet, then moves forward the same distance to swing the dog around into place, and then halts. The dog is helped around by the leash held in the left hand. Fewer steps are taken each time, and the collar is snapped harder until the dog responds instantly to the command "Heel."

When I tell my Shetland Sheepdog to go to heel position she obeys, but in a very sloppy fashion. She gets three-quarters of the way around and then sits at an angle. What is the best way to correct this?

Put the dog on leash. Hold the leash in the right hand but grasp it with the left a short distance above the dog's collar. Give the command "Heel." When the dog starts to move forward, drop the left hand past the body and hold it as far back as you can reach. With the arm still outstretched, give several hard jerks on the leash until the dog continues on far enough to make a good turn. At this point, the left hand lets go of the leash, and the trainer's side is patted to coax the dog to move closer to the left knee.

I entered my first obedience trial a short time ago and won second place. The judge told me I lost points when my dog heeled for a few steps on my right side instead of on my left. My Cocker has always had this habit and I can't break him of it.

When the dog sneaks in on the wrong side, kick backward with your right foot and catch him by surprise. A few such corrections, if they are sharp enough, should remind the dog to stay on the proper side.

We have a Collie that is a fast-moving dog. When he works in obedience trials he always walks slightly ahead of me. When I try to catch up to him he walks faster than ever. The judge always marks me down on this exercise.

When you train at home, don't hurry but walk slowly and move forward only a step at a time. The leash should be slack, and when the dog starts ahead, snap out the command "Heel" and give a hard jerk on the collar. Make a quick about turn or turn to the left and strike against him with your knee as you make the turn. One or two taps on the nose with the end of the leash will also make the dog hold back and adjust his pace to yours.

I have been training and exhibiting my Pomeranian with success, but she dislikes to heel and won't sit close to me. How can I keep her from staying so far away?

Because of the Pomeranian's size it is natural for her to protect herself. Remember, your feet appear big to her, and she doesn't like to be stepped on. Special care should be taken not to hurt her in any way by stepping on her paws or by taking a side step toward her when you halt. Frequently small dogs heel just as close as the larger ones, but, because there is more open space below the trainer's dress or coat, the small dog only appears to be farther away.

I have tried repeatedly to teach my Shepherd to go to "Heel" position when he is sitting in front of me, but no matter how much I signal or command him to "Heel," I end up my pulling him around with the leash. Is there any way to make the dog move when I tell him to so that he will not just sit and look at me?

When a dog is taught to go to "Heel" position, both hands are held in front of the trainer, waist high. The command "Heel" is given first, then immediately the left foot steps backward and the leash jerks the dog forward with a hard snap as both hands are dropped to the left side. With practice the dog should start to move the moment the left hand begins the downward motion.

What is the best way to get my Shepherd's attention while heeling? He won't look at me but is interested in everything around him. I jerk on the leash but get nowhere.

The best way to get your Shepherd's attention is to yank the leash in a series of jerks as hard as you can. Make a number of quick about-turns while heeling and several unexpected right and left turns. Always jerk the leash several times and not just once or twice. If you alternate a fast walk with a slow pace and then go into a quick run, you will catch the dog off guard and will be able to make even more corrections.

Whenever I am training my dog he grabs at my arm or at my hand in play. If I jerk away he even jumps up on me. How can I stop this?

You make the mistake of jerking away when he bites at you. Do just the opposite. Hold your arm still and use your voice to order the dog to stop. At the same time flip the end of the leash sharply across the dog's nose. One or two such lessons will convince him you mean business and that training is not a game.

Why is a dog trained to heel on the left side? I would like my dog to heel on both sides so he will always walk on the side toward the curb.

For police work the dog is trained to walk on the left side, between the officer and the criminal. This leaves the officer's right hand free to use his gun. At the same time, it places the dog near the criminal's right hand in case he tries to attack. For everyday use, right-handed people will have more control over the dog during the training period if the dog is on the left. Once the training is completed, the right hand can be used more freely with the dog on the left side out of the way. However, except for obedience competition at dog shows, there is no reason why your dog should not be trained to walk on either the right side or the left.

I have been training my Dalmatian in obedience, and he does very well on leash, but the moment I take the leash off he darts away. Do you have any suggestions?

Fasten the training leash to the collar and let it drag along the ground while you put the dog through his heeling exercises. When the dog tries to run away, step on the leash quickly and snap out the command "Heel." The leash may be replaced with a long piece of clothesline and the rope shortened a little every day. When your Dalmatian responds entirely to voice commands, take the line off completely and see what happens.

Does it make any difference which foot the trainer uses to step forward at the start of heeling?

If the dog works entirely by signals it will help if the trainer starts forward on the left foot. If a verbal command is given it is not so important because the voice controls the action.

Will you describe the difference between a left U turn and a left about-turn?

In the left U turn both the trainer and the dog turn to the left when making an about-turn. In the left about-turn, the trainer turns to the left but the dog turns to the right, going behind the trainer. The leash is passed in back of the trainer from the right hand to the left, then back to the right again.

I have visited our local training class and watched owners train their dogs. I notice that when some of the dogs are told to "Heel," the leash is jerked so hard it throws the dog off balance. Doesn't this practice make the dogs associate the command "Heel" with the unpleasant experience of being thrown off their feet?

Not if your timing is right: The command is given first and followed a split second later by the correction (in this case a jerk on the collar). A word of praise or a pat, given immediately, soon makes the dog forget the correction and puts him back in good spirits. He doesn't associate unpleasantness with the word "Heel" if the correction follows the command.

What is the advantage of having a dog finish an exercise by going around in back of the trainer?

No advantage except that it is a bit easier to teach. Once the dog is trained, though, there is really a disadvantage, because if the dog is on leash and the owner's arms are full of bundles, the leash entwines itself around the body when the dog, to get to "Heel" position, has to pass in back of the person.

Special Problems in Heeling

If a dog is attending a training school, should he be made to heel when walking along the street? In other words, how

*will he understand when he is being taken out to relieve
himself?*

If you want the dog to relieve himself, walk slowly, or stand
still and give the dog a little freedom. Otherwise, walk at a
normal pace and make the dog heel without letting him stop
at every hydrant or post he comes to and without sniffing the
ground constantly.

*My Weimaraner pushes up against me when we walk on the
street. I have jerked him away with the leash repeatedly
but it doesn't help. How close to the trainer should the dog
walk while heeling?*

A dog should walk as close to the trainer as he can without
touching him. Interference in any way should be discouraged.
Instead of using the leash to make the corrections, lift your
left knee (if the dog is on the left side) and bump him hard
every time he crowds you. Make several unexpected turns to
the left, and step into him as though by accident. This way the
dog should soon learn to keep his distance.

*My Beagle constantly sniffs the ground while heeling. I jerk
hard on the collar but it doesn't help. Is it usually difficult
to train a Beagle to keep his head up?*

Because they are hounds, Beagles are apt to keep their noses
close to the ground unless otherwise trained. An unexpected kick
along the ground under his nose when he begins to sniff, will
help teach your Beagle to keep his head up. At no time while
working must he be permitted to drop his head for an instant
without being corrected in one way or another, either by a jerk
on the leash, a gentle push with the foot, or by tossing something at the spot he is smelling, if he is not on leash.

*When my Cocker was a young puppy, he always galloped up
and down stairs ahead of me. Last week, when he was on*

leash, he tripped me and I fell. How can I stop him from dragging me up and down stairs?

With the dog on the left side and the leash held fairly short in the left hand, advance either up or down stairs one step at a time and use the word "Heel" accompanied by a sharp jerk on the leash. Every time your Cocker lunges ahead, stand still— repeat the command and give the correction again. A whack on the tip of the nose with the handle of the leash will also help to make the dog think twice before lunging ahead. Another method is to turn unexpectedly and walk in the opposite direction.

My Schnauzer comes when called and sits squarely in front of me, but he always goes to "Heel" position without waiting for me to tell him to. Have you any suggestions?

Put the dog back on leash, call him and make him sit in front of you. Step back, and call him again. Do this a dozen times or so without permitting him to go to "Heel" position. When you take the leash off, follow the same procedure. Do several recalls without completing the exercise. This will steady your Schnauzer down to wait for the command before going to "Heel" position.

Sitting

Will you please describe the method for training a dog to sit on command?

The training should be done on leash. Pull the leash tight with one hand to hold the dog's head up, then push down on the dog's hindquarters with the other hand until he goes to a sitting position. Always say "Sit." If the dog resists the downward pressure slap him sharply on the hindquarters, but keep the leash tight to hold the dog's head high. After he knows what you mean by the command "Sit," you can use a short jerk on the leash instead of a steady pull. This will make him sit more quickly. When he obeys willingly on leash, try taking the leash off. If he doesn't sit at once when told, pull up on the collar and slap him lightly on the rear end.

My Shepherd used to sit at an angle with his rear end away from me. I succeeded in breaking him of this habit, but now he sits in back of me at the opposite angle. I've tried pulling him forward but it doesn't help.

Instead of fighting the dog by pulling on the leash, take up the slack in the leash gradually when the dog starts to sit down. At the same time, kick backward with your right foot and tap him on his rear end to make him pull himself forward and sit straight. The correction is timed to catch the dog as he lowers himself to the ground, and it is not severe enough to cause the dog to swing too far in the opposite direction.

Our Chow has a habit of barging through doorways ahead of people and tripping them. Can we break her of this?

Teach her to sit on command. When you approach a doorway and she starts to push ahead tell her to "Sit," and walk on through the door. If you do this consistently, she will learn to wait when she comes to a doorway. Another method is to close the door carefully and catch the dog just behind the ears. Hold her momentarily while she struggles to free herself. Then release her and tell her to "Heel!"

My St. Bernard weighs almost 200 pounds, and I weigh 130. How can I make the dog sit down when I tell him? When I jerk his collar and push down on his rear end, I can't budge him.

You might just as well save your energy, because your dog is too big to be handled in the usual way. Use both hands on the leash just above the dog's collar. Pull up as hard as you can with both hands and hold him tight in that position until he sits down. When he obeys, release the collar immediately and praise him a great deal.

When a large dog, such as a Newfoundland or a Great Pyrenees, sits at an angle with his rear end away from the trainer

*what method of correction is used? They are too big to
pull around.*

This type of dog should be handled slowly and quietly. While
walking, tell the dog to sit and, at the same time, slide the left
hand back on the leash and hold it tight over the spot where
your hip pocket would be if you had a hip pocket. Step across
in front of the dog with your left foot to keep the dog in back
of your body. Hold him in this position until he sits down. When
he does, bring the left foot back to the normal position at the
side of the dog and slacken the leash gradually.

*Is it natural for a Pug always to sit on one hip? Mine does it,
and I am wondering if it is because she can't sit straight.*

Certain heavy-set breeds are inclined to sit on one hip, but
there is no reason why they cannot be made to sit straight. With
the leash held short in one hand, the free hand gives a sharp
whack on whichever hip the dog leans toward. If the whack is
timed to get the dog just as he sits down, the habit will be
broken more quickly.

*If a dog has formed the habit of sitting far back instead of
close to his trainer, what method of correction is suggested?
My Great Dane is too heavy to drag forward.*

An assistant should walk along quietly just in back of the dog
and carry a light bamboo rod or several short pieces of chain
in his hand. When the dog starts to sit down too far in back of
the trainer the pole is used to tap the dog on his hindquarters
or the chains are tossed at his rear end to make him move up.
The dog should be on leash and the timing is important, as the
correction is made just as the dog lowers his rear end to the
ground.

"Come-fore" and What It Means

*I frequently hear mention of "Come-fore." What is meant by
this expression?*

The "Come-fore" is used when a dog is taught to sit and face
his trainer. This position in front of the trainer is used so fre-

quently with every exercise it is a good idea to teach the proper "Come-fore" position during the first few lessons.

What command is given to the dog for the "Come-fore" exercise, and is there any special way to teach it?

Either the command "Come-fore" or "Come-front" may be used. The trainer walks with the dog at heel position with both hands on the leash just as when teaching the dog to heel. He then walks BACKWARD two or three steps and gives the command word "Come," at which time the trainer's left hand brings the leash close to his body, waist high, and holds it there until the dog sits down on command squarely in front of and close to the trainer. The first few sits should be as perfect as possible so that the dog will form the habit of doing this exercise correctly.

Every time I call my Dalmatian he comes so fast he almost knocks me over. How can I cure him of this and make him sit in front of me as he should?

Put the leash on your Dalmatian and train him to come and sit in front, as though starting to train him from the beginning. When he comes too quickly snap out the command "Sit" while he is still three or four feet away from you. At the same time, extend both arms forward full length and snap the leash hard. With practice, the dog should sit immediately when he hears the command. Later, when the leash is taken off, your voice can still control the dog and make him sit when he should.

My Collie comes so slowly when I call that everybody laughs at him in obedience trials. This is embarrassing. How can I hurry him up?

All breeds of dogs do not work in the same way. Collies are noted for the slow and deliberate way in which they obey. They are usually steady workers but take their own sweet time about doing things. Keep a few morsels of food—such as dog candy, pieces of cooked liver, or other tidbits—in your pocket. When you call your dog, give him a piece. If this doesn't speed him up, about the only thing left is to have the correction come from someone else. With several persons to help, form a circle and work the dog inside the circle. Do a series of "Comes" from every angle. Whenever the Collie is slow, the person in back of the dog should drop a chain on the floor, or toss a leash at the dog's heels to make him move faster. Your part will be to praise the dog more than ever and make him feel you are offering him protection from the terrible things that are happening.

When my Irish Setter does the "Come-fore" exercise, he always sits crooked. When I try to make him sit straight, he jumps away. What am I doing wrong?

If the leash is permitted to get slack when making the correction, the trainer will lose control of the dog. Keep the leash tight and hold the dog firm, then either slap the dog on the hip or tap him lightly with the toe of your shoe to make him straighten up. Once he is square, slacken up on the leash.

Sit and Sit-Stay

I notice in obedience trials how some dogs sit in front of their handlers very close and very square. My Shetland sits away from me and always at an angle. Will you advise me how best to overcome this wide and crooked sit?

Your Shetland should be put back on leash, and instead of being jerked to the correct sitting position, she should be pulled in gently and coaxed to sit close. Walk slowly backward and make her follow along in front of you as close as possible. Every few feet stop and make her sit. This training should be done every day until the dog no longer objects to coming in but will snuggle up close for a pat or a morsel of food.

My dog simply will not stay when I leave him on the "Sit-Stay" exercise. How can I correct this fault?

An assistant stands behind the dog and holds the leash rather slack while the trainer tells the dog to sit and stay and then walks away. If the dog moves, the leash is given a quick, hard jerk, after which the trainer returns to the dog and places him in position and commands him to stay again. If this doesn't work after numerous repetitions, you may have to use a leash and a long, light piece of rope, both fastened to the dog's collar. The trainer holds the rope and the assistant holds the leash, standing in back of the dog. In this way either one can make any necessary corrections.

My Doberman Pinscher never breaks on the "Sit" and "Down" when he can see me, but the minute I go out of sight he gets up. I have taken him back and made corrections but it doesn't help.

Go out of sight, but ask someone to stand where you can see him and where he can see the dog. When the dog moves, this person should signal so you can call out the correction without making an appearance. It will also be an advantage if, instead of your making the correction, the other person does it occasionally.

My Boston Terrier watches me so closely in all his training that on sit-stay he turns around and looks at me when I stand in back of him. Is this wrong?

If your dog turns just his head, that is all right because his attention is where it should be, but if he breaks the sit by turning his body, he must be corrected. At first, stand close to your Boston and correct him every time he shifts his body around. Gradually increase the distance until he remains in the position in which you have left him, no matter how far you move away.

When the dog is off leash is there a signal to make him sit when he lies down by mistake?

The proper signal is to hold the hand outstretched—palm up—and to flip the fingers upward in a quick motion. This motion was used to make the dog sit and stay in the beginning so he will not be confused when he receives it in the form of a correction.

Teaching the Stand

Is there any special way to train a dog to stand at heel position so it will not confuse him with the sitting at heel as required in obedience trials?

The proper way to teach the "Stand" is to carry the leash rather short in the right hand. The left hand drops gently down the dog's right side and is held underneath and just in front of the near back leg. The commond "Stand" is repeated several times. Once the dog gets the idea of what is expected of him the left hand moves forward gradually until, later on, it is held straight down in front of the dog's muzzle, palm back. This is the "Stay" signal, and unless the dog is given this signal or receives the command to stand he will sit at heel as he was taught to do in his early lessons.

My Corgi is quick to sit down when I stop, but I con't make her stand very well. How can I teach her to stcnd when I tell her to?

The size of the dog has a lot to do with your trouble. Place your Corgi on a table and pose her in the stand position while you repeat the word "Stand" over and over. Every time she starts to sit down, stand her up again. She will soon learn what is meant by the word "Stand." Later, when placed on the ground, she will obey the command more easily. A push up under her stomach may do the trick, or touch her lightly just in front of the near back leg. For persistent sitters, the leash is sometimes looped under the stomach, and the dog is held up in a standing position.

*How can I keep my Cocker Spaniel from biting my hand when
I touch him under the stomach to make him stand? He also
bites when I push on his hindquarters to make him sit.*

The dog should be placed on a table and your hands should
be run over all parts of his body freely. It may be necessary to
muzzle him at first until he accepts handling without resentment.
Any growls or attempt to bite should bring a severe reprimand.
Later, when you attempt to make him stand or sit on the floor,
the leash should be pulled forward and downward and held tight
enough to keep the dog under control should he try to turn
and grab your hand. The pressure from the collar falls on the
back of the neck, so it won't interfere with the dog's breathing.

*My Shetland Sheepdog receives high scores in all the obedience
exercises except the standing for examination. In this she
always fails because she will not permit a stranger to touch
her. I am getting desperate. Have you any suggestions?*

Since your Sheltie is obedient to your commands in all respects,
she should be made to "Stand-Stay" as frequently as possible,
while a number of strangers walk around her without touching
her. If ignored completely, she may overcome the feeling of fear.
Gradually, the strangers should brush against her accidentally,
or touch her in a disinterested manner, while you, in the meantime, firmly demand that she stay where she is without moving.
Persistence on your part may help your Sheltie overcome her
fear until she will finally let the strangers touch her.

Lie Down

What is the best way to make a dog lie down on command?

The trainer faces the dog and is about two steps away. The
leash is held in the left hand and is short enough so that it just
clears the floor. The right foot steps on the leash and pulls the
dog's head slowly downward, while the left hand pulls up on
the leash. At the same time, the command "Lie-down" is given,
and the right hand is raised above the shoulder and held there

in the "Down" signal. The trainer should stand erect, and although the foot only taps the leash gently at first to make the dog lie down, it must be done later with a snap in order to get instant results.

I trained my Shepherd to lie down by pulling the leash downward with my hand. Last week I saw a trainer demonstrate the "Down" but the foot was used instead. Is there any advantage in this method?

The advantages are that when the foot is used the dog is not so inclined to creep forward; the dog can be taught to respond more quickly to the command, and the trainer is able to stand in an upright position instead of leaning over the dog. Also, if a dog fights the "Lie down," you have better control over the dog and a better chance to make corrections by using the foot on the leash.

I am training my Cocker Spaniel at home, and she is very smart. She will do everything except lie down. On this she fights like a wildcat and yells as though she is being murdered. What is the best way to make her lie down?

Certain small breeds of dogs are apt to fight this exercise, but this is easily overcome. With the leash held in the left hand, and just clearing the floor, place the right foot over the leash so it slides freely under the instep. Pull the leash tight with both hands until the dog stops struggling. When she does this press down on her shoulders and push her to the floor. Release the pressure on her collar a little to see if she remains. If she doesn't remain, tighten the leash again. The important thing is not to let the leash get too slack so that you lose control. All motions should be done quietly and slowly. The command to lie down should be repeated in a low, firm voice. When you succeed in getting her down the first time, the next time will be easier. Ignore any squealing on her part. It is merely an expression of resentment.

My Great Dane is large and very strong. When I attempt to make her lie down by stepping on the leash, she lifts her head, and I lose my balance and end up on the floor myself. What am I doing wrong?

Before you give your Dane the command or signal to lie down, hold the leash firmly in both hands not too far from the dog, so that it just clears the floor. Step on the leash with the right foot so it slides freely under the instep, and put your full weight upon it. Quietly give the command to lie down and gradually pull the leash up with *both* hands and hold it tightly. If your weight is entirely on the right foot, your Dane will not be able to lift her head and throw you off balance. In attempting to get away, she may turn her body in different directions, but keep the leash tight and turn with her until she stops struggling and goes down quietly. Ease the leash slightly until you see if she is going to stay in the down position.

Every time I make my Irish Setter lie down, he leaps at me and tries to bite. How can I stop him?

Take your usual position for the down. With the leash in the left hand and the right foot on the leash so it will slide under the instep, hold the handle of the leash in the right hand with about eight inches dangling free. When your Irish Setter lunges forward, flip the end of the leash across his nose and give him a sharp whack. In the meantime, the left hand pulls the leash tight and takes up the slack so the dog can't reach up to grab you.

Why does my Cocker Spaniel creep forward when I signal him to lie down, and how can I best overcome this habit?

When your Cocker was first trained to lie down, perhaps the hand with which you gave the signal was held too close to the ground. If this was the case, the gesture could have been interpreted as a "Come" signal. The best way to correct this habit is to hold the right hand shoulder high; then, when the dog moves forward, drop your hand quickly and cuff him on the tip of the nose. One sharp cuff is worth several nagging ones, so if you want quick results don't be afraid to slap your dog.

If a dog will lie down on command when the leash is on, why won't he obey when he is off leash?

The fact that a dog does not obey when the leash is not there to make corrections is proof that he does not respond quickly enough to your commands. The next time do not wait for the dog to lie down by himself, but snap him down hard with the leash. Do this over and over until the dog drops instantly at the very first command or the moment he sees the hand start to go up for the down signal.

Training Your Dog to Stay

We have taught our Fox Terrier to heel and to sit when told, but he won't stay. We tell him to stay and put him back when he moves, but he always gets up and runs away.

The training should be done ON leash, not off. Every time the dog moves from a particular spot, the leash should be jerked harder and the command to stay repeated with a more threatening attitude. Remember, the harder the snap the quicker the results. Your Terrier should first stay while you face him, then while you walk around him. Later, he must remain still while you stand in back of him. Keep him sitting while you drop the leash on the floor; then make him stay while you walk across the room or go out of sight. A move on his part means another correction. It is only through constant corrections that your Terrier will learn his lesson.

Does it make any difference which foot the trainer uses to step forward with when the dog is left in a sitting position?

Yes. The right foot should move first, and there should be a slight hesitation before the next step is taken. Of course, the command "Stay" is given at the same time, and the left hand is dropped in front of the dog's muzzle as a signal that he is to remain where he is.

What is the best method to cure a dog from moving forward on the "Stand-Stay"?

When the left hand is dropped to the side with fingers extended, the palm of the hand bounces hard against the dog's nose, then is held quietly for a moment about three inches in front of the nose. If the dog continues to move, do it again and make each correction more severe.

How can a dog be cured of anticipating the recall? In obedience trials, my Cocker never waits for me to call her, but she comes the moment I turn and face her.

During the practice periods, the dog should be left in the sitting position, while you face the dog at a distance. Instead of calling the dog, return to her as in the "Sit-Stay" exercise. Do this over and over, until the dog is steady; then call her only occasionally. Anticipation is corrected the same way as breaking on the "Sit-Stay."

Clowns and Runaways

What makes dogs run away? My puppy is only seven months old but already he refuses to come when called.

Dogs run away for a number of reasons. It may be to romp and play, or it may be that he fears what will happen when captured. While the puppy is young the reward he receives for coming when he is called should always be as pleasant as possible, such as a pat or a kind word or a tidbit. He will then look forward to this treatment and respond willingly. To break the habit of running off, the older dog should be trained on leash. When left in the sitting position he is commanded to "Come," after which the leash is snapped sharply, and the dog is coaxed to come and sit in front of the trainer. This is repeated every day until the dog forms the habit of coming when he is called. If he ignores the command or tries to run away at any time, the leash is jerked harder than ever, but the dog still receives praise for coming to the trainer.

I am fourteen years old and have a Terrier puppy that loves to run and play. Jeff won't come when I call him, and everybody tells me I mustn't run after him. How else will I be able to get him?

The next time you call Jeff, sit down quietly on the ground and see what happens. Puppies have a great deal of curiosity, and Jeff will probably be no exception. If he approaches you don't reach out and grab for him because that will make him dart away from you again. Pat him instead; then slowly take hold of his collar. It would be wise to have a pocketful of biscuit or dog candy to encourage Jeff to come to you more often and to make him feel his trip was worth-while.

My Airedale is obedient in the house and in an enclosed area, but the moment he runs free I can never catch him. When I work him again on leash he obeys perfectly.

You will have to have assistance in training your dog not to run away. Get several persons to stand around in an enclosed training yard, each with several short pieces of chain in his hand. Give your Airedale his freedom; then call him to you. If he obeys no correction is necessary, but if he ignores your command or if he runs away, each person, in turn, should throw the chains at the dog's feet until he feels the only safe place to go is back to you—at which time you must make a great fuss over him. The training should be repeated until the dog comes to you on the first command. Increase the size of the enclosed area, and, later, try him in an open lot but not without assistance.

I have a dog that likes to clown. When I call him he thinks it is a game, and I can never catch him. I live alone, so have no one to help me. Do you have any suggestions?

Since you have no assistance, the best thing is to give your dog a strict course in basic obedience training until he obeys every command to come and does so without hesitating. Later, when the leash is taken off, the training should be so impressed on him that he will obey at once. If, instead, he starts playing, raise your hand and command him to lie down; then give the command "Stay" while you circle around him to heel position. Quietly reach out and snap the leash on his collar. Give him more training on leash before trying him without it again.

Training an Ill-Tempered Dog

Although my Wire Fox Terrier minds at home, when I take him to a training class or to a dog show where there are other dogs, he becomes hysterical and forgets all his manners. Do you think he will improve?

Your Terrier will improve over a period of time. Take him out where he can see other dogs more frequently and be very severe in your training when he acts up. Shortly before you go to the training class or to a dog show, give him an aspirin to calm him down and make him less excited.

I am an amateur instructor of a training class. We have a very bad Doberman that tries to bite when I make him obey. I can lift a small dog off the floor when he does this, but I am afraid of the Doberman because he is so big. Do you have any suggestions?

Make the Doberman wear a muzzle in training class until he learns to accept discipline. Later, when the muzzle is taken off, if he attempts to bite you, hold him up just as you would a small dog with both arms straight out from your body to keep the dog at a distance. At the same time, circle around slowly. This circling will throw the dog off balance so he will be in no position to attack. Lower him slowly and release the pressure on his collar when he quiets down.

Why will a dog so often obey a professional trainer but not his owner? My Bulldog does everything our training class director tells her to, but she behaves very badly when I handle her.

The answer is simple. The trainer knows what he is doing. The dog knows that he knows, and the result is *respect!* When you succeed in getting your Bulldog to respect you as much as she does the trainer, you will have no more trouble with her.

We have one dog in our training class which attacks every other. Some members have threatened to drop out unless this particular dog is kept away. Should this dog be dismissed?

If the dog has not associated with others or has had unpleasant experiences with them in the past, it may take a while for him to accept these dogs as his friends. Instead of working this particular dog in class the owner should sit on the side lines and make corrections every time the dog lunges forward. Corrections will have to be drastic if the owner wants to get results. As soon as the dog is able to associate with others without causing trouble he should be permitted to work in the lineup, and if he is muzzled perhaps the other members of the class will feel more secure. If the dog does not improve over a period of time, he should certainly be dismissed.

I have enrolled my dog in our local training class. I am anxious to do as well as the others, but my dog resents it when I make him mind. Last week he bit me. As a result I have become afraid of him and would like to know what to do.

Since your dog actually did bite you there is no doubt that his intentions are serious. A sharp cuff on the nose, which is the usual correction will probably make him worse than ever. Instead, handle the dog quietly but firmly. When he lunges hold him by the leash at arm's length with his front feet off the floor. Lower him only after his anger has subsided; then quietly pat him. Once the dog realizes that you are not afraid of him and biting brings the discomfort of being choked, he will avoid further attacks on you.

*I have been sick for about two months and, until recently, have
been unable to walk my big white Standard Poodle. I now
find that the person who walked him during my illness, permitted the dog to growl and bark at other dogs. In general,
my Poodle wants to fight. I am discouraged and do not know
how to get him over this.*

Your Poodle has merely formed a bad habit that must be
broken. I doubt very much that he would fight if given the
chance, because Poodles, as a rule, are not fighters. The best
thing to do is to walk the dog on a short leash on your left
side. Hold the leash in your right hand, about eight or ten
inches from the end. When your Poodle barks or growls, flip
the leash sharply across his nose and command that he stop. A
small switch can be used instead of the leash if you want. When
a dog lunges at another dog he is all keyed up and excited. The
whack on the nose will give him something else to think about
momentarily.

How to Encourage the Slow Dog

*Is it all right to use tidbits of meat or dog candy to get my dog
to work a little more willingly and to move faster during
his obedience training?*

Yes, an occasional tidbit is all right. The practice of giving
food as a reward for everything the dog does is not recommended.
The dog should be encouraged to obey because you ask him and
not for the reward of food alone. If a little meat or a piece of
dog candy helps to overcome a special training problem, by all
means use it.

Without the Leash

*I have been training my Kerry Blue for the past six weeks and
have had to keep him on leash because our neighbors object
to having him in their flower gardens. Do you think he has
had sufficient training to try him without the leash?*

If your training has been consistent, six weeks should be enough
time to teach your dog to heel properly and to keep him under

control. Before you take him off the leash completely though, try heeling in different places with the leash thrown loosely across your shoulder. If the dog obeys, drop the leash on the ground and see what happens. Should he make a dash for the flower garden you can step on the leash quickly and stop him short. You will know, then, just how much control you have over your Kerry Blue and if he can be trusted with the leash off.

Retracing Your Steps

I keep hearing people speak of the "review" exercise. Of what does this consist?

This refers to a review of the six major exercises that go to make up basic obedience training. The first is "Heeling," second the "Come-fore," third "Sit-Stay," fourth "Lie-Down," fifth "Come," sixth "Heel" (or "Finish"). Usually in this order, the review exercise is done first on leash, then off, and it should be a part of the dog's daily training whether the dog is a novice worker or one that is doing the more advanced exercises.

Retrieving

I want to teach my Collie to carry things in his mouth—a basket, or a folded newspaper, for instance. Would it be hard to do this?

Some dogs learn to carry things by themselves, others have to be taught. With the dog sitting in front of you, and on leash, drop the leash on the floor and step on it with your right foot. This will prevent the dog from backing away. Open the dog's mouth with your left hand, and place the folded newspaper in his mouth with your right hand. Once the article is in his mouth, take hold of the fold of loose skin under the throat to hold the dog's head up. Stroke his head and give him repeated commands of "Take it—take it—good boy—that's it!" If he struggles, hold the paper in his mouth by force until he stops fighting. Once he holds the article on command, you can teach him to walk with it more easily.

*Would you describe the obedience training dumbbell and tell
me how it is used?*

The obedience training dumbbell looks very much like the kind
of small dumbbell with which an aspiring weight lifter might
begin his training—that is, a dumbbell that would fit in one hand.
Unlike the muscle-developer type, however, the obedience training dumbbell is made of wood. Its size and weight will depend on
the size of your dog. It is used in training dogs to retrieve. In
all obedience trials, it is standard equipment. For example, in one
competition, the dumbbell is thrown over a hurdle, whereupon
the dog is commanded to retrieve it. The dog must leap over the
hurdle, pick up the dumbbell in his mouth, come back over the
hurdle, sit before his handler, and, on command, present the
dumbbell to the handler.

*My French Bulldog has always retrieved his ball in play and
lately is doing the same with his dumbbell. Is this all the
training that will be necessary to teach him to retrieve in
obedience tests?*

Most certainly not. The dog that retrieves in play obeys because
he wants to, not because you have told him to. The time will come
when he will not be in the mood to retrieve, and then you will
be on the spot. The dog that has been trained to retrieve through
obedience is dependable at all times. In your case, you have an
advantage over the owner whose dog isn't playful, and if you
combine the playfulness with straight obedience, you will have
a happy and reliable retriever.

*What is the best way to handle a dog that fights and barks
when the dumbbell is put in his mouth? My dogs yelps and
simply refuses to hold the dumbbell.*

With the dog on the left side, stretch the leash forward and step
on it with the right foot. This will prevent the dog from getting
away from you. Hook the fingers of the left hand under the chain
collar and grasp the flap of skin under the dog's throat. If, after

the dumbbell is placed in the dog's mouth, he starts struggling, lift up by the collar so the dog's front feet come off the floor. The right hand presses down on top of his nose to keep the mouth shut. The pressure from the collar is on the back of the neck so the dog can breathe freely and yet he cannot get away nor can he drop the dumbbell. When the dog ceases to struggle, lower him to the floor. After one or two fights, the dog should hold the dumbbell willingly.

What method is used to make a dog pick up the dumbbell or any other article? My Boxer will hold anything I give him, but he won't take it from me himself.

The chain collar is moved high up on the neck just behind the ears and with the ring on top. The left knee (in the case of small dog it is the left leg) supports the dog so he cannot twist away. The collar is gradually tightened until the dog gulps or swallows hard, at which time the dumbbell is eased in gently and the pressure released immediately. The comand "Take it" is repeated over and over, and the dog is praised when he obeys.

Should I permit my dog to play with his dumbbell at home? I am training him to retrieve and want him to enjoy it.

No. Never permit the dog to play with his dumbbell by himself. If you throw the dumbbell as you would a ball, insist that he bring it back to you. That is excellent training, and recommended to make a dog work gaily. At all other times the dumbbell should be kept out of reach of the dog, and he should be given toys, balls, or large shin or knuckle bones to play with instead.

What can be done with a dog that dislikes his dumbbell? My Cocker Spaniel retrieves balls and sticks but the moment he sees his dumbbell he loses interest.

When your Cocker retrieves his balls and toys, it means play. The dumbbell stands for work. Reverse the procedure. Use the toys, the sticks, or other articles he likes and force him to take them, to carry and to retrieve them on command. When the retrieving is done in play, use only the dumbbell. This will avoid dislike of any one object.

How can we train our Airedale to go fetch objects when commanded? He will carry almost anything when we put it in his mouth, but he won't go and pick things up.

It is difficult in this limited space to tell you how to train your Airedale to fetch objects upon command. Dispositions and circumstances vary and require different methods of training. The first step, in any case, is to teach your dog to reach out for an object held in your hand. With the collar placed high on his neck, just behind the ears, give the command "Take it" and jerk the collar sharply. Repeat this over and over until the dog reaches to take the article by himself from one of many positions such as sitting, lying down, or walking at "Heel." With practice he should later pick it up from the floor, even though it may be weeks later.

What is the next step to teach a dog to retrieve if he will take the dumbbell from the trainer's hand but will not pick it up from the floor?

The dog must respond immediately to the command "Take it" before you attempt to make him pick it up from the floor. If the dog is slow about reaching for the dumbbell, the jerks on the collar should be harder until he obeys without hesitating. Make him reach for the dumbbell while he is walking at "Heel." Gradually hold it lower and, later, drag it along the floor in front of the dog. When he will take the dumbbell from these different positions, he should pick it up from the floor with a bit more urging and several repeated jerks on his collar.

Every time my Welsh Terrier retrieves his dumbbell, he drops it at my feet in play and waits for me to throw it again.

This doesn't help to get a good mark in obedience trials, and I can't stop him from doing it.

Do a series of "Comes" on leash, while the dog holds the dumbbell. Make him sit in front of you each time but do not take the dumbbell away from him. If he drops it, correct him severely. Later, try the retrieve again with the leash, and when the dog returns to you, snap out the command "Sit-stay" before he has a chance to drop the dumbbell at your feet. In other words, prevent him as much as possible from dropping the dumbbell.

My Doberman retrieves his dumbbell willingly, but he drops it after he is sitting in front of me. How can I make him hold the dumbbell until I take it from him?

With the dog on leash and holding the dumbbell, leave him in the "Sit-stay" position, then call him. Every time the dumbbell is dropped the dog should be corrected sharply, either by a jerk on the collar or by a cuff on the nose, and comanded "Phooey!" This exercise should be repeated over and over until the dog no longer drops the dumbbell but waits for you to take it from him.

The newsboy on our route throws the paper on the front lawn. Our Labrador Retriever quickly learned to bring the paper into the house, but now he's bringing the neighbors' papers as well and sometimes their doormats, laundry, and children's toys. What shall I do?

When your Labrador is outside he should be watched, unknown to him, and if he approaches any article other than your newspaper, he should be scolded or startled so that he will associate something unpleasant happening when he takes things other than his own. Don't forget to praise him, though, when he picks up the correct newspaper.

My Golden Retriever works well in obedience, but I always lose out in the "Drop on Recall." Penny will obey the com-

*mand but is reluctant to do so. Is there any way I can make
her drop more quickly when she is coming toward me?*

Hold the leash wadded up in the right hand. When Penny
ignores the command to lie down, the leash should be tossed
just in front of her or dropped to the floor with a crash. If Penny
is the nervous type, do it gently so as not to frighten her. If she
still ignores you, the corrections can be more severe.

Jumping

How are dogs in obedience classes taught to go over the jumps?

At first, the jumps are kept very low, and the handler will invariably step over the jump with the dog, at the same time giving the
command "Hup" or "Jump." He goes back and forth several
times with the dog until the dog jumps freely at the command.
The leash is held in the right hand, but the left hand holds the
leash a few feet from the collar in order to guide the dog in the
direction of the jump. If the dog is stubborn and refuses to go
over, the leash is pulled tight, and the dog is forced to step over.

*I want to train my dog to jump over a stick but he thinks it's
a game and takes the stick in his mouth. How can I break
him of this playful habit?*

One would instinctively jerk the stick away when the dog makes
a grab for it. The next time, hold it still and order the dog, in a
firm tone of voice, to behave. At the same time, jerk the leash
backward with the left hand to emphasize the correction. When
he stops playing, urge the dog to jump.

What advantage is there in teaching a dog to jump over a stick?

It gives him exercise, for one thing. It also helps to prepare a
dog for the bar hurdle jump required in obedience trials. Most
dogs like to jump, and even jumping over a stick makes training
more interesting. It teaches them to leap off the floor on command
so that it will not be necessary to lift them in and out of cars,
over barriers, or onto the table for grooming.

Is it very difficult to teach a dog to retrieve over a hurdle? I would like my Boston Terrier to do this.

Teaching a dog to retrieve is what is hard—not teaching him to retrieve over a hurdle. If your Boston will pick up anything from the ground that you tell him to, and, if he obeys quickly and willingly, you should have little trouble making him do the same thing over the hurdle.

At the last two obedience tests my Terrier would go over the hurdle, but when he reached the dumbbell he would just stand and look at it and stare at the audience. He has learned that they always laugh and clap when he delays picking up the dumbbell. How can I break him of this habit?

The leash should be put on your Terrier but kept slack. If he hesitates at all, the leash is jerked hard, just as when you taught him to retrieve the dumbbell. No command is given, only the jerk on the collar. A few such lessons should discourage your dog from playing to the gallery. This same correction is used when a dog gets into the habit of returning over the hurdle without picking up the dumbbell.

Our Yorkshire Terrier is a bright little dog and would make a good pupil for obedience training. What worries me is that I have seen photographs of dogs performing in obedience tests, and the jumps which they go over appear to me to be much too high for a small dog to be able to clear. How high would my dog have to jump in such tests?

The height a dog must jump is determined by American Kennel Club rules. The requirement is that the hurdle be set at one and one-half times the height of the dog at the shoulders. The length of the broad jump is twice the height of the high jump. For instance, if your Yorkshire is ten inches high, he must clear a fifteen-inch high jump and a thirty-inch broad jump. This applies to all breeds except Bull Mastiffs, Great Danes, Great Pyrenees, Mastiffs, Newfoundlands, and St. Bernards. For these breeds the high jump is once the height of the dog at the withers or three feet, whichever is less.

My Miniature Poodle is an excellent jumper, but when I try him off leash, he always stops and waits a moment before he jumps. If I put him back on leash he jumps perfectly. What can I do to overcome this hesitancy?

Keep the leash slack, give him the command to jump, then snap the leash very hard. Do this several times even though the dog would ordinarily jump by himself. When you try him off leash again and give the signal with your left hand, snap out the command quickly, which should remind him of the correction he received on leash.

When my German Shepherd does the retrieve over the hurdle he always uses the top board to balance himself when he goes over. When I put him back on leash he clears it easily. How can I get him to do it when off the leash?

Set the top board of the solid hurdle so that it will spin around if the dog steps on it. When your Shepherd feels his secure footing give away underneath him he should clear the hurdle thereafter. Another suggestion would be to stretch a clothesline a little above the top board, as this would also move when the dog touched it and give him the same feeling of insecurity.

My Doberman Pinscher jumps the broad jump very well, but he makes a wide circle when he returns to me. Is there any way I can cure him of this?

Put the dog back on leash, and stand at the side of the jump in the usual manner. Give the command to jump—but keep the leash slack. The moment the dog lands on the opposite side call out the command to "Come," and, a second later, snap the leash as hard as you can. Two or three such corrections, if they are timed properly, should break your Doberman from circling wide on the return.

Is there any way to cure a dog from cutting the corners when he jumps the broad jump?

To correct this habit the trainer stands ahead of the hurdles instead of at the side. When the dog jumps and crowds the trainer upon landing, the left knee is raised quickly to the side and knocks against the dog with force. If the corrections are timed right, the dog should soon learn to keep his distance even when the trainer stands at the side of the hurdle. To avoid cutting corners in the first place, train the dog to take the broad jump as part of his "Heel" exercise. He will form the habit of jumping in a straight line as the action continues forward, and the dog is not tempted to cut the corners as he turns back toward his trainer.

At every obedience trial I miss out on the broad jump, because my Great Pyrenees won't take it. He is too heavy to pull over. Have you a suggestion?

Work the dog on leash. Shorten the overall length of the broad jump so your dog can clear it freely. Have him take the jump while heeling. Later, leave him in the sitting position in front of the jump while you stand on the opposite end. Call him over and give the leash a quick snap. After several such lessons, try standing at the side and hold the leash in both hands. The left hand guides the dog over, and the right hand takes up the slack. If he refuses to jump, go back to his first lessons and practice some more. An assistant can help by holding a long pole parallel to and 18 inches above the first hurdle. The dog will learn to jump higher this way. In difficult cases, it would be worth building a special jump. A bar hurdle fastened to one of the regular hurdles and constructed so it would tip over when the dog knocked against it would train him to jump high and wide.

Tracking and Trailing

Is there a difference between a dog that tracks and one that trails?

When a dog tracks, he follows the broken path that results from the laying of the track. The disturbed ground over which the person walks or an object is dragged holds the scent and makes it easy for the dog. When a dog trails he follows the scent left by a body as it passes through undisturbed air. This airborne scent settles toward the ground and falls on the grass, on the leaves, and on the ground itself.

In a tracking test must a dog follow exactly where the person walked in order to qualify? I have sometimes seen a judge mark a dog "Not Passed" because the dog was a number of feet off the trail, although he was definitely working, and if permitted to continue would undoubtedly have found the article at the end of the trail.

A dog that is tracking footsteps will follow the line of the track more accurately than the one that is trailing a scent that descends on the surrounding objects. Unless a judge knows whether the dog is tracking or trailing a certain amount of leeway should be permitted.

Can every breed of dog be trained to follow a person's scent?

The long-nosed breeds of the Working, Hound, and Nonsporting groups are natural scenters. Probably most sporting dogs can be trained to follow a person's scent provided they are not tempted by stray game. Terriers have good noses but they must be taught to concentrate. The breeds that have short noses, such as the English Bulldog and the Pekingese, have great difficulty doing nose work.

What odors or conditions, if any, affect a dog's scenting powers when he is trailing or tracking?

Any strong odors, such as tar or gasoline, or any moving objects, such as shifting leaves and running water, will affect a dog's power to follow the trail accurately.

Does the time of day affect the dog's power to scent?

Definitely. Late in the afternoon or early in the evening, when the dew begins to fall and the air is heavy, are best. Early morning, before sunrise, is also a good time of day. Once the sun comes out and the moisture evaporates, scenting becomes more difficult. The hot, dry part of the day is the hardest of all.

Will a heavy rainfall destroy a scent?

Heavy rains will not destroy scent, but will temporarily lessen it. Once the rain stops, the scent is still there.

Do dogs ever backtrack when following a trail?

A good tracking dog should not backtrack but should keep on following the strongest and most recent scent. State police have gone so far as to say that a well-trained dog never backtracks at any time.

How long will a scent remain so that a dog may follow a trail?

Dogs have been known to follow trails that were more than a week old.

Is it true that a dog cannot follow the scent of a person that wears rubbers or rubber-soled shoes?

If this were true, dogs would be unable to track down many criminals and lost children. It is doubtful if they always wear leather-soled shoes. It may be a little more difficult for a dog to follow the trail left by rubber soles, but it is not impossible, since the scent descends from the body and not merely through the soles of the shoes.

Recently I saw a trick where a dog picked out one special dollar bill from among others. I would like my Poodle to do this. Is it hard to teach?

The trick is known as scent discrimination. The dog is trained to pick out an article entirely by smell. In other words, a person gives the dog the scent by putting his hand over the dog's nose. The dog, in turn, selects the article that corresponds to that smell. A dog must first learn to retrieve different articles on command before he can be trained to distinguish between them. Encouraging scent discrimination in the form of play is a good way to start teaching this exercise. For instance, when a dog is taught to pick up a glove and then to hunt around for the glove when it is hidden, he will invariably bring back the same glove, even if it is dropped alongside a second glove. Later the training is done on leash to make the dog more reliable.

Sending Him Away

How is a dog taught to do the "Send-away" in the directional jumping exercise in the Utility Class? I have tried by placing food at the end of the ring but with little success.

The "Send-away" should be taught as systematically as all other training. The dog should be put on a long line and given the command "Go." The line is taken in by a second person. When the dog reaches the other end of the ring, the trainer tells him to sit, then walks over to him and rewards him with food or praise. An automatic fishing reel that will take in the slack line is a good way to teach this exercise. When the dog walks away from the assistant, who holds the reel, the spring is wound up. When the dog is sent by the trainer, the line pulls him gradually without jerking the collar. The exercise is done at first without using the hurdles. When the dog obeys the command to "Go" and does it willingly, and is under control, he is then permitted to take the jumps on the return trip.

Was the "Send-away" used in obedience trials prior to 1950?

Yes. The Send-away was used in England in obedience trials as far back as 1934. The exercise was done so that the dog would continue to go away from the trainer as long as the trainer's arm remained outstretched. If the dog looked back and saw the arm dropped to the side, he stopped. The dog was then commanded to lie down, then was recalled to the trainer.

I have tried doing the "Send-away," but have no control over my dog when he is at a distance. He runs from one side to the other, gets tangled in the line, and won't sit when told.

A dog trained to do the "Send-away" must first be thoroughly trained in all preliminary exercises. When he doesn't respect the trainer's command to sit and starts running around the ring, the dog needs more basic training.

When I send my dog away from me for the directional jumping, although he obeys, his tail is down and he looks very unhappy. Is there any way to cheer him up in this exercise?

Since the dog obeys but is unhappy about it, try sending him for something he will enjoy going for. This may be for food, or a pat and a word of praise from someone he likes. As he becomes less depressed, the dog should be stopped on command while he is still some distance away from the reward he anticipates.

Dogs As Guards

I want to train my dog for protection work and to guard my property. How do I do this?

Teaching a dog to attack on command is highly specialized training and should not be done by the amateur. You can, however, teach your dog to bark and give warning. Encourage him every time he growls at a stranger or at any unusual noise. He will soon get the idea that he has your approval and will act accordingly.

Should a dog that has been trained for protection be kept in the home as a children's companion?

A dog that has been trained professionally to attack and to guard should be considered a dangerous weapon. It is not wise to keep such a dog as a pet, especially where there are children.

Is it possible to train every dog in protection and guard work? My Sheltie is quiet by nature, and I thought training him to attack would improve him and make him more aggressive.

Training will not change a dog's temperament. If a dog is not aggressive in disposition, training will not make him so. If a dog is inclined to be shy he will learn to bark and give warning very easily, as he will do that much for his own protection, but a timid dog can never be made to attack in the working sense.

A friend wants to give me a dog that was used by the Army for sentry work. The dog has been de-trained since his release from the service. Do you think it is safe to take him?

Many dogs used for guard and sentry work during the war had their natural protective instincts sharpened, but not to the point where they would attack of their own volition. Such a dog is not dangerous to have around the house as a pet.

Training Him to Use His Voice

What is the best method to train a dog to speak on command or on signal?

The owner must first find one of several ways to get the dog excited so he will bark of his own accord. This may be through play or asking for his dinner or from jealousy of another dog. Every time the dog barks, the trainer commands "Atta-boy. Speak." In this way, the dog will associate the word "Speak" with the noise he makes. Later, the training collar is used, and the dog is kept under control, while the trainer again gets the dog excited and keyed up to the point where he will give voice. The raised index finger is the signal to speak.

If a dog is trained to speak on command, will this make him more noisy than usual?

The dog that is trained to speak on command can also be trained to stop speaking when told. Such a dog should be quieter around the house rather than noisier, unless he has learned that by barking he gets what he wants and uses barking to demand attention.

Why was the "Speak on Command" dropped from the obedience trials at dog shows? This seemed such a useful exercise.

The owners of the Sporting breeds do not want their dogs to give voice in the field. They feel that if a dog is taught to speak he may speak by himself at an inopportune moment. Since obedience training is intended for all types of dogs, the "Speak on Command" exercise was dropped, as it was considered detrimental to the training of certain breeds.

My friend's dog, a Sheltie, barks when he wants to go outdoors. Can I train my Pointer to do the same?

Undoubtedly your friend's Sheltie taught himself to ask for what he wants. Barking comes naturally to some breeds. The Pointer can be taught to do the same, but it will be more difficult. He must be trained to use his voice and to make a sound, even though slight, when you command him to speak. Once he does this, if you make him speak every time he wants to go out, it will become a habit and later on he will demand attention by himself.

My eleven-year-old Beagle died last year, and now I have a new puppy, five months of age. The old dog had one habit I'd like the youngster to acquire—he barked whenever the telephone or the doorbell rang, which was a help, as my hearing is poor and I often don't hear the bell ring. None of us can remember how the old dog acquired this trick, and would like to know how to teach the new one the same thing.

A noisy dog by nature acquires the habit of barking at every sound. Encouragement is all he needs. If your new puppy seldom barks you must teach him to speak on command, as described on page 356. Once he understands the meaning of the word "Speak," station a second person outside the door and ask him to ring the bell, and give the dog the command to speak when the doorbell rings. Barking at the sound of the bell will become a habit, and the dog will do it automatically.

Training Clubs and Classes

Where can one find out where training classes are located and whom to contact about such classes?

Information on the location of training classes in your vicinity and whom to contact for further details may be obtained by writing to the American Kennel Club, 221 Fourth Avenue, New York 3, New York.

How does one go about forming a training class?

Find someone who is able to act as training director. This may be some person who has trained his own dogs, or who has attended training classes at one time or another. It may be someone who worked with the war dogs during the war or who has assisted in a training kennel. The instructor must be a leader, able to handle groups of people and to take the initiative at all times. With such a person as instructor, and with the aid of books and training films now available, a class can be formed and results obtained in at least preliminary training. The advanced work will be more difficult.

If a dog graduates from a training class and receives a diploma, does that mean that he has won his C. D. title?

No, obedience titles are awarded only by the American Kennel Club. A dog must receive scores at three different shows, of more than 50 per cent of the available points in each exercise, with a total score of 170 or more. A certain number of dogs must compete, and the points must be awarded by three different judges.

A training class has just been formed in our neighborhood. Would it be of advantage to join this class?

Yes. Training classes offer the opportunity to work with other dogs. Even though the animal behaves well at home, he may be obstreperous when out in company or in the presence of other dogs. Training classes keep up interest in training because there is a competitive spirit in trying to do as well as the others in the class. Also, one has the advantage of working under a trainer who will assist the owner with difficult training problems.

What is the difference between a training class and a training club and how do they operate?

Training classes may be sponsored by any civic-minded group of people such as the Lions Club, the S.P.C.A., the Boy Scouts, etc. The participants are not required to be members of the sponsoring organization. Training clubs consist of a group of people, all members of the club, with elected officers and yearly dues. Training clubs may become members of the American Kennel Club with representation by a delegate and a voice in forming the governing rules and regulations for obedience trials.

What You Can Expect to Pay

What is the average cost to enroll a dog in a training class? I want to train my dog but can't afford to pay a great deal.

The cost of enrolling a dog in a training class will vary from five dollars to twenty-five dollars for a nine- to twelve-weeks course. If the classes are sponsored by an organization such as the S.P.C.A. or the Humane Society, the cost is usually lower, because such organizations look upon the classes as a public service. If the training classes are run by a local training club the cost may be higher. Fifteen to twenty-five dollars per dog would be a fair price for classes run by a club.

If I decide to have my Scottie trained while he is boarding this summer, about how much can I expect to pay for his training?

The usual charge for obedience training is made by the week, and the average cost is twenty-five to thirty dollars per week, which includes the cost of boarding. For a six- to eight-week period the cost to you would be approximately a hundred and fifty to two hundred dollars. For this amount your dog should be well trained in basic obedience and given some advanced training as well.

Recently we formed an obedience-training club. If we hold a trial how much will it cost to get permission from the American Kennel Club?

The fee for holding an Obedience Specialty Show is twenty-five dollars. Before permission is granted by the American Kennel Club to hold a licensed show, your club must first hold two sanctioned matches at least six months apart. If an Obedience Trial is held as part of an All Breed Show instead of as a separate show the fee is fifteen dollars.

When There Is More Than One Trainer

Should more than one person—such as a husband and wife—handle the same dog in a training class?

During the first part of the dog's training, until he knows what it is all about, it is best for one person to do the actual teaching. Later, other people should handle the dog, provided they use the same signals and commands. Only when the dog has respect for every member of the family will he be a well-trained dog.

I have been criticized for permitting other people to play with my trained dog and to put him through the obedience exercises. Do you think this will interfere with the dog's regular work?

Not seriously. Even if your dog makes mistakes with other people, he will probably do his usual good work when you handle him again.

About Professional Trainers

Are people that train dogs professionally licensed to do so?

Unfortunately, people that train dogs for other people do not have to be licensed. Until such time as they are, the best way to choose a trainer for your dog is through the recommendation of a reliable third person.

My friend is anxious to have a professional trainer obedience train her dog. Where can she get the necessary information and how will she know if such a trainer is reliable?

Since obedience training is relatively new, a careful investigation should be made before sending a dog to be trained. The training of dogs is not controlled at present, and selecting a trainer must be done entirely through recommendation, either by a reputable person or by someone who has had his own dog trained. The American Kennel Club or your local kennel club will furnish you with a list of people who do training. By making a few inquiries on her own and by visiting the training kennels your friend can make a decision.

I am a member of a training club where the training director collects the enrollment fee for each dog and keeps the money as remuneration. Some of us feel it would be better for the fees to go into the club treasury and the training director to be paid by the club.

The last arrangement seems the only sensible plan to follow. All enrollment fees, the club dues, the proceeds above the cost of holding match trials, etc., are part of the income that clubs depend on to meet expenses.

What to Expect of the Training Class

Our local training club offers a nine-week course in training. I have enrolled my Bedlington in the fall class. How well will Trinka obey at the end of this time?

One cannot expect to have a dog progress as well in a training class as she would in the hands of a professional trainer. When trained privately, it requires six to eight weeks for basic training. The dog would be given intensive work every day and not just one evening a week such as you will probably do in class. Professionals train six days a week for at least half an hour each day, and they know how to handle the different breeds and how to meet the various problems that come up. By the end of the nine-week course, if you have practiced every day, your dog should know the different basic steps of obedience and should obey your commands in one fashion or another, but the principal thing will be that you yourself will have learned how to make the dog mind.

Easy Tricks to Teach Your Dog

Can any dog be taught to do tricks?

Any healthy dog can learn to do a few tricks for his own and his owner's amusement.

Should small dogs be taught the same tricks as large dogs?

Some of the tricks which a large dog can perform easily are too difficult for a small dog. There are tricks which are suitable for little dogs which seem rather silly and undignified for big dogs.

Will it ruin my dog for obedience work if he learns to do "parlor tricks"?

No, because if the commands used are entirely different he will understand what is expected of him. There are several obedience exercises which can be utilized as tricks. Jumping, retrieving, staying, can be worked into stunts if the owner wishes.

What is the simplest trick to teach a dog?

Probably to shake hands. Decide which command you wish to use—"Shake hands" or "Give me your paw." Let the dog sit or stand, facing you, give the command and then pick up his paw and hold it for a moment. Tell him he is a bright boy. If you do this five or six times a day, he should be offering you his paw on command within a short time.

How do I teach my dog to sit up?

Don't try to teach this until the dog is six or seven months old, as his back may not be strong enough before this. Prop him up in the corner of an upholstered chair or in the corner of a room (be sure the floor isn't slippery), take both front paws in your left hand, and lift him to an erect sitting position, and hold a tidbit just above his nose with your right hand. When he is in the correct position, give him the tidbit. To do this four or five times a day is enough at first. Some dogs seem to have a natural sense of balance and practically teach themselves this trick, others require many lessons before it is mastered.

Is it difficult to teach a dog to "play dead"?

Not if he has learned the obedience exercise "Stay." Roll him on his back and tell him "Stay dead." If he moves, put him back in position and repeat the command until he understands that he must hold the pose.

I'd like to teach my Fox Terrier to jump through a hoop. Please tell me how.

First teach him to jump on command, using a broom stick or golf club. The command may be "Jump!" or "Hup!" Next, get a barrel hoop which is large enough for him to pass through easily. Be sure the hoop has no nails or large splinters which might hurt your dog. To be safe, it is a good idea to wrap the hoop with cloth, cellophane tape, or adhesive tape. Put the dog's leash on him and pass it through the hoop. Hold the hoop in your left hand about a foot in front of him and a few inches off the ground. Give the command "Rowdy, Hup!" and guide him through the hoop, using the leash. Tell him he's doing fine, whether it's true or not. After a few practice sessions the hoop can be raised and the leash discarded.

Why do so many obedience-minded people object to teaching a dog a few simple tricks?

It is doubtful that many obedience people object to teaching a dog a few tricks, but what they do resent is obedience itself being referred to as tricks or stunts. As a matter of fact, the obedience-trained dog will take to performing tricks more readily and with a great deal more gusto than the untrained dog.

Qualifications for Judging Obedience Trials

How does one become a judge at dog show obedience trials? There are so few judges in our section that I would like to take out a license to judge at dog shows.

To become an obedience judge you must first write to the American Kennel Club. They will send you the necessary papers to fill out. If you meet the American Kennel Club's requirements your name will be published in their official publication, the American Kennel Gazette, for comment, favorable or otherwise. The next step is acting as an apprentice judge under licensed judges. If the reports on these shows are satisfactory, your name is again published in the Gazette and is placed on the A.K.C. list of approved judges.

Part Three

●

DOG BREEDING, SHOWS,
and
FIELD TRIALS

CHAPTER *12*

Breeding Dogs

Before you make up your mind that you are going to breed your dog, there are certain things you should know. First of all, the bitch must be of suitable age—that is, mature but still young. This is particularly important if the prospective litter is her first one. Proper house and yard space for the puppies is essential. The size of the breed enters the picture here, for the pen or yard that would be spacious for three or four Cairn Terrier pups just would not do for a litter of German Shepherds.

We take for granted your knowledge of the fundamentals of the general care and nutrition of dogs—you may need other knowledge and skills too. You should be prepared to devote your entire time and attention to the project, should it meet with misfortune in the form of whelping difficulties, a Caesarean, or an inadequate milk supply on the part of the dam. You may be confronted with the patience-trying task of caring for a litter of orphaned pups. These prospects are worrisome, it is true, but they are, after all, possibilities, not probabilities. The outlook becomes more encouraging when you consider the fact that more than 90 per cent of all bitches whelp their puppies with little or no trouble to themselves or their owners, have more than a sufficiency of good milk, and are devoted and competent mothers.

Like any other interest into which you put your whole heart, dog breeding has its problems and its drawbacks, but, in our opinion, there is no more absorbing and rewarding avocation if you have a true love of fine dogs.

Bitches and Breeding

How long is the period between mating and the birth of puppies?

Nine weeks. This may vary with individual bitches. For some the period of gestation is sixty-one days, while others may carry their puppies for sixty-four or sixty-five days.

When may we expect our female Cocker to be in heat for the first time?

This varies with individual bitches and with different breeds. Bitches of the small, early-maturing breeds may be expected to come in season when they are as young as six months. Females of the large breeds are often eleven months or over a year old before they come in heat.

Should a bitch be mated the first time she comes in season?

Only if the bitch is well past one year of age and fully matured when she comes in season for the first time. The fact that she is in heat and apparently ready for mating does not mean that a bitch is physically mature enough to be subjected to the strains of pregnancy, whelping, and nursing a litter of puppies.

How often do bitches come in heat?

Most bitches come in heat at intervals of six months. This varies with individuals, though, as there are perfectly normal, healthy bitches who have cycles of five, seven, or nine months. There is one breed, the Basenji, which comes in season but once a year, usually in the fall. A debilitating illness is sometimes the cause of a bitch's not coming in season on schedule. A change of environment may also bring about a delay.

How long does the average bitch's period of heat last?

Usually from eighteen to twenty-one days.

Can a bitch be mated and become impregnated at just any time during her period of being in season?

No. During the first eight or nine days she will usually refuse the advances of male dogs, though they are attracted to her. From the tenth to the fourteenth or fifteenth day of the period she will be interested in males, receptive to them, and will even attempt to escape confinement in her efforts to find a mate. If a mating takes place during this middle part of the period it usually results in puppies. After the receptive phase has passed, the bitch may still be said to be in season, as she will continue to be a magnet for lovelorn males, but the period is waning, and she will usually fight them off, as she did during the first few days.

How can I tell when my bitch is about to come in heat?

You can't always. Some bitches will have a bigger appetite than is normal, starting about a week before coming in season, and there is usually a slight swelling of the vulva about five or six days before there is any discharge. Once a bitch is actually in heat, her condition is indicated by a bloody discharge. This first phase usually goes on for eight to ten days, after which the flow lessens and fades to a pinkish or creamy color. It is when the discharge has abated that the bitch will be flirtatious and playful with males and is ready for mating.

Can a bitch be bred every time she comes in season?

She can be, but she certainly should not be. Once a year is often enough. A bitch that is bred too often will age prematurely, and her puppies will be weedy and lacking in vigor.

How does a bitch behave when she is ready for mating?

She will behave like a hussy. She will flirt, play around, and do all she knows to entice and excite the male. When the male sniffs and licks her, she will "flag" her tail, that is, lift it away from her body to one side, or over her back.

Our young Sheltie bitch behaves in a very peculiar way. In full season and ready for breeding she will encourage the attentions of the male, flag her tail, and even back up to him, but if he tries to mount her she jumps away from him and either squeals as though hurt or snaps at him. How should we handle her?

Young bitches often behave this way at their first mating, probably because of timidity. If you are positive that you are mating her at the right time (and the behavior you describe would certainly indicate it), muzzle her so that she cannot bite you or the male and hold her firmly so that she is not able to spring away from the male. If the male is inexperienced you will have a difficult time. Usually it takes a veteran stud dog to cope with a flighty maiden bitch. If he is a beginner too, he may become discouraged by her yipping and growling and give up his attempts to breed her.

Best Age for Breeding

What is the best age to mate a bitch for the first time?

Much depends on the breed of the bitch. Bitches of the small breeds, which are fully developed at eighteen months of age, may be mated when they are a year and a half, two, or two and a half years of age. Bitches of the larger breeds, taking two or two and a half years to achieve their growth, should not be mated before they are two years of age.

Male Disposition and Breeding

When we bought our male Beagle it was with the understanding that the kennel from which we purchased him could use him three times for breeding. Since then a friend has told us that we should try and get out of this agreement because it will ruin our dog's disposition to be mated—that he will become surly, forget his house manners, and no longer be a nice pet. Is this true?

Not in the least. Mating your dog will not spoil or change his temperament in any way at all. Thousands of male dogs that have been frequently used at stud are lovable, gentle, well-behaved house pets.

Our Collie was hit by a car last year and her pelvis was broken. She is as good as ever now, and we would like to breed her. Do you think she will be able to have puppies normally?

It would be risky to breed a bitch that has had her pelvis broken. Breaks of this kind often heal in such a manner as to cause constriction. More than likely your bitch would need a Caesarean.

Finding a Mate

Our Clumber Spaniel bitch is almost three years of age, and we want to breed her before she is much older. We have been trying to find a mate for her, but because this is an unusual breed, have not been able to. How can we locate a stud dog of this breed?

By writing to the American Kennel Club, 221 Fourth Avenue, New York 3, New York. As is often the case with the less common breeds, you will probably have to arrange for the breeding by correspondence and then ship your bitch to the owner of the stud. Air transportation has made the shipment of dogs a quick and easy affair, so you need not worry about subjecting your bitch to an unpleasant experience. When shipping a female for breeding, send her on her way at such a time that she will have a day or so in which to settle down before the mating takes place. Also take care that she does not arrive at her destination on a Saturday or Sunday, when delivery services are often curtailed or nonexistent.

*What is the usual cost of the stud fee for breeding a bitch to a
registered dog?*

It is almost impossible to set an average, because in some
breeds the fee for a male of championship status is as low as
fifteen or twenty dollars. In the more popular breeds the usual
fee is thirty-five dollars for a nonchampion male and fifty for a
champion. If a dog is a famous show winner or is the sire of
many champions, the fee may be seventy-five or a hundred dollars.

*Don't you think it's rather greedy for the owner of a male dog
to charge a fee for the use of his dog in breeding? After all, it
doesn't cost the owner anything for his dog to mate a bitch.*

When the owner of a bitch pays a fee for the services of a
fine male dog, he is purchasing the hereditary factors which that
dog carries. An outstanding stud dog often represents years of
patient and careful selective breeding on the part of his owner.
The owner is certainly entitled to some return for the time,
money and thought he has invested in obtaining a dog of unusual
quality.

What is meant by "breeding for a puppy"?

It means that instead of paying a stud fee, the owner of the
bitch allows the owner of the sire to take his pick of the puppies
when they are six or eight weeks of age. This may seem like a
very smart and economical way of doing things, but it has its
disadvantages. It often happens that the owner of the sire will
select the very puppy that the breeder wants for himself. Sometimes, when this occurs, a cash payment will be accepted instead,
but should the stud owner insist on taking the particular puppy
he wants, he is perfectly within his rights and nothing can be
done about it.

*Our Doberman bitch is the daughter of a famous show winner,
and her pedigree contains the names of many champions.
We want to breed her to a fine male in the hope of getting*

some puppies good enough to show. How do we go about locating a suitable mate for her?

If you can get in touch with the breeder of your bitch his advice on the selection of a sire would be valuable. He should be familiar with the bloodlines behind your bitch and would know what characteristics are in need of emphasis and what faulty tendencies may exist which need correction. If this is not possible, attend a dog show and talk to the breeders and fanciers you meet there. Take along a copy of your bitch's pedigree and give as realistic an appraisal as possible of her shortcomings and virtues.

My female Pomeranian was bred to a dog belonging to a friend. I promised the friend a puppy in lieu of the usual stud fee. If there is only one puppy in the litter who gets the puppy?

Under such unusual circumstances, the courteous gesture would be for the owner of the male to release you from your promise and to accept the regular stud fee instead.

What does the phrase "To approved bitches only" mean when a male dog is advertised at stud?

It means that the owner of the stud reserves the right to refuse to breed his dog to a bitch he considers unsuitable because of her pedigree or conformation. This is done to protect the male dog's reputation as a sire. If a fine male is bred indiscriminately to bitches with serious faults or undesirable family background, the resulting puppies are liable to be of such poor type that they are a disgrace to their sire.

The Sire

What is meant by the term "proven sire"?

A proven sire is a male dog that is known to be fertile and has sired several litters of puppies.

When a bitch is bred to a proven sire and fails to conceive puppies, is it because of some physical defect on her part?

Most breeders and veterinarians believe that in the majority of cases where a bitch "misses," the reason is either that her cycle varies widely from the normal, or she has some physical peculiarity or ailment which makes it difficult or impossible for her to get in whelp.

Can a male dog with one testicle sire puppies?

Yes, but most breeders avoid using a stud with this deficiency, as it is an inheritable characteristic, and many of those who have made a study of canine genetics believe the condition (known as monorchidism) to be the first step along the way to cryptorchidism (the condition of having no visible testicles) and consequent sterility.

Wolves, to which dogs are related, are naturally monogamous, taking one mate for life. Why is it then that dogs are polygamous in their instincts?

It is probably the influence of the dog's long and close association with mankind—the practices of those who breed dogs have dimmed the natural canine tendency to be monogamous. In spite of this, many male dogs do show a definite preference for certain females and will sometimes refuse to mate with others.

Last spring I bred my bitch to a champion stud dog, paying the fee at the time of the mating. She did not have any puppies. I want to repeat the breeding when she is next in season. Will I have to pay the same stud fee again?

No, unless it was distinctly understood that there was to be no return service. The usual arrangement is that should the first service prove unsuccessful, one additional service will be given free, provided that the stud dog is still in the possession of the same owner.

When Puppies Are Wanted

When is the best time to mate a bitch in order to insure her having puppies?

Usually the tenth, eleventh or twelfth days. We say usually, because this is true of most bitches. There are bitches that will accept the advances of a male on the sixth or seventh day of their heat period and conceive puppies if a mating takes place. We know of bitches that have had litters as a result of matings that occurred as late as the fifteenth or sixteenth days of their season. The most reliable indication is the bitch's attitude toward the male. If she is playful, flirtatious and encourages rather than resents his attentions, the time is probably right.

The last time our Scottie bitch was in season we decided to breed her. A friend of ours has a good male Scottie which was to be the sire of the puppies. When our bitch had been in heat for ten days we took her to our friend's house, closed the two dogs in the garage and left them together for twenty-four hours. We had no puppies. What do you think was the trouble?

Probably no mating took place at all. A competent breeder would not consider for a moment any such casual procedure as simply turning a dog and a bitch loose together. An inexperienced male (especially if he is of a short-legged breed) can seldom manage to breed a female without skilled assistance and even verbal encouragement. If he should be able to, there is a very real risk of his being injured. To insure a satisfactory mating, you had better obtain the cooperation of a qualified breeder who will know how to handle the dogs.

We have tried to mate our pair of Cockers without much luck. What can we do to help?

Try the bitch with the dog on the tenth or eleventh day of her season. Let the dogs play and romp and watch the female's behavior. If she indicates readiness, and the male shows signs of being sexually aroused and attempts to mount her, try this: have one person kneel or sit on the floor, holding the bitch's head steady in one hand and bracing her under the abdomen with the other hand or a knee; this will prevent her from sitting down and keep her from moving forward when the male puts his forepaws on her hindquarters.

It is most desirable that the persons assisting be well-known to the male. Many males, even experienced stud dogs, become shy if a stranger attempts to interfere or to handle them or the bitch. If the male has trouble effecting an entrance, it may be necessary to maneuver the bitch's rear so that he can make contact. Be sure the footing is not slippery. If there is a difference in the height of the dogs, place a door mat or folded blanket under the hind feet of whichever one needs elevation, in order to equalize the variance.

Do not permit the dog to exhaust himself. If he tries to breed the bitch for a few minutes with no success, take him into another room for a while and let him calm down a bit before he makes another attempt. No matter how inept the male's efforts may be, *don't* lose patience with him. Pet him, talk to him reassuringly, stroke his back vigorously, pat the bitch's rump in an inviting manner, and do all you can to keep him from becoming discouraged. If all efforts fail, you had better have the bitch examined by a veterinarian. It occasionally happens that a bitch has a constrictive formation of the vagina which makes mating impossible unless the condition is remedied by dilation.

Our Boxer bitch has been mated twice, and both times she has failed to have puppies. The dog to which we bred her has sired several litters, so we don't think it's his fault. She is healthy in every way, and we can't understand why this has happened.

A problem like yours is one that only a veterinarian can solve, for the explanation may be any one of several. It may be that the bitch has been mated too early or too late in her season, she may have a hormone imbalance, a vitamin deficiency, a heavy worm infestation, or ovarian cysts.

Litters—Sex and Size

Do some breeds have larger litters than others?

Yes, the larger breeds usually have more puppies per litter than the small breeds. When a bitch of one of the small breeds has an oversize litter, it is a serious drain on her to provide sufficient nourishment for so many puppies. The owner will have to help by supplementary feeding of the puppies with a milk formula if they are not to be weaklings and their mother a wreck.

Which parent influences the number of puppies in a litter, the sire or the dam?

The dam. Although a fertile male releases enough sperm cells in a single breeding to fertilize millions of ova, there will be only as many puppies in a litter as a bitch has ripe egg cells (ova) at the time of mating.

Is it possible for a litter to have two different sires?

A single puppy can have only one sire, but should a bitch mate with two different males during her period of heat, it is possible that some of her egg cells may be fertilized by one dog and some by the other one.

Is there any way to influence the sex of a litter of puppies?

There are many theories about ways and means of controlling the sex of puppies—that is, of breeding litters of mostly males or mostly females, depending on the breeder's wishes, but none of them has ever proved practical. If you hear it claimed that if a bitch is douched with an alkaline solution just before mating her puppies will be males, you can put it down to wishful thinking, because it just does not work out that way.

Are there more male puppies born than females?

Yes. Records show that the ratio is about one hundred and twenty male puppies to every hundred females.

How Dogs Link in Mating

Is it true that the male and female become linked together when they are mated?

It is a characteristic of the animal family which includes dogs, wolves, jackals, and foxes, that a tie takes place during the act of copulation. The sexual organ of the male dog has a knoblike enlargement at the base which becomes swollen with blood during the act of mating. This swelling makes it impossible for the male to withdraw sometimes for as long as an hour, though, usually, the tie lasts for about fifteen or twenty minutes. Most breeders consider a mating in which there is no tie as inadequate, although there have been cases in which puppies resulted from tieless breedings. Once a tie has been accomplished, the dog and the bitch should be held so that there will be no struggling to pull apart. This is especially important with bitches that are inclined to be snappish, as the male is relatively helpless in this situation and the bitch may bite him.

Pregnancy

Are there any tests to determine whether or not a bitch is pregnant?

The laboratory examination known as the "frog test," which is used to test for human pregnancy, will reveal whether or not a bitch is in whelp. About three ounces (80 cc) of the bitch's urine is needed to make the test which can be performed by any laboratory which specializes in urinalysis, blood tests, etc. By X-raying the bitch a week or two before she is due to whelp, one can learn how many puppies to expect in the litter.

Is artificial insemination ever used in the breeding of dogs?

It is becoming increasingly common. The procedure is an intricate one and should not be attempted except by a veterinarian.

WHELPING CALENDAR

A bitch mated on the date given at the left side of each column of figures will be due to whelp her litter on the date shown at the right side of the same column. These figures are based on a pregnancy period of sixty-three days. Variations of two or three days, one way or the other, are not unusual.

Jan. Mating	Mar. Whelping	Feb. Mating	April Whelping	March Mating	May Whelping	April Mating	June Whelping	May Mating	July Whelping	June Mating	Aug. Whelping	July Mating	Sept. Whelping	Aug. Mating	Oct. Whelping	Sept. Mating	Nov. Whelping	Oct. Mating	Dec. Whelping	Nov. Mating	Jan. Whelping	Dec. Mating	Feb. Whelping
1	5	1	5	1	3	1	3	1	3	1	3	1	2	1	3	1	3	1	3	1	3	1	2
2	6	2	6	2	4	2	4	2	4	2	4	2	3	2	4	2	4	2	4	2	4	2	3
3	7	3	7	3	5	3	5	3	5	3	5	3	4	3	5	3	5	3	5	3	5	3	4
4	8	4	8	4	6	4	6	4	6	4	6	4	5	4	6	4	6	4	6	4	6	4	5
5	9	5	9	5	7	5	7	5	7	5	7	5	6	5	7	5	7	5	7	5	7	5	6
6	10	6	10	6	8	6	8	6	8	6	8	6	7	6	8	6	8	6	8	6	8	6	7
7	11	7	11	7	9	7	9	7	9	7	9	7	8	7	9	7	9	7	9	7	9	7	8
8	12	8	12	8	10	8	10	8	10	8	10	8	9	8	10	8	10	8	10	8	10	8	9
9	13	9	13	9	11	9	11	9	11	9	11	9	10	9	11	9	11	9	11	9	11	9	10
10	14	10	14	10	12	10	12	10	12	10	12	10	11	10	12	10	12	10	12	10	12	10	11
11	15	11	15	11	13	11	13	11	13	11	13	11	12	11	13	11	13	11	13	11	13	11	12
12	16	12	16	12	14	12	14	12	14	12	14	12	13	12	14	12	14	12	14	12	14	12	13
13	17	13	17	13	15	13	15	13	15	13	15	13	14	13	15	13	15	13	15	13	15	13	14
14	18	14	18	14	16	14	16	14	16	14	16	14	15	14	16	14	16	14	16	14	16	14	15
15	19	15	19	15	17	15	17	15	17	15	17	15	16	15	17	15	17	15	17	15	17	15	16
16	20	16	20	16	18	16	18	16	18	16	18	16	17	16	18	16	18	16	18	16	18	16	17
17	21	17	21	17	19	17	19	17	19	17	19	17	18	17	19	17	19	17	19	17	19	17	18
18	22	18	22	18	20	18	20	18	20	18	20	18	19	18	20	18	20	18	20	18	20	18	19
19	23	19	23	19	21	19	21	19	21	19	21	19	20	19	21	19	21	19	21	19	21	19	20
20	24	20	24	20	22	20	22	20	22	20	22	20	21	20	22	20	22	20	22	20	22	20	21
21	25	21	25	21	23	21	23	21	23	21	23	21	22	21	23	21	23	21	23	21	23	21	22
22	26	22	26	22	24	22	24	22	24	22	24	22	23	22	24	22	24	22	24	22	24	22	23
23	27	23	27	23	25	23	25	23	25	23	25	23	24	23	25	23	25	23	25	23	25	23	24
24	28	24	28	24	26	24	26	24	26	24	26	24	25	24	26	24	26	24	26	24	26	24	25
25	29	25	29	25	27	25	27	25	27	25	27	25	26	25	27	25	27	25	27	25	27	25	26
26	30	26	30	26	28	26	28	26	28	26	28	26	27	26	28	26	28	26	28	26	28	26	27
27	31	27	May 1	27	29	27	29	27	29	27	29	27	28	27	29	27	29	27	29	27	29	27	28
28	Apr. 1	28	2	28	30	28	30	28	30	28	30	28	29	28	30	28	30	28	30	28	30	28	Mar. 1
29	2	29	3	29	31	29	July 1	29	31	29	31	29	30	29	31	29	Dec. 1	29	31	29	31	29	2
30	3			30	June 1	30	2	30	Aug. 1	30	Sept. 1	30	Oct. 1	30	Nov. 1	30	3	30	Jan. 1	30	Feb. 1	30	3
31	4			31	2			31	2			31	2	31	2			31	2			31	4

*At what stage of a bitch's pregnancy should the owner be able
to tell she is carrying puppies?*

In a normal pregnancy there is usually a visible enlargement
of the abdomen by the end of the fifth week after mating. Experienced breeders are sometimes able, by palpation (feeling with
the hands), to distinguish the lumps in the bitch's uterus, which
are the developing puppies, as soon as three or four weeks after
the bitch has been bred. It is not a wise idea for the novice
breeder to poke and prod at a bitch's abdomen, attempting to
detect the presence of unborn puppies. He probably wouldn't
be able to find out anything anyway, and he might hurt the bitch.

*We have a Shepherd bitch who has given us two litters of nice
puppies, but the last time she was bred she fooled us. She
gave every indication of pregnancy up until two weeks before
her puppies were due, then she slimmed down, never had
any milk and looked and acted as though she had not been
pregnant at all. A breeder we know told us this sometimes
happens to older bitches, and that what happened was that
the bitch conceived puppies in a normal way but resorbed
them. Is there anything that can be done to prevent this
happening another time?*

Most veterinarians are willing to admit that they know very
little about either cause or prevention of the resorbtion of fetuses.
There is a belief that it can be averted by administration of
female sex hormones at regular intervals during the bitch's pregnancy. It might be worth trying.

*If a bitch that is in whelp changes hands, who is considered the
breeder of her puppies—the person who owned her at the
time she was mated or the person who owns her when the
litter is born?*

Whoever owns or leases a bitch at time of mating is recognized
as the breeder of her puppies, no matter who may own her when
the litter is born.

Taking Care of the Expectant Mother

Should a pregnant bitch have any particular kind of diet?

It is important that the diet of the bitch in whelp be complete and balanced. It should be rich in protein, in other words, concentrated, rather than sloppy or bulky. One or two all-purpose vitamin capsules and a tablespoonful (more or less according to the size of the bitch) of di-calcium phosphate should be added to her food daily. If you are in any doubt about the adequacy or balance of your bitch's feeding, consult your veterinarian and ask him to give you a list of the necessary foods and food supplements. The reason for the emphasis on proper nutrition of a pregnant bitch is that it has been found that there is a definite connection between improper or inadequate diet and trouble at the time of whelping. It has also been proved that puppies from a well-nourished mother have more resistance to disease.

During the last three weeks of pregnancy the bitch may enjoy her food more if her daily allowance is divided into two meals rather than fed in one large meal. It is imperative that the bitch not become constipated. If necessary, small amounts of mineral oil or milk of magnesia may be added to her food.

Why is it so important that a bitch be treated for worms before she is mated?

Because a bitch in whelp that is infested with worms can transmit them via the blood stream to her unborn puppies and the pups' chances for survival will be poor. Whole litters have been lost at the age of two or three weeks because the puppies were wormy at the time of birth.

How much exercise should a bitch in whelp be allowed or given?

During the first four or five weeks a pregnant bitch may be permitted a normal amount of activity. As she becomes heavier she will not want to exercise much, nor should she be forced to if disinclined. Do not make the mistake of coddling her to the

point where she puts on too much weight and becomes soft and
flabby. Activities to be avoided are strenuous running and jumping, racing up and down stairs, leaping on and off furniture, or
in or out of automobiles—in fact any sort of gymnastics which
might result in a hard bump or a fall. Take care that she does
not become wet or chilled.

*We plan to breed our Corgi bitch the next time she comes in
season. What special treatment or care should she have?*

It is vital that she be in good condition when bred. Her diet
should be the very best you can afford to give her. Waiting until
a bitch is in whelp and then starting to feed a rich, balanced
diet is too late. The conditioning program should get under
way two or three months before she is in season. One month
before she is due to be in heat have your veterinarian examine a
specimen of her stool for worms and, if there is evidence of
their presence, get rid of them. If she is fat, reduce her by
means of diet and exercise. Fat bitches often fail to conceive and
if they do, are likely to have a terribly difficult time whelping
the puppies.

*Can a bitch be safely treated for worms after she has been
mated?*

Yes, if it is done within the first two or three weeks of pregnancy.

Whelping Difficulties of Different Breeds

*Are some breeds more inclined to have whelping difficulties
than others?*

Yes. Breeds having heads which are blocky or exaggerated in
size frequently require Caesareans in order to have puppies.
Bulldogs and Boston Terriers are two examples of breeds in
which troublesome births are the rule rather than the exception.

Preparations for Delivery

Is any special bed or box necessary for a bitch that is having puppies?

Most breeders use a whelping box for the bitch while she is having her puppies and during the time they are nursing. A properly constructed box seems to comfort the bitch, making her feel protected, and serves to keep the little ones from becoming scattered and chilled. A square box with three high sides (twelve to eighteen inches), and one low side (four to six inches) which the bitch can easily step over, usually proves satisfactory. Its dimensions should be such that the bitch can stretch out full length on her side and have several inches to spare at either end. Boxes which are so constructed as to make it impossible for the mother to get away from the puppies when she chooses are to be avoided. There should always be a low side or an exit for her use.

WHELPING BOX WITH A HINGED COVER

During the actual whelping, several layers of spread-out news-papers may be used for bedding, the top layer being pulled off as it becomes soiled. Once the family has arrived, and is contentedly nursing, a more comfortable surface should be provided. A bitch that is a good mother will usually push her puppies together in the middle of the whelping bed and then curl her body around them. If given loose bedding, she will paw at it until it is saucer-shaped so as to make a nest for her babies. An arrangement similar to this can be made of shredded newspaper piled on the floor of the box and slightly hollowed toward the center, with a piece of mattress pad or a cotton crib blanket laid on top and thumb-tacked down at the edges. This is preferable to using loose blankets or pads, as it prevents the puppies from getting under the bedding and possibly smothering. It is important that the covering used over the newspapers be washable, as it will require frequent changing.

What is the right temperature for the whelping box?

About seventy degrees for newborn puppies. A chilled puppy is usually a dead puppy. If the room where the whelping box is placed is cooler than this, it may be necessary to supply extra warmth with hot-water bottles or an electric heating pad. If either of these are used they should be covered with two or three layers of a thick towel or piece of blanket, fastened with safety pins. When checking the temperature of the puppy room, be sure to test it at floor level where the puppies are. Bitches of some of the hardy breeds of northern origin could probably have their puppies in a snowdrift and both mother and litter would survive, but the average well-cared-for house pet and her puppies are not so tough and will do better if given warmth and protection.

I have heard stories about people preparing elaborate whelping boxes for the birth of puppies, and then the mother dog had her litter in a corner of the cellar. How can a person be sure the puppies will be born where he wants them born and not in some inconvenient, dirty place?

About two weeks before the puppies are due, start having the bitch use the whelping box as her bed. Place her regular mattress or blanket in it to make it seem more homelike. By the time the pups arrive she will be accustomed to it and will seek it as a refuge.

When the Puppies Arrive

Is there any way to tell if a bitch is going to have her puppies within the next two or three days?

About forty-eight or seventy-two hours before the litter is born, the bitch's shape changes. Her abdomen, instead of looking barrel-shaped will sag pendulously. Her breasts redden and become enlarged, and often there is milk present for a day or two before the puppies are born. She may start scratching and rooting at her bedding in an effort to make a nest.

What are the signs which indicate a bitch is going to start whelping her puppies inside of a few hours?

The surest sign is a definite drop in temperature. The normal temperature will go down two or three degrees, about twelve to eight hours before actual labor begins. If you plan to use this method of forecasting, it is wise to check ahead of time to ascertain the bitch's normal temperature, for it varies with individuals. Other signs are restlessness and digging and scratching at her bed or the floor.

Experienced matrons will usually refuse food just before whelping and may ask to be let outdoors every few minutes to relieve themselves. Females whelping for the first time often will eat a meal and then vomit it. Bitches that are great pets will frequently wander about the house aimlessly, hide under furniture, whimper, and indicate they want attention. Such behavior should not be mistaken for true labor. It is usually caused by nervousness and bewilderment and is only a preliminary to the delivery of puppies.

How does a bitch behave when she goes into labor?

She will usually be on her side, and there will be definite
sharp contractions of the abdomen and flanks. Generally, she
pants and her facial expression is drawn and worried. She may
make efforts to expel a puppy for a few minutes, then rest for a
short period and try again. There is almost always a longer period
of labor before the birth of the first puppy of a litter than
preceding the arrival of the other puppies. Just before each puppy
emerges there will be a pronounced distention of the band of
skin between the vulva and anus.

The Length of Time for Whelping

*How long does it usually take for a bitch to give birth to a litter,
provided that the whelping goes along in a normal way?*

A litter of one or two puppies may be born in as short a time
as half an hour. When the litter is large, it may be twenty-four
hours before all the pups are whelped. Three or four hours is
considered an average time for the birth of a litter of five or
six puppies.

*What is the average length of time between the arrival of each
puppy during whelping?*

At first, depending on the size of the litter, puppies may
arrive anywhere from fifteen minutes to half an hour apart. As
the whelping continues, the length of time may increase from
one to two hours. It has been known for a last puppy to be born
almost twenty-four hours after the beginning of whelping, but
this is unusual.

Helping With the Delivery

*Should a bitch be left to herself when whelping puppies, or is
it better that someone stay with her?*

Someone should stay with her. There are several reasons for
this. Each puppy is born enclosed in a membranous sac which
looks rather like cloudy cellophane. This sac must be removed

immediately so the puppy can start breathing. Most bitches will busy themselves at once stripping away the membrane with their teeth and freeing the puppy. However, there are occasional young and inexperienced bitches who look upon their newborn pups with utter astonishment and seem to have no idea of what they should do for them. This is where help is needed, and quickly, in breaking and removing the membrane if the puppy is not to suffocate.

The mother will usually bite through the navel cord to sever it, but she often needs help here too. If she leaves too long a piece of cord, she may keep pulling at it with her teeth and cause an umbilical rupture. The attendant can prevent this by cutting the cord about an inch or an inch and a half from the puppy's navel. Attached to each puppy by the navel cord is the mass of soft, spongy tissue called the afterbirth. If all is going well, the afterbirth will be expelled right after the puppy emerges. It may happen that the navel cord breaks during the birth process and an afterbirth is retained. The bitch, if left alone, will usually eat the afterbirths, so unless she is watched there is no way of knowing if she is rid of all of them or not. It is terribly important that an afterbirth be discharged for each puppy, for if one remains in the uterus it will be only a matter of a few days before the mother dies of peritonitis. Should an afterbirth be unaccounted for, veterinary help should be obtained at once.

Is it wise for the owner to try to help in any way if a bitch is having difficulty in whelping?

Whether or not to advise an inexperienced person to attempt to assist in the delivery of puppies is a rather thorny question. There are people who, though they have never seen puppies born before, are so naturally deft and discerning that they can be a real help to the mother. Others are so helplessly heavy-handed that, if they attempt to help, they will probably injure the mother or break a puppy's neck.

There are one or two situations in which the owner can and should help if he feels sufficiently self-confident. Puppies are usually born headfirst but occasionally onė gets turned around, comes hind end first, and the mother has trouble. If a puppy is partway expelled and then seems stuck, grasp what you can of the unborn puppy with a soft turkish towel wrapped around your hand and try to ease him out. It is important that the pulling be very gentle and that you coordinate it with the mother's efforts at expulsion.

When a puppy has been born and the afterbirth is retained, if the assistant can grasp the cord connected to it and pull it at the same time the mother strains, he may be able to extract it. The cord is slippery and fragile so a light touch is required. Should the cord slip away or break, one can only hope that the missing afterbirth will come with the next puppy.

Bitches that are naturally good mothers will lick and nuzzle their newborn puppies until they are warm and dry and ready to nurse. Should a bitch fail to do this, the helper should rub the puppy dry with clean cloths and then place it where it can reach the milk supply.

Sometimes, if one or two pups have been born and nothing further seems to happen for a long period, it speeds matters if the bitch is made to get to her feet and lie on the opposite side from the one she has had against the floor.

When to Seek Professional Help

Under what circumstances should the help of a veterinarian be obtained in the birth of puppies?

If a bitch has been in labor for an hour without being able to give birth to a puppy, professional help should be sought without delay. Further efforts on her part may only bring on exhaustion and complete inability to whelp. Injections of Pitruitrin to stimulate the muscular contractions of the uterus, or the use of instruments, or manual manipulation may be in order. Such measures are not to be undertaken by the amateur, as they require skill and experience, and should be left strictly to the qualified veterinarian.

The First-born

Should the first puppy born be left with the mother while the rest of the litter is being born?

The first puppy can be left with the bitch and allowed to nurse until she shows signs of going into labor again. When this starts the pup can be placed in a box (a corrugated cardboard grocery box serves well) lined with clean old towels or blankets) and warmed by a hot-water bottle or electric pad wrapped in a piece of blanket or flannel. The bitch will usually be calmer if the pups are permitted to nestle against her and nurse between the periods of labor.

Defective Puppies

Is there any way to tell if newborn puppies are physically defective?

There are some defects which are immediately noticeable. A puppy born with a cleft palate will be unable to nurse and usually worries his mother almost to distraction by continual crying. You can discover this defect by putting your finger in the pup's mouth and feeling the roof of it. If the roof is not properly closed over, the puppy will not survive and should be destroyed. Another deformity which makes a puppy unable to obtain nourishment is a harelip. This is a split which divides the upper lip and prevents the puppy from sucking. Puppies with this malformation are considered impossible to raise and are usually destroyed.

Puppy Blindness

I understand that puppies are born blind. How old are they when their eyes open?

The number of days before puppies' eyes are fully open will vary from ten to fourteen days. The eyes will have a bluish cast at first and seem rather weak. They should not be subjected to strong light for at least ten days after opening.

Reviving a Newborn Puppy

Can anything be done to revive a puppy that is apparently dead when born?

Rubbing the puppy with a rough towel, using short brisk strokes, will sometimes start respiration. Manipulation of the forelegs forward and backward for several minutes often helps. Be sure the mouth is clear of mucus, and keep the puppy warm while working over him.

The Afterbirth

Should a whelping bitch be permitted to eat the afterbirths or should they be taken away from her?

Opinions differ. The only food an undomesticated mother dog received for the first few days after whelping, when she would not leave her puppies, was that contained in the afterbirths. Nature provided this way of cleaning up the whelping quarters and of cleaning the female internally, since the afterbirths act as a laxative. Because modern dogs receive such good care this nourishment is not necessary to them. But no harm is done if a bitch does consume one or more of the afterbirths, and many breeders allow their bitches to eat them if they want to.

Attending the New Mother

What should be done for the mother when she is finished having her litter?

Take her away for a few minutes, even though she won't want to leave the babies, and while she is gone, clean up the whelping box and provide clean, comfortable bedding. If her coat is soiled, sponge it off and dry her. Let her return to the puppies and give her a bowl of warm beef broth or milk. Put the bowl right in the box so she will not have to move away from the little ones to reach it and leave a dish of cool water close to the box. Hang a "No Visitors" sign on the door of the room and, no matter how much your friends or their children coax, don't let them or any other person who is not a member of the household view the puppies. The presence of strangers is most upsetting to a bitch with new puppies. Tell the would-be visitors that the puppies aren't very cute (and they aren't—they look like blind rats at first) and that a visit will be much more fun in about five or six weeks.

Can a bitch that has had a Caesarean nurse her puppies?

Most veterinarians make the incision for a Caesarean in such a way that the bitch will be able to nurse her puppies.

Nursing Problems

Should a bitch that is nursing puppies be given large quantities of milk in order to aid her milk production?

Meat is more important to a lactating bitch than milk. Many bitches suffer from loose bowels when given a great deal of milk, and if this is the case the milk should be eliminated. Meat (with fat added, if it is lean), cereal or prepared dog food, vitamins and minerals are the main items necessary to a bitch that is nursing a litter. The diet should be generous in order to compensate for the nourishment the puppies are taking from her.

Is there any way to keep a bitch from becoming thin and run-down from nursing her puppies?

Giving her all the food she will eat during this period will help. If the litter is a large one it will be less of a burden for the mother if the pups are given supplementary feeding with a nursing bottle using the formula given on page 122 in the chapter "Menus for Your Dog." By the time puppies are three weeks old, their nails are usually as long and as sharp as cat's claws. Because the pups place their front feet against their dam's abdomen and pump as they nurse, the bitch often becomes scratched and sore. To prevent this, keep the sharp points of the nails cut down. Take the puppy in your lap, and hold him on his back with his head pointed away from you. Ordinary scissors may be used, as the nails of young pups are quite soft.

What are nursing fits?

Nursing fits is the commonly used name for a convulsive condition known as eclampsia which occurs in lactating bitches. It is caused by the rapid loss of calcium from her system while she is nursing puppies. It is also believed that a maladjustment of the parathyroid glands may be involved. Experienced breeders have noticed that an attack of this sort often coincides with any loud or unusual noise, disturbance, or excitement. (This is one of the reasons it is so strongly advised that visitors be kept away from nursing bitches and their puppies.) The symptoms are violent trembling, rigidity of the muscles, a wild-eyed expression, and a skyrocketing temperature. Veterinary help must be obtained as quickly as possible. The usual treatment is a big dose of calcium gluconate administered directly into a vein, after which the convulsions subside in about ten minutes.

Baby Care

When should puppies be weaned, and how does one go about it?

Puppies can be weaned as young as three weeks, though the usual practice is to start them between the fourth and fifth weeks. The earlier age is recommended in the case of orphan puppies, or if the litter is large and the mother is becoming worn out with them.

To teach puppies to lap, prepare a batch of puppy formula, heat it to lukewarm, and pour it in a soup plate or pie pan. Place the pan on the floor and dip each puppy's mouth into the mixture. There will be much spluttering at first and more of the formula will be on the puppies than in them. The lesson will go better if the mother has been away from the pups for a couple of hours beforehand, so that their appetites are sharpened. After several face dunkings the puppies will usually start to lap.

Give them two such meals the first day, three the second, and by the third or fourth day the number can be stepped up to four. By the fourth day, dry baby cereal can be added to the formula, and the mother should be kept away from them entirely during the day but allowed to sleep with them at night.

When the puppies are between five and six weeks old, chopped beef can be added to their diet. They may scorn this strange food at first and have to be induced to sample it from little dabs held out on a finger to them. When they are eating the meat with eagerness, their regime can consist of two milk meals and two meat meals a day. Viosterol or cod-liver oil and mineral supplements can be added to the meat, and when the pups are eight weeks old cereal or kibble may be mixed with the meat.

Do puppies derive enough moisture from the milk they are given or should they have water available besides?

As soon as puppies are eating solid foods, a pan of clean water should be provided that they can reach at all times. When they are first given water they may be inclined to "tank up" and try to drink the pan dry, but they will soon realize that the water is not milk and will drink only as their thirst dictates.

Should a litter of young puppies be fed from the same dish or should each have his own dish?

When puppies all eat from the same pan, the competition seems to spur their appetites. However, they should be watched when fed this way, as the larger and stronger puppies may get more than their share while the smaller ones are pushed aside and do not get enough. If this happens, either the pups should be separated when fed, or the smaller ones should be taken aside and given extra food to make up for their litter-mates' gluttony.

Does their early environment and treatment have any permanent effect on puppies's dispositions?

Yes. *The Journal of Genetic Psychology* has reported that the period from three to ten weeks of age is a critical time in the emotional and mental development of puppies. If, during this period, they are protected from rough handling, loud noises, or frightening experiences of any sort, the possibility of their turning out to be nervous or timid will be greatly lessened.

Should a puppy be picked up by the scruff of the neck?

Picking up a puppy by taking a big handful of the loose flesh over his withers and supporting him under the stomach with the other hand will do him no harm, but many puppies seem to dislike being handled this way and may become hand shy as a result. A better method is to place one hand under the puppy's chest with the forefinger between the front legs and the other under his bottom. Never, never should a dog be picked up by having his front legs grasped. It will be painful to him and may do such injury to his shoulders that he will be lame for the rest of his life.

Is it true that puppies are immune from distemper as long as they are nursing?

Apparently, but the moment they are fully weaned they should be given temporary serum injections every two weeks until they are old enough for their permanent inoculations.

Do all puppies need to be treated for worms?

Almost without exception. When the pups are six weeks old, stool specimens should be checked by a veterinarian and worming treatments given if necessary. Most breeders worm their puppies at six weeks of age and again when they are eight weeks old,

Docking Puppy Tails

What is the correct age for docking the tails of the breeds where this is a requirement?

Tails are usually shortened when puppies are three days old. The reason for performing this operation while the puppies are very young is because the bones are still soft at this time and the docking causes little pain. At the same age dewclaws, if present, are removed from the hind feet. These thumblike appendages on the inside of the hind legs are a handicap to hunting breeds and are considered a disfigurement to most others. The only breeds in which dewclaws are left intact are the Great Pyrenees, the Briard, and the St. Bernard.

Although tail-docking and the removal of dewclaws are simple procedures, unless a breeder has had a good deal of experience, the operation should be done by a veterinarian. Take the mother away from the puppies while the tails are being shortened, for any whimpering (there is usually but a single yip) she may hear will distress her. When she returns to her puppies, keep a careful watch that she doesn't lick the tail stumps and prevent them from healing. Small puppies cannot afford the loss of blood which will be caused by such stimulation, and it may be necessary to keep her away except for periodic nursing sessions, until scabs have formed. Monsell's Solution dabbed on the newly cut tails is usually effective in stopping bleeding.

Tail-docking Chart

Breed	Length
Affenpinscher	Leave 1 joint.
Airedale	Take off little more than $\frac{1}{2}$
American Cocker Spaniel	Leave little less than $\frac{2}{3}$
Bouvier des Flandres	Leave 2 joints
Boxer	Leave $\frac{1}{8}$
Brussels Griffon	Leave $\frac{1}{3}$
Clumber Spaniel	Leave $\frac{1}{4}$
Doberman Pinscher	Leave $\frac{1}{8}$
English Cocker Spaniel	Remove $\frac{3}{5}$
English Springer Spaniel	Leave $\frac{1}{4}$
English Toy Spaniel	Leave $\frac{1}{4}$
Field Spaniel	Leave $\frac{1}{4}$
German Shorthaired Pointer	Leave $\frac{2}{5}$
Giant Schnauzer	Leave 3 joints
Irish Terrier	Leave $\frac{3}{4}$
Kerry Blue Terrier	Remove full $\frac{1}{3}$
Lakeland Terrier	Leave $\frac{1}{2}$

Miniature Pinscher	Leave ⅛
Miniature Poodle	Leave 1 inch
Miniature Schnauzer	Leave 3 joints
Norwich	Leave ⅓
Old English Sheepdog	Leave 1 joint
Pembroke Welsh Corgi	Leave 1 joint
Rottweiller	Leave 1 joint
Sealyham Terrier	Remove full ⅓
Smooth Fox Terrier	Remove full ⅓
Standard Poodle	Leave 1¼ inch
Standard Schnauzer	Leave 2 joints
Sussex Spaniel	Leave ⅓
Toy Poodle	Leave ¾ inch
Weimaraner	Leave 1½ inch
Welsh Springer Spaniel	Leave ⅓
Welsh Terrier	Remove a little more than ½
Wire Fox Terrier	Remove full ⅓
Wire-haired Pointing Griffon	Leave ⅓

Cropping Their Ears

Which breeds have their ears cropped, and at what age should it be done?

Breeds which by tradition have part of their ear flaps removed so that the remainder will stand in smart, erect points are: the Boston Terrier, the Bouvier des Flandres, the Boxer, the Brussels Griffon, the Doberman Pinscher, the Great Dane, the Manchester Terrier, and all three sizes of Schnauzers.

The cropping may be done at any time between seven and ten weeks of age, with eight weeks being the preferred time.

We are raising our first litter of Boxers and I have been considering cropping their ears myself. I have a book which gives directions for the operation. Would you advise me to attempt it?

No. Ear-cropping requires not only a knowledge of anesthesia and surgical technique, but experienced judgment as to the eventual size of the puppies and what proportion of ear will best balance with each pup's head when he is mature. The amateur who attempts this job will find he has not only involved himself in what is little short of a piece of bloody butchery, but his pups' good looks may be irreparably marred as well.

Raising Orphans

Is it possible to raise puppies if their mother dies in whelping them?

It is, but the breeder who undertakes to substitute his care for that of the litter's own mother should realize he is confronted with a task which will require every shred of patience and determination he has.

The ideal solution for such a problem is to locate a foster mother. Your veterinarian, the local humane society, or a nearby breeding kennel may be able to help in the search. Puppies of the smaller breeds have been raised by cats as foster mothers. If a foster mother with a loving heart and plenty of milk is found, be sure she is clean and free of external parasites before introducing her to her adopted children. She will take to the strange puppies more readily if some of her milk is squeezed out and smeared on the pups. This will make them smell familiar to her and she will generally start licking and mothering them. If she shows any hostility, she must not be left alone with the pups and they should only be allowed with her for nursing and then removed.

In case a foster mother is unavailable, the breeder will have to supply the warmth, nourishment, and body massage which is normally provided by a mother. The puppies will need a warm bed, smaller than a whelping box, and with four high sides for greater warmth. A wooden or cardboard carton will do. An elec-

tric heating pad, turned on low and well wrapped in towels will
keep the bed cozy. A hot-water bottle can be used but will require
frequent refilling. Newborn orphan puppies need to be fed every
three hours, *day and night,* until they are a week or eight days old.
This means the setting of an alarm clock and many, many weary
midnight warmings of formulas and patient bottle-holding
sessions.

The formula used may be that given in "Menus for Your Dog,"
or one of the dehydrated commercial products especially prepared
for weaning puppies. There are dried-milk preparations intended
for human babies which will do in a pinch and are available at
most drugstores. The puppy weaning foods are good and nourishing but the feeding directions which accompany them should be
ignored. We know of one which states that once every eight hours
is often enough to feed newborn orphan pups. If such a schedule
were followed the puppies would be screaming with hunger and
colic in very short order.

The next problem is to get the formula into the orphans. A
doll's nursing bottle, usually obtainable in the ten-cent stores or
toy departments, or a baby bottle fitted with the smallest size
nipple will serve the purpose. Many breeders use a medicine
dropper but this has its dangers. If the fluid goes into the puppy's
mouth faster than he can swallow it, he will choke. If milk gets
into his lungs, the result will be pneumonia. If one is willing to
squirt the fluid into the pup's mouth literally drop by drop, a
medicine dropper is safe. Otherwise, a bottle with a nipple should
be used. When using the bottle method, after a little practice,
one can usually fill two bottles at once and feed two of the pups
at the same time, which shortens the feeding sessions considerably.

There is more to raising orphan puppies than just keeping them
warm and fed. Newborn pups (this is true of several other
mammals, too) are unable, of their own volition to urinate or
defecate. If you have ever watched a bitch with a very young
litter, you may have noticed that whenever a puppy whimpers,
the first thing the mother does is to lick it under the tail or
between the legs. This external stimulation enables the puppy to
relieve itself. Orphan puppies, if they are to survive, must have

this attention. A wad of cotton dabbed with olive oil or petroleum jelly can take the place of the mother's tongue. If a puppy has just been fed and still cries as though hungry or in pain, he usually needs help in emptying himself. By the time the litter is eight days old, the feeding schedule can be changed to every four hours and the pups may be able to relieve themselves without help from you. They will still have to be wiped off frequently and their soiled bedding changed quite often.

By the end of the second week the litter should be able to go all night without a feeding, if the last meal at night is fairly late and the first one in the morning is early. By three weeks of age, to the enormous relief of their human foster mother, they can begin to learn to lap from a dish. Once the transfer from bottle to pan has been made, their care will seem simplicity itself compared to the ordeal of the first twenty-one days. We know of no organization which awards medals to people who successfully raise orphan litters, but there should certainly be one, and the breeder who accomplishes such a stint is justified in giving himself a pat on the back.

Canine Birth Control

How can we safeguard our Setter bitch from an undesirable mating taking place when she is in season?

By the strictest confinement possible during the entire period. A fenced yard is not always a safe place for a bitch in season, for even small male dogs often display an ability to scale fences like cats when there is an enticing female on the other side. If the bitch is taken out, it should be on a leash. She should not be permitted one minute of freedom. Few private homes can provide the virtual imprisonment that is necessary at such times, for if some member of the household inadvertently leaves a door unlatched—zip! the bitch is off and on her way to amorous adventure, leaving her owners to face the prospect of a litter of mongrels. The safest means of all for avoiding such accidents is to take your bitch to a boarding kennel or veterinarian's establishment, where the

building and fencing are designed to provide maximum protection.

*Can anything be done to prevent the birth of puppies when a
bitch has accidentally mated with a mongrel or a dog of another breed?*

A remedy for mésalliances employed by old-time breeders was
to douche the bitch with two quarts of a mixture of one-half
vinegar and one-half water. The douching must be administered
within a very short time after the mating and is far from being 100
per cent effective in preventing conception. A more advisable
measure is to take the errant female to the veterinarian with all
possible haste. By means of injection treatments he may be able to
bring about a termination of the pregnancy.

*There are several commercial products advertised in dog maga-
zines which claim that a bitch in season will not attract male
dogs if daubed with these substances. Would you consider it
safe to let a bitch in season run loose if one of these pre-
ventives had been used on her?*

No, not at all. There are male dogs so ardent that they would
mate with a bitch in season, without hesitation, even if she were
soaked from nose to tail in a repellent oil or liquid. Not only are
such repellents unreliable, their odor is sickeningly unpleasant to
the bitch.

*Why is it that male dogs will always find a house where there is
a bitch in heat, and hang around it? Is there any way to avoid
this?*

Although the owner will not notice any odor at all about a
bitch in season, the place where she is confined will attract males
if she is allowed to urinate close to the premises. If your bitch
is small, carry her a hundred yards or so away from your house
before putting her down. This will avoid a concentration of the
exciting scent which draws males. In case your bitch is too large

for carrying, walk her rapidly and don't permit her to stop to relieve herself until you are some distance from your own property.

When our Miniature Schnauzer bitch is in season we keep her in an unused room of our house but take her outdoors for exercise. We have trouble at these times with male dogs prowling around the house. A neighbor suggested that we cover the floor of the room with newspapers and not let her out at all until her period has passed. It seems like a good idea, but we are afraid that perhaps she would become unhousebroken if we do this. What do you think?

Being obliged to relieve herself indoors might ruin the house manners of a very young bitch, but it would probably not demoralize your mature, thoroughly house-trained Schnauzer at all.

We own a pair of Collies, brother and sister. We always send the female to a boarding kennel while she is in season. When she comes home from the kennel, even though she is completely past being in heat, the male dog gets so excited over her that he refuses to eat for several days and may even become so wrought up he lifts his leg on the furniture. What is causing this?

The odor of the bitch's discharge is probably noticeable to the male dog, particularly if it has soiled her coat or skin. When you bring her home from the kennel bathe her, using one of the new deodorant type soaps and give her a final rinse with a creolin or pine oil solution.

False Ideas About Breeding

We have been told that if a bitch is to be healthy and live out her full span of years she must be allowed to have a litter or two of puppies. Is this so?

No, it is not true at all. Many, many thousands of unspayed

bitches have never had puppies and have lived normal, healthy, full-length lives.

My father spent his boyhood in a part of the south where there is great interest in Coon Hounds and Foxhounds. He tells me that the hound dog men believed that if a bitch was hunted vigorously while she was in whelp her puppies would be fine hunters. Do people who have made a study of heredity in dogs agree with this idea?

No, they don't. The bitch's activities while pregnant will not in any way serve to increase or decrease the intelligence, instincts, or abilities of her puppies. In fact, strenuous hunting can be dangerous for a bitch in whelp, as a fall or blow may kill one of her unborn puppies which will then decompose and cause a serious infection.

Would it be a mistake to breed our Golden Retriever bitch? She is a beauty but has a disfiguring scar from a hunting accident. We are worried that her pups might be blemished in some way.

Any marks or scars which your bitch has acquired during her lifetime will not have any influence on her puppies. There are many breeds of Terriers which have had their tails docked for unnumbered generations but the puppies are still born with long tails which have to be docked. The factors which will affect the puppies are the hereditary characteristics which their dam and sire received from their parents and will pass on to their progeny.

Is it true that if a purebred bitch has an accidental mating and gives birth to a litter of mongrels she is ruined as a producer of purebred puppies?

No. This is a very common and persistent misbelief about dogs. It is always unfortunate for a fine purebred bitch to waste her substance on the development and birth of a litter of mongrels, but it does not in the least affect her future usefulness as a matron, nor will any puppies she has in later litters be blemished or marked in any way because their mother has been the dam of crossbreds.

I remember hearing about a law of saturation which affects the breeding of dogs. The theory is that if a bitch has three or four litters sired by the same male, each successive litter will look more like their sire and less like their dam. Will you please explain how this system operates?

This theory is completely erroneous. Nothing would be more pleasing to breeders who are interested in fine show dogs than to have such a process take place, as it would make the breeding of champions so easy. All one would need to do would be to mate a brood bitch to the same topflight champion male every time she was bred in order to eventually produce whole litters of pups that were dead ringers for their handsome papa.

We own an Irish Setter that seems to have no hunting instinct at all. We have been informed that this is because his mother died when he was a two-day-old puppy and the litter was raised by a Collie foster mother. Because the foster mother was not of a bird-dog breed it spoiled the natural abilities of the puppies. Could this be so?

No, it couldn't. Many orphan puppies have been raised by cats, but they don't grow up meowing any more than human children want to eat grass because they are nourished on cow's milk. The reason your dog is lacking the instinct to hunt is that he didn't inherit it.

Inbreeding and Line-breeding

What is the difference between line-breeding and inbreeding?

Line-breeding and inbreeding are different degrees of the practice of mating animals which are related to one another. To breed a bitch to her grandsire would be considered line-breeding. To breed her to her full brother or to her sire would be inbreeding. In other words, inbreeding is an intensification of line-breeding.

Is it true that inbreeding is usually the cause of dogs being nervous or vicious?

No. Many shy or emotionally unstable dogs are the result of the mating of two completely unrelated parents, both of whom may have had temperaments which made them totally unfit for breeding. Inbreeding is a dangerous practice in the hands of the inexperienced, for it intensifies faults as well as virtues, but it is through inbreeding that the finest and most prepotent sires and dams are produced.

Registering the Litter

What does one have to do to register a litter of puppies?

First, write to the American Kennel Club and ask for a litter registration application and for individual registration applications for as many puppies as there are in the litter. These blanks are furnished free of charge. To complete the litter registration it is necessary that the signature of the owner of the sire be obtained. Other information is supplied by the owner of the litter, unless the bitch changed hands while she was in whelp, in which case the signature of whoever owned her at the time she was mated will be required. It is important that the application blank be fully completed and, except for signatures, all the writing be in very clear, legible printing or typewriting. The fee for registering a litter is two dollars. The puppies may be registered individually anytime after the litter is registered at a cost of two dollars each.

As of January 1, 1960, the American Kennel Club revised its registration fees, for the first time in twenty-six years. An extra charge of $2.00 for registering a dog over 18 months of age was dropped. Also dropped were "breeder specials", the submission of a litter application with individual applications of all dogs in the litter, at a lower registration fee. Since 1960, the fee has been $2.00 for the registration of all litters and $2.00 for the registration of all individual dogs which are members of registered litters, regardless of age.

Can anyone besides whoever owned a litter when it was born register the puppies?

Only the owner of a litter at birth may register that litter, but a person buying a puppy from a registered litter may register the puppy individually, provided the application blank is properly signed by the registered owner of the litter at birth.

Are there any restrictions on the name a dog is given when he is registered?

Duplication of names is not permitted nor will a name be accepted which is longer than twenty-five letters. A registered kennel name may not be used by any person other than the owner of that name without his permission.

How soon after their birth may a litter be registered?

If the owner wishes, he may file a litter registration application the very day the puppies are born. Most breeders wait until the litter is a month or two of age before registering it.

Can a dog's name be changed after it has been registered?

No.

Is it advisable for the owner of a litter to register the puppies individually himself or should he let the people who acquire the puppies do it?

It is usually more satisfactory for the breeder to register his puppies himself. The purchasers of puppies may bestow names upon them which are distasteful to the breeder, or neglect to register them at all. The only way to be sure a puppy is properly registered with a suitable name is for the breeder to attend to it himself.

Breeding as a Business

Within the past year or so, several of my friends have bought puppies as pets, paying prices ranging from fifty to over a hundred dollars. Judging from this, it appears to me that a pleasant and easy way to make a living would be to raise and sell puppies of some popular breed. Are there any reasons why this isn't a good idea?

It is a wide-spread delusion among people who have never had much to do with dogs that the breeding and selling of purebred dogs is a lucrative and undemanding business. For most people who breed dogs it is not a business at all. It is a hobby, and not a cheap one. If there is an occasional year when they break even on kennel expenses, it is cause for rejoicing. There are extremely few kennels that can provide sufficient income to support a family on puppy sales alone. This is not to say that a living derived from dogs is an impossibility. There are professional dog people who own comfortable homes, send their children to college, and live very well indeed, but the revenue which makes these things possible is usually derived from the service end of the dog business— boarding, bathing, grooming, stud fees, training, conditioning and handling for the show ring, field trials, or obedience competition.

The hazards and uncertainties of dog breeding are numerous. Bitches may miss, for no apparent reason, or else give birth to only one or two puppies when one had every reason to expect a fine lusty litter of six or eight. Prospective puppy buyers have an infuriating habit of wanting a dog of an age, color, or sex which the breeder hasn't on hand, even though his kennel is loaded with healthy, salable young stock. The market for puppies is a fickle one. At times, the demand is so brisk that there are three buyers for every pup you can raise; then again, there will be a period during which puppies can hardly be given away. But no matter what the condition of the market, the expense and labor necessary for maintenance are constant. There is always the danger of disease, which can entail large veterinary bills, render puppies unsalable, or even wipe out a whole kennel almost over night. These are only some of the reasons that, to be profitable, a kennel must offer services or accommodations for which there is a steady demand, rather than be dependent on puppy sales as a major source of income.

CHAPTER *13*

What You Should Know About Dog Shows and Field Trials

Though you may never enter your own dog in a bench show or field trial, or perhaps not even attend one of these events, you probably have wondered just what purpose they serve, whether your dog is eligible to take part in them, or how a champion earns his title. This chapter is intended to answer such questions and give you a broader understanding of the more popular forms of competition in which dogs are featured.

Theoretically, dog shows are for the purpose of the improvement of purebred dogs. In recent years in the United States, there have been between five and six hundred annual dog shows at which championship points have been awarded, and it is a fact that these shows have done a great deal to stimulate interest in better-looking, sounder purebred dogs, and have brought public attention to the merits of the well-bred registered dog. Besides furnishing an absorbing hobby to thousands of dog fanciers and breeders, dog shows present the dog-loving public with the opportunity to view colorful sporting events in which the dog is the star. For the serious breeder, a dog show serves both as a showcase for the results of his efforts and skill, and a measuring stick for the merits of his stock as compared to that of other owners.

If you would like to own a show dog but fear that he might not make a good pet, let us hasten to add that a very high percentage of the dogs exhibited in the dog shows of today are house pets living on very close terms with their owners. In short, it is entirely

408

possible for a dog to be of sufficient excellence to win in the show ring, and also to be an intelligent, affectionate pet and companion.

Kinds of Dog Shows

What is the difference between an all-breed show, a limited show, and a specialty show?

An all-breed show provides classes for all the breeds which are recognized by the American Kennel Club. Limited breed shows have several variations. Such a show may have classes for forty or fifty breeds, or it may confine its entries to dogs of one particular variety group, such as the Toy Group or the Terrier Group. A specialty show is for dogs of a single breed.

Are there any classes in which dogs of breeds not recognized by the American Kennel Club may be exhibited?

At all-breed shows the miscellaneous class is provided for dogs of such breeds. The list usually includes Akitas, Australian Heelers, Australian Kelpies, Belgian Malinois, Border Collies, Chinese Crested Dogs, Russian Owtchars, Shih Tzus, Soft-Coated Wheaten Terriers and Spinoni Italiani.

In what way do benched and unbenched dog shows differ?

At benched shows each dog is assigned a numbered stall where he remains during the show hours except for the time he is being groomed, is in the ring being shown, or is in the exercise pen. At unbenched shows no rows of benching are provided, and the dogs may remain in crates or in their owner's cars when not competing in the ring. From the spectator's viewpoint, a benched show is a more orderly and interesting exhibition, as it furnishes an opportunity of seeing all the dogs entered and enables you to locate without difficulty whatever breed or breeds you may particularly like.

Eligibility for the Dog Show

Are there any age restrictions for dogs exhibited at point shows?

No dog under six months of age may be entered at a show where championship points are awarded.

Must a dog be registered with the American Kennel Club in order to compete in a dog show?

This is the American Kennel Club's ruling on the subject:

"If the owner of an apparently purebred dog shall be unable to supply all the information necessary for registration, and can and does furnish proof acceptable to the American Kennel Club that such dog is ineligible for registration such dog may be listed with the American Kennel Club for the purpose of being shown or exhibited at dog shows and may be shown for life without being registered upon payment of a listing fee on each occasion upon which it is entered. A dog eligible for registration likewise can be listed with the American Kennel Club for the purpose of being shown or exhibited at dog shows, but may only be shown at three separate events before application for registration is made. A listing fee must be paid on each occasion if the dog is shown without its registration number."

At the present time the listing fee is twenty-five cents.

How to Enter Your Dog in a Show

How does an owner go about entering his dog in a bench show?

To enter a dog in a bench show you must obtain an entry blank, which, properly filled out, should be sent, together with the entry fee, to the show superintendent in time to reach him before the closing date for entries for that show.

How can an owner obtain entry blanks and premium lists for dog shows?

Each issue of the American Kennel Gazette contains a list of licensed dog show superintendents. A letter to any of these organizations requesting that your name be placed on their mailing lists to receive premium lists and entry blanks for their shows will insure getting the entry blanks in ample time to make entries for whatever shows you may be interested in.

The American Kennel Gazette, Popular Dogs, and several other dog magazines print lists which give the dates and locations of the shows to be given in the near future and the names of the secretaries of show-giving clubs. Entry forms and premium lists may be obtained by writing to the secretary of whatever club's show you wish to enter.

The Entry Fee

What does it usually cost to enter a dog in a show?

It varies with the size and type of show. Match shows generally charge an entry fee of fifty cents to one dollar. Fees for point shows are usually six to eight dollars. An additional charge of twenty-five cents used to be added to the entry cost of a point show. This was the recording fee which went to the American Kennel Club. This charge has been discontinued.

Grooming the Show Dog: Legally and Otherwise

Don't you think that it is very wrong and artificial to have dogs' coats plucked and trimmed for show ring competition?

Forbidding the plucking and grooming of dogs' coats for show competition would be as unreasonable as ruling that the young lady entrants in a beauty contest should not be allowed to go to the hairdresser before parading for the judges. Naturalness is all very fine, but many breeds look more like mops than dogs if their coats are not properly trimmed and groomed.

I have heard that many of the dogs exhibited in dog shows have their coats dyed to improve the color and are painted up with powder, mascara and other cosmetics. Is this so?

A few years ago the changing of show dogs' looks by means of dyes and cosmetics was quite prevalent. At the present time, however, the American Kennel Club has strict rulings against such practices, and judges are expected to withhold any award from dogs whose appearances have been faked. The use of preparations, such as talcum or chalk, to clean a dog's coat is permitted, but every bit of the cleaning material must be brushed out of the coat before the dog is taken into the ring.

How Championships Are Won

How does a dog become a champion?

When a dog has won fifteen points in bench show competition he is given the title of champion. Points are awarded to the male and female in each breed placing Winners Dog or Winners Bitch. The number of points won depends on the number of dogs or bitches competing in the regular classes. The fifteen points must include two major wins (three or more points) awarded by two different judges, and one or more of the balance of the points must be won under a third judge. The maximum number of points which a dog can win at any one show is five, so it is impossible for a dog to gain a championship in fewer than three shows, and, in most cases, a dog is shown many more times before he accumulates the necessary points.

What is a dual champion?

A dog that has won both a bench show and a field trial championship is called a dual champion.

When a dog or bitch places Winners, can the owner tell how many points the win is worth?

Yes. The American Kennel Club has set up a schedule of points toward championship governing each breed, which is printed in the catalog of all point shows held under the club's rulings. Breeds which have consistently large show entries have a higher point rating than those which are not shown in such great numbers. For example, there must be nineteen male Collies competing in the regular classes for the Winners Dog to be credited with a three-point win, but in Greyhounds it requires only four dogs in competition for the winning male to get three points. In some breeds the rating differs between the sexes. For example, in Irish Setters, if twelve males are shown, the Winners Dog is awarded three points, but there must be thirteen bitches present for the Winners Bitch to receive three points. The above examples are quoted from the present point schedule for the section of the country known as Division I, East and North.

Because the popularity of many breeds varies with the different sections of the country, the A.K.C. has modified the point schedule to fit the conditions of five major areas. They are: Division I, East and North; Division II, West and South; Division III, California; Division IV, Pacific Northwest, and a fifth schedule governs Hawaii. An illustration of the variance of the ratings affecting different sections is that, at the present time, in a show held in Division II, an entry of twenty German Shepherds in competition in either sex will have a three point rating, while in Division III, in the same breed, there must be thirty-six males or thirty-eight females competing for the Winners Dog or Winners Bitch to get three points. From time to time the Kennel Club adjusts the point schedules as the show entry figures of different breeds rise or fall.

Does the owner of a dog that has won a championship receive anything in recognition of the dog's title?

When a dog earns a championship the American Kennel Club sends the owner a handsome certificate attesting to the dog's status as a champion of record.

If a dog wins a championship and then is entered for Specials Only Classes at shows and is defeated, does he lose his title?

No. He retains his status as a champion.

What is the point of continuing to exhibit a dog at shows after it has won the title of champion?

It enhances the prestige of a kennel to have a dog in competition that can consistently win Best of Breed or Best of Variety awards over other champions. In the case of a male dog, he will be more in demand as a stud and will command larger fees if he has an impressive show record.

Does the dog or bitch that is awarded Reserve Winners receive any championship points?

No. Points toward championship are credited only to the Winners Dog and Winners Bitch.

What is the reason for the awards of Reserve Winners Dog and Reserve Winners Bitch?

Should the dog or bitch which is awarded Winners be disqualified and the win cancelled, the Reserve Winner is awarded the championship points and any ribbons, prize money, or trophies which are offered for winners. A dog's wins may be cancelled if he is entered in a class for which he is not eligible or if the owner's name stated on the entry blank is not in accordance with the recorded registration on file with the American Kennel Club.

Are there dog shows at which no championship points are awarded?

Yes. They are known as match shows and are more informal than shows at which points are awarded. Dogs need not be entered ten days or two weeks in advance, as is required by point shows, but may be brought to the show and entered any time up to the start of the judging. A match show may be for one breed only or for all breeds. Champions are not allowed to compete, and at many match shows any dog having more than two points toward a championship is excluded. Because they provide the same atmosphere and mechanics as point shows without the long hours and air of tension, match shows provide the best possible experience and training for young dogs being readied for championship competition. They are also helpful to an inexperienced owner who needs practice in the technique of handling.

What is meant by the term "regular official classes of the American Kennel Club"?

The regular official classes are the classes into which the dogs competing in each breed are divided. They are Puppy, Novice, Bred by Exhibitor, American-Bred, Open, and Winners.

The Puppy Class is for dogs not less than six and not more than twelve months of age. To be eligible for this class a puppy must have been whelped either in the United States of America or in Canada. At large shows this class is often divided into two divisions, one for puppies six to nine months of age and another for those nine to twelve months of age.

The Novice Class is for dogs six months of age and over which have never won a first prize in any regular official class (including Winners), except puppy classes. Dogs entered in this class must have been whelped either in the United States or **Canada.**

The Bred by Exhibitor Class is for dogs six months of age and over which are owned by the person or persons on record with the American Kennel Club as their breeders. (A dog's breeder is the owner or lessee of the dog's dam at the time she was mated.) A dog entered in this class may be shown in the ring in this class only by the owner or a member of his immediate family, i.e., husband, wife, mother, son, daughter, brother, sister.

The American-bred Class is for dogs six months of age and over, born in the United States of America as a result of a mating which took place in this country. Champions may not be entered in this class.

The Open Class is for dogs six months of age and over, American-bred or imported. Champions may be, but seldom are, entered in this class.

The Winners Class is made up of the first prize winners of the Puppy, Novice, Bred by Exhibitor, American-bred, and Open Classes. Two prizes are awarded in this class, Winners and Reserve Winners.

These classes are each divided by sex. The winner of the male classes being called Winners Dog and winner of the classes for females being termed Winners Bitch. The winning dog and bitch compete for the prize of Best of Winners. Whichever wins this award then goes into the class known as Specials Only, to contend against whatever champions are entered. The winner of this final class is designated Best of Breed or Best of Variety.

Is a dog or bitch entitled to more points for being awarded Best of Winners?

The dog or bitch placing Best of Winners is entitled to the number of points based on the number of dogs or bitches competing in the regular classes, whichever is greater. For instance, if there is a two point entry in males, and a four point entry in females, and the Winners Dog is awarded Best of Winners, he is credited with a four point win. The Winners Bitch does not lose her four points if this occurs, nor would she have gained any points by being placed over the male.

The Best in Show

How, out of all the dogs entered in a show, is one dog singled out to be awarded Best In Show?

A dog show is an elimination contest. First, all the dogs of each breed compete with the other specimens of their breed for Best of Variety or Best of Breed. At a show, for example, where sixty breeds are represented, by the time the best of each breed is chosen, only sixty dogs out of a total entry of six or seven hundred remain eligible to contend for higher honors. If there were fifty Boxers entered in the show, the dog winning Best of Breed would still be in competition, the other forty-nine having been eliminated.

After the best of each breed has been selected, the six variety groups, Sporting, Hound, Working, Terrier, Toy, and Non-sporting are judged. Here the dogs that have won best in their respective breeds meet the other breed winners. The six dogs that place first in each of these groups make up the final group from which one dog is selected for the final and highest honor of Best in Show.

*Why is it that so often the winner of Best in Show is a dog of
one of the more popular breeds?*

The more popular a breed is, the greater the number of high
quality specimens of that breed in circulation and being shown.
A dog that is able consistently to win Best of Breed in competition,
and that belongs to one of the popular breeds which runs to large
show entries, is almost bound to be a fine specimen and, consequently, stands a good chance to win in group and Best in Show
competition.

Who Does the Judging?

*Are there any rules about who may or may not judge at dog
shows?*

Yes. The American Kennel Club's rules state that "Any reputable person who is in good standing with the American Kennel
Club may apply for leave to judge any breed or breeds of purebred dogs which in his or her opinion he or she is qualified by
training and experience to pass upon." The Kennel Club will not
grant judging licenses to people in certain occupations. Those who
may not judge are: persons employed as solicitors for kennel advertising; salesmen for organizations which sell dog food, dog remedies or kennel supplies; persons employed in and about kennels;
professional dog dealers; persons residing in the same household
with a professional handler; professional show superintendents.
Professional handlers are not permitted to judge except at two
types of shows: sanctioned match shows and specialty club shows
which are held as separate events, that is, not in connection with
all-breed shows.

*If a person has never judged, but feels confident of his ability
to do so, how does he become eligible to accept judging invitations?*

By obtaining an application form for a judging license, filling
it in, and submitting it to the A.K.C. for approval. The application form in present use reveals a great deal about the applicant's

knowledge of dogs, experience, and personal history. If the information given in the application is satisfactory, it is tentatively approved, and the name of the applicant and the breed or breeds he wishes to be licensed to judge are published in the American Kennel Gazette. If, after the applicant's name has been published, there are no objections raised against him which are serious enough to prevent his approval, he is classified as an apprentice judge.

Before an apprentice is licensed he must serve three times as an apprentice under three different licensed judges. He will retain the rating of apprentice for six months after the approval of his application. At the end of the six months period and after the three apprentice assignments have been served, the applicant will be licensed to serve as a judge. After having gone through this routine in four different breeds, a judge may be licensed for additional breeds without serving an apprenticeship.

This apprenticeship system for licensing judges became effective in January, 1949. Those who held judging licenses before its institution may be approved to judge additional breeds by submitting satisfactory applications and are not obliged to serve apprenticeships.

Are exhibitors allowed to question a judge as to the reasons for his placements?

Certainly, and most judges are glad to explain their decisions.

What are the qualifications for being a group judge?

Before a judge is permitted to judge a group he must be licensed to pass on certain "key breeds" within that group. For instance, in order to judge the Working Group it is required that a judge be licensed for six of the twenty-eight breeds of that group which must include Boxers, Collies, Doberman Pinschers, German Shepherds, Great Danes. The sixth breed may be any one of the remaining twenty-three breeds.

Must a judge be licensed for all breeds in order to be eligible to judge Best in Show?

No. Persons eligible to judge one or more groups are also qualified to select Best in Show.

Does the American Kennel Club select the judges which are to officiate at each dog show?

No, it licenses judges, but the actual selection of a judging panel is left to the show-giving club.

Are dog show judges paid for their services?

There are both amateur and professional judges. Amateurs receive no fee for judging but are entitled to remuneration for transportation costs, money spent for hotel accommodations, and other expenses incurred in connection with a judging assignment. Professionals, most of whom are licensed to judge all breeds, charge a set fee for their services and, in cases where much traveling is necessary, may require that their expenses be paid too.

What is a "specialist" judge?

The term is used to describe a judge who, by reason of long experience in breeding or showing, is an expert in one particular breed—in other words, a specialist in one breed.

Faults—Serious and Minor

Why is it that the standards by which dogs are judged rate certain faults as very serious or even disqualifying, while other faults are considered only minor?

In most cases, the faults which are regarded as very serious are those which impair the dog's usefulness as a hunter or worker, or which have proved themselves to be very difficult to eradicate in breeding. Minor faults are those which constitute only a slight physical handicap or which can be easily eliminated by judicious breeding.

How do dog show judges decide whether one dog is better than another one?

Every breed which is recognized by the American Kennel Club has a written standard of perfection which describes, point by point, the physical conformation which is considered ideal for that breed. When a judge examines a class of dogs, he is presumably measuring each specimen against the ideal, and whichever dog comes closest to conforming to the standard for its breed will be placed first.

In watching dog show judging I have noticed that most judges pay a great deal of attention to how a dog looks when the handler trots it up and down the ring. Why is this?

Because a clever handler can pose a well trained dog so that it looks like an almost perfect specimen of its breed while it is standing still. The action of a dog, that is, walking or trotting, if closely observed, often reveals unsoundness or defects which may not be apparent when the dog is posed.

Honest Judgment in Dog Shows

Is there much dishonesty in the judging of dog shows?

Very little, though to hear a minority group of chronic bad losers tell it, the dog show world is riddled with dishonesty, favoritism, bribery, politics, and ignorance. Judges who show favoritism or who play politics in the ring usually eliminate themselves in fairly short order. Their drawing power for entries wanes as their reputation for unfair judging spreads, and their invitations to judge become fewer and farther between. Judges are, after all, only human, and it is inevitable that mistakes in placements are made occasionally, but the vast majority of these errors are honest ones. Usually, when one hears accusations against a judge they come from the sort of exhibitor who regards his dog's defeat as a personal affront and then displays his lack of sportsmanship by telling all who will listen that the judge is a crook.

Professional Handlers

Are professional handlers licensed?

Yes, by the American Kennel Club. The Kennel Club has ruled that any person who accepts payment for handling dogs for others must hold a license.

Are there different dog show classes for amateur and professional handlers?

No. Dog shows are one of the few sports wherein amateurs and professionals compete on equal terms.

Don't you think an amateur who shows his dog himself has very little chance of winning in competition with professional handlers?

The amateur (and there are many of them) who is willing to spend the amount of time and effort that a professional does in developing his skill in handling and in training and conditioning his dog has just as good a chance of winning as does the professional, if his dog is of real show quality. Naturally, the owner who brings an untrained, out-of-condition house pet into the ring is not liable to win much.

Can any dog owner learn to be a good handler?

Some people are too nervous and self-conscious to ever handle a dog well. Nervousness is transmitted right down the leash, and a jittery handler will make his dog jittery too. Large dogs, if they are to be shown to advantage, require a handler who is strong enough and in good enough physical condition to be able to manage them without struggling, and who can keep pace with them when moving. Most people can acquire a certain degree of handling skill if they work at it, but the really top handler seems to be born, not made. A flair for showmanship and the knack of "getting the most out of a dog" are the extras which distinguish a superior handler.

The First Dog Show in America

The date 1874 is a milestone in the history of purebred dogs in this country, for it was during that year that both the first dog show and the first field trial were held in America. The dog show was a casual affair, arranged as an added attraction at a meeting of the Illinois State Sportsmen's Association in Chicago. The entries were all dogs of the sporting breeds—Pointers, Setters, and perhaps some Spaniels. Just how the judges arrived at their decisions is cause for speculation, for this was ten years before the organization of the American Kennel Club, and the written standards by which dogs are judged today were nonexistent.

Haphazard as this first show must have been, the idea caught on and before the year was out three other shows were staged, one at Oswego, New York, another at Mineola, Long Island and a third at Memphis, Tennessee. The Memphis event was a combined bench show and field trial, and the field trial is considered to be the first organized competition of this sort in the United States. It is recorded that the winner of the trial was a black Setter (possibly a Gordon) named Knight. These first four shows were open only to dogs of the sporting breeds. All-breed competition got its start in January 1875, when a show was held at Detroit, Michigan, at which classes were offered for dogs of every breed.

The Purpose of Field Trials

What is the purpose of field trials?

The main purpose of field trials is to encourage the breeding and training of better hunting dogs. As a sport field trials have become enormously popular, providing, as they do, interest and excitement for both participants and spectators.

For those who like dogs and have an interest in sports, a field trial provides a fascinating demonstration of dogs of the sporting breeds competing under actual hunting conditions. Unlike the dog show, where perfection of physical conformation is emphasized, the field trial stresses excellence of performance.

Kinds of Field Trials

Are all field trials alike, or do they hold special trials for certain breeds?

Field trials fall into two general classifications, those for hounds and those for dogs of the sporting breeds, and are further subdivided as follows:

1. *Hounds.* Field trials are held for five of the breeds in this group: Beagles, Coonhounds, Dachshunds, Basset Hounds, and Foxhounds.
2. *Sporting dogs.* Trials are conducted for almost all of the breeds in this classification. These tests fall into three separate divisions: Bird-dog trials, Retriever trials, and Spaniel trials. The breeds which participate in each classification are as follows:
   A. *Bird dog trials.* Pointers, English Setters, Irish Setters, German Shorthaired Pointers, Brittany Spaniels, Gordon Setters, Wirehaired Pointing Griffons, Weimaraners.
   B. *Retriever trials.* Labrador Retrievers, Chesapeake Bay Retrievers, Golden Retrievers, Irish Water Spaniels, American Water Spaniels, Curly Coated Retrievers, Flat Coated Retrievers.
   C. *Spaniel trials.* American Cocker Spaniels, English Cocker Spaniels, English Springer Spaniels.

For the sake of equalizing and, at the same time, sharpening competition, events and entries in field trials are usually grouped into classes arranged according to several factors. The puppy stake is for dogs not older than 18 months, the derby class for dogs not over 30 months of age, and the all-age for dogs of any age. Gun-dog and shooting dog classes are for dogs which are used as all-round personal shooting dogs, the amateur class is for dogs handled by non-professionals, while the open places no limitations on the status of the handlers. Futurities are limited to young dogs which have been entered far in advance, sometimes before birth. Winners stakes are open only to dogs which have placed first, second, or third in a previous trial. Championships are trials which are held to determine a regional or national champion.

What the Dogs Do in Field Trials

What are the dogs required to do during a field trial?

Requirements vary with the different classifications. Hounds, which are run only on furred game, are expected to use their noses in tracking and to give tongue when trailing. Bird dogs must find birds, hold a steady point, honor or "back" points made by their running mates, and remain steadfast at the flight of the bird and the shot. Retrievers are called upon to demonstrate complete obedience to the orders of their handlers and must plunge without hesitation into the iciest water or the thorniest underbrush when commanded to "go fetch." Spaniels are required to find and flush birds and then retrieve the game when it is shot down.

Field Trial Sponsors

Who sponsors field trials?

Most field trials are given by clubs or associations of persons interested in hunting dogs.

Are any measures taken to make sure that a field trial is conducted fair and square?

When the entries for a trial have closed, a drawing is held (usually the night before the trial) to determine which dogs shall run in the trial together. This procedure insures that there shall be no partiality concerning the time of day a dog performs or which dog shall be his brace mate.

The Field Trial Spectator

Do you think that a mere spectator would find anything of interest at a field trial, or is it a highly technical affair that would only interest somebody who had a dog in the competition?

From the point of view of a judge or an owner who has a dog in the competition, the field trial is, indeed, a highly technical affair, requiring the attention and judgments of experts. But for all concerned—judge, owner, and spectator—the field trial is also an interesting and thrilling experience, whether the trial attended be for hounds, bird dogs, or retrievers. Usually there is no admission charge, though it may be necessary to rent or borrow one of the horses which are generally available at such events in order to view properly the swift-running, wide-ranging contestants in the big bird dog trials. Spaniel, hound, and retriever trials are easily followed without equine transportation. No one with a drop of sporting blood can fail to be deeply stirred when, for the first time, he hears "the sweet cry of hounds," watches the perfect coordination and control of a well-trained retriever and his handler working together, or sees the dash and style of a top flight bird dog in the field.

Sources of Official Regulations

I assume that there are rules and regulations governing the procedures at field trials and dog shows. Who sets up these rules?

Bench show competition comes under the jurisdiction of the American Kennel Club, as do field trials for Beagles, Spaniels and Retrievers. Trials for bird dogs are run under the rules and regulations of the Amateur Field Trial Clubs of America. The official publication of the events held under A.K.C. rulings is the American Kennel Gazette, while news of bird dog trials is published in the weekly journal, The American Field.

The American Kennel Club

What is the purpose of the American Kennel Club?

To quote from its charter, the objects of the American Kennel Club are: "to adopt and enforce uniform rules regulating and governing dog shows and field trials, to regulate the conduct of persons interested in exhibiting, running, breeding, registering, purchasing and selling dogs, to detect, prevent and punish frauds in connection therewith, to protect the interests of its members, to maintain and publish an official stud book and an official kennel gazette, and generally to do everything to advance the study, breeding, exhibiting, running and maintenance of the purity of thoroughbred dogs."

Can an individual be a member of the American Kennel Club?

No. The American Kennel Club is not a club in the sense that individual persons hold memberships. It is an association composed of around 300 member clubs, which may be all-breed clubs, specialty clubs, field trial clubs, or obedience clubs. Each member club is entitled to representation in the form of a delegate.

Does the American Kennel Club take disciplinary action against those who do not abide by its rules and regulations?

Yes. The penalties imposed may range from a reprimand or fine to suspension for life from all privileges of the A.K.C.

Has the American Kennel Club more than one office?

No, its only offices are in New York City. It is, however, represented by Trial Boards which act for the club in matters of discipline. Each Trial Board consists of three members, one of whom is usually an attorney. The eight boards are located in Boston, New York, Chicago, Los Angeles, Philadelphia, the Pacific Northwest, the Southeastern and Southwestern areas.

CHAPTER 14

A Dictionary of Dog Terms and Phrases

Like most people who are close followers of a sport or hobby, dog folk have an argot of their own. The conventional slang of the dog world may well seem like another language to the inexperienced dog owner, and when a seasoned fancier starts talking about hocks and withers and flews, the average dog lover is likely to find the conversation unintelligible. Even the American Kennel Club approved standards for each breed are presented in language which is in need of interpretation for the benefit of the layman. To help solve his problem, this chapter provides definitions of the less familiar terms employed in describing the various physical features, faults and virtues of dogs, the nicknames of various breeds, and the phraseology of the dog show, obedience test, and field trial, and other perplexing words of interest to dog lovers.

Abbreviations Commonly Used in Dog Show Reports

B.	Bitch
B.Am.B.	Best American bred
BB.	Best of breed
BiG.	Best in group
BiM.	Best in match
BiS.	Best in show
BoS.	Best of opposite sex to best of breed or best of variety
BV.	Best of variety

BW.   Best of winners

E.   Exhibition or exhibitor

J.   Judge

M.   Male

RB.   Reserve winners bitch

RM.   Reserve winners male

S.   Specials

WB.   Winners bitch

WM.   Winners male

— *A* —

Account For: A fox-hunting term. When a fox has either been killed or run into its den, it is spoken of as having been accounted for.

Acquired Characteristics: Characteristics which are developed through habit or environment rather than through heredity.

Acquired Immunity: An immunity from a disease, resulting from vaccination or from a previous attack of that disease which renders the body resistant to it.

Action: The way in which a dog walks, trots, or runs.

Adel: Nobility. The word is German and is frequently used by fanciers of the German breeds to describe a dog with great style and elegance. In other words, "the look of eagles."

A. K. C.: Abbreviation for American Kennel Club.

Alaunt: Name of a now extinct breed of large mastifflike English hunting and fighting dogs. Probable ancestor of the modern Mastiff and Bull-Mastiff.

Albinism: Deficiency of coloration of coat, nails, nose. A congenital condition.

Albino: An animal which lacks normal pigmentation. Characterized in dogs by blue or gray eyes, flesh-colored noses and white, or white and mottled coats.

All Rounder: A judge who is licensed to pass on all and any of the breeds which are accorded American Kennel Club recognition.

Almond Eye: A slantingly set, oval eye, pointed at the ends. Typical of the Bullterrier.

Alsatian: The English name for the German Shepherd.

Alter: To castrate a male or spay a female.

American-bred:

1. A dog born in the United States of America from a mating which took place in the United States of America.
2. A dog-show class for American-bred dogs only.

Amniotic Fluid: The fluid with which the unborn puppy is surrounded in the uterus.

Anal Glands: A pair of small secretory organs situated on either side of the anal opening.

Angulation: The degree of angle existing between two bones of the leg or shoulder which meet at a joint. Usually referring to the femur and fibular tibia—upper and lower thigh bone—angle, or the angle between the shoulder blade and upper arm.

Anticipating: An obedience term describing the action of a dog that performs an exercise before the command for that exercise is given by his handler.

Apple-Headed: Having a domed or rounded skull. Typical of the English Toy Spaniel and Chihuahua.

Apron: A frill of long hair below the neck and on the forechest. Typical of the Collie.

Articulation: The joints or junctures of the bones and cartilages.

APPLE-HEADED

Ascob: Abbreviation for "any solid color other than black." A variety division of the Cocker Spaniel.

Atavism: Reversion to primitive habits and instincts.

Ataxia: Unsteadiness of gait. A reeling or staggering gait is usually considered a symptom of a brain or spinal cord injury or disease.

Awards: Placings in classes at dog shows, field trials, or obedience tests.

— B —

Babbling: Giving tongue when not on the trail of game.

Baby Teeth: Same as puppy teeth.

Back or Backing: Term used to describe the action of a bird dog coming to a point upon sighting another dog at point on game, thereby "honoring" the other dog's point.

Backtracking: Running a trail backwards.

Back-Yard Breeder: Small-scale breeder who raises one or two litters a year.

Back-Yard Champion: A dog which looks and acts like a top-notcher when at home but refuses to show to advantage when in a dog show.

Bad Mover: A dog which walks or trots awkwardly, stiffly or in a cow-hocked manner. A dog whose gait lacks freedom or soundness.

Bandog or Bandogge: An obsolete term for a large watchdog kept tied by day and turned loose at night.

Bandy-Legged: Having front legs which are sprung outward, or hind legs which are too wide apart at the hocks.

Bat Ears: Ears which stand erect, pointing slightly outward like a bat's.

Bawl: A hound bay that is characterized by a prolonged, drawly note. Coonhounds are frequently described as having bawl voices.

Bay: The musical, prolonged barking noise made by hounds when trailing game or when game has been brought to a stand.

Beard: Bushy thick whiskers.

Beefy: Heavily muscled, fat and thick through the hind quarters.

Belton: A coat coloration consisting of a white background, heavily flecked with a darker color. Freckles of black, gray, orange-tan, or lemon are the most frequently seen. An English Setter whose coat is flecked with blue-gray is called a Blue Belton; if the flecks are orange-tan the term used is Orange Belton.

Bench: A slightly raised platform, divided into individual stalls used for exhibition of dogs entered in dog shows.

BENCH AT A DOG SHOW

Bench Show: A dog show where benching is provided for the entrants. The term is also used commonly to mean any dog show.

Bench Show Committee: The committee of a show-giving club, which is responsible for all arrangements for the show and the enforcement of A. K. C. rules at the show.

Best of Losers: Dog-show slang for getting a "Best of Opposite Sex" award for a dog with which one hoped or expected to win "Best of Breed."

Best of Winners: The dog or bitch which is placed first when Winners Dog and Winners Bitch are brought together in competition.

Big Going: Descriptive of a bird dog that ranges at considerable distances from his handler when seeking game.

Bird Dog: Any of the breeds that are used in hunting birds. Usually Pointers or Setters.

Bird-of-Prey Eye: A yellow eye having the cold expression typical of hawks and vultures.

Birdy: An adjective used to describe a bird dog who has a good nose—scenting power—and unusual bird-finding ability.

Biscuit: A pale fawn color.

Bitch: Female dog.

Bitchy: Descriptive of a male dog which is overrefined in general conformation, giving an impression of femininity.

Bite: The meeting of the teeth; the set of the teeth. See also: *even bite, overshot, pincer bite, undershot.*

Blacktongue: A disease caused by a deficiency of vitamin B. The name of the disease is derived from the fact that the tongue becomes discolored during the advanced stages of the disease.

Blanket: A dark marking, usually black, extending over the back and sides from the withers to the base of the tail.

Blaze: A white mark running up the middle of the foreface and between the eyes. Often seen in St. Bernards.

Blinking: A bird-dog term describing the action of a dog that either finds birds, points, and then goes away and leaves them before they are flushed, or deliberately passes them by even though he is aware of their presence. A serious fault.

Blocky:
  1. Descriptive of a head which is square or boxlike in formation. Characteristic of the Boston Terrier.
  2. Descriptive of a chunky, square body.

Bloom: The glossy sheen of the coat of a dog in good condition.

Blue: Bluish-gray color.

Bob-Tail: Nickname for the Old English Sheepdog.

Bolter: A bird dog which goes out of control, runs away from his handler and hunts for his own pleasure.

Bossy: Overdeveloped and thick through the shoulders.

Brace:
  1. A pair of dogs of the same breed.
  2. Two dogs which run together in the same heat in a field trial.

Brace Class: A special class, usually held only at the larger dog shows, for two dogs of the same breed belonging to one kennel or owner. The dogs need not be of the same sex. It is desirable that the two dogs be well matched in color, size, and general type.

Bracelets: Strips of long hair encircling the lower legs of Poodles clipped show-style.

Brag Dog: A hunting dog—usually a bird dog or hound—whose hunting ability is so much the pride and joy of his owner that the owner boasts about the dog.

Bred by Exhibitor Class: Dog-show class in which the dogs competing must be owned by the person—or persons—who bred them. Champions are not eligible for this class.

Breech Birth: A birth in which the puppy's hind feet appear first rather than the head.

Breeching:

1. Long, profuse hair on the thighs.
2. The tan markings of the inside and back of the hind legs of black-and-tan marked dogs. Typical of the Manchester Terrier and the Doberman Pinscher.

Breed Club: An organization composed of breeders, fanciers, and exhibitors who are interested in the same breed. Examples: The American Sealyham Terrier Club, The Great Dane Club of America.

Breeder: The breeder of a dog is the person who owned or leased the dog's dam at the time she was mated.

Breeding Terms: An arrangement between two breeders wherein one of them leases a bitch for breeding purposes, or undertakes the boarding and care of a bitch and her litter in return for a cash consideration or a specified number of her puppies.

Brindle: A coat color showing a mixture of light and dark hairs. Usually the effect is one of irregular stripes of the darker hair.

Brisket: The forechest. The section of the body in front of the chest and between the front legs.

Broad Jump: An obedience test exercise wherein a dog is required to clear a broad jump made up of low hurdles spaced so as to cover a distance equal to twice the height of the high jump set for the particular dog. An Open Class exercise.

Broken Color: Descriptive of a coat which is all one color, or shades of one color which is broken by stripes, patches or spots of white.

Broken-Up Face: Foreface showing receding nose, deep stop, projecting lower jaw, and pronounced wrinkles. Characteristic of the Bulldog and Pekingese.

Brood Bitch: A bitch kept for breeding purposes.

Brush: A tail covered with thick, bushy hair. Characteristic of the Collie. The tail of a fox is always called his brush.

Bull-Necked: Unusually thick, heavy, or muscular through the neck.

Burning Scent: A freshly made, easily followed trail.

Burr: The irregular inner formation of the ear.

Butterfly Nose: A nose showing two colors. Usually black or dark brown, spotted with flesh color.

Button Ears: Ears which fold over to the front and are held close to the head. Typical of the Fox Terrier.

— C —

Call-Name: Name by which a registered dog is known and called at home or in the kennel. Usually a shorter and easier name than a registered name.

Camel Back: A back showing so much roach or hump as to appear crippled.

Campaigning: Extensive showing of a dog.

Caniche:

1. The French word for Poodle.
2. A Poodle which is midway in size between the Miniature and Standard varieties. In this country the Caniche is considered too small to be a representative Standard Poodle and oversized for a Miniature.

Canine Teeth: Long, strong pointed teeth just behind the incisors. Sometimes called "fangs." They correspond to the eye teeth of humans.

Carp Back: An arched back.

Cast: The circle or swing made by a hound in an effort to pick up a trail it has lost.

Castration: Removal of a male dog's testicles.

Cat Foot: A short, round, compact foot. The knuckles should be high like those of a cat. A good English Foxhound has feet of this type.

Catalogue: Book published by show-giving club, listing name, ownership, birthdate, parentage, registration number, and breeder of every dog entered at the show; also judging schedule, prizes offered, and other pertinent data.

C.D.: Abbreviation for Companion Dog, a title given by the American Kennel Club to dogs which have made three qualifying scores in Novice A or Novice B classes at recognized obedience trials. This is the first of the obedience degrees it is possible for a dog to win.

C.D.X.: Abbreviation for Companion Dog Excellent, a title given by the American Kennel Club to dogs which have won C.D. degrees and have made three qualifying scores in Open A or Open B classes at recognized obedience trials. This is the second of the obedience degrees it is possible for a dog to win.

Chamois Ear: A soft, thin ear.

Champion:

1. A dog which has won 15 points in dog-show competition under American Kennel Club regulations. The 15-point total must be made up of two wins of 3 or more points, these two wins to be awarded by two different judges, the remainder to be awarded by at least one other judge. Five points are the maximum which a dog can win at a single show.

2. Dog which has won a field-trial championship for his performances in such competitions.

Character: The combination of correct physical conformation, good expression, and desirable temperament which make up a typical representative of a breed. Outstanding specimens are often described as having "a lot of breed character."

Charlie Chaplin Feet: Feet which turn out.

Chasing: A bird-dog term for running after flushed birds. A deplorable habit.

Cheap Champion: A dog whose championship title has been won in areas where the point rating is low and competition is not of a high caliber.

Check:

1. A Boxer whose white markings are more extensive than is considered correct for the breed.

2. A hound term denoting the point where a trail is temporarily lost and later recovered.

Check Line: A piece of light, strong rope, about thirty feet in length, with a snap at one end. Used in controlling bird dogs in training and also for obedience work.

Cheek: Fleshy portion of the side of the head, below the eyes, and above and behind the mouth.

Cheeky: Heavy, rounded development of the cheeks. Seen in Bulldogs.

Cheese Champion: A dog of relatively poor quality that has managed to win a championship usually by means of extensive campaigning and a good deal of sheer luck.

Chest: The portion of the body behind the brisket and in front of the abdomen.

China Eye: A light-blue eye.

Chiseling: Well-defined, delicately modeled contours of the head.

Chokebored Nose: Bird-dog term used to describe exceptionally keen scenting powers. Dogs with noses of this type are capable of scenting birds at a great distance.

Chops: Thick, pendulous upper lips which hang below the line of the lower jaw. Typical of the Bloodhound and Bulldog.

Chorea: A nervous disease characterized by twitching of the muscles or jerking. A frequent aftermath of distemper.

Circuit: A series of dog shows in the same general area arranged on consecutive dates. A well-planned circuit gives handlers and exhibitors the opportunity to compete at several different shows within a short period of time.

Class Dog: A dog which has not won his championship and is competing in the regular classes to win points for the title.

Clipper Burn: A sore or chafed area of a dog's skin resulting from any of three causes: the use of dull or defective clippers, clipping too closely, an extra sensitive skin.

Cloddy: Low, thickset in conformation.

Close Action: A gait which is characterized by the hocks coming close together when the dog is walking or trotting.

Close-Coupled: Short-backed, or short-bodied.

Coat: The hair covering a dog's body.

Cobby: Compact and muscular in build. The expression comes from the short-backed sturdy conformation of the cob type of horse.

Cold-blooded Dog: A dog which to all appearances is a purebred dog but which is not registered and has no pedigree.

Color Breeding: The mating of individual dogs for the purpose of producing puppies of some particular color or combination of colors.

Colostrum: The first milk secreted by a bitch following whelping.

Common: Lacking in aristocracy and elegance.

Condition Powder: A mixture of drugs and herbs used as a tonic and general conditioner. Very popular with British dog fanciers.

Conditioning: Feeding, exercising, and grooming in order to bring a dog in top physical form.

Conformation: Structure.

Congenital Characteristics: Characteristics which exist at birth or which date from the time of birth. Congenital characteristics are those which are believed to be acquired during development in the uterus as differentiated from hereditary characteristics which are those transmitted by the germ plasm.

Corky: Compact in conformation. Active and alert in temperament. Often used to describe terriers.

Coupling: Portion of body between forequarters and hindquarters.

Cow Hocks: Hocks which point inward toward one another. A definite indication of structural unsoundness.

Cowlick: A patch of hair growing in the opposite direction from the lay of the rest of the coat.

Crank Tail: A short tail curving down and then away from the body.

Crest: The convex upper arch of the neck.

Crisscross Inheritance Theory: An erroneous

COW HOCKS

breeding theory maintaining that female puppies inherit the physical characteristics of their sire and male puppies inherit those of their dam.

Cropped Ears: Ears from which a portion has been cut off to cause them to stand in erect points. This operation is performed on many breeds in the United States and Europe but has been forbidden in England since 1895. Two examples of the breeds which are almost always seen cropped in this country are Great Danes and Boxers.

Crossbred or Crossbreed: A mongrel whose parents are both purebreds but of different breeds.

Croup: The portion of the dog's back just in front of the root of the tail. Also called the rump.

Cry: The baying of hounds on the trail.

Cryptorchid: A male dog with no visible testicles.

Cull: A puppy of substandard quality or one with disqualifying faults.

Culotte: Long, bushy hair on the upper parts of the hind legs. Typical of the Pomeranian.

Cushion: Thick heavy fullness of upper lips and foreface. Characteristic of the Bulldog.

Cutting Bite: See *scissors bite.*

— D —

Dachsie: Nickname for the Dachshund.

Dam: Mother, female parent.

Dappled: A coat color with irregular rings of a darker shade.

Daredevil: Nickname for the Irish Terrier.

Delegate: Person chosen by a member dog club to be its representative to the American Kennel Club.

Depth of Thigh: Width and thickness of the thigh.

Derby:

1. A bird dog not yet thirty months of age.
2. A field-trial Beagle is considered a derby during the entire year following the year during which it was whelped.

Derby Stakes: Field-trial class for bird dogs not yet thirty months of age.

Derby Year: Period during which a bird dog is over eighteen months of age and not yet thirty months of age.

Dewclaws: Superfluous claws on the inner side of the legs just above the foot.

Dewlap: Loose, pendulous skin under the chin and throat. Characteristic of the Bloodhound.

Diehard: Nickname for the Scottish Terrier.

Dimple: A small depression on either side of the forechest. Characteristic of the Dachshund.

Dingo: Wild dog native to Australia.

Dishface: A foreface which is concave from the eyes to the nose tip. The effect is one of being hollowed out and the nose appears to turn up slightly. Often seen in Pointers.

DISHFACE

Disqualifying Fault: A fault so serious that it disqualifies a dog from bench-show competition. Examples: a Samoyed with a black or black spotted coat; a German Shepherd with hanging hound-type ears; a Miniature Schnauzer measuring more than fourteen inches at the withers.

Distemper: A virus disease which kills more puppies and young dogs than any other ailment. Public enemy number one to dog health.

Distemper Teeth: Teeth which are pitted or ringed by areas having no covering of enamel. The marks are usually discolored. The condition is caused by the dog having been ill of a disease accompanied by high fever during the teething period.

Dobe: Nickname for the Doberman Pinscher.

Docking: The practice of shortening tails by cutting. Cocker Spaniels and Fox Terriers are two of the breeds whose tails are commonly docked.

Dome: Rounded portion of the upper skull.

Dominant Characteristic: A characteristic of one parent which manifests itself in the offspring to the exclusion of any contrasting characteristics from the other parent.

Double Coat: A coat consisting of a soft, dense, furry underpart and a coarser, profuse outercoat. Collies and Old English Sheepdogs have coats of this type.

Down and Stay: An obedience test exercise wherein the dogs are required to lie down and stay put by themselves for a definite length of time.

Downfaced: Having a foreface or muzzle which slants downward from the stop to the nose tip. Characteristic of the Bull Terrier.

Down in Pastern: A weakness of the joint of the foreleg just above the foot, evidenced by this part of the leg (the pastern) sloping back from the foot and joining the foreleg at an angle rather than perpendicularly. Considered a sign of faulty structure or poor condition in most breeds.

Drop Ears: Soft pendulous ears which hang flat to the head.

Dropper: A crossbreed produced by the mating of a Pointer and a Setter.

Dry: Free of superfluous flesh.

Dual Champion: A dog which has won championships in both dog show and field trial competitions.

Dudley Nose: A pink or yellowish nose.

Dysplasia: A condition in which the femur bone is displaced from the hip socket.

— E —

Ear Canker: An ulcerated condition of the inner ear, often occurring in dogs with long hanging ears.

Ear Fringes: Long silky hair forming fringes on the edges of the ears. Typical of Spaniels and Setters.

Earrings: Same as tassels.

Earth: The den of a burrowing animal.

Earthstopping: Filling in the burrow of a fox or badger with dirt or rocks in order to prevent the animal from taking refuge there.

Easy Keeper: A dog of good health and temperament which is easily kept in proper physical condition.

Eclampsia: Convulsions which sometimes occur in lactating bitches. Often called "nursing fits."

Eczema: A skin ailment which may be either of the acute and moist type or chronic and dry type. Occurs most frequently during hot weather.

Elbows: The joints at the tops of the front legs next to the body.

Elegance: The combination of aristocratic bearing and symmetry of conformation.

Elephant Action: Lumbering, shuffling manner of walking or trotting.

Enter:

1. Fox-hunting term meaning to start young Foxhounds with the pack for the first time.
2. To enroll a dog for competition in a dog show, field trial, or obedience test.

Enteritis: Inflammation of the bowels.

Entry: A dog which is participating in a dog show, field trial, or obedience test.

Entry Blank: A form which must be filled out and filed in advance in order for a dog to compete in a dog show, field trial, or obedience test.

Even Bite: Meeting of the front teeth at the edges with no overlap. Same as a pincer bite.

Ewe Neck: A neck showing a concave line from the back of the skull to the withers.

Exhibition Only: A special classification for dogs which are entered and benched at a dog show without competing in any classes.

Expression: The expression of the eyes and face which indicate a dog's intelligence, character, and emotional make-up. It is considered extremely important in the judging of dogs that a dog have the expression which is typical of his breed. For example, the standard for the Beagle calls for a "gentle and pleading" expression, while an expression that is "full of fire, life, and intelligence" is considered correct for the Fox Terrier.

External Parasites: Fleas, lice, ticks.

Eye Teeth: Same as canine teeth.

— F —

Faddist: A fancier or judge who is "hipped" on some particular point of a dog's anatomy. Examples: the judge who will not give a high award to a dog with yellow eyes no matter how perfect a specimen the dog may otherwise be; or the fancier who considers a good coat more important than any other feature.

Faking: Altering a dog's appearance by means of surgery, dyeing, chemicals, drugs, or cosmetics. Strictly against the rules of the American Kennel Club. At one time extensively practiced in order to improve the appearance of show dogs.

Fall: Long hair, like bangs, overhanging the face. Typical of the Skye Terrier.

Fallow: Pale yellow color.

False Point: The act of pointing in the direction of underbrush or other cover where there is no game.

Fancier: A person interested in the breeding and showing of dogs, usually of some one particular breed.

Fangs: Long canine teeth; eye teeth.

Fawn: A rich, light golden-tan.

Fear Biter: A dog that bites because of a nervous, unstable temperament.

Feathers: Long, silky fringes of hair on the ears, chest, abdomen, legs, and tail. Typical of the Irish Setter.

Feist: Small mongrel. Usually of the Terrier type.

Felted Coat: A coat which has formed into dense mats and wads.

Fetch: A command ordering a dog to retrieve.

Fiddle Face: An elongated, pinched foreface.

Fiddle Front: Term for crooked or bandy forelegs. This type of build, viewed from in front, shows elbows that turn out, pasterns that turn in, and Charlie Chaplin front feet.

Field Dog: A dog used for hunting or field trials.

Field Trial: A competition held under natural conditions for testing the hunting ability of bird dogs, Spaniels, Retrievers, or hounds.

Finish: To win a championship. A dog who has won the required fifteen points for this title is spoken of as having "finished his championship," or "completed his championship."

Fire: Sparkling, lively expression of the eyes.

Fire House Dog: Nickname for the Dalmatian.

Flag: Tail, particularly one which is fringed or bushy.

Flanks: The loin and upper thighs.

Flashy: Spectacularly attractive in either conformation or movement.

Flat-Sided: Lacking proper roundness through the ribs.

Flecked: A coat color lightly marked with small spots of a darker shade. Usually white with brownish-orange or gray-black flecks.

Flesh Nose: Pinkish or tan nose.

Flews: Pendulous upper lips. Characteristic of the Bloodhound and Bulldog.

Flush: To approach game birds in such a manner as to cause them to take wing.

Fly Ears: Ears pointing in opposite directions or carried askew.

Flyer: A dog, usually a youngster, of unusual promise as a show prospect.

Foreface: The portion of the head from the eyes to the nose tip.

Foul Color: A color which is uncharacteristic of a breed and therefore undesirable. Examples: A white Boxer, a solid black Bulldog, a Welsh Terrier with extensive white markings.

Foundation Stock: The original bitches and dogs with which a kennel makes its start.

Fowler's Solution: A tonic containing arsenic. Its use is fairly widespread among English breeders and fanciers for conditioning show dogs, particularly those breeds which should carry a heavy coat. Poisoning can result from its continued use.

Frenchie: Nickname for the French Bulldog.

Frill: Long hair under the neck and on the forechest. Characteristic of the Collie.

Frog Face: A foreface which is typified by an extending nose, a receding lower jaw and overshot teeth. The term is usually applied only to short-faced breeds such as the Boxer or Boston Terrier.

Front: The front legs and fore part of the body.

F.T. Ch.: Abbreviation for field trial champion.

Full Cry: The loud, full-throated baying of hounds when on a hot trail.

Full Eye: A round, slightly protruding eye.

Full-Mantle Dog: Descriptive of a St. Bernard whose coat has no white collar or markings breaking the dark coloration of neck, shoulders, back, and sides.

Fur-and-Feather Dog: A sporting dog which will hunt and point birds, and which can also be used for trailing furred game such as raccoons, rabbits, and 'possums.

Furnishings: Thick, fringed or long portions of the coat. Examples: the chin whiskers which are typical of the Schnauzer; the heavy hair on the backs of the legs of the Kerry Blue Terrier; the ear fringes and leg fringes of the Cocker Spaniel.

Furrow: An elongated depression in the center of the skull extending from the occiput to the stop.

Futurity: A class for which dogs are entered while still very young puppies, or even before birth, and which is judged when the dogs are one year or eighteen months of age. Entry payments are made at stipulated intervals to keep each dog's entry in effect and the accumulated money is divided into prizes when the class is judged.

– G –

Gait: Manner of walking, trotting, or running.

Gay Tail: A tail which is carried straight up.

Gazehound: An obsolete term for hounds which pursue their game by using their eyes rather than their noses. Now known as "sight hounds."

Gestation: Period of pregnancy.

Giving Tongue: Baying when on the trail of game.

Good Doer: A dog of keen appetite, general good health and vigor, which is easily kept in top physical condition.

Good Nose: Fine scenting ability.

Goose Rump: A rump which slopes sharply down from the hip bones to the root of the tail.

Ground Color: The background color of a parti-colored dog.

Group: One of the six divisions into which the American Kennel Club has, for purposes of dog show competition, classified all recognized breeds. They are: Sporting Group, Hound Group, Working Group, Terrier Group, Toy Group, and Nonsporting Group.

Grizzle: A steel gray color, or black-and-gray mixture.

Gun-Barrel Front: Absolutely straight front legs.

Gun Dogs: All the Setter breeds, Pointers, Retrievers, and Spaniels.

— H —

Hackney Gait: A high-stepping lively gait.

Handler: Person taking a dog into the ring at a dog show, or the person managing a dog competing in a field trial or obedience test.

Hard-Bitten: Tough and contentious in disposition. Often applied to terriers of a fiery temperament.

Hard Loser: Dog-show exhibitor, obedience test competitor, or field trial competitor who is a sorehead when his dog does not win.

Hardmouthed: Descriptive of retrievers who clamp down on, chew, tear, or "muss up" game when picking it up or carrying it. A serious fault.

Harefoot: Long, narrowish foot. The toes are deep knuckled and held tightly together.

Harelip: An upper lip which is divided by a slit running from its front edge up to the nose. Puppies born with this deformity are almost impossible to raise as they are unable to nurse.

Harlequin: Black-and-white coloration. The background is white and the black portions are small, irregular, "torn" patches distributed over the entire body.

Harsh-Coated: Having a stiff, wiry coat.

Haunches: Back portion of the thighs. The dog's "sitting surface."

Haw: The red membrane inside the lower eyelid which is often prominent in breeds having heavy wrinkled faces that pull the eyelids down. Examples: Bloodhound, St. Bernard.

Hazel Eye: A light-brown eye.

Heel: Command used to order a dog to walk close to his handler's side with his head no farther forward than the handler's knee.

Heeling: Describing the action of a dog walking at his handler's side with his head on the level of, or in line with the handler's knee.

Heel Free: An obedience test exercise wherein a dog is required to heel (walk at his handler's side) without a leash.

Height: The measurement from the highest point of the shoulders (withers) to the ground.

Herding Drive: The natural instinct to herd sheep, cattle, or ducks, which is inborn in many dogs of the breeds which are used for these purposes.

Hie On: Field-dog command sending a dog out to seek game.

High-Stationed: Standing high off the ground. Leggy.

Hocks: The joints of the hind legs between the second thigh and the pastern.

Hocky: Same as cow-hocked.

Honoring: Same as "backing."

Hot Spots: Kennel term for hairless, raw patches in the coat which often appear during hot weather.

Hound Colors: Black, tan, and white.

Hound Marked: Descriptive of the coat color of Fox Terriers having black-and-tan markings on a white background similar to the markings of Foxhounds.

Houndy: Showing the characteristics considered typical of hounds such as long, soft, low-hanging ears, gentle expression, deep muzzle.

Hucklebones: The top of the hip joints.

Humerus: The upper arm. The bone between the shoulder blade and the elbow.

Hup: Word of command used for bird dogs, meaning "down." Also, command used in obedience training when ordering dog to jump.

Husky: Common name applied to all sled-dog breeds. Properly only used for Siberian Husky.

— I —

Import: Any dog bred and born in another country and brought into the United States of America.

Inbreeding: The mating of dogs that are closely related. Examples: breeding a bitch to her litter brother, breeding a male to his own daughter.

Incisors: The small, even, "biting off" teeth at the very front of the upper and lower jaws.

Internal Parasites: Worms.

International Champion: A dog that has won bench show or obedience titles in more than one country. Examples: The United States of America, and Canada; or England, and the United States of America.

Interseason Periods: The time between the "in-heat" periods of a bitch.

In Heat: Same as in season.

In Season: Ready for breeding. A bitch is spoken of as being in season during the semiannual periods which she will allow a male dog to mate with her.

In Shouldered: Narrow-fronted.

In Whelp: Pregnant.

Iris: The colored portion of the eyes.

— J —

Jones Terrier: Frequently used name for the Norwich Terrier.

Judge: Person officiating at dog shows, field trials, or obedience tests, making awards and placements.

— K —

Kelpie: An Australian sheepherding breed. Considered one of the best breeds for handling sheep.

Kennel:

1. Building where dogs are kept.
2. All the dogs belonging to one kennel owner.

Kennel Blindness: Utter inability to see any faults of temperament or conformation in one's own dogs. Fairly common among breeders and exhibitors.

Kennel Name:

1. A name registered with the American Kennel Club by means of the proper application and payment of a fee. This gives the registered owner of that name the sole rights to its use in connection with the registration and exhibition of dogs. For example: If Mrs. A. Collie Owner registers the kennel name of Fairchance then that name is hers alone to use as a prefix or suffix when registering puppies, and dogs of her breeding will be identified by such names as Fairchance Floradora or Hasty of Fairchance. When Mrs. Owner exhibits her dogs she may enter them as being owned by the Fairchance Kennels.
2. A short simple name by which a dog is known in the kennel or at home. Most dogs' registered names are too much of a mouthful to make good call-names. Consequently, a dog whose registered name was Ch. Fairchance Fantasy would probably be called something as simple as Ginny or Dot at home.

Kink Tail: Short, twisted tail. Typical of the Bulldog and Boston Terrier.

Kissing Spots: Contrasting markings on the cheeks. Typical of several toy breeds.

Knee: The joint of the front leg between the pastern and the forearm.

Knuckled Over: Having front legs which bend forward at the knee joint.

— L —

Lab: Nickname for the Labrador Retriever.

Lactation: Period during which a bitch is producing milk.

Lady Pack: A pack of hounds made up entirely of bitches.

Landseer: A Newfoundland whose coloring is other than solid black. Usually white with black or bronze.

Layback: A receding nose which is accompanied by an undershot jaw. Typical of the Bulldog.

Leather: The skin of the soft pendulous ears of certain hound breeds—Foxhounds, Bloodhounds, Dachshunds.

Leggy: Disproportionately long-legged.

Lemon: Pale yellow color.

Lengthy: Long in body.

Licensed Show: A show held under American Kennel Club rules and awarding points toward championships.

Light Eyes: Eyes which are yellowish in color.

Line: The trail made by game.

Line Breeding: The mating of dogs which are related. Examples: breeding a male dog to his granddaughter; or breeding a male and female both having the same dog as their maternal grandsire.

Linty Coat: A coat that is cottonlike in texture.

Lippy: Having lips which are too pendulous or thick.

Listing Fee: A fee of twenty-five cents charged for the entry at a dog show of a dog not registered with the American Kennel Club.

Litter: All the puppies brought forth at one time by a bitch.

Liver Color: A dark reddish-brown color.

Loaded: Showing undesirable thickness or heaviness through the neck, withers, and shoulders.

Lofty Tail: A tail which is carried high.

Loin: The portion of the body between the last rib and the hind legs.

Long Down: An obedience test exercise wherein the dogs are required to lie down and stay put by themselves for a definite period of time.

Long Sit: An obedience test exercise wherein the dogs are required to sit down and stay put by themselves for a definite period of time.

Low-Set Ears: Ears which are attached more to the side than on top of the head.

Lumber: Superfluous flesh or bone.

Lurcher: A crossbreed purposely produced for hunting by English gypsies and poachers. The cross is usually a Greyhound on one side and a Retriever, large Terrier, or Collie on the other.

— M —

Maiden Bitch: A bitch which has not produced a litter of puppies.

Major Win: A show win giving a dog three or more points toward his championship.

Mane: Long profuse hair on the neck and throat.

Mantle: A St. Bernard term denoting the dark portion of the coat covering the shoulders, back, and sides of the body.

MASK

Mask: Dark coloration of the muzzle. Commonly seen in Boxers, Afghan Hounds, Great Danes.

Match Show: An informal dog show where no points toward championships are awarded.

Matron: Brood bitch.

Mats: Thick wads of felty hair which occur in the coats of long-haired dogs through lack of combing.

Meat Hound: Hunting dog which can always be depended on to find game.

Member Show: A dog show given by a club which is a member of the American Kennel Club.

Mendelian Law: The law governing the inheritance of character-istics in animals and plants, which was discovered by the Austrian, Gregor Mendel.

Merle: A blue-gray color marbled with black.

Merry Tail: High-held wagging tail.

M.F.H.: Abbreviation for Master of Foxhounds.

Middle Piece: The portion of the body between the shoulders and hindquarters.

Milk Teeth: A puppy's first set of teeth.

Miscellaneous Class: A class offered at a dog show for several rare breeds which do not have American Kennel Club recognition but which are known to be purebreds.

Mongrel: Dog whose ancestry consists of a mixture of different breeds.

Monorchid: A male dog with but one visible testicle.

Mops: Long thick hair on the paws.

Mouthy: Unnecessarily noisy.

Moyen: A Poodle which is midway in size between a Miniature and a Standard.

Mug Hunter: Avid exhibitor whose one aim is to collect as many ribbons and trophies as possible.

Mustard Color: A yellowish-tan color.

Mutant: A dog whose physical conformation is not similar to that of his immediate ancestry and who has the ability to transmit this dissimilarity (or change) to his or her offspring.

Mute Trailer: A hound which does not give tongue when trailing game.

Mutton-Shouldered: Having shoulders which are too thick and heavy.

— *N* —

Nasolabial Line: A shallow groove between the nostrils which extends down the upper lip to its edge.

Newf: Nickname for the Newfoundland.

Noseband: A band of white encircling the muzzle. Typical of the St. Bernard.

Novice Class: A dog-show class for dogs which have never won a first prize except in the puppy class.

Novice A: An obedience trial class for purebred dogs of any breed and of either sex which have not won the title C.D. Companion Dog) . Dog entered in this class must be handled by the owner or a member of his immediate family. No professional trainer or handler, nor any kennel employee is allowed to compete in this class.

Novice B: An obedience trial class for purebred dogs of any breed and of either sex which have not won the title C.D. (Companion Dog) . Dogs in this class may be handled or exhibited by either an amateur or a professional.

$$-O-$$

Obedience Trials: Tests held under A. K. C. regulations, open to purebred dogs of any breed and of either sex, wherein dogs are put through various required exercises and are scored by a qualified judge on their performance. Obedience trials may be held either separately or as part of an all-breed show, and either indoors or outdoors.

Occiput: A knoblike bone at the top of the skull between the ears. Particularly prominent in the Bloodhound.

Oestrum: The biannual periods during which a bitch will accept a dog for mating.

Offal: Portions of animal carcasses considered unfit for human consumption.

OCCIPUT

Open A: An obedience trial class for purebred dogs of either sex and of any breed which have won the C.D. (Companion Dog) degree in obedience Novice Classes. Dogs must be handled by their owner or a member of his immediate family. No professional handler or trainer, or any kennel employee is allowed to compete in this class.

Open B: An obedience trial class for purebred dogs of either sex and of any breed which have won the C.D. (Companion Dog) degree in obedience Novice Classes. Dogs in this class may be handled or exhibited by either an amateur or a professional.

Open Class: A breed class at a dog show in which there are no restrictions and wherein any purebred dog that is over six months of age may compete—champions, imported dogs, American-bred dogs, puppies. Usually the stiffest competition in a breed is to be found in this class, with the exception of the Specials Only class.

Open Face: A common, expressionless face. Usually lacking proper chiseling and refinement.

Open Trailer: A dog, especially a hound, that bays when on the trail of game.

Otter Tail: A thick, tapering tail similar to that of the otter. Characteristic of the Labrador Retriever.

Out at Elbow: Having elbows that stand away from the body.

Outbreeding: The mating of two dogs that are of the same breed but who are totally unrelated, in other words, from entirely different families.

Overshot: Descriptive of a dog's mouth wherein the upper jaw protrudes beyond the lower jaw and the front teeth do not meet properly. A mouth of this type is similar to a shark's and gives a dog a rather "chinless" expression.

OVERSHOT

— P —

Pack: The portion of a Poodle's coat covering the rump and hindquarters, which is clipped to about an inch in length, when the dog is trimmed in the English Saddle style. Also, a group of hounds which regularly hunt together.

Pad: The sole of the foot.

Paddler: A dog which walks or trots with an awkward swinging-out motion of the front feet.

Paper Foot: A foot with a thin, flattened pad.

Parasite: A general term meaning any small animal living on or within the body of another animal. The commoner parasites which infest dogs externally are fleas, ticks, and lice; and the several types of worms internally.

Pariah: Scavenger dog of the Orient.

Parti-Color: A coat color consisting of two or more distinct colors appearing in clearly defined markings.

Parturition: The act of whelping.

Pastern: The section of the lower leg between the knee and the foot of the foreleg and the hock and foot of the hind leg.

Pattern: The design of long and short hair into which a Poodle's coat is clipped.

Pedigree: A written record of the names of a dog's ancestors.

Peke: Nickname for the Pekingese.

Penciling: Markings consisting of thin black lines against a tan background. Marks of this type are seen on the feet of Manchester Terriers, the pencil marks running up each toe.

Pepper and Salt: A coat color which is an even mixture of gray and black hair.

P.H.A.: Abbreviation for Professional Handler's Association, an organization of licensed handlers formed for the purpose of encouraging ethical conduct and competence among its members.

Pickup: Light, springy, quick action of the feet in walking.

Pigeon-toed: Having feet which point in toward one another.

Pig-eye: An unusually small squinty eye, which generally gives a dog an unattractive expression and often indicates a bad temperament.

Pig-jaw: A jaw which is overshot to an exaggerated degree.

Pigmentation: Coloration, usually referring to the darkness of nose, eye rims, and toenails.

Pile: The dense undercoat of breeds having a double coat.

PIGEON-TOED

Piley: Description of a coat containing both soft, short woolly hair and long crisp hair, the softer portion forming a very dense undercoat. Typical of the Dandie Dinmont Terrier.

Pincer Teeth or Pincer Bite: Front teeth of the upper and lower jaws which meet at the edges rather than overlapping when the mouth is closed. The juncture is similar to the manner in which the cutting edges of wire cutters come together.

Plucking: Removal of dead or superfluous hair from the coat with a trimming instrument. Usually referring to wiry Terrier coats.

PINCER TEETH

Plume: A tail with long profuse hair. Typical of the Pomeranian and Pekingese.

Plum-pudding Dog: Nickname for the Dalmatian.

Pointing Breeds: The breeds which "freeze" into position when hunting birds, their noses pointing toward the found game. Breeds which handle birds in this manner are the Brittany Spaniel, the Pointer, all the Setters, the German Short-haired Pointer, the Weimaraner, and the Wire-haired Pointing Griffon.

Point of Shoulder: Most forward portion of the shoulder. The joint of the shoulder blade and upper arm.

Point Rating: The schedule fixed by the American Kennel Club of the points toward a championship which are awarded to the winner's dog and winner's bitch of each breed in competition at a dog show. The points awarded are based on the actual number of dogs or bitches competing in that breed.

Points: Units of credit toward championship.

Police Dog: Any dog which has been trained to do police work. Also a common (but wrong) name for the German Shepherd.

Pom: Nickname for the Pomeranian.

Pompon: The tuft of hair left on the end of a Poodle's tail.

Poor Doer: A dog of picky appetite, usually of nervous, jumpy temperament, and almost impossible to get into good condition.

Posing: Placing a dog in the standing position which will display him to the best advantage.

Potlicker: Hillbilly name for a more or less worthless mongrel hound dog.

Pottering: Hunting back and forth over the same ground again and again in an indecisive manner. A cardinal sin in bird dogs and Beagles.

Premium List: A printed list describing the prizes offered at a dog show, obedience test, or field trial, and naming the judges who are to officiate.

Prick Ears: Ears which stand stiffly erect. Typical of the Scottish Terrier.

Professional Handler: Person licensed by the American Kennel Club to show dogs owned by others and to accept payment for these services.

Proven Bitch: A bitch which has produced one or more litters of puppies.

Proven Stud: A male dog which has sired one or more litters of puppies.

Puppy: A dog not over twelve months of age.

Puppy Match: An informal, unbenched dog show where no championship points are awarded. Numerous classes for puppies and grown dogs that have won no points are offered. Puppy matches may either limit their entries to dogs owned by members of the show-giving club or may be open to all comers.

Puppy Stakes: Bird-dog field-trial class for dogs not over eighteen months of age.

Puppy Teeth: The needle-sharp first set of teeth which drop out when the puppy is around four months of age, to be replaced by the permanent second set of teeth.

Put Down: Not given a high award.

— Q —

Qualifying Score: An obedience test score of 170 points or better.

Quarters: Hindquarters.

Quick: The live, fleshy portion of the toenail.

— R —

Rabbit Dog: Colloquial name for the Beagle.

Racy: Lean, long-legged and speedy-looking in structure. Examples: Greyhound, Whippet.

Rangy: Elongated and muscular in structure.

Ram's Nose: A slightly arched muzzle, the line from the stop to the nose tip being moderately convex when seen in profile.

Rattail: A long, pointed tail with short, thin hair on it.

Reach of Neck: Length and musculature of neck.

Reachy: Built so that the hind feet and forefeet are far apart and cover considerable ground, long in neck. This type of structure is typical of the Greyhound.

Recall: An obedience-test exercise wherein a dog is placed, seated, at one end of the ring. The handler goes to the other end and then calls the dog to him at the judge's command.

Recessive Characteristics: Hereditary characteristics which do not appear in the offspring when present in only one parent.

Red: Reddish-brown coat color.

Registration: Process of listing a dog's name, birth date, ownership, and parentage with an organization maintaining a recognized stud book, and having a number and certificate assigned as proof of the dog's being a purebred specimen of his breed.

Reh Pinscher: Original name of the Miniature Pinscher. Pronounced *Ray Pinscher*.

Reserve Winner: Dog placed second in a Winners Class.

Reversion: The reappearance of ancestral traits and characteristics.

Ribbed Up: Showing desirable roundness through the ribs.

Ringtail: A tail which describes almost a complete circle.

Roachback: A back showing a convex curvature from the withers to the base of the tail.

Roachy: Having a roached back.

Roman Nose: A foreface showing a convex line from the stop to the nose tip when seen in profile.

Rose Ear: An ear which folds backward and shows part of its inner surface.

Rounded: Descriptive of ears which have been shortened and trimmed to a round edge by cutting. Usually practiced only on Fox-hounds to prevent the ears from being cut and torn by briars and underbrush.

Ruff: Long profuse hair on the neck and shoulders. Characteristic of the Chow Chow and the Collie.

Runner: A dog-show employee who aids judges and stewards by calling the competing dogs into the ring for their classes and acting as a liaison agent between the judging ring, and the benching and handlers' sections.

Running Gear: Legs and feet.

Runt: Undersized specimen.

Russian Wolfhound: Borzoi.

— S —

Sable: Dark brown slightly shaded with black.

Saddle: 1. A solid black marking which extends over the shoulders, back, and upper flanks. A frequently seen marking of Beagles.

2. The part of the body directly behind the ruff which is clipped into two closely trimmed crescent shapes when a Poodle's coat is trimmed in the English Saddle style.

Sammy: Nickname for the Samoyed.

Sanctioned Match: Same as match show.

Scapula: The shoulder blade.

SCISSORS BITE

Scissors Bite: Meeting of the teeth wherein the upper front teeth slightly overlap the lower front teeth, and the inner surface of the upper teeth touches the outer surface of the lower teeth.

Scottie: Nickname for the Scottish Terrier.

Scratch Pack: A hound pack made up of dogs belonging to various owners.

Screw Tail: Short kinky tail. Characteristic of the Bulldog.

Scrotum: The pouchlike sac containing the testicles of the male.

Sealy: Nickname for the Sealyham Terrier.

Second Thigh: The portion of the hind leg between the hock and the stifle.

Seek Back: An obedience-trial exercise, requiring that a dog find and retrieve an object which his handler has dropped. A Utility Class exercise.

Self-colored or Self-marked: A dog that either is all one color, or else is one color with faint lighter shadings of the same hue as the only markings.

Self-hunt: Bird-dog term describing the act of a bird dog hunting for his own amusement and pleasure without human supervision.

Semiprick Ears: Ears which are carried erect with the tips pointing down and forward. Typical of the Collie.

Septum: The bone between the nostrils.

Set On: The juncture of the tail and the body.

Shearing Bite: Same as a scissors bite.

Shelly: Having insufficient depth or spring of rib. Too light through the body.

Sheltie: Nickname for the Shetland Sheepdog.

Short Coupled: Short in body.

Short Sit: An obedience test exercise wherein the dogs are required to sit down and stay put by themselves for a definite length of time.

Shot-breaking: Bird-dog term describing the action of a dog who breaks away or chases birds when a shot is fired.

Show Lead: A thin, lightweight leash with a loop and sliding clasps forming a collar at one end.

Shy: Nervously timid.

Siblings: Progeny of the same parents, not necessarily of the same litter.

Sickle Tail: A long tail which is carried up and curving forward in a semicircle.

SHOW LEAD

Skip: Nickname for the Schipperke.

Skully: Thick and coarse in skull.

Slab Sided: Flat-ribbed.

Sled Dog: Any of the breeds used as draught animals in snowy regions. Examples: Siberian Husky, Alaskan Malamute, Eskimo, or Samoyed.

Sleuth Hound: Old name for the Bloodhound.

Sloping Shoulder: A shoulder which is obliquely angulated and laid back.

Smooth Coat: A coat consisting of short, sleek, close-lying hair.

Snipey: Shallow, narrow, or too sharply pointed in the muzzle.

Soft-mouthed: Same as tender-mouthed.

Sound: Well put together and properly balanced in structure.

Spay: To remove by surgery the reproductive organs of a female.

Specials Dog: A dog who has won his championship and is entered in the Specials Only class to compete for Best of Breed or Best of Variety awards.

Specials Only: A dog-show class in which none but champions may be entered.

Specialty Club: Same as a breed club.

Specialty Show: A show put on by a breed club or specialty club, offering unusually generous prize money and trophies for the breed which the club sponsors. Specialty shows usually attract large entries, and winning at a show of this type is considered a great honor. Specialty shows may be held either in conjunction with all breed shows or as separate affairs.

Spectacles: Dark markings encircling the eyes. Typical of the Keeshond.

Splash: 1. A Boston Terrier whose coat has more extensive white markings than are considered desirable for his breed.

2. A St. Bernard whose coat has white as a background color.

SPLAY FOOT

Splay Feet: Feet which have spreading, open toes and are flat and thin in the pads.

Sport: A dog who does not resemble his sire or dam or litter-mates.

Spread: The width of chest between the shoulders. Usually applied to Bulldogs.

Spring of Rib: Roundness of the ribs.

Squirrel Tail: A short tail which curves forward over the back.

Stance: A dog's natural way of standing.

Standard: A written description of theoretical
physical perfection for a specimen of a
given breed. Each breed which is recognized by the American Kennel Club has
a standard of perfection which has been
approved by the Kennel Club. The more
closely a dog conforms to the standard
for his breed, the finer specimen he is
considered to be.

SQUIRREL TAIL

Standoff Coat: A double coat with the long outer hair standing
away from the body. Typical of the Pomeranian, Collie, Chow
Chow.

Steady: Descriptive of a bird dog who remains in pointing position
after the birds he has found have been flushed and a shot fired.

Stern: Tail. Usually a hound's tail is referred to as his stern.

Steward: A person assigned as an assistant to a judge at a dog show
or obedience trial. The steward's task is to check on entries being in their proper classes, the awarding of prize money and
trophies, to inform the judge of absentees and other details
not connected with the actual placement of the contestants.

Stifle: The thigh joint of the hind leg. The joint just above the
hock.

Stilted Action: A stiff, constrained manner of walking or trotting;
a gait which lacks freedom and elasticity. Usually caused by
lack of proper angulation.

Stop: The dip at the juncture of the foreface and the forehead.
Very pronounced in short-faced breeds such as the Pug, Boxer,
and Bulldog.

Straight Behind: Having hind legs which do not show sufficient
bend at the stifle and hock joints. A fault in most breeds.

Straight Hocks: Hocks which show no bend when viewed from
the side.

Straight in Shoulder: Having shoulders and upper arms which
meet with insufficient angulation.

Stud: A male dog used for breeding purposes.

Stud Fee: A fee paid to the owner of a male dog for the privilege of breeding a female to the dog.

Substance: Physical solidity. Bulk.

Superintendent: A professional arranger and manager of dog shows.

Sway-backed: Having a concave line along the spine. Sagging between the withers and base of tail.

— T —

Tallyho: A hunting cheer meaning "Game is in sight."

Tassels: Long, unclipped hair left on the ear tips of Bedlington Terriers.

T. D.: Abbreviation for Tracking Dog, the title awarded to dogs that have passed tracking tests.

Team Class: A special class, usually offered only at the larger shows, for four dogs of the same breed belonging to one kennel or owner. The four dogs need not be of the same sex, but it is important that they match well in size, color, and general type.

Teckel: Commonly used German name for the Dachshund.

Tender-mouthed: Having the ability to carry game without puncturing or tearing its skin. An important attribute of retrievers.

Terrier Front: Forequarters which are characterized by very straight pasterns and forelegs and upright shoulders.

THINNING SHEARS

Thinning Shears: Scissors with blades resembling the teeth of a comb. Useful for thinning out thick portions of the coat without giving it a hacked appearance.

Thorax: Chest.

Throaty: Having an excessive amount of loose skin under the throat.

Throwback: A dog that does not resemble his litter-mates and whose physical traits and characteristics seem to be derived from distant ancestors rather than his parents or grandparents.

Thumbmarks: Small circular black markings on a lighter background, which appear as though they might have been made by a human thumb that had been dabbed on an ink pad and then pressed against the coat.

Ticked Coat: A coat with small splashes of a darker color against a white background. The splashes are known as ticking.

Tidying: Trimming, clipping, or plucking a coat in order to give it a neat appearance.

Tied-in Elbows: Elbows which are so closely knit to a dog's body that they prevent freedom of movement.

Tight Lips: Lips which fit closely against the teeth and jaws with no suggestion of pendulous flews or chops.

Tilted Jaw: A lower jaw, which, when viewed from the front, is tilted to one side or the other—not horizontal.

Timber: Bone, particularly that of the legs.

Title: A championship won either in field trial or bench show competition or an obedience degree awarded for three qualifying scores in obedience trials.

Tongue: Noise made by hounds when scenting game.

Topknot: A clump of long hair on the top of the head. Characteristic of the Dandie Dinmont Terrier.

Topline: The line from the top of the skull to the base of the tail when the dog is seen in profile.

Torn Coat: Descriptive of a St. Bernard coat with white markings breaking the basic dark color of the mantle.

Trace: A stripe of darker hair running down the back of a solid-colored dog. Often seen in Pugs and red Dachshunds.

Tracking Drive: Natural ability and instinct to trail game or humans.

Training Collar: A slip collar with a ring on each end. The collar is made so that it tightens on the dog's neck if he lunges against it.

Transmitter: A sire or dam with ability to pass along his or her own qualities to his or her offspring.

Trappy: Smart and animated.

Tricolor: A coat color consisting of black, tan, and white.

Trimming: Clipping or scissoring a dog's coat in order to create a trim, graceful silhouette.

Trousers: Long, heavy, shaggy hair on the legs. Typical of the Afghan Hound.

True Action: A sound, rhythmic gait.

Tuck-up: The sharp rise of the underline of the abdomen just back of the ribs and under the loin. Characteristic of the Greyhound and Whippet.

Tulip Ears: Ears which are carried erect with a slight forward curvature.

Typey: Showing the conformation, expression, and other characteristics which are considered desirable and representative of a breed.

— U —

U.D.: Abbreviation for Utility Dog, a title given by the American Kennel Club to dogs which have won C.D.X (Companion Dog Excellent) degrees and have made three qualifying scores in the Utility Class at recognized obedience trials.

U.D.T.: Abbreviation for Utility Dog Tracker which signifies that a dog has won a Utility Dog degree and has passed a tracking test as well. This is the highest award that it is possible for a dog to win in Obedience Test Trials.

Undershot: Descriptive of a dog's mouth having lower front teeth which project beyond the upper front teeth. The opposite of overshot.

Upface: A foreface that tilts upward as in the Bulldog.

Upper Arm: The part of the front leg between the elbow and the shoulder blade. The humerus.

UNDERSHOT

Upright in Shoulder: Having an obtuse angle between the upper arm and shoulder. Same as straight in shoulder.

Upsweep: The upturning portion of the lower jaw of short-faced breeds—Bulldogs, Pugs, etc.

Utility Class: An obedience trial class for purebred dogs of any breed and of either sex which have won the title C.D.X. (Companion Dog Excellent) in obedience Open Classes.

Dogs in this class may be handled or exhibited by either an amateur or a professional.

— V —

Varmint Expression: Keen, piercing, beady-eyed expression considered desirable in many Terrier breeds.

Vent: 1. Patch of light colored hair under the tail.

2. Rectum.

Vermin Dog: Any dog which is proficient at killing rats and mice.

— W —

Walleye: An eye which is either blue or blue with the iris broken by brown or black. Often seen in Blue Merle Collies and Harlequin Great Danes.

Waster: A dog of scrawny, sickly constitution. A poor doer.

Weak-fronted: Showing structural defects of the forequarters, such as loose shoulders or elbows, weak pasterns, or bandy front legs.

Weak in Pastern: Same as down in pastern.

Weaving: Crossing of the front feet when walking or trotting.

Weedy: Scrawny, lacking in bone and general substance.

Well Let Down: Having a desirable degree of angulation of hock and stifle joints.

Well Put Down: Descriptive of a show dog that is properly groomed and in top-notch condition.

Well Sprung: Well-rounded through the ribs.

Wet Neck: A neck having a dewlap or other superfluous skin.

Wheaten: A light yellowish, cream, or fawn color.

Wheelback: Same as roach back.

Whelping: The act of giving birth to puppies.

Whiptail: A long, slim, straight, tapering tail. Typical of the Pointer.

Whiskers: Long, stiff, downhanging hair on the foreface and jaws. Typical of the Miniature Schnauzer.

Whitecoat: Same as a runner.

Whup or Whoa: Command word used to order a bird dog to stop.

Wide-going or Wide-ranging: Descriptive of a bird dog that ranges far out from his handler in seeking game.

Winners Bitch: The bitch which is placed first in the class made up of the first prize winners of the five regular official classes offered for females.

Winners Class: Class in which the first place winners of Puppy, Novice, Bred By Exhibitor, American-bred, and Open classes compete for championship points. Only two placements are made in this class—Winners and Reserve Winners.

Winners Dog: The dog which is placed first in the class made up of the first prize winners of the five regular official classes offered for males.

Wire Coat: A double coat in which the outer coat is composed of dense, crisp, harsh-textured hair. Typical of the Wire-haired Fox Terrier.

Withers: The point at the top of the shoulder blades where the neck joins the body.

Wolf Color: A coat coloration which is an evenly distributed mixture of black, brown, and gray.

Wrinkle: Loose folds of skin on the head and sides of the face. Characteristic of the Bloodhound, Bulldog, St. Bernard.

Wry Mouth: A lower jaw which is not horizontal when viewed from the front. It is tilted to one side or the other and does not line up properly with the upper jaw.

— Y —

Yard Work or Yard Training: First steps in the training of a sporting dog when such commands as "sit," "heel," and so on, are taught as a preliminary to actual schooling on game.

Yorky: Nickname for the Yorkshire Terrier.

Index

· A ·

• F •